Recycling and Waste

An exploration of contemporary environmental policy

Dr MATTHEW GANDY

Lecturer in Geography
School of European Studies
University of Sussex

Avebury Studies
in
Green Research

Aldershot · Brookfield USA · Hong Kong · Singapore · Sydney

Published by
Avebury
Ashgate Publishing Limited
Gower House
Croft Road
Aldershot
Hants GU11 3HR
England

Ashgate Publishing Company
Old Post Road
Brookfield
Vermont 05036
USA

British Library Cataloguing in Publication Data

Gandy, Matthew
    Recycling and Waste: Exploration of
    Contemporary Environmental Policy –
    (Avebury Studies in Green Research)
    I. Title II. Series
    363.72

ISBN 1 85628 542 1

Printed and Bound in Great Britain by
Athenaeum Press Ltd, Newcastle upon Tyne.

Contents

Figures

Tables

Abbreviations

ACC	Association of County Councils
ADC	Association of District Councils
ACRA	Aluminium Can Recycling Association
AMA	Association of Metropolitan Authorities
ARC	Amey Roadstone Company
AVG	Abfallverwertungsgesellschaft m.b.H.
CA	Civic Amenity
CIPFA	Chartered Institute of Public Finance and Accountancy
CCT	Compulsory Competitive Tendering
CLWDG	Central London Waste Disposal Group
COPA	Control of Pollution Act 1974
DEn	Department of Energy
DoE	Department of the Environment
DTI	Department of Trade and Industry
DSD	Duales System Deutschland

DSO	Direct Services Organisation
EDF	Environmental Defense Fund
ELWA	East London Waste Authority
EPA	Environmental Protection Act 1990
ERRA	European Recovery and Recycling Association
GAL	Grüne Alternative Liste
GLC	Greater London Council
HEW	Hamburger Electricitätswerke
HDPE	High-density polyethylene
IFEU	Institut für Energie und Umweltforschung
IföR	Institut für ökologisches Recycling
INCPEN	Industry Council for Packaging and the Environment
IPCC	Intergovernmental Panel on Climatic Change
ITU	Ingenieurgemeinschaft Technischer Umweltschutz
LAMSAC	Local Authorities Management Services and Computer Committee
LAWDC	Local Authority Waste Disposal Company
LB-HSR	Landesbetrieb Hamburger Stadtreinigung
LCC	London County Council
LPAC	London Planning Advisory Committee
MBI	Market-based instrument
MBO	Management buy-out

MCC	Metropolitan County Council
MSW	Municipal Solid Waste
MVA	Müllverbrennungsanlage
NAWDC	National Association of Waste Disposal Carriers
NLWA	North London Waste Authority
NFFO	Non Fossil Fuel Obligation
NUPE	National Union of Public Employees
OECD	Organisation for Economic Co-operation and Development
ÖTV	Öffentlicher Dienste, Transport und Verkehr
PET	Polyethylene terepthalate
PVC	Polyvinyl chloride
RDF	Refuse Derived Fuel
ROSS	Refuse Operations Simulation System
SELCHP	South East London Combined Heat & Power Ltd
SCLSERP	Standing Conference on London and South East Regional Planning
SELWDG	South East London Waste Disposal Group
SERPLAN	South East Regional Planning Conference
SWLWDG	South West London Waste Disposal Group
T&GWU	Transport and General Workers Union
TWA	Thames Water Authority
VKR	Veba Kraftwerke Ruhr

WCA	Waste Collection Authority
WDA	Waste Disposal Authority
WILJOG	Waste in London Joint Officers Group
WMAC	Waste Management Advisory Council
WRA	Waste Regulation Authority
WRWA	Western Riverside Waste Authority

Glossary

Air classifier	A centralised sorting technology
Blue Box	A collect system of recycling where mixed recyclables are collected from households and sorted at a centralised plant
Bring system	A recycling system where householders bring recyclables to on-street collection facilities or recycling centres
Calorific Value	The energy value of waste
Civic amenity site	A site provided by local authorities where the public may bring their bulky waste, as set up under the 1967 Civic Amenities Act and the 1978 Refuse Disposal (Amenity) Act
Clinker	The stony residue of burnt coal
Collect system	A recycling system where recyclable materials are collected directly from households either as mixed or separated fractions of recyclable materials
Cullet	Broken glass for recycling into new glass containers
Demunicipalisation	Term used to refer to the privatisation or contracting out of local government services

Dual-bin system	A more elaborate routine waste collection service where householders separate their waste into two fractions, typically putrescibles and the remainder
Dust Destructor	Term often used for incineration plants before the 1940s
Fly-tipping	The illegal dumping of waste, often on derelict land
Garchey system	A disposal system where kitchen waste directly enters the sewerage system
Hammer Mill	Pulveriser to reduce the volume of waste
Holsystem	A comprehensive kerbside collection system for all recyclable waste fractions
Leachate	The products of waste as it degrades at landfill sites, released either in the form of a gas or contaminated water
Kerbside collection	The 'collect' system of recycling (see above)
Müllgebühr	Separate annual charge to individual households for the collection and disposal of their waste
Municipal waste	The waste derived predominantly from individual households, commercial premises and street cleansing
Post-consumer waste	Waste produced by individuals and households in the consumption process
Primary Recovery	The recovery of materials rather than their calorific value (see above and also Secondary Recovery)
Pre-consumer Waste	Waste that has been generated in the production process

Putrescible Waste	Organic waste which is compostable (mainly kitchen and garden waste)
Pyrolysis	A process by which organic compounds are broken down into simpler compounds by heating in the absence of oxygen
Recycling Centre	A facility to which members of the public can bring a range of recyclable materials
Refuse Derived Fuel	Waste that is processed before incineration to produce storable fuel in the form of pellets
Secondary Materials	Materials which have already been used in the production process. Examples include scrap metals and waste paper
Siedlungstruktur	Categories of housing types used for the purposes of waste management planning
Tipping	The dumping of refuse on open sites before the widespread use of landfill and improved monitoring procedures
Totting	The removal of valuable items from the waste stream such as non-ferrous metals
Transfer station	Where waste cannot be delivered direct to nearby landfill sites by the collection vehicles, transfer stations are used to enable the bulk haulage of waste by road, rail or by river to disposal sites

Acknowledgements

I would first like to acknowledge the financial support of the Economic and Social Research Council (ESRC) and the Erasmus Programme, without which this study would not have been possible. My thanks also to the Deutscher Akademischer Austauschdienst (DAAD) for funding an intensive German language course taken at the Goethe Institute in Schwäbisch Hall during the summer of 1989. I would like to thank my PhD supervisors at the LSE: Dr Michael Hebbert for his conscientious and supportive role throughout the project and Dr Yvonne Rydin for her invaluable suggestions in the final stages of the research. I want also to acknowledge the support and encouragement of the LSE postgraduate community, and particularly Peter Wicks for advice over research methodology.

The successful completion of this study would not have been realised without the co-operation and help of many people in London and Hamburg. I am particularly grateful for the assistance of Jeff Cooper in the London Waste Regulation Authority, Mike Newport of the Jamestown Road Recycling Centre in Camden and the Hillmann family with whom I stayed in Hamburg. I would also like to acknowledge the essential supporting role provided by the library staff at LSE, the Greater London History Library and the Institute for Ecological Recycling in Berlin. Special mention must also be made of Dr Chris Fernandez in the LSE statistical advisory unit who provided detailed advice on the quantitative data analysis and Sue Rowland at the University of Sussex for assistance with the preparation of the maps of Hamburg. Finally, a special thank you to Maria, Mike and Billie.

Introduction

The study of municipal waste is of particular interest for the analysis of environmental policy because it is predominantly comprised of post-consumer waste produced by individual households. A focus on recycling allows an examination of the potential impact of new forms of environmental policy associated with the promotion of 'green consumerism' through individualised forms of public participation and political action and the application of market-based policy instruments. The political salience of recycling can be illustrated by the UK Government's public commitment in 1990 to raise levels of household waste recycling to 25 per cent by the year 2,000 as part of a new environmental strategy set out in their White Paper *This Common Inheritance* (DoE, 1990b):

> The Government is setting the challenging target of recycling half of our recyclable waste by the end of the century. That is around 25 % of all household waste. (DoE, 1990b p. 199)

The contemporary interest in increasing the level of recycling, raises two central issues to be addressed in this book: firstly, whether this national target is achievable under the contemporary legislative and policy making framework in the UK; and secondly, the identification of the underlying barriers to higher rates of materials recycling, involving a critical examination of current debates within the recycling and waste management literature, and the use of a comparative case study in the city of Hamburg.

The study of waste and recycling

The study of waste is a neglected area within the social sciences though waste management issues have been extensively examined within other disciplines, particularly engineering. At an early stage in this study I decided that a survey of the users of recycling facilities to examine their motivations and patterns of participation would not be a very fruitful exercise, since this has already been extensively carried out (see Coggins et al., 1989a, 1989b; Hay et al., 1990; Vining and Ebreo, 1990). Another heavily trodden path in waste management and recycling research is the technical and economic appraisal of different policy options (see Ball, 1988; Barton, 1989; OECD, 1983; Pearce and Walter, 1977; Pieters and Verhallen, 1986; Turner and Thomas, 1982). I wish to argue that the development and contemporary pattern of recycling is better understood through an examination of underlying political factors affecting the development of different waste management options. This requires a consideration of the historical emergence of waste management as a key aspect of local government services since the late nineteenth century and the contemporary process of demunicipalisation[1] of waste management activity since the early 1980s. The more overtly political approaches to waste management research have thus far been applied mainly to the study of toxic waste issues and the disposal of radioactive waste (see Bernstoff, 1989; Blowers et al., 1991; Lubjahn et al., 1988) and have not been widely extended to the analysis of municipal household waste.

Sources of data

Primary data for the study was gained from semi-structured interviews with key agents in recycling and waste management in London and Hamburg along with a comprehensive questionnaire survey of recycling activities in the London Boroughs[2]. London was chosen as the main focus for the study because it generates the biggest concentration of municipal waste in the UK, and has consistently faced both economic and environmental difficulties in its waste management, as revealed by the historical material presented in Chapter Three. A further feature of interest, is that in 1986, the regional waste disposal authority for London, the GLC, was abolished, and replaced by sixteen Waste Disposal Authorities. This allows a number of organisational and administrative aspects of recycling to be introduced into the analysis.

Since 1986, the collection of household waste in London is handled by thirty three Waste Collection Authorities composed of the thirty two London Boroughs and the Corporation of London, with the former waste regulation and toxic waste management functions of the GLC passing to a new body, the London Waste Regulation Authority (LWRA). As a consequence of these changes, London has shown a wide variety of responses from its thirty three Waste Collection Authorities and sixteen Waste Disposal Authorities, allowing an analysis of local variations in the organisation and effectiveness of recycling policy, and their relationship to wider developments including the evolution of the legislative framework for waste management at a national and international level. The London Boroughs form the focus of the research in London because they have been the co-ordinators of recycling policy since GLC abolition, a role which places them between individual citizens who wish to participate in recycling and the nexus of different agencies involved in materials recovery.

The exploratory interviews and preliminary data analysis revealed that the existing quantitative data on recycling in the London area are incomplete and unreliable. For example, the SERPLAN regional planning forum for the South East has complained of the declining standard and 'inconsistencies and inaccuracies' of the annually collected data on the collection and disposal of waste by the Chartered Institute of Public Finance and Accountancy (SERPLAN, 1988a p. 5). A further difficulty for the study of waste management in London is that since 1987, all quantitative data has become confidential as a result of the compulsory competitive tendering provisions contained within the 1988 Local Government Act, encouraging local authorities to keep the financial aspects of their waste management operations secret to help protect their own workforce from bids by outside contractors. The other sources of quantitative data compiled by the Department of the Environment and the London Waste Regulation Authority also show missing or unreliable data sets. Indeed, the new LWRA database on recycling in the London area had no information on eleven boroughs in the year 1989-90.

As a result of the lack of any London-wide comprehensive quantitative data, a questionnaire survey was carried out in the London Boroughs between April and August 1990, in order to generate as much data as possible, and a response was eventually obtained from all the London Boroughs and the Corporation of London. In addition to the collection of primary data, a wide variety of material was gained from specialist libraries and archives. Of particular value were the libraries at the Institute of Wastes Management in Northampton and at the Institut für ökologisches Recycling (IföR) in Berlin. The historical material on London was derived largely from the Greater London History Library in Finsbury and the GLC Modern Records Office at Globe House.

A conceptual framework for the analysis of recycling

The conceptual framework is the means by which the phenomena under investigation are to be explained. It clarifies the substantive connections between the empirical data collected in the fieldwork and the processes which are argued to have generated them. An initial complexity in this study was the need to combine analysis of the impact of wider political and economic changes, such as the evolving legislative framework and policy context for waste management and recycling, with local case study analysis of the range of factors affecting the development of recycling in practice. This has been done by combining the study of the changing political and economic context for municipal waste management with the analysis of contemporary case studies of recycling in two contrasting urban areas.

This study adopts a non-positivist theoretical framework, in recognising that in the social sciences, empirical phenomena are the manifestation of processes or laws which are historical rather than universal, and that explanation (rather than the description of empirical regularities) cannot be grounded in an inadequate epistemological conception of the relationship between fact and theory (Bowen, 1979; Chouinard et al., 1984; Lukes, 1981; Trigg, 1985). These theoretical concerns are particularly relevant to the study of waste and recycling because of the predominance of positivistic technocratic analyses or behaviouralist and pluralist approaches, all of which exhibit an epistemological attachment to ahistorical methodological individualism (Fay, 1981). The fundamental point of departure recognised here, between positivist and non-positivist positions, is the recognition that human societies are an 'open system' with no possibilities for laboratory style experimental replication, and that all research is internal to society which is itself evolving through time (Bhaskar, 1989). An objective of the fieldwork has been to mount an effective empirical challenge to the dominance of technocratic, positivist and behaviouralist analysis within the existing recycling and waste management literature, and to add to the theoretical debate over the research of environmental problems more generally.

In the next chapter I argue that the dominant positivistic, technocratic and pluralist approaches to the study of environmental problems fail to provide an adequate explanation of the cause of environmental degradation (and hence any solution). A politically and historically informed approach allows an effective integration of empirical research on policy in practice with wider theoretical issues concerning political change and the evolving legislative framework. The empirical research employed a mix of intensive and extensive techniques (Massey and Meegan, 1986; Sayer, 1992) used in a complementary fashion to generate as much valuable research knowledge as possible, in what is an under-researched area with limited and often unreliable data available. In interpreting the fieldwork, the realist conceptual distinction has been made between the use of intensive research (semi-structured interviews) to identify causal mechanisms, and the use of extensive research (the questionnaire survey) to identify empirical regularities (Gregory, 1986). Where quantitative techniques have been used (correlation and regression analysis) these have been used to enable more precise descriptions of empirical data, and not as a positivist explanatory (or predictive) tool (Hay,

4

1979; Keat, 1979).

In summary, the conceptual framework treats the cities of London and Hamburg as contingent urban settings within which the development and contemporary pattern of recycling and waste management has been examined. The aim has been to trace the connections between the contemporary evolution of recycling and waste management and the changing context for environmental policy making. This in turn allows a better explanation of the underlying barriers to raising levels of materials recycling towards technically achievable levels.

The use of Hamburg as a comparative case study

At a national level, the UK and Germany have been found to be very useful as the basis for comparative research (see Boehmer-Christensen and Skea, 1992; Hall, 1983; Kunreuther and Linnerooth, 1983; Peacock, 1984; Rüdig, 1986), and the case for comparative research into environmental policy and planning issues has been widely made (see Badaracco, 1985; Brickman et al., 1985; Clawson and Hall, 1983; Enloe, 1975; Masser and Williams, 1986). Germany provides a number of features of direct relevance to the debate over recycling and waste management. The growth of a powerful environmentalist movement has seen wide ranging legislative developments during the 1980s, and most studies have indicated higher rates of recycling in Germany in comparison with the UK. The academic debate over alternative waste management strategies has also been advanced further within the German literature, providing a number of alternative perspectives to the predominance of technical and cost-benefit analysis type studies typical of the Anglo-American literature.

A German case study was used in order to clarify and develop a number of themes and issues identified in the London. Hamburg was chosen for this study because it is the largest city in Germany, with the exception of Berlin, which would have been unsuitable for analysis because of the overwhelming impact of issues surrounding German reunification. The exploratory interviews and preliminary data analysis suggested a city with similar socio-economic and morphological features to London, but where the political pressure for recycling and higher standards in waste management was significantly greater. As early as 1978, for example, environmentalist political groups achieved 4.6 per cent in the elections to the Hamburg senate and the German Green Party has been represented continuously in the Hamburg Senate since 1982 (Hülsberg, 1988; Müller-Rommel and Poguntke, 1990).

The structure of the book

This introductory chapter has described the aim and methodology of my study, and set out the conceptual framework for the analysis.

In the next chapter, I give an overview of the environmental debate and different conceptions of environmental policy. I note that the 1970s neo-Malthusian emphasis on the 'limits to growth' has been supplanted by a focus on sustainability through the integration of environmental and economic policy making. I argue that the contemporary promotion of market-based policy instruments is a corollary of wider shifts away from Keynesian to neo-liberal patterns of public policy with profound implications for environmental protection.

In Chapter Two, a range of technical, economic, political, institutional, social and other factors influencing the development of recycling and waste management is reviewed. Particular emphasis is given to the difficulties in achieving high rates of recycling in large urban areas and the problems facing municipal waste management. The diverse rationale for recycling is linked with the diversity of environmentalist thought described in Chapter One, and contemporary recycling is clarified in terms of the different methods of recovering materials from the waste stream. A hierarchy of recycling options is set out, emerging in later chapters as a key dimension to the debate over the legitimate definition and rationale of recycling activity. The promotion of materials recycling is evaluated as a potential element in environmental policy making and the debate over the use of different kinds of policy instruments is extended with an examination of alternative strategies to raise levels of recycling.

In Chapter Three, the historical development of waste management and recycling in London since the mid-nineteenth century is described. This allows a range of additional contextual issues including political change and the evolution of the legislative framework for waste management to be introduced. The relationship between the practice of waste management and the administrative structure of local government is identified as a key factor neglected within the existing literature.

In Chapter Four, the analysis of the quantitative data on recycling activities in the London Boroughs is presented along with material gained from the semi-structured interviews. The pattern of recycling is analysed in relation to a range of issues identified in the literature and a distinction is drawn between local factors accounting for differences in the level of recycling between the London Boroughs and wider underlying factors constraining the overall development of recycling across London.

In Chapter Five, the discussion is extended to include analysis of wider developments within waste management which have fundamentally altered the context for materials recycling. I argue that the absence of a national waste policy and strategic planning, coupled with the increasing role of the private sector in municipal waste management, will favour the development of energy recovery technologies rather than the recycling of materials within the hierarchy of potential recycling options.

In Chapter Six, the main themes emerging from the study of London are developed through a comparative case study of the city of Hamburg. It is shown how a political choice has been faced between two waste management strategies: an increasingly market-led approach based around the construction of a new incineration plant and the recovery of energy from waste; and an alternative strategy advanced by radical environmentalists, focused on the maximum promotion of materials recycling and waste reduction at source. Although the city is able to achieve substantially higher rates of recycling than London, there appears to be a political and economic threshold beyond which it is increasingly difficult for the recycling rate to be increased any further. The limits to recycling policy in local government are shown to have led to a modification of the state role at a national level in Germany in order to tackle the politically contentious issue of packaging waste.

Finally, in the concluding chapter, the existing literature is re-interpreted in the light of the study findings. It is concluded that contemporary recycling policy is marked by a divergence between three distinct positions: an emphasis on waste reduction at source; a renewed focus on materials recycling, involving new forms of state intervention at a national level; and a market-led pressure to move the policy emphasis away from materials recycling and towards the profitable generation of electricity from waste.

Notes

1   I use the term demunicipalisation to describe the process whereby the operational aspects of municipal waste management are being increasingly handled by private sector waste management companies. A key theme examined in this book is the impact of this process on the prospects for raising levels of materials recycling.

2   The research carried out for this book consisted of a questionnaire survey of each the London Boroughs in 1990, the interviewees being the local government officers responsible for the development of recycling in each local authority. In addition, 93 exploratory and semi-structured interviews were carried out with key agents involved in recycling and waste management in London and Hamburg from 1989 to 1992. The formulation of the survey within the overall research design followed the procedure of Mann (1985) from pre-pilot open interviews, through a series of pilot versions of the survey before the production of the final survey. The questionnaire survey had a dual function, combining the collection of quantitative data for the London Boroughs and also additional qualitative data such as anecdotal material. Because of the small number of potential interviewees, the 32 London boroughs and the Corporation of London, and the length and complexity of the survey, face-to-face interviews were used rather than a postal survey in order to achieve a high and accurate response (a 100 per cent response rate was eventually achieved). There were several important difficulties with the survey. In many boroughs, financial data was no longer publicly available as a result the introduction of compulsory competitive tendering and local authorities seeking to keep the cost of their service provision confidential. In a small number of boroughs, notably in Conservative controlled Harrow, Wandsworth and Westminster, the interviewees were not permitted to answer the overtly political questions referring to the abolition of the GLC and the impact of restrictions in local government expenditure on recycling. An additional problem for a survey of this type, is that the questions covering more technical issues and complex legislative changes present difficulties in some authorities where little in the way of formal policy exists for waste management, combined with wide variations in the knowledge and experience of the interviewees.

1 The environmental debate

In this chapter, I examine the post-war debate over the causes and appropriate policy responses to the environmental crisis, as the conceptual and practical background to this study. Concern over the wastage of materials and energy is shown to be a consistent element in environmental concern since the late 1960s and early 1970s, but the emphasis of the debate has shifted from 'limits to growth' type fears towards finding new ways of integrating economic and environmental policy making.

I begin by outlining the background to the growth of environmental concern over the post-war period and the complexity and diversity of the different strands of thought lying behind the contemporary 'greening' of public policy. The influence of socio-economic change and political shifts in public policy on the growth of market-based environmental policy is considered. Finally, the relationship between different interpretations of the cause of environmental problems and the current debate over appropriate policy responses is examined, conceived in terms of a distinction between market-based and non market-based conceptions of the environmental crisis.

The recognition of an environmental crisis

In the period up to the end of the eighteenth century three general notions concerning the relationship between humankind and nature were identified by Clarence Glacken: the idea of a designed earth created by divine forces; the idea of environmental influence on human culture; and the impact of human activity on the natural environment. For Glacken, the appreciation of the human impact on the environment was less well developed until the latter part of the nineteenth century, a period marked by the widespread recognition of the environmental consequences of human activity, as illustrated by the publication of *Man and Nature* by George Perkins Marsh in 1864 and the influential writings of John Ruskin, William Morris and others, at a time of rapid urban growth and increasing industrial activity (Glacken, 1967; Williams, 1986).

After the second world war, the deleterious human impact on the environment accelerated rapidly, with increasing scientific evidence of an environmental crisis. In the late 1950s and 1960s, for example, a number of post-war developments associated with mechanised agriculture became the focus of public concern, including the contamination of ecosystem food chains with pesticides (Carson, 1962; Dempster, 1968; Prestt, 1970) and the destruction of wildlife habitats and declining biotic diversity (Hawksworth et al., 1974; Rose and Wallace, 1974). The post-war period also saw recognition of the threat to human health from air pollution caused by the burning of fossil fuels, leading to the 1956 Clean Air Act in the UK and US Clean Air Act of 1970.

In the late 1960s there was wide media coverage of disasters such as the 1967 Torrey Canyon oil spillage and the 1968 Minamata Bay mercury poisoning in Japan. These and other incidents gave impetus to a burgeoning environmental movement in many developed economies. In the period from the late 1960s to the early 1970s a wide range of environmental organisations were founded, including the Conservation Society, Friends of the Earth, Greenpeace and Population Concern. In 1972 the first environmentalist political party was formed in Tasmania, and by the mid-1980s there were twenty three green political parties contesting national elections (Parkin, 1989; Seager, 1990).

The 1972 UN Stockholm Conference on the Environment was the first international recognition of the need for global action to protect the environment. In the same year, the publication of the *Blueprint for Survival* called for radical measures by governments and was endorsed by an impressive panel of leading academics from within the natural sciences (Goldsmith et al., 1972). The environmental debate of the early 1970s was focused on the perceived incompatibility between continued economic growth and environmental protection, typified by the 'limits to growth' thesis of the Club of Rome (Forrester, 1970; Meadows et al., 1972; Mesarovic and Pestel, 1974). Uncontrolled population growth was frequently identified as the underlying cause of the crisis (Ehrlich, 1970; Ehrlich and Ehrlich, 1970; Hardin, 1968, 1974) and many of these studies claimed that there would be an imminent exhaustion of the earth's 'carrying capacity' for the human population. The pessimistic projections of the limits to growth school were taken very seriously by policy makers and formed a central element in public debate. The analysis was rooted in the natural science discipline of biology and its emerging sub-discipline of ecology:

Geometric increases in number can always overtake the size of the cake that technical ingenuity can devise. Perhaps ecology's first social law should be written - All poverty is caused by the continued growth of population. (Colinvaux 1980 p. 196).

Attention was also focused on the wastage of energy and resources in industrialised societies. Research suggested that the US, for example, was facing the first serious peace-time shortages of essential raw materials (Ballard, 1974) and it was predicted that future demand for minerals could only be met by huge inputs of energy during extraction and processing (Dunham, 1974). Figures on primary energy usage indicated that oil consumption in the period 1960-1970 in the OECD nations was equivalent to total oil produced before 1960 and that coal consumption since 1940 exceeded all the coal produced in the preceding nine centuries (Hubbert, 1976). The key policy document to emerge from the 'limits to growth' period of environmental concern was the *Global 2,000 Report* commissioned by president Carter in 1977, which in its opening paragraph warned that:

If present trends continue, the world in 2000 will be more crowded, more polluted, less stable ecologically, and more vulnerable to disruption than the world we live in now. Serious stresses involving population, resources, and the environment are clearly visible ahead. Despite greater material output, the world's people will be poorer in many ways than they are today. (US Council on Environmental Quality, 1982 p. 1).

Yet by the time of its publication, the political and economic context for environmental policy had begun to shift, and many of the basic premises behind the neo-Malthusian pessimism of the 'limits to growth' period were being widely questioned.

The decline of neo-Malthusianism

From the mid-1970s onwards the 'limits to growth' thesis was subjected to sustained criticism from across the political spectrum. From the political left, the criticism focused on the social and economic consequences of limiting economic growth (Beckerman, 1974) and the ethical implications of socio-biological and neo-Malthusian arguments against Third World aid and development (Bradford, 1989; Harvey, 1974). Marxist analysts took issue with the application of positivist and empiricist methodology to the study of human society, leading inevitably to neo-Malthusian type conclusions (see

11

Harvey, 1974; Sandbach, 1980). David Harvey, for example, highlighted the relationship between ideology and science, in discounting the objectivity and impartiality claims associated with many so-called 'scientific' analyses of environmental problems:

> The use of a particular scientific method is of necessity founded in ideology,....and any claim to be ideology-free is of necessity an ideological claim. (Harvey, 1974 p. 256).

From the political right, the ecological pessimists were criticised for exaggerating the rate of resource depletion and systematically underestimating human ingenuity and technological change (see Simon, 1981; Simon and Kahn, 1984). Indeed, the weaknesses in this early work were instrumental in the Reagan administration's rejection of the findings of the *Global 2000 Report*. The technological critique has also been pursued within the political-economy based literature, where the link between environmental sustainability and the potential for economic development is depicted as a dynamic relationship rather than a static relationship as implied in much of the early 1970s 'limits to growth' and neo-Malthusian literature:

> ...the frontiers of sustainability are constantly shifting. Developments in bio-technology, for example, leave open the possibility that resources can be produced from nature without permanently harming the biosphere. There is nothing inevitable about the destructive progress of science. (Redclift, 1987 p. 203).

The mid to late 1970s were marked by mounting economic, social and political difficulties facing the OECD nations which heralded a waning of environmental concern (Rüdig and Lowe, 1983; Sandbach, 1980). The poor economic situation of stagflation and declining profitability in many developed economies was also exacerbated by substantial oil price rises, which contributed to cost-push inflation and lower rates of growth in the core economies. An important consequence of the price rises for primary energy sources was that the relationship between energy consumption and rates of economic growth altered through the widespread adoption of energy conservation measures. Research suggested that the US economy in the early 1970s had an energy efficiency of only 1 to 2 per cent, with a concentration of waste within the transport, commerce and domestic sectors. For Ayres and Narkus-Kramer (1976) this revealed that the neo-Malthusians had neglected to examine the scope for energy conservation, since there was 'no fixed relationship between the extent to which final demand is satisfied and the quantities of physical materials and energy required' (Ayres and Narkus-

Kramer, 1976 p. 1).

Following the oil price rises of the 1970s, there was an 18.9 per cent improvement in energy efficiency in Western Europe between 1973 and 1983, and contrary to earlier expectations oil prices fell by almost 25 per cent in real terms from 1981 to 1985 (Odell, 1985; Financial Times Survey, 1991a). The implications of the changing relationship between rates of resource depletion and economic growth served as an important rebuttal of the arguments which held that economic growth and environmental protection were intrinsically incompatible policy goals. Shortages of resources were also seen increasingly in terms of geo-politics rather than a result of natural scarcity, which was underlined by a general weakening in producer cartels for a range of primary raw materials since the early 1970s (Crow and Thomas, 1983).

The 1980s emphasis on sustainable growth and development has emerged, therefore, from the ashes of the 1970s debate over finite resources, as many of the previously held assumptions about the relationship between economic activity and environmental degradation have been refuted. The new wave of environmental concern during the 1980s can be characterised as being distinct from the earlier wave of interest in the late 1960s and early 1970s. In addition to the repudiation of simplistic neo-Malthusian assumptions, there has been a growing critique since the 1970s of the limitations of conventional economic policy making. For example, attention has focused on the failure of conventional economic indicators such as GDP to distinguish between economic activity which is harmful or beneficial to the environment. Research has indicated a growing burden of expenditure in developed economies to tackle the consequences of environmental degradation, as shown in Figure 1.1 for West Germany from 1975 to 1987. To avoid this economic and environmental burden, it is maintained that the full ecological and social costs of economic activity must be integrated into decision making, since a pre-condition of sustainable development or the 'ecological modernization of industrial society' would be a transformed information base for policy making (Leipert and Simonis, 1990 p. 4).

There are a number of variants of the term 'sustainability' in widespread use, all of which denote a difference in policy emphasis in terms of the degree of fundamental reorientation in current policy which is required. A broad distinction can be made between the 'sustainable growth mode' and 'sustainable development mode' (Turner, 1991a), the latter requiring fundamental economic restructuring and the integration of environmental ethics into economic policy making. These environmental ethics include the recognition of poverty, social needs and North-South development issues. Similarly, O' Riordan (1989), distinguishes between 'sustainable utilization' within the current market economy framework, and 'sustainability', which

Figure 1.1: Expenditure on environmental protection in West Germany

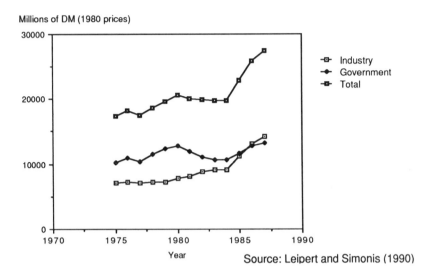

Millions of DM (1980 prices)

Source: Leipert and Simonis (1990)

would involve a radical transformation of society. Above all, the concept of sustainability has enabled the combination of previously polarized positions on the environment and economic growth, even if there has been little practical impact on environmental policy making (Owens and Owens, 1989). Yet despite the intense interest in the 'catch all' concept of sustainability since the late 1980s, conventional economic indicators such as GDP are still used across the political spectrum, in order to evaluate the efficacy of public policy (see Coates and Hillard, 1986; 1987).

By the late 1980s the emphasis of the environmental debate had shifted towards the need for international agreements, the implementation of tougher environmental legislation, and the increased use of economic policy instruments in order to integrate environmental policy into mainstream market-based economic policy. The 1980s focus on sustainability and alternative forms of economic policy has emerged from the perceived limitations of both neo-Malthusianism and conventional economic policy making. However, the sustainability consensus masks important differences in both the interpretation of the causes of environmental problems and the promotion of different policy strategies, as suggested by the diversity of environmentalist thought illustrated in Table 1.3.

14

The re-emergence of environmentalism in the 1980s

During the 1980s public attention was drawn to new scientific evidence of the seriousness of an environmental crisis encompassing: climatic change and ozone depletion; the effects of 'acid rain'; the destruction of tropical rainforests and mass extinctions of fauna and flora; the impact of unprecedented levels of air, sea and land pollution; the continuing threats to agricultural production from growing desertification and soil erosion; and more recently, fears over the safety of food and water for human consumption (see Brown, 1991; IPCC, 1990; Koopowitz and Kaye, 1983; McCormick, 1989; Myers, 1980; Seager, 1990). In addition to these identifiable processes of environmental degradation, there was a series of major environmental catastrophes, including Bhopal, Chernobyl, and the Exxon Valdez oil spillage, acting as a further catalyst to public concern.

There has also been a growing environmental role for international organisations as a continuation of the 1972 UN Stockholm Conference, in recognition of the need for co-operation between nation states in order to achieve sustainable growth and development. The United Nations has become increasingly involved in environmental policy, as reflected by the UN Environment and Development Programme's Brundtland Commission of 1987, and the major UN Rio Conference held in June 1992 (UN, 1987). Other international developments include the Brandt Commission of 1983 and the World Conservation Strategy of 1980, drawn up by the International Union for the Conservation of Nature and Natural Resources (IUCN) (Brandt Commission, 1980; World Wildlife Fund, 1983). The European Community has steadily increased the scope of its environmental policy making, as indicated by the EC sponsored 'European Year of the Environment' in 1987, the launch in 1992 of the Fifth Action Programme on the Environment, and the increasingly comprehensive range of directives aimed at improving environmental standards in its member states (Burgues, 1992; Haigh, 1987).

The renewed growth of environmentalism in the 1980s can be shown by a number of indicators: the increasing priority afforded to the environment in surveys of public opinion (Blowers, 1992; Porritt and Winner, 1988); the widespread greening of politics and formation of environmentalist political parties, as suggested by the elections to the European Parliament shown in Table 1.2; and a series of major international conferences and efforts to reach international agreements, including the 1987 Montreal Protocol on CFC emissions and the 1988 Conference on the North Sea. In the UK alone, membership of environmental organisations ranging from Friends of the Earth to the Royal Society for the Protection of Birds, has risen substantially during the 1980s, as illustrated in Table 1.1. These clear indications of a rise in environmental concern in the 1980s should, however, be set against important

15

Table 1.1: The growth of environmental groups in the UK during the 1980s

| | Individual membership | | % Change 1980-89 |
	1980	1989	
Greenpeace	10,000	320,000	+ 3,100
Friends of the Earth	12,000	120,000	+ 900
World Wildlife Fund	51,000	202,000	+ 296
Ramblers	36,000	73,000	+ 103
National Trust	950,000	1,750,000	+ 84
CPRE	27,000	44,500	+ 65
RSNC	140,000	205,000	+ 46
RSPB	321,000	433,000	+ 35
Total	1,547,000	3,147,500	+ 103

Source: McCormick (1991)

electoral setbacks at a national level for Green Parties in Germany, Sweden and the UK in the early 1990s, indicative of a partial waning of environmental concern in the face of pressing political and economic difficulties largely absent in the late 1980s.

The political goals of these different environmental groups are very diverse, ranging in the UK from the more conservatively inclined Council for the Protection of Rural England to radical left-oriented groups such as the Labour Countryside Campaign and the Ramblers (see Lowe et al, 1986). The split in environmentalist opinion is seen very clearly in the divide between the fundamental *fundis* wing and the pragmatic *realos* wing of the German Greens (Müller-Rommel and Poguntke, 1990). On the right of the environmental movement, there are claims that Green politics has been hijacked by the left (Bramwell, 1989; Capra and Spretnak, 1984). This is illustrated by reference to the defection of leading conservative environmentalists, such as Herbert Grühl, from the European Green Movement. It is also claimed that the worst environmental degradation has been a result of central planning:

In reality, it is socialist planning and economic policies, both under socialist and corporative capitalist parties, that have proved to be the most wasteful consumers of resources...The claims of the new Red ecologists that more of the same - 'changing social relations of property', 'taking resources from private ownership' will somehow produce an ecological millennium, show that ecologism has already lost its way. (Bramwell, 1989 p. 235).

Table 1.2: The electoral success of Green Parties in the elections to the European Parliament

	1979	1984	1989	Green Parties in 1989
Belgium	3.4%	8.2%	14.3%	AGALEV ECOLO-V REGEBO
Denmark	-	-	-	-
France	4.4%	6.7%	10.6%	The Greens
Greece	(Not in EC)	-	1.5%	Alternative Ecologists Ecological Movement
Ireland	-	0.5%	3.7%	Green Party
Italy	-	-	6.2%	Green List Rainbow Greens
Netherlands	-	6.9%	7.0%	Rainbow Party
Portugal	(Not in EC)	(Not in EC)	14.9%	United Democratic Coalition
Spain	(Not in EC)	(Not in EC)	2.8%	Green List (LV) Ecological Greens (VE) Green Party (PV) Green Alternative (AV-MEC)
United Kingdom	0.1%	0.5%	14.9%	Green Party
West Germany	3.2%	8.5%	9.3%	The Greens Ecological Democratic Party Ecological Union

Source: Mackie (1990); Mackie and Craig (1985).

Some environmentalists welcomed the process of de-industrialisation since the early 1970s as the natural precursor of a post-industrial and ecologically sustainable society, based around the adoption of decentralised human-scale technologies. However, the identification of the 'industrial super-ideology' (Porritt, 1986 p. 350) as the root cause of environmental problems has been criticised as a variant of 1950s and 1960s style liberal pluralism in political science by structuralist and political-economy interpretations of the environmental crisis. The concept of post-industrial environmental utopias is rejected as based on an inadequate conception of the social and economic organisation of capitalist societies (Frankel, 1987; Weston, 1986):

They (the post-industrialists) argue that the class-based society of the classical capitalist era has been replaced by a highly complex 'industrial society' in which economic interests are simply one of many countervailing factors in the distribution of resources...The society they wish to replace - the 'industrial society' - does not exist. (Weston, 1986 p. 28).

The attack on materialist culture and the 'industrial society' has been a central element in environmentalism since nineteenth century romanticism, and is allied with conceptions of the implicit superiority of rural as opposed to secular urban ways of life (Williams, 1986). The development of urbanism and cities has been characterised as an underlying cause of alienation from nature (Rozcak, 1979) and as a contributory factor in the development of socially stratified societies and militarism (Mumford, 1961).

The left of the environmental movement has seen the diversity of environmental politics as an indicator of its failure to mount a coherent challenge to the underlying causes of environmental problems:

The very fact that environmentalism now draws support from such a wide spectrum of political opinion is evidence of its failure to threaten the status quo...A campaigning environmentalism, based upon an understanding of the social construction of our physical surroundings, would have been in direct confrontation with the capitalist system. (Weston, 1986 p. 15).

The eco-socialists like Joe Weston have argued for a combination of environmental protection and social justice, stressing for example, the job creation potential of environmental protection technology and labour intensive 'soft' technologies (Griesshammer, 1985; Howells, 1986; Ryle, 1988; Williams, 1986). Eco-socialism has also been identified with the more pragmatic policies of environmental Keynesianism, for the regeneration of industrially depressed areas with public spending on environmental policy and was promoted in the mid-1980s as an alternative to monetarism and neo-liberal policies for economic restructuring (see Labour Party, 1986; Ossenbrügge, 1988; SPD, 1986).

The eco-socialists have been particularly powerful within the fundamentalist wing of the German Greens, and their radical agenda can be illustrated by the writings of Rudolf Bahro, who ultimately resigned from the German Green Party in 1985, in opposition to their repeated compromises and alliances with the existing political establishment:

The existing world order impoverishes half of humanity, forces whole nations below the basic subsistence level, and everywhere smothers local cultures, makes hundreds of millions of people landless and unemployed, destroys the fertility of the land, extends the deserts, fells the rain forests, and drives one country after another into state bankruptcy and towards military dictatorship....An ecological and social type of economy demands a completely different system of production: small units, locally integrated and self administered, with soft technologies which save resources and spare the environment. The present big industrial infrastructure for the flow of energy and materials, must be dismantled. (Bahro, 1986 pp. 36-40).

In the early eighties, it was widely argued that opinion within industrialised societies could be categorised into two main groups, ecocentrist and technocentrist, on the basis of their response to the environmental crisis (see O'Riordan, 1981; Pepper, 1984; Sandbach, 1980). The ecocentrists stressed the need for decentralised and low technology based social organisation, while the technocentrists continued to promote existing patterns of production and consumption, hard technological solutions to environmental problems, and no radical changes to society. However, a number of developments since the mid-1980s have served to weaken the clarity of this distinction, including the advent of 'green consumerism'; the emerging political consensus over the goal of environmental sustainability, which has clouded the distinctiveness of the 'green' alternative; and the rift between the fundamentalist and pragmatic wings of the environmental movement.

Thus far, this chapter has described the rise of environmentalism and environmental concern as if it were simply a response to environmental change but socio-economic changes within the developed economies have also facilitated and shaped its development. Rising affluence, for example, has allowed the growth of 'post-materialist' values (Cotgrove and Duff, 1980; Inglehardt, 1981) and a greater demand for 'positional goods' such as environmental amenity (Hirsch, 1977). The growth of a new middle class associated with the rise of service sectors in the economy has been linked with the emergence of new political demands since the 1960s encompassing feminism, lesbian and gay liberation, environmental protection and quality of life issues (Esser and Hirsch, 1987; Lash and Urry, 1987)

Despite the diversity of environmentalist thought, as illustrated in Table 1.3, the membership of the environmental movement is overwhelmingly drawn from professional and managerial occupations (Cotgrove and Duff, 1980; Lowe and Goyder, 1983; Lowe et al, 1986). This apparent anomaly can be explained by important political differences within the middle class, as in the distinction between more conservatively inclined nature

Table 1.3: Western environmentalist thought : A typology

School of thought	Central tenets	Key proponents
Cornucopians	No major problems perceived. Easily solved by human ingenuity and economic development.	Simon (1981) Simon and Kahn (1984)
Managerialists and technical fixers	The use of organisational or technical solutions, such as the use of nuclear energy to combat energy shortages and global warming.	Feiss (1963) Haefele (1974)
Market-based approaches	The use of MBIs to internalise environmental cost externalities and harness market forces.	Elkington (1987) Pearce et al (1989; 1991)
Institutional reform school	Promotion of sustainable development by better integration of environmental policy with economic development. Focus on N.-S. dimension and need for change in global monetary and trade policy.	Brandt Report (1981) UNEP Brundtland Commission (1987)
Environmental Keynesianism	Emphasis on the employment creation potential of public expenditure on environmental protection.	Griesshammer (1984) SPD (1986)
Post-industrialists and liberal pluralists	Industrialism seen as underlying problem. Focus on need to change individual attitudes.	Capra and Spretnak (1984) Porritt (1984)
The Limits to Growth school	The promotion of scientifically based public policy and reduced growth of populaion and the world-economy.	Meadows et al (1972) Goldsmith et al (1972)
Socio-biologists and authoritarian ecology	The promotion of neo-malthusian ideas and social darwinism in public policy.	Bramwell (1988) Colinvaux (1980)
Deep Ecology	The preservation of wilderness areas and the centrality of nature to all policy making.	Devall and Sessions (1985)
Gaia hypothesis	The promotion of homeostatic and sustainable policies.	Lovelock (1979)
Utopian socialists and anarchists	The transformation of society into numerous decentralised and largely self-sufficient communities. The promotion of 'soft' technologies.	Bahro (1982; 1986) Croall and Rankin (1981)
Orthodox Marxists	Environmental degradation seen as an inevitable consequence of the capiatalist mode of production	Harvey (1974) Sandbach (1980)
Post-marxist political economy	Environmental problems seen as stemming from structural features in the economy and society which need to be examined from a historically based political-economy perspective.	Hecht and Cockburn (1989) Ossenbruegge (1988) Redclift (1987)
Feminist Perspectives	Domination and destruction of nature seen as a corollary of women's oppression under patriarchy	Shiva (1988)

Source: Gandy (1992b).

conservationists and heritage preservers and the radical left oriented anti-nuclear protesters (Cotgrove, 1982). Indeed, the divergence of political views within the middle class since the 1960s can be conceived as an example of class de-alignment in political identification (Franklin, 1985; Särlvik and Crewe, 1983). Further studies suggest that many of the members of the ostensibly non class-based green movement can be characterised as 'political outsiders' in relation to established class structures and social relations, and are often employed in the public service sector of the economy (Cotgrove and Duff, 1980; 1981).

The re-emergence of environmentalism and the rise of 'green consumerism' in the 1980s should be placed in the context of the socio-economic restructuring in the developed economies which has been necessitated by growing economic difficulties in the OECD nations since the early 1970s. In the 1980s, for example, there has been a trend towards what may be termed 'positional' or luxury goods. This diversification of 'positional' goods corresponds with the product differentiation and market niche creation which is integral to the economic shift from Fordism to post-Fordist flexible accumulation and economies of scope rather than of scale (Cooke, 1988; Lipietz, 1992; Scott and Storper, 1986). The shift from the mass consumption of consumer durables to individualised consumption, can be illustrated by the development of environmentally friendly products which are more expensive than their environmentally damaging alternatives, not because they are necessarily more expensive to manufacture, but because they serve an elite consumer market where price is less of an object:

> The frenetic pursuit of the consumption dollars of the affluent has led
> to a much stronger emphasis upon product differentiation under the
> regime of flexible accumulation. (Harvey, 1989a, p. 269).

An important question is how far the nature of western environmentalism and environmental policy has been shaped by the wider socio-economic changes which have aided its development. Since the early 1970s, the developed economies have undergone a set of socio-economic, political and cultural changes, which many social scientists believe are interrelated and not readily explicable in terms of existing conceptual frameworks (Pratt, 1990; Smart, 1993). This has led to a key theoretical debate at present within the humanities and the social sciences, concerning a postulated shift from modernism to postmodernism. The phenomenon of postmodernism has been associated in particular with the demise of orthodox Marxist political economy and 'grand theory'; changing cultural styles in architecture and art; a disaffection with the modernist Enlightenment project; and the emergence of 'flexible accumulation' and post-Fordism in response to the economic crises of the 1970s in the core OECD economies (see Harvey, 1989a, 1989b; Jencks, 1986; Nairne, 1987; and Soja, 1989).

The body of work arising from the socio-economic restructuring and postmodernity debate serves as a heuristic device to enable a number of complex issues surrounding the socio-economic developments of recent years to be addressed coherently, rather than in a piece-meal unconnected fashion. The relevance of this debate to environmentalism in the 1980s rests on a number of interrelated developments: the increase in aggregate world consumption within a market economy of extended global reach; the collapse of state socialism and the discrediting of state intervention in the economy; space-time compression and improvements in communications technology; the emergence of 'green consumerism' as a form of elite lifestyle politics within developed economies; and the growth of a cultural anti-modernity, associated with a lack of faith in science and technology and the decline of Modernism and socialism as a secular emancipatory ideology (Nairne, 1987; Pepper, 1989; Smart, 1993).

The rise of individualist politics in the 1980s has become integrated into environmental concern through the increasing emphasis on the need to adapt individual behaviour and patterns of production and consumption to assuage environmental fears. Indeed, the growth of 'green capitalism' and 'green consumerism' has been widely welcomed in the technocratic and liberal pluralist sections of the green movement, as a key aspect of environmental policy, which can harness the 'enlightened self-interest' of consumers (see Elkington, 1987; Elkington and Hailes, 1988; Porritt and Winner, 1988; Seymour and Giradet, 1988). In this respect, therefore, the promotion of 'green consumerism' and market-based environment policy has closely followed the socio-economic shifts towards more individualised forms of political expression and a more fractious and splintered politics associated with the decline of class-based mass political parties (Esser and Hirsch, 1987; Lash and Urry, 1987).

However, the postmodern condition of new flexible patterns of economic activity is of paradoxical significance for environmental policy, since it is a political and cultural adaptation to the perceived economic and political failure of the Modernist project, which had previously given some degree of legitimacy to the role of planning and state intervention in public policy. As a result, therefore, the current direction of environmental policy is being shaped by the economic and political inability of the state to take a major role in the implementation of policy under the shift from Keynesianism to neo-liberalism since the late 1970s with its emphasis on the use of market-based rather than regulatory policy instruments. In the next chapter these developments are explored further through the process of demunicipalisation in local government services, as part of the evolving political and economic context

22

for recycling within the privatisation of municipal waste management.

Competing conceptions of environmental policy

In order to examine the environmental debate in greater detail, it is necessary to disentangle the main strands of thought which underpin the diversity of environmentalist views, illustrated in Table 1.3, and which inform different approaches to environmental policy making. There are broadly three different groups of interpretations of the cause of the environmental crisis and appropriate policy responses identifiable in the literature: firstly, there are the dominant market-based and technocratic approaches; secondly, there are humanistic, pluralist and behaviouralist approaches; and thirdly, there are the structuralist political-economy approaches. Figure 1.2 suggests that these three approaches can be distinguished epistemologically in terms of their theoretical conception of society, and practically, in terms of the degree and nature of societal change which would be necessitated in order to protect the environment. The typology adopted here is based loosely on Emel and Peet (1989) and can be considered in conjunction with the philosophical distinction between positivism, humanism and structuralism used widely within human geography and the social sciences (see Johnston, 1983).

In the following sections, the review of different interpretations of environmental problems is used to clarify the debate over environmental policy, and in particular, the relative role of market-based and regulatory policy instruments. I argue that the most important cleavage within the spectrum of environmental thought and policy making concerns the conceptualisation of the role of the market and the degree and nature of state intervention in the economy.

Technocratic and market-based approaches

The market-based approach can be conceived as a variant of 'technocentrism' within the technocentrist/ecocentrist distinction (O'Riordan, 1989). In the past, technocentrism has been frequently associated with the search for managerialist and 'hard' technological solutions, often promoted and financed by the state. An example is the advancement of 'nuclear parks' in response to the 1970s energy crisis (Häfele, 1974). Technocentrist approaches saw solutions in terms of engineering based technical 'fixes' but since the late 1970s and 1980s the technocratic emphasis has shifted towards market-led technological developments based on the relative profitability of different policy options. The decline of nuclear power as a result of the extension of market forces into strategic technological decision making can be viewed as

Figure 1.2: The relationship between different conceptions of environmental problems and policy

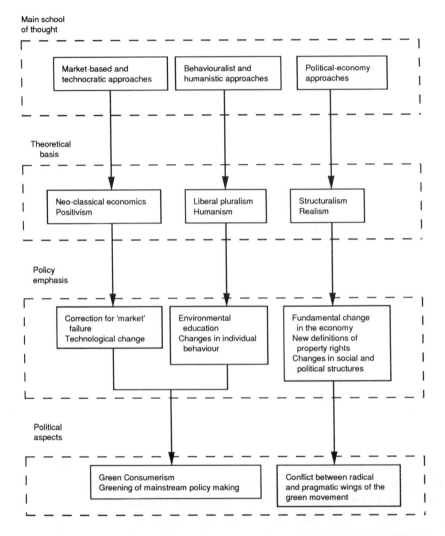

Source: Gandy (1992b)

an example of this process.

Until the 1980s, however, the policy debate had tended to discuss regulatory instruments to the relative exclusion of economic instruments: there has been a tendency to see fiscal measures and regulation by the state as direct alternatives (Owens et al., 1989). Economic policy instruments have emerged as a fundamental component in the new environmental consensus for sustainability, based around market-based conceptions of policy (see Pearce et al., 1989; 1991; 1993). It should be noted that a large section of the environmentalist movement has also embraced the development of 'green consumerism' and market-based policies, particularly the liberal pluralists and pragmatic wing of the green movement, as illustrated in Figure 1.2, where the emphasis on individual responsibility and action has become easily incorporated into 'green consumerism' and the use of market-based policy instruments to modify consumer behaviour.

A central concern emerging from the 1970s literature was whether the market could provide for the future. For Roberts (1974), the market could not consider long-term resource scarcity because it was only concerned with short-term profitability, as illustrated by the built-in obsolescence of consumer durables. However, other commentators began to develop an alternative perspective based around the notion that the market could provide for the future if it operated efficiently in the absence of various sources of 'market failure' which lay behind environmentally damaging economic activity (Page, 1977). The market-based approach to environmental policy is based on the belief that a properly functioning market economy is the best allocator of goods and resources, yet the market does not currently extend adequately to the use of natural resources and environmental externalities:

> Environmental goods like clean air and clean water are not exchanged in unregulated markets: they have no price, so there is no incentive for economy in their use. While 'free' to the individual, they are scarce to the community, and therefore become degraded. Pollution can be seen in this context as an externality - a cost of economic activity which can be imposed by some parties on others without compensation. Intervention to create a 'market' in clean air or clean water - by creating property rights in the environment or imposing effluent charges - will in theory internalise these costs and correct the market failure which leads to pollution. (Owens et al., 1990 p. 4).

The effective operation of market mechanisms must therefore be brought about by the internalisation of the environmental costs associated with production and consumption. Button and Pearce (1989), for example, argue that the costs of urban environmental policy are not adequately incorporated into decision making as a result of a combination of 'market failure' and the role of government interfering with the 'private optimum'. However, the market-based position does not conceive of the state's role as entirely negative, since state intervention is frequently necessary in order to allow the market to function effectively.

A key component in many market-based instruments (MBIs) is the use of the 'polluter pays principle' whereby costs are imposed on individual polluters as a disincentive to continue with the polluting activity (though some polluters may choose to ignore such incentives, see BANC, 1990). The different means by which the costs of polluting activity can be internalised can be further differentiated. The OECD has recently classified the range of economic instruments available for environmental policy into five categories: charges, subsidies, deposit-refund systems, market creation and financial enforcement incentives (Opschoor and Vos, 1989). In the case of the application of the 'polluter pays principle', by using pollution taxes or charges, there are two main theoretical arguments put forward: firstly, that of 'allocative efficiency' whereby a tax or charge achieves desired environmental quality at minimum economic cost (those who can most cheaply reduce pollution do most of the pollution control); and secondly, the 'innovative incentive principle', whereby a charge must be paid on all units of pollution, providing a continual incentive to develop better means of pollution control (Owens et al., 1990).

Criticism of market-based approaches to environmental policy has questioned a number of fundamental tenets held within the neo-classical economic paradigm, as well as the effectiveness of these policies in practice. For example, in order for a market to achieve optimal resource allocation, a range of conditions would have to be met, including the economic rationality of producers and consumers and perfect mobility of the factors of production, yet these conditions do not hold in reality (Emel and Peet, 1989). Despite these types of criticisms of the difference between the theoretical basis of neo-classical economic analysis and the nature of the market economy as it exists, many resource economists claim that technological and allocative efficiency can be attained with appropriate government intervention to correct for market failure (Button and Pearce, 1989; Pearce et al., 1989).

For MBIs to be effective there is a need for the development of sophisticated cost-benefit analysis (CBA) methodologies, extending monetary value to the 'total economic value' of the environment, and moving beyond narrow conventional economic indicators such as GDP. This would, according to David Pearce, include three different kinds of use value: direct use values (e.g. timber and eco-tourism); indirect use values (e.g. air quality); option and quasi-option values (e.g. the retention of resources for future generations); and also non-use existence values (e.g. the protection of the blue whale). As a parallel project, methodologies would be developed to determine the intensity of preference by measuring the willingness of consumers to pay for environmental protection.

There are perhaps four main arguments as to why the use of a monetary valuation of the environment may be an effective aspect of environmental protection: the economic argument can be seen as an additional argument to scientific analysis of environmental problems; the economic argument is a more powerful tool for political lobbying than moral arguments, as the dominant language of social power, and is now widely employed by environmentalist pressure groups; money can also be portrayed as a universal notion of value; and finally, research has suggested that the conservation and sustainable utilisation of resources may be worthwhile in purely economic terms irrespective of other social and ecological concerns (Pearce, 1991).

However, there are a number of concerns both practical and methodological, with the use of monetary valuations as the basis for policy making. The assignment of monetary values to components of the environment assumes an atomistic view of the environment as a collage of different pieces to which property rights may be attached, but this fails to determine who has rights to what and the basis on which property rights are to be allocated. Note, for example, how multinational corporations are currently hardening their views on property rights to control the results of plant and animal breeding in order to secure long-term profitability within the global agricultural sector in the face of economic uncertainty (Harvey, 1992; Holmberg et al., 1993). A further consideration is the positivist conception of knowledge shared by both the natural sciences and also the emerging sub-discipline of environmental economics with its theoretical basis in neo-classical economics, since many of the factors which need to be incorporated within comprehensive cost-benefit analysis procedures are intrinsically subjective and 'indeterminate' (Adams, 1974; BANC, 1990; Rosenhead and Thunhurst, 1979; Self, 1975). The CBA procedure becomes even more uncertain when applied to the 'option values' of resources for future generations since money is not a constant value over time and economic crises periodically herald a devaluation of assets from previous periods of economic activity (Harvey, 1992).

Under market-based models of decision making, the distributional issues of income disparities both within and between nations are given inadequate attention. Neglected areas include the nature of democratic procedures for public decision making and the impact of Third World debt and the terms of trade for basic commodities (BANC, 1990). If the neo-classical analogy of 'money votes' is used to show how decision making takes place in the market place, it is clear that many people are relatively, if not completely, disenfranchised from environmental decision making. The application of the 'polluter pays principle' to reduce environmentally damaging activity may also be socially regressive, especially when used to discourage the profligate consumption of fuel and other basic essentials. A further distributional issue is the impact of 'green' taxes on raw materials usage and energy resources in developing countries and the concern that 'green taxes' are ultimately paid for by the public as additional forms of indirect taxation (Williamson, 1974). Pollution taxes may also cause negative wider macro-economic effects including increased inflation and reduced international competitiveness, an argument used against the introduction of a Carbon Tax in the UK to counter global warming, where there are fears over the employment impact in the high energy consuming industries (McGavin, 1991).

Non market-based approaches

A number of alternative conceptions to that of the neo-classical economic and technocentric approaches move the focus towards more overtly subjective and ethically oriented positions. The necessity of considering non-economic factors in the application of economic or technical engineering based solutions to resource management problems has long been recognised in the field of natural hazards (Emel and Peet, 1989). This is linked to a recognition of the diversity of interpretations which exist of both the causes and possible solutions to environmental problems:

> What we have is not the real (environmental) risks versus a whole lot of misconceptions of those risks but the clash of plural rationalities each using impeccable logic to derive different conclusions (solution definitions) from different premises (problem definitions). (Thompson, 1986 quoted in Redclift, 1987 p. 202).

An important alternative to the market-based analysis is the range of political-economy perspectives. These are marked by their focus on the structuralist economic and political features of society, and in particular, on the historical emergence and contemporary operation of the global market economy. Michael Redclift, for example, notes that environmental rationalities are not only socially constructed, but are 'supported by social groups with different degrees of power and with conflicting economic interests' (Redclift, 1987 p. 202).

Structuralist political-economy approaches are characterised by the rejection of the findings of positivist 'value-free' ahistorical analysis and individualist humanistic interpretations of social change. The historical dimension is seen as a critical aspect of any explanation of environmental degradation, with emphasis on processes such as the internationalisation of the global environment through the extension of capitalist exchange values into cultures based around traditional use values for natural resources (Redclift, 1987). There are a range of political-economy based arguments arising from the analysis of the historical development and contemporary operation of the global market economy. These studies suggest that capitalist economic development and environmental sustainability are intrinsically incompatible, and that an extension of market mechanisms and value-free 'scientific' rationalisations of environmental problems would ultimately only exacerbate the environmental crisis (Bahro, 1982; 1984; Redclift, 1987; Sandbach, 1980; Weston, 1986).

There were a number of Marxist studies in the 1970s, showing how environmental concern had been dissipated by legislative measures. Examples include Walker and Storper's (1978) study of the 1970 Clean Air Act in the US (and the failure of government regulation and planning in practice), and Sandbach's (1980) interpretation of the 1974 Control of Pollution Act in the UK as a 'legitimation' strategy by the Government. Environmental 'reformism' was viewed as a legislative 'end of pipe' response to the growing political salience of environmental concern, with little practical impact on the cause of environmental problems. More recently, the UN Brundtland Commission has been criticised for its failure to address the necessary shifts in power and institutional alignments which could allow sustainability to become a practical reality and therefore overcome the underlying barriers to environmental protection (O'Riordan, 1989).

Structuralist political-economy perspectives on the environment have developed substantially during the 1980s. Orthodox Marxist interpretations of economic development and environmental degradation have themselves been widely criticised by new political-economy perspectives. Principal concerns with the earlier studies include: the reliance on a labour theory of value (Martinez-Alier, 1987); failure to give sufficient weight to the impact of patriarchy on the environment, particularly in a Third World context (Shiva, 1986; 1988); the primacy of economic determinism in explanation (Corbridge, 1986); sterile 'epistemological confrontation' with other interpretations (Corbridge, 1986); the neglect of environmental degradation under state socialism; and insufficient attention given to the role of technology in extending the 'frontiers of sustainability' (Redclift, 1987).

In the last decade, there have been a number of studies of how structural causal mechanisms operate in producing local or regional manifestations of the environmental crisis. Examples include soil degradation in different societies (Blaikie 1985; Blaikie and Brookfield, 1987); famine in Nigeria (Watts, 1983); deforestation in the Amazon basin (Hecht and Cockburn, 1989); and the environmental pollution facing the inhabitants of Mexico City (Redclift, 1987). These studies stress the importance of the historical development of contemporary phenomena, and also the interplay of economic and political forces at both a regional and global level of resolution.

Conclusion

This chapter has attempted to unravel some of the complexities and contradictions within the contemporary environmental debate. I argue that beneath the diversity of different perspectives, there is a conceptual distinction to be made between the use of market-based and non market-based conceptions of the causes of environmental problems. This in turn informs the discussion over the appropriate use of different policy instruments, and in particular the degree and nature of state intervention in the market. I suggest that this focus on the market/non market dimension is a more useful conceptual framework than the influential ecocentrism/technocentrism distinction widely employed in the literature of the 1980s. The Western phenomenon of 'green consumerism' and the focus on market-based policy instruments can be best interpreted as a coalescence between the emphasis on 'individual responsibility' within the behaviouralist and pluralist environmental perspectives and the ideological shift towards market-based interpretations of the cause of environmental problems as a corollary of wider developments within public policy since the 1970s.

In the next chapter, the theme of the theoretical and practical aspects of different approaches to environmental policy is elaborated further with an examination of policies to reduce the wastage of materials in household waste. The pattern of municipal waste management and recycling in developed economies is outlined as the practical focus of this study, and a range of key issues are identified as the basis for the analysis of recycling in London and Hamburg.

2 Waste, recycling and environmental concern

The post-war period has seen a dramatic increase in the production of waste, reflecting unprecedented global levels of economic activity. The increase in the waste stream can be attributed to a number of factors: rising levels of affluence; cheaper consumer products; the advent of built-in obsolescence and shorter product life-cycles; the proliferation of packaging; changing patterns of taste and consumption; and the demand for convenience products (Crowther, 1974; Galbraith, 1958; Packard, 1960). The scale of increased personal consumption in the UK over the post-war period can be illustrated by the fact that in 1957 less than 20 per cent of all households had a refrigerator, yet by 1987 over 95 per cent of households had this consumer durable, and in the case of car ownership, this had risen from under 25 per cent of households in 1957 to over 60 per cent of households in 1987 (Elkington and Hailes, 1988) and the UK now produces double the amount of waste it produced in 1965 from municipal and industrial sources (Financial Times Survey, 1990).

The post-war period has seen not only an increase in the size of the waste stream, but also a steady increase in the cost and logistical difficulties of municipal waste management. In global terms, it is the larger cities which present the greatest challenge for the handling of municipal wastes, since they represent a geographical concentration of waste production coupled with ever scarcer opportunities for its cheap and safe disposal: many US cities now face a tax burden for their solid waste management which is exceeded only by education and roads.

Waste categories and definitions

The idea of waste arises from the perception that material by-products of production and consumption have no further value, especially within affluent

31

Figure 2.1: Total waste production in the UK

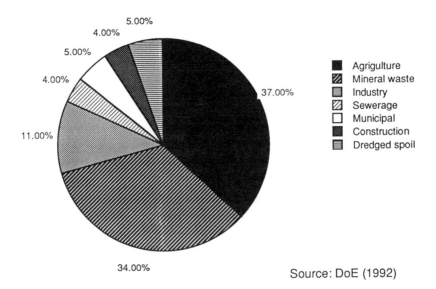

Source: DoE (1992)

developed economies and among richer citizens of developing countries. Any definition of waste is therefore related to the material needs of a given society or community, and is a dynamic historically determined concept. In any discussion of waste issues it is important to recognise that there are no reliable comparative figures for global waste production, particularly for developing countries, and that the most reliable information is available for the OECD nations with more sophisticated data gathering procedures. There is at present no internationally recognised classification system for waste categories, although the European Community and the OECD are developing new systems to facilitate the implementation of new legislation and international guidelines:

> The definitions of waste, their hazards, recommended treatment and the boundaries between them and recyclable materials is in flux...A number of national definitions exist and no two are alike. (Holmes, 1989 p. 6).

It is possible, however, to distinguish between several broad categories of waste within the total waste stream of developed economies. In the case of the UK, in the late 1980s, some 700 million tonnes of waste were produced. Figure 2.1 shows that of this total, 37 per cent comprised agricultural wastes, disposed of as straw and silage; mineral waste, accounted for 34 per cent,

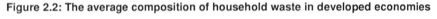

Figure 2.2: The average composition of household waste in developed economies

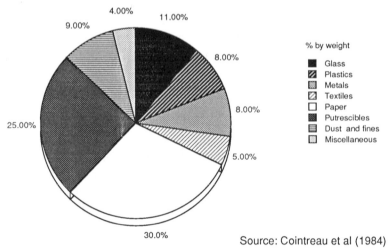

4.00%

11.00%

9.00%

8.00%

% by weight

■ Glass
▨ Plastics
▦ Metals
▨ Textiles
☐ Paper
▨ Putrescibles
▤ Dust and fines
▧ Miscellaneous

25.00%

8.00%

5.00%

30.0%

Source: Cointreau et al (1984)

disposed of on land; controlled industrial wastes, known to the local authority Waste Disposal Authorities (WDAs), made up 11 per cent of the total and were generally disposed of by landfill or incineration; sewage waste made up 4 per cent of the total, and was disposed of at sea; municipal and medical wastes amounted to just 5 per cent of the total waste stream, and were disposed of by landfill or incineration; a further 4 per cent was derived from construction and demolition activity; and finally, there was 5 per cent of dredged spoil, which was disposed of at sea (DoE, 1992). It is of interest that only 3 per cent of the total waste stream is derived from household sources, and this is an important issue to bear in mind when considering the potential contribution of household waste recycling to environmental policy.

Figure 2.2 shows that the average contents of household waste in developed economies now contain around 30 per cent paper and cardboard; 24 per cent vegetable matter; 11 per cent glass; 9 per cent dust and cinders; 8 per cent plastics; 8 per cent metals; 5 per cent textiles; and a further 4 per cent of miscellaneous and unclassified fractions. Each of these major fractions can be further differentiated in terms of different materials and their origin. In the case of metals, over 80 per cent of waste metals are ferrous, the non-ferrous scrap consisting primarily of aluminium, copper, zinc, tin, lead, and various alloys (DoE, 1991a; ITU, 1989). The composition of waste varies spatially as a result of a number of factors: the level of urbanisation; the degree of prosperity and the local employment structure; the housing type and urban morphology; and the time of year (affecting the proportion of garden waste, for example). Note that the municipal waste stream also includes quantities of waste from trade and commerce, in addition to household waste. As a consequence, any study of household waste necessarily involves a consideration of the municipal waste stream, and much of the available data for developed economies does not distinguish between these different sources of municipal waste.

The material categories of the municipal waste stream in developed economies can be usefully divided into three main classes for the purposes of waste management planning: firstly, there is combustible waste, which makes up approximately 50 per cent of the waste by weight; secondly, there are non-combustibles, which account for roughly 20 per cent by weight; and thirdly, there is the putrescible material which constitutes around 30 per cent by weight, and includes some paper as well as vegetable waste (Barton 1988; Newell, 1991). The two most important overall characteristics of household waste for energy recovery are derived from the moisture and ash content and the calorific value. The calorific value determines the potential for incineration with energy recovery, as an alternative means of waste disposal. The average calorific value of municipal solid waste stands at around 10.8 MJ/kg assuming a moisture content of 20 to 30 per cent by weight, which compares with around 30 MJ/kg per tonne for coal and 40 MJ/kg per tonne for industrial fuel oil. However, the calorific value of different waste materials varies from nil in the case of glass and metals, to 37.0 MJ/kg for mixed plastics, as illustrated in Table 2.1.

Table 2.1: The calorific value of municipal waste

Waste fraction	MJ/kg
Plastic	37.0
Textiles	16.0
Paper and card	14.6
Dust and cinders	9.6
Putrescibles	6.7
Glass	nil
Metals	nil

Source: WARMER Bulletin (1991)

Municipal waste management

The pattern of household waste recycling cannot be understood independently of the wider practice of municipal waste management, since the recovery of re-usable materials from the waste stream can be conceived as an alternative to the routine collection and disposal of waste. Within developed economies, the emergence of a legislative framework for waste management can be traced to the public health fears associated with rapid industrialisation and urbanisation in the nineteenth century (see Evans, 1991; Melosi, 1981; Soper, 1909 and Chapter Three). Until the 1930s, waste management in developed economies was quite straightforward: household rubbish was burnt in a basic incinerator or dumped on an open tip. Industrial wastes were not as numerous or complex as they are now, and were often deposited on a site acquired by the owner of the factory where they originated or disposed of along with household and other wastes (Financial Times Survey, 1990).

The collection of municipal waste

The collection of municipal waste is a typical service provided by local government, which either directly employs labour for the task or uses private sector companies on a contractual basis. Since the 1970s, the use of private companies for the collection of waste has been increasing in developed economies and these changes form an important element in the changing policy context for recycling, examined in Chapter Five.

The technical and logistical aspects of waste collection vary in a number of respects: the design of the dustbins and the collection vehicles; the time and frequency of the collection service; and the particular arrangements used for congested urban areas, as illustrated in Table 2.2. A key dimension to the analysis of waste collection is the administrative and organisational relationship between the collection and disposal of waste and the interrelationship between the practice of waste management and the structure of local government. A further theme of interest is the rise of political concern since the mid-1970s over levels of state expenditure and the cost of local government services, focusing attention on the economic efficiency and productivity of waste collection (Stewart and Stoker, 1989) and forming an important factor behind the process of demunicipalisation of local government services (see below).

Waste disposal by landfill

At the beginning of the 1990s, most municipal refuse is disposed of by tipping at so-called landfill sites. However, this option is faced with growing

Table 2.2: The collection of household waste

The organisation of waste management	Size of the administrative units The degree of integration with waste disposal
The design of dustbins or other receptacles	Wheeled or standard bins Single or multiple bins systems (for paper or organics) Containers for mixed recyclebes Separate containers for different recyclables Paladins (shared bins for appartments)
Collection vehicles	Vehicle adaptations and technical aspects Compartmentalised vehicles for segregated wastes Component recycling (CR) systems
Operational aspects	Alternative approaches: *Public sector workforce (DSOs in the UK)* *Management buy outs (MBOs)* *Publicly owned corporation s e.g. LB-HSR in Hamburg* *Private sector waste management companies (small firms or specialist multi-national companies with interests in other aspects or municipal service provision*
Economic aspects	Net cost of waste collection
Arrangements for bulky household waste	Kerbside collection services Civic amenity type facilities
Integration with sewerage and management of wet wastes	Garchey system for kitchen wastes
Logistical aspects	Frequency of collections Special arrangements for high rise appartments

Source: Gandy (1992a)

political and economic difficulties. Landfill has been criticised as a viable disposal option because it produces toxic leachates which can contaminate water supplies and also produces combustible landfill gas from the anaerobic decomposition of putrescible waste. These gases, once they have entered the atmosphere, act as greenhouse agents, and one kilogram of methane is believed to be up to 60 more powerful than carbon dioxide in its contribution to global warming, and constitutes some 16 per cent of greenhouse gases (Foley, 1991). It has been estimated that landfill gas emissions account for 21 per cent of UK methane gas emissions, being the third most important source after agriculture (33 per cent) and coal mining (29 per cent) (*WARMER Bulletin*, August 1991).

Past landfill methods, particularly the co-disposal of household waste and miscellaneous hazardous wastes derived from industry, were common in the developed economies until the mid-1970s and this practice has contributed to public opposition to the construction of new landfill facilities (Forester, 1991; Gore, 1992; Klinski, 1988; Norton-Taylor, 1982). In the US, for example, public pressure and new legislation have resulted in a rapid decline in the number of landfill sites, and under legislation in 1984, the US Environmental Protection Agency issued the most stringent landfill regulations in US history. The US Environmental Protection Agency reported that in 1979 there were over 16,000 landfill sites in operation, but by 1988 the number had decreased to around 5,500 as a result of tighter controls and the exhaustion of existing sites (Forester, 1991). The cost of waste management has been rising steadily in many developed economies since the early 1970s (Leipert and Simonis, 1990) and in the US, for example, the average cost of landfill per ton rose from $10.80 to $26.93 in the six year period 1982-88 (Forester, 1991). The consequence of these developments is that the new generation of landfill sites is different from the sites of the past: they are larger and further away from centres of population; they are much more closely monitored; their operation often involves advanced technical methods of pollution control; and some sites extract landfill gas as a source of fuel, serving as a source of income for the site operators. Landfill 'bio-gas' is now widely used for the production of heat or electricity, or for conversion into higher quality fuels such as liquid natural gas. Of the 242 landfill gas schemes which are operating world-wide, 55 per cent of projects generate electricity. The USA was the first country to exploit landfill gas in the 1970s, and by 1989 there were 87 operational schemes. In western Europe there were 140 schemes running, including 74 in Germany, 33 in the UK and 20 in Sweden (Richards, 1989).

Disposal by incineration

The first systematic incineration of municipal refuse was tested in Nottingham in 1878 and it rapidly became a key component of waste disposal in Europe from the late nineteenth century onwards (Tucker, 1977). Present day incineration is the high temperature burning of waste, from which the waste heat can be used for CHP heating schemes and also for the production of electricity. Incineration facilities have had an increasing role in waste management in the developed economies since the early 1980s: there are now over 500 incinerators for municipal solid waste within the European Community, of which more than 80 per cent have energy recovery facilities (*WARMER Bulletin*, January 1990). It is now the dominant method of waste disposal for a small number of developed economies, notably in Denmark, Japan, Luxembourg, Sweden and Switzerland.

The environmental concerns associated with incineration emissions and the related problem of the increasing quantities of toxic wastes in the municipal waste stream grew rapidly in the late 1970s (Klinski, 1988). Emissions concerns focus principally on dioxins and furans produced from chlorine containing compounds such as plastics, and bleached paper. Some dioxins such as terachlorodibenzo-p-dioxin, are among the most toxic molecules yet identified, and research has indicated alarming levels of these carcinogens in mothers' milk in the vicinity of incineration plants (see Gore, 1992; Hoffman et al., 1986; Meister, 1990; Rappe et al., 1986; Spill and Wingert, 1990; and WEN, 1989, on the human health hazards of incineration plants). In 1986, Sweden became the first country to issue dioxin regulations, and by 1987 there were eleven air pollutants regulated in West Germany with the stipulation that any furnaces violating emissions limits for one hour must be closed. The year 1989 saw the introduction of an EC Directive (89/369/EEC) on incineration emissions which will accelerate the rationalisation and technical developments within this branch of the waste management industry.

The other main impact is from toxins, particularly heavy metals left in the residual ash after burning. The production of heavy metals is mainly from dry cell batteries, paint, and lighting fixtures. As a result of the concentration of heavy metals in the residual incineration ash, this is now treated as hazardous waste in Sweden (Pollock, 1987) and there are moves in the US to prevent the co-disposal of incineration ash with municipal waste at landfill sites (Underwood et al., 1987; Gore, 1992). Further concerns focus on the contribution of these plants to the formation of acid precipitation from the emission of nitrous oxides released from the burning of organic wastes.

There have, however, been improvements in incineration technology since the 1970s with research and development concentrated in Europe and encouraged by the increasingly tough state and EC level emission controls (*WARMER Bulletin*, January 1990). Proponents of incineration argue the emissions problems with dioxins can be technically solved and that the generation of electricity reduces the use of fossil fuels and therefore contributes towards a net reduction in the greenhouse effect (Tabasaran, 1984; Porteus, 1990). Other research has claimed that incineration emissions are insignificant in relation to total air pollution in developed economies (Halbritter et al., 1984) and that toxins can be reduced by the separation of plastics from the rest of the waste stream by recycling activities (Shiga, 1975).

The demunicipalisation of waste management

In Chapter One I described how the shift towards neo-liberalism in the 1980s has affected the environmental policy debate. The decline in Keynesian patterns of post-war economic and social policy associated with the decline in Fordist and collectivist socio-economic structures, has seen a transformation in the role of the state in public policy (Martin, 1987; Ossenbrügge,1988). The key development of interest here is the attempted 'recapitalisation' of the OECD economies in the 1980s, marked by an extension of market forces and the 'rolling back' of the state. This has resulted in increasingly tight controls on public expenditure, a decline of strategic planning, and cut backs in social welfare programmes (Ambrose, 1986; Lipietz, 1992; Martin, 1986). The changes during the 1980s have been particularly significant in local government, where the role of municipal authorities has been substantially modified to reduce the national and local tax burden on the 'wealth creating' private sector (Fincher, 1989; Stewart and Stoker, 1989). In the UK, for example, there was an expansion in local government employment of 69.7 per cent between 1961 to 1975 and state expenditure as a share of GNP rose from 42.1 per cent in 1961 to 57.9 per cent in 1975 (Stoker, 1989). Figure 2.3 shows how expenditure on the collection and disposal of municipal waste has risen sharply since the 1930s and this area of local government services has been a key target for the reduction of public expenditure (Stewart and Stoker, 1989).

The root of the contemporary process of demunicipalisation in waste management can be traced to the mid-1970s, when the existing structure of municipal waste management in the public sector, especially in the US, began to be increasingly criticised on a number of grounds: the growing environmental controls and technical complexity had left many local municipalities in the operational role of only waste collection; the spiralling costs of waste collection and waste disposal were a growing tax burden; the complexity of new developments in waste management was exceeding available expertise in local government; and the combination of these developments, along with new demands for resource recovery, required new administrative structures for waste management which could effectively handle data gathering and policy development, benefit from economies of scale, and invest in new programmes for the recovery of materials and energy (Goddard, 1975).

The main concern was the high and rising costs of waste collection. In the mid-1970s, waste collection constituted over 70 per cent of the overall costs

Figure 2.3: Expenditure on municipal waste collection and disposal in the UK

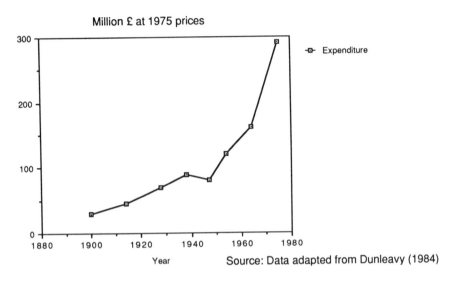

Source: Data adapted from Dunleavy (1984)

of municipal waste management in the US, and this was attributed to labour costs in the public sector:

> A publicly operated collection agency tends to be less cost and efficiency conscious than a private one, especially if Solid Waste Management is funded out of tax revenues. This usually results in excessively large crew sizes, abuse of sick leave, and the fostering of unionism to counteract the market power of the government. (Goddard, 1975 p. 335).

It is clear from the writings of Goddard, Savas and others, that the political and economic rationale for the demunicipalisation of waste management was rapidly gathering ground in the 1970s. It is important to note, however, that the alternatives were not always seen in terms of a simple dichotomy between the public sector and the private sector, but rather a wide spectrum of potential organisational forms ranging from tendered franchises to publicly owned non-profit making corporations. The private sector waste management industry has been taking an increasingly active role since the early 1980s for three main reasons: the decline in the operational role of the municipal public sector and the increased use of private contractors; the rising cost and technical complexity of municipal waste management, which is providing new market opportunities; and an ideological shift in public policy

40

towards the active encouragement of the private sector role in waste management as a corollary of wider shifts towards neo-liberal policy making. Analysts at Citycorp Investment Bank have predicted that as a result of legislative changes, the price for disposal of non-hazardous waste in UK landfill sites will rise by 15 per cent a year and that the total value of the waste disposal business in England and Wales could increase by at least 10 per cent a year. A similar pattern is predicted by the Paribas Capital Markets, the international equity research group, for the whole of western Europe. They consider that charges for disposing of industrial and municipal waste are likely to double in western Europe by the end of the century as a result of tougher environmental legislation:

> The waste management industry is going through the greatest transformation in its history as a result of the large increase in public concern for the state of the environment...Governments have been spurred to take action and the trend is towards stiffer national regulations for the control of all wastes...The growth in the amount of waste being handled and the increasing sophistication of the techniques being used means that waste management is very big business. (Financial Times Survey, 1990 p. I).

The growing cost and technological sophistication of waste management has already begun a major restructuring of the industry as smaller firms are 'squeezed out' by their larger competitors. In the UK, for example, increased operational costs are forcing a rationalisation of the highly fragmented waste management industry, which has over 4,000 companies on some estimates and it is predicted that the large industry shakeout in the waste management industry will be accompanied by a wave of acquisitions, similar to those that transformed the US waste industry in the 1970s when environmental standards were raised (Thomas, 1990a). As a result of the changing context for waste management, the industry has been undergoing a diversification and internationalisation of its activities. A sectoral restructuring is taking place in response to the growing value of the market for handling municipal waste. This can be illustrated by the closer integration of the private sector provision of a whole range of municipal services ranging from energy supply to water and sewerage, both within and between nations and the emergence of technologically advanced engineering and environmental control technologies as a key sector within the industrial core of many developed economies.

Recycling as an alternative to waste disposal

The diverse rationale for recycling

There are a variety of environmental justifications for recycling which can be found in the literature: the conservation of finite resources as a move towards 'steady state' or sustainable economies (Daly, 1977; Hayes, 1978; Schumacher, 1974; Thomas, 1979, 1984; Young, 1991); the reduction of energy consumption in production (Castle, 1986; Cointreau et al., 1984; Lindberg and Akagi, 1974); the limiting of pollution emissions involved in the production process, and in the disposal of waste (IföR, 1988); and the environmental education benefits of participation in recycling (Castle, 1986; GLC, 1986b). The relative importance of these different environmental objectives also varies: the saving of energy is usually seen as paramount over the recovery of materials, if there is to be a trade-off between the two goals (Boustead and Hancock, 1984; Schertz, 1984). Furthermore, the recycling of different components from the waste stream has a differential environmental impact depending on which materials form the focus of recycling policy, as illustrated in Table 2.4 comparing the pollution associated with the processing of primary and secondary raw materials.

Global environmental aims feature widely within the rationale for promoting recycling at local, national, and international levels. It is of interest, that most of these potential environmental benefits relate to global or regional problems such as the reduction of greenhouse gas emissions from the production process and landfill sites, yet the location and operation of recycling facilities also have a local environmental impact, suggesting that comprehensive recycling programmes may involve a trade-off between local and global environmental objectives. This dilemma is explored further with the analysis of the use of bottle banks in Chapter Four.

A number of economic arguments can also be found in the literature, particularly the claim that recycling may reduce of the costs of waste disposal for urban areas which face fewer cheap landfill opportunities (EDF, 1987; McClaren, 1992; Pollock, 1987; SIRR, 1975). The income derived from the sale of materials is also seen as a useful additional source of income for local government, voluntary organisations and others involved in recycling activities (Castle, 1986). A number of other macro-economic benefits can be found in the literature: the reduced balance of payments deficit in raw materials (Butlin, 1977; Chandler, 1983; Cointreau et al., 1984); and increased geo-political resource security against producer cartels, which was a frequent argument in the literature of the 1970s (Hayes, 1978; Risch, 1978). A further consideration is the global impact of western resource use on the Third World and the connection between equity in resource management and

Table 2.3: The objectives of recycling policy in developed economies

Environmental Objectives	Key Proponents
Integral part of 'steady state' or sustainable economies	Daly (1977)
Reduced energy consumption in the production process	Chapman (1974); Schertz (1984)
Reduced pollution emissions in the production process and from the disposal of waste	IfoR (1988; 1989)
Environmental education benefits	Castle (1986)

Economic Objectives	Key Proponents
Regeneration of urban economies	Elkin and McClaren (1990)
Reduced expenditure on waste disposal	EDF (1987); Pollock (1987)
Income for charities and local authorities from the sale of materials	Castle (1986)
Reduced balance of payments deficit in raw materials	Chandler (1983); Dyson (1974)
Geo-political resource security against producer cartels	Hayes (1978); Risch (1978)

Social Objectives	Key Proponents
Employment creation in economically depressed areas	Vogler (1981); SPD (1986)
Promotion of 'soft' technologies and decentralised forms of social and economic organisation	Hahn (1991)
Employment creation for the long-term unemployed and for handicapped persons	Turner and Thomas (1982)
The fostering of positive 'social norms' in the community	Vining and Ebreo (1990)

Source: Gandy (1992a)

economic development (Redclift, 1987; Trainer, 1986).

A frequent social justification for recycling is the potential job creation, especially for depressed areas with high unemployment (Chandler, 1983; EDF, 1987; Jacobs, 1969; Letcher and Sheil, 1986; Vogler et al., 1981). The employment potential of recycling depends on the nature of the scheme adopted, with the highest employment associated with low technology community-based schemes: it has been estimated that for every 600 tonnes of waste, one job is created by recycling (Quigley, 1987 quoted in EDF, 1987) compared with 0.4 jobs if the waste is sent to landfill (Rockefeller Institute,

Table 2.4: Environmental benefits derived from substituting secondary materials for virgin resources

% reduction	Aluminum	Steel	Paper	Glass
Energy usage	90-97	47-74	23-74	4-32
Air pollution	95	85	74	20
Water pollution	97	76	35	-
Mining wastes	-	97	-	80
Water usage	-	40	58	50

Source: Letcher and Sheil (1986)

1986). Examples include the advocacy of community based industries for paper making in preference to the capital intensive paper industry (Sweetman, 1979) and similar arguments have been made for small-scale glass making (Vogler, 1980). Job creation has also formed part of most alternative 'ecologically' oriented waste management strategies, and is a key element in the environmental Keynesianism associated with the red/green arguments of the mid-1980s introduced in the last chapter.

Recycling is often portrayed within the environmentalist literature as integral to the conception of an alternative society founded on small-scale community based industries and commune type human settlements (see Bahro, 1986). The aim is to create self-sufficient sustainable urban communities based around local production for local consumption from local resources. Community based recycling and waste reduction have also been conceived as a practical example of a 'soft' technological path for waste management (Norton, 1986) and the distinction between technocentric 'hard' and ecocentric 'soft' technology has been framed in terms of the choice between incineration technologies for energy recovery and community scale recycling initiatives focused on materials recovery. This perceived choice between incineration and recycling has led to local political conflict in Japan (NIES, 1978), Germany (Burkard et al., 1988; Spill and Wingert, 1990), the US (Gore, 1992), and the UK (*Environment Business*, 5/5/93). This political conflict over the choice between different waste management strategies is examined further in Chapter Six through the case of Hamburg.

Contemporary recycling is frequently portrayed as a 'hierarchy' of potential options within waste management, as illustrated in Figure 2.4. Each of these stages within the recycling hierarchy varies in terms of its potential environmental impact, both locally and globally; the levels of public participation required; the capital and operational costs involved; and the degree of technological sophistication. The general term 'resource recovery' is often used to refer to both materials recycling and incineration with energy recovery, yet there are important distinctions between these options in terms of their complexity, cost, and political implications for environmental protection.

The first step within the hierarchy of options is waste minimisation and waste prevention in the production process and this is seen as integral to alternative 'ecologically' based waste management strategies (IföR, 1988; Moser, 1990). Waste reduction can either refer to a reduction in the toxicity of waste (qualitative waste reduction) or to a reduction in the quantity of waste produced (quantitative waste reduction) (Forester, 1991; Moser, 1990). The Berlin based Institute for Ecological Recycling (IföR) claim that some 90 per cent of pollution results from the production process, and not in the eventual disposal of products (see Koptytziok and Oswald, 1988). From this perspective, the recycling of materials and also the reduction of waste volume and weight through incineration cannot properly be referred to as waste prevention.

The second step, where the production of wastes is unavoidable, is their re-use within the production process itself. This is easier than post-consumer recycling, since uncontaminated and economically handleable quantities of waste are in proximity to industry as potential new raw materials. Indeed, some items sold as recycled products are made in just such a way, and contain no post-consumer waste, whereas in other cases there may be a mixture of pre- and post-consumer wastes which have been recycled. The economic and logistical advantages of recycling within the production process are reflected in the higher rates of industrial recycling in comparison with the recycling of similar materials from the municipal waste stream.

The third stage, is the re-use and repair of products to prolong their usefulness before entering the waste stream, including the use of returnable beverage containers and the elimination of built-in obsolescence in consumer durables. In the case of returnables, which have been widely argued for by environmental groups, there is debate over the trade-off in overall objectives between energy saving in their cleaning and transportation in comparison with the manufacture of new containers. The political aspects of pursuing different

Figure 2.4: The hierarchy of recycling options

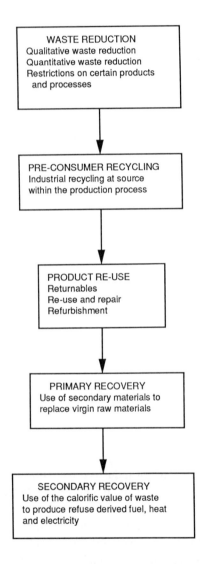

WASTE REDUCTION
Qualitative waste reduction
Quantitative waste reduction
Restrictions on certain products
and processes

PRE-CONSUMER RECYCLING
Industrial recycling at source
within the production process

PRODUCT RE-USE
Returnables
Re-use and repair
Refurbishment

PRIMARY RECOVERY
Use of secondary materials to
replace virgin raw materials

SECONDARY RECOVERY
Use of the calorific value of waste
to produce refuse derived fuel, heat
and electricity

Source: IfoR (1988) and Porteus (1987)

options within the recycling hierarchy is an important issue, since product recycling and the mandatory use of returnables is strongly opposed by the private sector, as being incompatible with the principles of a free market economy (Cointreau et al., 1984; Hooper, 1984; Troge, 1984).

The fourth stage is the primary reclamation of materials to create new raw materials. This forms the main focus of this book and of contemporary recycling policies within OECD nations and includes a variety of measures, such as the collection of waste paper and glass cullet, the magnetic separation of ferrous scrap at some incineration plants and waste transfer stations, and the production of compost from putrescible waste. The primary recovery of materials can be carried out by three main methods, as shown below in Table 2.5. It is useful to distinguish between: 'collect' or kerbside schemes; 'bring' systems based around the use of on-street collections facilities such as bottle banks and recycling centres; and centralised sorting plants, which have sometimes been linked with the production of refuse derived fuel (RDF) or other secondary recovery technologies, as shown in Table 2.5. These three organisational approaches ('bring', 'collect', and centralised sorting) differ in the levels of public participation required; the extent and nature of the costs incurred; the potential levels of materials recovery which can be attained; technical and logistical difficulties in their implementation; and the relative role of 'hard' and 'soft' technologies.

The fifth stage is the recovery of energy from the calorific value of materials. This includes the production of refuse derived fuel (RDF); the use of incineration plants integrated into combined heat and power systems (CHP); the recovery of landfill gas as a fuel source; and high temperature pyrolysis of tyres and plastics. The secondary recovery option of incineration is highly contentious in terms of its legitimacy as a form of recycling (see IföR, 1988; 1989) and is widely criticised from within the environmental movement because of emissions and residual ash concerns.

The technical limits to materials recovery

The potential for recycling is frequently highlighted by the analogy of 'urban mines', since post-consumer waste contains basic raw materials, often in a more concentrated form than their naturally occurring precursors (Boustead, 1989; Jacobs, 1969). Estimates of the theoretically achievable recycling rate for municipal waste vary depending on different evaluations of both the composition of household waste, the degree of materials contamination, and the technically obtainable recycling rates for individual materials. Estimates range from about 40 per cent by weight, as an upper technical limit excluding contaminated materials and putrescibles (Barton, 1989) to about 80 per cent by weight for household waste (EDF, 1987; Hahn, 1991; Young, 1991).

Table 2.5: A comparison of different organisational approaches to recycling

Method of recovery	Advantages	Disadvantages

'Collect' systems
 	
e.g. kerbside collection
 	
    multiple wheeled bin systems
 	
    dual bin systems for 'wet' and 'dry' wastes
 	
    Grune tonne system
 	
    Blue Box system
	High levels of materials recovery
	
	Wide range of materials can be recovered, including putrescible wastes and toxics
	
	Low levels of materials contamination
	
	High levels of public participation
		High capital costs
		
		High labour costs
		
		Reliant on continuous public cooperation
		
		Difficult in congested urban areas

'Bring' systems
 	
e.g. on-street collection facilities for glass
 	
    recycling centres and civic amenity sites
 	
    Component recycling (CR) systems
	Low labour costs
	
	Low capital costs
	
	Local government can take a purely enabling role
		Low levels of materials recovery
		
		Local environmental impact
		
		Difficult in congested urban areas
		
		Difficult to provide high density of facilities in areas of low population density
		
		Contamination of materials

Centralised sorting plants e.g. transfer stations with mechanical separation technologies or manual sorting	Low labour costs Can be combined with the production of refuse derived fuel or energy recovery technologies No changes needed in the arrangements for waste collection	High capital costs Political opposition to plants, especially when combined with incineration Moderate levels of materials recovery but problems of contamination Difficult for small municipal authorities to fund and operate without reliance on the private sector May require hand sorting of mixed waste

Source: Adapted from Boustead (1989) and Cooper (1990b).

Almost all calculations of potential recycling rates over 50 per cent assume that the recycling programme extends to the major fraction of the waste stream derived from putrescibles, as illustrated in Figure 2.2, and that use is made of expensive kerbside collection schemes, as set out in Table 2.5. The figures which are available suggest wide disparities in the recycling rates for different OECD nations, both for municipal waste as a whole and for its separate components, as suggested by Tables 2.6.

Table 2.6: Glass recycling in Europe

Country	Tonnes Collected	% recycled in 1991
Switzerland	199,000	71
Netherlands	360,000	70
Germany	2,295,000	63
Austria	156,000	60
Belgium	223,000	55
Italy	763,000	53
Sweden	57,000	44
France	987,000	41
Denmark	60,000	35
Finland	15,000	31
Portugal	50,000	30
Turkey	54,000	28
Spain	310,000	27
Ireland	16,000	23
Greece	26,000	22
Norway	10,000	22
United Kingdom	385,000	21
Total	385,000	46

Source: WARMER Bulletin, May 1993.

The debate over packaging is central to waste management, since packaging contributes about 35 per cent of the weight and 50 per cent of the volume of household waste in the developed economies (EDF, 1987; Hooper, 1984). However, the factors affecting the growth of packaging lie largely outside the control of local and regional governments who are responsible for managing the municipal waste stream, and the packaging policy debate is focused on national and international policy towards the packaging, retail and marketing sectors of the economy. Trends within retailing associated with the growth of supermarkets and the rise of mass consumption have led to the increased use of smaller one-way containers for food and beverages, which would formerly have often been sold in larger returnable containers or without any packaging in the case of many bakeries and greengrocers (Schmidt-Alck and Strenge, 1988). Indeed, over 80 per cent of packaging waste in developed economies is now calculated to be derived from food and beverages (Gehrke, 1988).

Concern has focused, since the late 1960s, on the rise in the quantity and variety of packaging over the post-war period; the increasing proportion of materials which are difficult to recycle, such as mixed plastics and laminated cartons; and the environmental impact of packaging. As a result of these concerns, there have been calls from within the environmental movement for state controls on superfluous and non-returnable packaging (see Jordan and Wessel, 1988; Kopytziok, 1988a). The production and use of plastics in the OECD nations has more than quadrupled since the late 1960s and world-wide production is doubling every twelve years. In the developed economies, they now make up around 8 per cent of the municipal solid waste stream by weight, as shown in Figure 2.2, and about 18 per cent by volume (*WARMER Bulletin*, January 1990; Wirth, 1988). The rapid rise in the use of plastics reflects their unique advantages in terms of their chemical and physical properties, especially for packaging and plastics manufacturers are now targeting metal cans as their next major market opportunity for expansion (Pollock, 1987). Plastics are primarily produced from non-renewable oil and gas, and are replacing materials which can be much more easily recycled, such as glass and metals. The production of plastics involves four times the energy used in glass manufacture, greater pollution emissions than in paper or glass production, and there are serious emissions concerns over the recovery of the chemical constituents of plastics by pyrolysis and the energy value through incineration (Wirth, 1988). As a result of these difficulties, many environmentalists have argued for the reduced production of plastics, and the banning of potentially toxic polymers such as PVCs (Die Grünen, 1989; Wirth, 1988).

The argument for returnable containers is based on the contribution of one-way containers to the volume of waste, their environmental impact, and the wider costs to society. It has been shown that the proliferation of smaller one-way containers has involved a four-fold increase in waste compared with the use of larger returnable containers, and that on a one-for-one basis, returnables handle, on average, forty times as much volume of products as one-way containers (Schmidt-Alck and Strenge, 1988). The positive impact of returnables is dependent on a sufficient number of cycles between the consumer and retailers and producers (Bojkow, 1984) and technical developments in returnable packaging during the 1980s have lowered the number of cycles needed in order to have a positive environmental impact (Golding, 1989). In terms of the economic impact, it is maintained that the job losses in the one-way packaging industry would be more than offset by employment created within the recycling and waste management sector. An example would be the creation of community based industries for the reclamation, renovation and repair of goods (Burkard et al., 1990). In contrast, the packaging lobby has consistently claimed that packaging provides benefits in terms of safety, enhanced quality and convenience, and in particular, reduced food spoilage (see for example British Plastics Federation, 1989; INCPEN 1987; *WARMER Bulletin*, September 1990). It is contended that advances in packaging technology have made it lighter and increasingly efficient in terms of both materials and energy usage (Falk, 1988), and that with the partial replacement of glass by plastics, the weight of packaging in municipal waste has declined in recent years (Hooper, 1984; Troge, 1984).

The problem of packaging derived waste raises three key issues in waste management: firstly, the practical difficulties in influencing the size and composition of the municipal waste stream; secondly, the ideological debate surrounding the degree and extent of state intervention in the production process, retail and marketing; and finally, the complexities of the production and consumption pattern involved in the creation and disposal of waste and the difficulties in evaluating the environmental impact of alternative kinds of packaging.

Public participation

Public participation is essential for 'bring' and 'collect' systems which rely on the sorting of waste by households rather than the use of centralised sorting plants, as set out in Table 2.5. The increased role of public participation in recycling reflects the growing emphasis of environmental policy on individual responsibility and the enlightened self-interest of consumers, as described in the last chapter. Yet as Pollock argues 'consumer awareness of the effects of purchasing decisions on waste volumes, disposal needs, and the environment is only slowly emerging' (Pollock, 1987 p. 9) and it is consequently difficult to evaluate the ultimate limits to public participation. A recurring theme in the recycling literature is the identification of the factors which determine differences in public participation. There are three main elements in this discussion: firstly, the general psychological aspects to participation in different types of schemes; secondly, the effect of different socio-economic household characteristics on their likelihood to participate; and thirdly, the general level of environmental concern in society.

The highest rates of participation have been recorded for mandatory kerbside schemes in affluent small towns, where householders are required to set out separated fractions of their waste for collection (EDF, 1987). In Woodbury, New Jersey, and Solingen in the Federal Republic of Germany, between 85 and 95 per cent of residents have participated in seven category separation schemes, for paper, glass, plastics, metals, hazardous waste, putrescibles, and the remainder (EDF, 1987; Hedlund, 1988). In the case of 'bring systems' based on the use of on-street collection facilities, a central question is the influence of the density of collection facilities on the rates of public participation. This affects the ease of participation, since a low density of facilities involves longer average distances for households to the facilities, and this makes participation more difficult for the old, the disabled, and households which lack access to a car. If facilities are positioned at convenient sites such as supermarket car parks this can also increase participation and limit unnecessary extra journeys, therefore reducing energy consumption if a car is used to transport the materials. With 'bring systems', there is evidence of a trade-off between the density of on-street facilities and the level of materials recovery, up to a limit beyond which it becomes extremely expensive to raise participation rates any further, as suggested by Figure 2.5. Yet it is also suggested that a lower density of facilities yields lower levels of materials contamination, because only the most motivated citizens will make the effort of bringing their recyclable waste[1].

There have been a number of studies from a behavioural psychology perspective examining the motivation of participants in kerbside collection schemes. There is, for example, a debate over effects of different kinds of inducements on the rate of participation. Raymond De Young's study of recyclers in Michigan, found that the intrinsic satisfactions associated with environmentally responsible behaviour contributed to citizens' sense of well-being and that conservation behaviour might be carried out without the need for an external reward such as a financial inducement (De Young, 1986). There is also evidence that participation will rise if the scheme is sponsored by, or donates its proceeds to a charitable organisation. In San Francisco, for example, a fourfold increase in usage of on-street collection facilities and recycling centres was reported when the proceeds were given to AIDS charities (EDF, 1987). The charitable aspects of recycling activities clearly

Figure 2.5: The influence of bottle bank density on glass collection

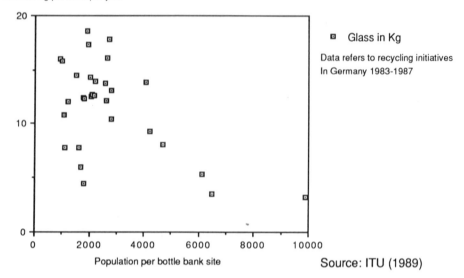

Glass in Kg per head per year

Population per bottle bank site

Glass in Kg

Data refers to recycling initiatives
In Germany 1983-1987

Source: ITU (1989)

play an important role in encouraging both public participation and also the involvement of voluntary sector organisations who can derive some income from the sale of materials.

In contrast, other research suggests that financial inducements are always necessary to gain the participation of less environmentally motivated 'non-recyclers' (see Vining and Ebreo, 1990) Inducements can take a number of forms, ranging from the use of savings in waste disposal costs to cut local taxes (though this assumes that recycling reduces the costs of waste management), to the provision of incentives to individual households. A further recycling inducement is the use of direct charges to citizens for their waste collection service based on the volume or weight of waste collected, which has been used by some municipalities in the Netherlands, New Zealand and the US (Cooper, 1989b; Forester, 1991). In the town of Hoofddorp in the Netherlands, dustbins have even been fitted with a special measuring device for this purpose (*The Guardian*, 23rd October 1991). This is a clear example of the 'polluter pays principle' applied directly to individual households, yet there are difficulties with the use of 'end of pipe' direct charging for consumer waste. It is doubtful, for example, whether households should be held financially responsible for waste derived from unnecessary packaging or toxic materials, and the use of direct charges for essential municipal services is socially regressive, a theme returned to in the concluding chapter.

The morphological structure of urban areas has consistently emerged as a key determinant of levels of public participation in recycling schemes. A number of factors have been identified: the levels of congestion for the provision of recycling facilities; the amount storage space within individual dwellings; and the psychological effect of shared bins for waste collection (Pieters and Verhallen, 1986). Studies have found that shared bins, such as paladins for high rise housing, present a psychological barrier to effective participation, because of their relative anonymity (ITU, 1989; Scheffold, 1984). However, these differences cannot be attributed only to the psychological effect of anonymity in urban architecture, since there are additional socio-economic factors which might be expected to influence rates of participation.

The analysis of the influence of socio-economic structure on recycling raises a number of methodological difficulties. These arise in part from the relationship between important factors such as housing density with levels of socio-economic deprivation. The relative importance of different features associated with shared bins or paladins is unclear, since their use indicates both the physical characteristics of dwellings such as lack of space and the presence of common areas, and also socio-economic features, such as higher levels of deprivation in much inner urban high rise housing. For example, a study of 'green bin' systems in Germany found that the failure of the green bin system in high rise housing areas could be attributed to a combination of five main factors: the housing structure and degree of anonymity; the social structure and levels of deprivation; the degree of environmental awareness among householders; the extent of public information on the scheme; and the frequency of collections (Scheffold, 1984).

The economic viability of recycling

An important rationale for recycling is claimed to be its potential to cut waste disposal and collection costs, and also to generate a net income from the sale of materials. In order to examine the cost of recycling schemes in comparison with other waste management options, it is necessary to examine how the overall costs of municipal waste management are distributed. The usual pattern within developed economies is that the collection of municipal waste is more expensive than its disposal, a result of the operational costs, especially labour, and also in many cases the capital investment required in new vehicles and other equipment. This pattern can be observed in the US (Forester, 1991), the UK (Holmes, 1989), and Germany (ITU, 1989).

A number of studies have examined the economic viability of recycling.

Some analyses of recycling have argued that the economics of comprehensive 'collect' systems, such as kerbside schemes, are very favourable. An analysis of a proposed comprehensive recycling programme for New York City, by the Environmental Defense Fund, suggested that given 1985 market prices and efficient collection arrangements, a 40 per cent recycling rate would be less expensive per ton than incinerating an equal quantity of waste and landfilling the residual ash (EDF, 1985). Similarly, the California Waste Management Board has claimed that the average cost of collection and disposal to be $60 per ton, while the net cost of kerbside recycling was only $40 per ton (EDF, 1987). However, many other studies have suggested that kerbside collection schemes are invariably more expensive than 'bring' systems and routine collection and disposal of waste by landfill or incineration (Beal, 1992; Birley, 1992; Thiel, 1988). These issues are explored further in Chapter Six in the case of Hamburg.

The economics of recycling can be improved in comparison with alternative means of waste disposal, by the use of surcharges and rebates. For example, a surcharge can be applied on all waste disposed of by landfill or incineration instead of recycling. The second method, is the payment of a rebate or incentive payment directly to recyclers by municipalities, in recognition of savings in waste collection and disposal. This is most frequent where the collection of waste is carried out by a separate tier of local government. In the UK, for example, some Waste Disposal Authorities have been giving rebates to their Waste Collection Authorities to encourage recycling, a practice now formally extended to all local authorities under the recycling credit provisions of the 1990 Environmental Protection Act. This is usually calculated on a per tonne basis for the marginal cost savings created by the diversion of materials out of the municipal waste stream by recycling activity. This source of income is especially important where the savings in waste disposal costs amount to more than the intrinsic value of the recovered materials, as a consequence of weaknesses in the secondary materials market (see below).

The secondary materials market

The economic viability of recycling initiatives is a function of the cost of setting up and running the scheme, offset by any savings in collection and disposal and income derived from the sale of materials. The secondary materials market is, therefore, a key determinant of the economic viability of recycling schemes, but the value of different materials varies greatly, from £5 or less per tonne for waste paper to over £700 per tonne for aluminium, as indicated by Table 2.7. The main contemporary factors behind the weakness of the secondary materials market include: the mis-match between the supply

Table 2.7: Revenue from sale of recyclable materials

Commodity	Weight per tonne of recyclables	Estimated value per tonne	Potential revenue per tonne of recyclables
Paper and board	515 Kg	£5	£2.60
Plastics	70 Kg	£25 - 75	£1.75 - 5.30
Glass	280 Kg	£20 - 30	£5.60 - 8.40
Ferrous scrap	120 Kg	£20 - 30	£2.40 - 3.60
Aluminum	15 Kg	£600 - 800	£9.00 - 12.00
Total	1000 Kg	-	£21.00 - 39.00

Source: DoE (1991a)

of recycled materials and demand for recycled products, which has followed increased recycling efforts for some materials; the competition with virgin raw materials, which often enjoy extensive state subsidies; and the difficulties of ensuring consistent supply of uncontaminated materials in economically handleable quantities.

Evidence suggests that recycling has been hampered by the secondary materials market throughout the post-war period. The problems have, however, affected some materials to a greater extent than others, and prices for materials have tended to fluctuate in response to a range of different factors. In an important study, Darnay and Franklin (1972) showed that the level of recycling had progressively declined over the post-war period in the US. They attributed this decline to the difficulties faced by the secondary materials industry, especially for paper, textiles and rubber, dominated by small-scale, often family run enterprises, finding it increasingly difficult to compete with virgin materials because of rapid technological developments in the capital intensive extractive industries for the processing of raw materials. It was increasingly difficult and expensive to collect recyclables from householders, for whom sorting wastes had become a repugnant activity. Meanwhile, virgin materials had improved steadily in quality and were increasingly competitive in price. Furthermore, the waste stream now included increasing quantities of materials which were difficult to reclaim, such as plastics and composite items, for which no secondary materials market existed. Similar processes of decline within the secondary materials industries have also been described in the UK. In the case of tyres, the only major market for recycled rubber, carpet underlay, collapsed in the 1960s and early 1970s with the advent of plastic foam-backed carpets (Newell, 1990). Another example is textiles recycling, long established in the UK, yet demand for recycled fabric and fibre waste has fallen over the last 20 to 30 years and many textile reclaimers have been forced to cease trading. Post-consumer textile waste now comprises a complex mixture of natural and synthetic fibres. As a result, the identification, sorting and grading of textile waste for different end uses are labour intensive operations and textile wastes are increasingly exported to countries where sorting costs are lower than those in the UK (DoE, 1991a).

The most important recent example of a price collapse is the glut of low grade waste paper which currently prevails in Europe and North America, and has driven down prices as shown in Figure 2.6. In the UK, the swamping of the market for low grade paper has seen prices fall rapidly in the late 1980s and early 1990s (see Chapter Four) and an earlier flooding of the market in Germany saw a 70 per cent price fall during 1985 alone (Jordan and Wessel, 1988). This has led many paper recovery schemes into bankruptcy and meant that large quantities of waste paper collected for recycling by the general public have been dumped for landfill[2]. Several factors have contributed to the current weakness in the waste paper market: the increased participation in recycling by the public during the current wave of environmental concern; the attempts in Germany and especially in the US to mandatorily increase the recycling of paper, which has swamped the world market with cheap exports, given a boost from the falling value of the dollar; the dearth of capacity in the de-inking and paper reclamation industry; the competition with high quality cheap virgin pulp imports; and the high demands that merchants and mills have been stipulating for quality of waste paper in the face of uncertainty over the marketing of recycled paper products (Jordan and Wessel, 1988). The state of the waste paper market has deteriorated still further since the 1990s as a result of world recession lowering the demand for paper products and price cuts for virgin pulp in an attempt to stimulate demand by the depressed paper industry now facing a spate of bankruptcies in North America.

The capacity of secondary materials markets to absorb the collected materials could be improved by a variety of policy instruments aimed at different stages in the cycle of production and consumption. A number of policy measures have been promoted by environmentalists, including government procurement of recycled products; state support for recycling as an economic development strategy; the use of economic incentives such as 'green taxes' to modify consumer behaviour; and export promotion (EDF, 1987; Langer, 1979). The US, for example, saw its waste paper exports increase by a factor of ten between 1970 and 1987, reaching a total of 4.3 million tonnes or 19 per cent of total US waste paper collections (EDF, 1987). The growing wastepaper demand, especially in NICs such as South Korea and Taiwan, can be explained by a number of factors: the rising literacy rates; fast rates of economic growth; the high quality of imports of

Figure 2.6: The price of waste paper and board in the UK 1985-1991

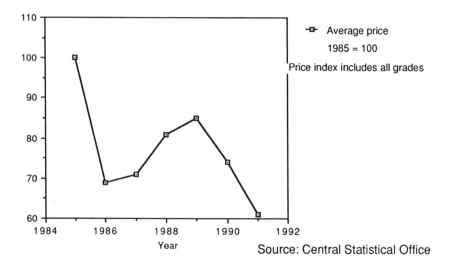

Source: Central Statistical Office

western waste; local shortages of indigenous softwoods for pulping; the 50 to 80 per cent higher capital cost of pulp-based mills in comparison with recycling mills; energy savings in production; and low wages making hand-sorting more economical than in the OECD nations (EDF, 1987; Pollock, 1987).

Competing approaches to recycling policy

In this section, the connections between different conceptions of the environmental crisis and appropriate policy responses identified in the last chapter are related to different policy strategies to raise levels of recycling. Just as there is a useful distinction to be made between the hierarchy of recycling options, as illustrated in Figure 2.4, there is an equally important (and growing) distinction between recycling and waste management policies on the basis of their relative emphasis on market-based and regulatory policy instruments. Whilst it is misleading to draw a false distinction between the use of market-based and regulatory instruments as direct alternatives, Table 2.8 shows that the market-based and non market-based distinction helps to distinguish between the variety of different policy responses to the low level of waste recycling in comparison with technically achievable levels.

Through much of the post-war period, waste management policy has been dominated by developments in engineering and related fields of applied sciences (see Greenberg, 1976; Skitt, 1972). More recently, the technocratic based approaches have been modified to include developments in cost-benefit analysis, mathematical modelling, and in the 1980s the application of market-based policy instruments. The market-based position maintains that low levels of recycling are a function of 'market failure' from four main sources: monopoly pricing power; cost externalities of economic activity; distortions in the tax system and state expenditure; and non market price systems (Page, 1977). The market-based policy instruments seek to modify human behaviour through the price mechanism and include product charges on waste disposal, the use of rebates or credits in recognition of waste disposal costs, and various deposit-refund systems (see Brisson, 1992; Turner, 1991b; Turner, 1992). The contemporary market-based approach to raise levels of recycling is focused on the need to internalise the full range of environmental externalities associated with the costs of alternative means of waste disposal. Other research has identified the degree of state support for virgin raw materials as a more important source of market failure (Curlee, 1986; Williamson, 1974) but the focus of contemporary policy has been on the internalisation of the costs of waste disposal. This instance of 'market failure' is to be tackled with a tougher regulatory role for the state in order to allow waste management to respond to the 'real' cost of different waste disposal options (DoE, 1990b; DTI/DoE, 1992; Turner, 1990; 1991b; 1992). It is claimed that the current trend towards increasing waste disposal costs operates as an economic incentive to recycle in the sense that low landfill costs have previously acted as a disincentive to expand recycling (see EDF, 1987; Lambert and Laurence, 1990; Pollock, 1987). This argument is now often made within the environmentalist literature and by mainstream policy makers, where it is assumed that recycling will prove progressively more attractive as improved environmental standards in waste management force up the cost of waste disposal:

> As landfill costs continue to rise because of space constraints and stricter environmental regulations, and as the high capital costs of incinerators and their pollution control technologies sap city budgets, the appeal of recycling will inevitably grow. (Pollock, 1987 p. 27).

In contrast, the alternative non market-based approaches seek to maximise recycling up to a technically achievable level with an emphasis on the use of regulatory rather than market-based policy instruments (see Hahn, 1991; IföR, 1989). This is frequently presented as an alternative political strategy to the predominance of market-based 'hard' technologies in waste

Table 2.8: Market-based and non market-based recycling policy

Market-based policies	Non market-based policies
Green taxes and fiscal measures to influence behaviour of producers and consumers	Regulatory measures
Differential indirect taxation for recycled and non recycled products	Mandatory recycling schemes
Taxes on certain products and packaging materials to reflect their environmental impact and discourage their use	Controls on one-way packaging Controls on superfluous packaging Controls on non-recyclable products
The use of direct charges to households for the collection and disposal of their waste, based on either weight or dustbin size	Restrictions or bans on toxic products or processes Restrictions on what may be thrown into the municipal waste stream
Deposit-refund systems	
Marketable permit systems	
Corrections for market failure in waste policy	Central tenets
1. Monopoly pricing power:	Focus on maximisation of materials recovery rather than energy recovery
Competition policy	Focus on reducing the size of the waste stream and tackling waste production at source
2. Cost externalities of economic activity:	
Internalising the costs of waste management to encourage recycling and waste reduction	Policy emphasis on the use of kerbside collection systems to maximise materials recovery
Rebates or credits for savings in waste collection or disposal	Integration of policy with wider aims such as employment creation and the promotion of 'soft' small-scale technologies
3. Distortions in tax system and state expenditure	
Removal of state subsidies for virgin raw materials and the use of a virgin raw materials levy	Links with political demands for alternative forms of social and economic organisation
4. Price systems	
Ensuring that transport costs of both virgin and secondary raw materials are undistorted and reflect marginal costs	
Central tenets	
Policy emphasis on voluntary recycling schemes and the use of cheaper 'bring' systems for materials recovery	
Opposition to state intervention unless to correct for market failure	
Extension of definiton of recycling to include the energy recovery of calorific value	

Source: Partly based on Kopytziok (1988b); Page (1977); Turner (1991b; 1992).

management and in environmental policy more generally. The alternative non-market or ecologically-based approaches to waste management differ from the market-based approaches in a number of respects: environmental criteria are seen as more important than economic criteria in policy making; the state is expected to play a much more interventionist role, beyond the correction of 'market failure' and including the banning of certain products or processes; there is a holistic desire to see the wider integration of waste management across all sectors, including municipal, industrial and agricultural wastes, and the extension of waste management policy to all stages of the production and consumption cycle; there is a greater emphasis on waste reduction and attempts to limit the generation of wastes at source; and the promotion of recycling is seen as part of a wider process of achieving a fundamental political transformation of society (Kopytziok, 1988b).

Conclusion

This chapter has illustrated the close interconnection between factors affecting the recycling of household waste and the pattern of municipal waste management in developed economies. The wide-ranging rationale for recycling was shown to mirror the diversity of environmentalist thought described in the last chapter.

The promotion of contemporary materials recycling can be conceived as a choice between three organisational approaches: the 'bring' system; the 'collect' system; and the use of centralised sorting. It was noted that the highest rates of materials recovery are obtained by the use of 'collect' systems and that each of the different organisational approaches raises a different set of political, economic, technical and other issues. A question of interest is why the level of materials recycling is significantly lower than technically achievable levels, given the wide range of environmental, economic and social arguments for recycling advanced in the literature. An important research theme is the identification of the factors which account for these wide differences in the rates of recycling achieved in ostensibly similar market economies which share many socio-economic features in common.

A range of factors in the literature which are claimed to limit the extent of materials recycling were considered. The debate over the most appropriate policy response to low levels of recycling was shown to be a corollary of the wider debate over the use of different kinds of environmental policy instruments, and in particular, the relative efficacy of market-based and regulatory policy instruments. In the next chapter, the discussion is furthered with an examination of the development of municipal waste management and recycling in London, which forms the main empirical focus of this book. The historical material enables a number of the earlier themes to be more fully developed in relation to the evolving political and legislative context for urban waste management.

Notes

1   Interview with Dr Joachim Wüttke, Umweltbundesamt, Berlin, 18th September 1990.

2   Though there is uncertainty over the extent of landfilling of paper collected for recycling, the practice was alleged by Friends of the Earth and a number of local government officers in the London Boroughs.

3 An historical overview of waste management and recycling in London

London has had a tumultuous history in its waste management, an understanding of which is necessary for the analysis of the contemporary pattern of recycling activities. This chapter provides a historical and contextual examination of the development of waste management in a large urban area in a developed economy. The discussion of the earlier chapters is extended to include a range of political, legislative and organisational issues which have affected waste management and recycling.

I show how the growth of London necessitated the development of a complex waste management infrastructure in order to co-ordinate the transfer of collected wastes to increasingly distant landfill sites in the interests of public health and economic efficiency. A number of important developments in London are described: the rise of incineration to become the dominant form of waste disposal in the County of London before its decline and partial re-emergence under the GLC; the eventual emergence of strategic planning and centralised co-ordination in waste management for London; and a shift of recycling activity from local authority run kerbside collection schemes to cheaper 'bring' systems based around individual participation.

The development of waste management

A clear chronology can be traced in the development of waste management for London, beginning with the demands for organised street cleansing in order to allow free passage along highways and at a later stage to protect public health. The advances in street cleansing led eventually to arrangements for the collection of waste from individual households, leading in turn to the emergence of different means of waste disposal. This sequence of developments occurred against a background of a rapidly growing city (and a growing municipal waste stream) and a political struggle over the reform of local government for London.

The origins of waste management in London

In 1500, only 10 per cent of the population of England lived in towns, and any refuse that was not re-used, burnt or buried by the householders themselves was thrown out into the streets. Yet by the first census of 1801, the proportion of the English population living in towns had risen to 26 per cent, and the existing ad hoc arrangements for street cleansing were quickly overwhelmed by the rapid growth of towns and cities that accompanied the industrial revolution:

> It was no longer possible for most of the old corporations to cope, and in the new industrial areas the corporations did not even exist. Thus by the early nineteenth century the condition of the streets was probably worse than it had been in the preceding centuries. (Eedle, 1971 p. 161).

The deteriorating conditions of life in eighteenth century London led to demands for a greater degree of co-ordination and better standards in the management of London's waste, through the role of a London-wide authority. In 1752, for example, Corbyn Morris described the alarming levels of mortality for London, and observed that:

> As the preservation of the health of the people is of great importance, it is proposed that the cleaning of this city should be put under one uniform public management, and all the filth be carried into lighters, and conveyed by the Thames to proper distances in the country. (Quoted in the Herbert Commission 1960 p. 168).

Yet, to a statutory authority of 1835, urban cleansing remained a matter of convenience for free passage along highways, which was reflected in the provisions of the 1839 Metropolitan Police Act and its legal sanctions against the leaving of any materials in the main thoroughfares of London (GLC, 1975b; Winter, 1989). It was not until the mid-nineteenth century that there was widespread recognition of the connection between dirt and disease and some indication of the squalid urban conditions in London during the mid-nineteenth century is given by contemporary accounts. For example, a survey in 1849 by the surveyor, Thomas Lovick, into improved 'mechanical and economical methods of street cleansing' in Soho, central London described how:

Many of the streets and courts in which these experiments were performed, were (before cleansing) in a most filthy and insalubrious condition; the surface coated with   mud, and strewn with offal and refuse of the most disgusting nature; in the interstices   between the paving, and in hollows formed by its partial settlement, stagnant foetid liquids had collected, charging the atmosphere with their offensive exhalations. (Metropolitan Commission of Sewers, 1849 p. 4).

It took the repeated cholera epidemics of the 1830s and 1840s, together with the investigations of the Poor Law Commissioners to give birth to the public health movement of Chadwick, Southwood-Smith, Cochrane and others. In 1842, for example, Edwin Chadwick recommended that public authorities should undertake removal of all refuse from habitations and streets, a change which had to wait until the Public Health Act of 1875. The Health of Towns Society was established in 1844, followed by the formation of the Health of London Association, which campaigned for a central public health agency for London. In 1847, the Health of London Association argued that it was futile to treat drainage, sewerage, street-cleansing and water supply as though they were separate issues and that the only hope for a comprehensive approach to the problem was to set up some kind of over-riding central authority (Winter, 1989; Wohl, 1983).

The acquisition of a metropolitan police force and advances in paving and draining technology suggested that there might now be solutions to the problem of street cleansing. Under the first Public Health Act of 1848, the General and Local Boards of Health were established, and the indiscriminate dumping of refuse in the streets was prohibited (Corrie, 1969). A report by the Metropolitan Sanitary Commission in 1847, emphasised the desirability of combining the control of water supply with control of drainage, sewage and refuse-disposal services. Seven years after the first public health legislation, came the initial attempt at an organised waste management service for London (Barker, 1946). This was instituted under the provisions of the Metropolis Management Act of 1855 (Townend, 1982), which primarily concerned itself with the reconstruction of London's inadequate sewerage infrastructure (Olsen, 1964).

With the 1858 Local Government Act, the powers of the Local Boards of Health were extended to undertaking contracts not only for street cleansing, but also for the removal of house refuse from premises and the cleaning of privies, ashpits and cesspools. A new department of central government was set up in 1871, the Local Government Board, which along with the Public Health Acts of 1872 and 1875, divided England into Urban and Rural Sanitary Districts - the precursor of the latterday Waste Collection and

Disposal Authorities. In the case of London, the Urban Sanitary Authorities were to be the town councils in the numerous municipal boroughs and under the 1875 Public Health Act every Sanitary Authority was required to undertake or contract for the removal of house refuse from premises when required by the Local Government Board. This was to be carried out on approved days by the Sanitary Authorities, and each householder was obliged to place their refuse in a moveable receptacle, which constituted the first legal recognition of the dustbin (GLC, 1975b).

The period of the London County Council

London grew very rapidly during the latter part of the nineteenth century, as shown in Figure 3.1, and the existing local government structure appeared increasingly inadequate to the task of satisfactory waste management and other public health needs. In introducing the Metropolitan Management Bill of 1855, for example, Sir Benjamen Hill estimated that London was governed by no less than ten thousand commissioners and 250 different local acts (Barker, 1946).

The late nineteenth century saw growing demands for some kind of London-wide government. The League for Municipal Reform and other pressure groups called for one unified system of government for London under a single authority, democratically elected and possessing adequate powers:

> In many places, and notably in districts which had become densely peopled with the poorest of the poor, there was not even a pretence of management, no public or quasi-public body existed at all for any sanitary purposes... Miscellaneous bodies of paving commissioners, lighting commissioners, turnpike boards, directors of the poor, etc., were scattered at random over the town without regulations for their guidance, no attempt at uniformity of administration, no board of union, no security for the proper performance of their functions. (Firth, 1888 quoted in Barker, 1946 p. 10).

Initially, it was the problem of co-ordinating highways maintenance and the direct emptying of sewage from London's three million inhabitants into the Thames which had led to the formation of the Metropolitan Board of Works in 1856, representing the first functional centralisation of service provision for the rapidly expanding city. In 1889 the Metropolitan Board of Works was replaced by the London County Council with a jurisdiction over the Administrative County of London, comprising the 29 Metropolitan Boroughs, as shown in Figure 3.2. During the period of the London County Council,

Figure 3.1: The population of London 1801-1931

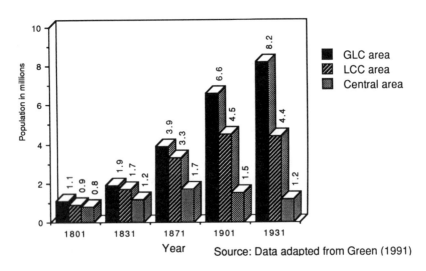

Source: Data adapted from Green (1991)

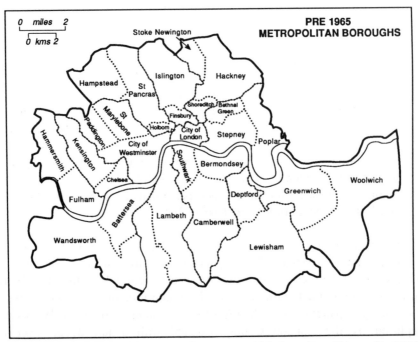

Figure 3.2: The London County Council and Metropolitan Boroughs 1889

from 1885 to 1965, refuse collection and disposal became the responsibility of the individual Metropolitan Boroughs, and the London County Council had no operational role in either the collection or the disposal of waste. Within the Greater London area as a whole, there were now some ninety five separate local authorities (Metropolitan Boroughs, County Boroughs, Non-County Boroughs, Urban Districts and Rural Districts) individually carrying out the collection and disposal of their waste. The new London County Council passed a bye-law in 1893, making it compulsory for house refuse to be removed from all premises in London at least once a week. This replaced the existing arrangements whereby 'dustmen perambulated the streets and removed the refuse on the application of the occupiers of the houses' (Soper, 1909 p. 61). The compulsory collection of refuse met with some opposition when first introduced: in 1905, for example, some six thousand households in Hackney were refusing to permit their waste to be collected (Soper, 1909).

During the late nineteenth century, the use of incineration plants or 'dust destructors' as they were then known, began to emerge as the main means of waste disposal in the 29 Metropolitan Boroughs rather than the earlier practice of dumping the refuse on open tips. An important reason for the growing use of incineration was the Metropolitan Boroughs' wide ranging service delivery role, including the provision of electricity. From the 1880s onwards the Metropolitan Boroughs began to exercise their powers for electricity and gas supply (which were taken away in 1947 and 1948) and by the turn of the century six boroughs were producing electricity from waste incineration, as shown in Figure 3.3, a trend pioneered by the Metropolitan Borough of Shoreditch with its motto of 'more light, more power' (Goodrich, 1904; Mander and Golden, 1991). Indeed the Shoreditch plant commissioned in 1896, was the first of its kind in the UK and the plant was re-opened successfully in the winter of 1947 as a result of the coal crisis (Schomburgk, 1975).

Figure 3.3 shows that by the turn of the century, incineration had become the dominant form of waste disposal in the County of London and it was increasingly seen as superior to refuse tipping on both environmental and economic grounds. Goodrich, for example, berated the impact of the existing 'filthy and insanitary system of disposal' by refuse tipping in proximity to housing, its spoliation of the countryside, and its associated public health risks (Goodrich, 1904 p. 26). In particular, Goodrich argued for the economic superiority of incineration for London's waste disposal and urged the use of incineration as the only acceptable alternative to tipping:

> It cannot be deemed satisfactory when large Metropolitan Boroughs inflict their filth upon smaller communities in Urban Districts, and such a method does not even possess the saving grace of economy.

The system is most expensive, and it has been clearly demonstrated wherever destructors have been erected, with the exception of Battersea, that the cost of disposal has been materially reduced...So increasingly difficult is it becoming to get rid of London's waste that the destructor is generally recognised to be the only solution. It is quite certain that if it were not possible to inflict the filth upon the urban communities, the London of to-day would be far better equipped with destructors than is the case. (Goodrich, 1904 p. 176-177).

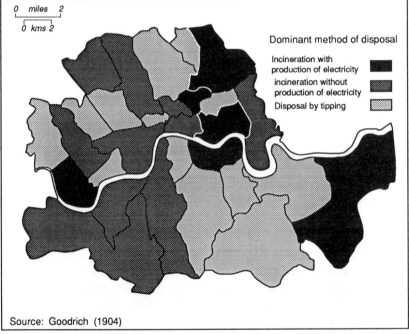

Figure 3.3: The production of electricity from municipal waste by the Metropolitan Boroughs in 1904

By the time of the first world war, it was clear that the formation of the LCC and the operation of the new waste collection and disposal responsibilities of the Metropolitan Boroughs had not yet succeeded in establishing a satisfactory system of waste management for London. The use of incineration began to decline and had not eliminated the much maligned practice of refuse tipping: by 1914, only the boroughs of Fulham, Hackney, Shoreditch and Stoke Newington relied exclusively on incineration, and the remaining 24 Metropolitan Boroughs were using tipping for all or part of their waste stream (Local Government Board, 1914). Fourteen mainly riparian boroughs, transported their waste to tipping sites by barges from wharves along the river. Five boroughs relied on rail to transport their waste to tipping sites outside the LCC area (Camberwell, Deptford, Islington, Lewisham, and Southwark, all of which lacked direct access to the river, with the exception of Southwark). Only two boroughs, Poplar and Woolwich, recorded the disposal of some of their refuse on tips within their boundaries. One clue as to the cause of this decline in the use of incineration is that by the 1920s there was a growing disparity in the costs of incineration in comparison with tipping, as suggested by Table 3.1.

Table 3.1: The costs of waste disposal in the Metropolitan Boroughs 1925-26

	s.	d.
Incineration	7	10
Tipping with river transfer	6	4
Tipping with rail transfer	5	2
Tipping direct to tipping sites	4	1

Source: Ministry of Health (1929)

The debate over London's waste management began to be conceived again in terms of the inadequacies of the fragmentary administrative structure. A report to the Shoreditch Electricity Committee in 1926 argued for a voluntary centralised scheme whereby all of London's waste could be disposed of by the use of larger more sophisticated incineration plants in order to overcome the problem of waste tipping:

A unified scheme of disposal should be carried out by having the refuse disposed of in large central destructors, probably four for the whole of the London area...By a combination of the authorities concerned, including possibly the LCC, a centralised scheme could be devised and worked co-operatively with success and economy. (Metropolitan Borough of Shoreditch, 1926 p. 1).

Interestingly, the report acknowledged that the use of incineration did create its own set of difficulties in densely populated areas. Attention was drawn to the problem of emissions (evidently not yet tackled satisfactorily, despite the earlier optimism of the 1880s); traffic congestion from the delivery of waste; and the lack of space on the incineration sites for the recovery and storage of reclaimed materials and useful by-products of combustion such as clinker.

In addition to emerging difficulties with the widespread use of incineration, the problem of uncontrolled tipping of waste and the lack of co-operation between different local authorities was becoming increasingly serious. A key problem for inner London was the co-ordination of transfer facilities for those boroughs which could not conveniently take their waste in collection vehicles directly to incineration plants or to tipping sites. A conference on London Cleansing held by Westminster City Council in 1914 called for the formation of boroughs into groups for the sharing of depots, landfill sites and the use of water frontage; and the need for rail rolling stock to allow the conveyance of refuse at reasonable fixed charges per ton. It was resolved that 'these proposals are of the greatest importance from a sanitary and financial point of view, as affecting the whole of London, and that steps be taken at once to bring them into effect' (quoted in Tee, 1937 p. 240). Apparently little or nothing was done, for in 1922 the Ministry of Health, after numerous complaints about the impact of the tipping of London's waste, called a conference of the LCC and the Metropolitan Borough Councils. The result was the issue of the 'controlled tipping' letter by the Ministry of Health on the 26th July 1922, which instructed local authorities to improve the practice of refuse tipping. Despite this intervention of central government, the situation deteriorated further, with increasing and insistent complaints, especially from the County Councils which bordered on the County of London, and in 1925 a deputation from the LCC urged upon the Minister of Health the need for an investigation by the Ministry into the disposal of household and other wastes in the London area.

In 1925, the Ministry of Health set up a full inquiry under their Inspector of Public Cleansing, Mr J.C. Dawes, which yielded the 1929 Dawes Report into Public Cleansing in the County of London (Ministry of Health, 1929). The investigation covered the whole field of cleansing operations in London and concluded by recommending the setting up of a central cleansing body to deal with the County of London and the densely populated areas adjoining it. Dawes had found serious deficiencies in the arrangements for both waste collection and disposal. In the case of waste collection he recommended the compulsory use of covered 'dustless' collection vehicles and that there be some kind of satisfactory container for household waste provided and maintained out of the rates:

> 200 years ago a service for the collection of refuse had been instituted and was paid for by the householders themselves, and from the records it is learned that the refuse was set out in tubs, boxes, baskets and other vessels. It is extraordinary that this method of temporarily storing refuse is still in evidence in parts of London...the provision of proper non-absorbent metal containers was in some boroughs as low as 5 per cent. (Ministry of Health, 1929; quoted in Tee, 1937 p. 243).

The arrangements for the disposal of waste were found to be equally wanting:

> it is alleged that the local authorities whose refuse was conveyed to some of the dumps took little or no interest in the methods of disposal adopted by their contractors, who appeared to operate on the sole principle of dumping the greatest amount in the shortest time. (Department of Health, 1929; quoted in Tee, 1937 p. 244).

Dawes criticised the system whereby boroughs 'contracted out' of their responsibilities for the hygienic disposal of house refuse and drew attention to the insanitary state of the tipping sites used by London: 'the reeking masses at South Hornchurch, taken together comprise the worst refuse dump in Britain and by far the biggest' (Ministry of Health, 1929 quoted in Robson, 1939 p. 31). Figure 3.4 shows that by 1925-26, seventeen of the Metropolitan Boroughs were reliant on private contractors for their waste disposal.

Dawes also found that the 29 boroughs into which the County of London was divided had no practical advantages in planning terms for the purposes of public cleansing, and in 21 instances, the house refuse collection vehicles of one authority passed into the district of at least one other authority during the process of collecting and disposing of waste. The local officers employed by the twenty-nine cleansing authorities took a purely parochial view of their duties and no-one had responsibility to consider the cleansing service of the city as a whole in order to obtain higher standards and greater economic efficiency. The main recommendation within the Dawes report, was for a centralised body to co-ordinate waste disposal in the interests of both public

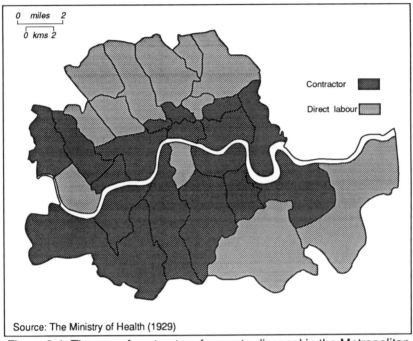

Source: The Ministry of Health (1929)

Figure 3.4: The use of contractors for waste disposal in the Metropolitan Boroughs 1925-26

health and economic efficiency. It was noted in the 1930s, for example, that the cost of the collection and disposal of London's annual production of 2,200,000 tons of municipal waste was equivalent to a third of the average charge on the rates and that costs were markedly higher in the Metropolitan Boroughs than in other urban authorities in England and Wales (Robson, 1939).

In March 1929, the Minister of Health, Neville Chamberlain, appointed a Departmental Committee to consider the Dawes Report. Evidence was submitted by various interest groups including the County Councils and the Association of Metropolitan Borough Engineers and Surveyors. In November 1930, the final report of the Chamberlain Committee recommended in favour of a central organisation, and repeated all the main criticisms in the Dawes Report noting that 'London as a whole has not kept pace with the great advances that have been made in the science and practice of public cleansing' (Ministry of Health, 1930 p. 5). The system of contracting was again condemned and the committee recommended that the local sanitary authorities and the central body should be empowered to terminate all contracts subject to compensation.

The 1930 Ministry of Health report was then considered by the Metropolitan Boroughs Standing Joint Committee, a body containing representatives from all the Metropolitan Borough Councils. On the key question of the centralisation of refuse disposal, 18 boroughs voted against and 11 in favour, showing that there was a clear majority of constituent boroughs against the delegation of responsibilities in waste disposal to a central authority. Finally, on the 16th June 1932, the Minister of Health wrote to each borough stating that it was not practicable at that time to legislate for the centralisation of London cleansing under one authority (Tee 1937 p. 242). However by July 1932, the Minister of Health was forced to convene a conference, at which he stated that the waste disposal situation had deteriorated markedly since the Dawes Report of 1929. He asked whether a system of co-operation between the boroughs could be achieved, preferably on a voluntary rather than a compulsory basis.

In 1934, the Ministry of Health Cleansing Committee reported a number of difficulties: many boroughs were continuing to refuse to accept outside waste from other boroughs for their incinerators; the financial crisis of 1931 had delayed a wide range of new investments and improvements; and there was continuing incidence of uncontrolled tipping, which was reflected by a series of local legislative efforts by County Councils in the early 1930s to protect themselves against the tipping of waste. Essex County Council's Bill of 1932-33, sought to prohibit the tipping of refuse in the County of Essex without the written consent of the County Council and the District Council. At the time, Essex received one third of the total refuse produced in London and no less than 23 local authorities petitioned against the Bill (Robson, 1939). Similar legislative efforts were also made by Surrey County council in 1931 and by Middlesex County Council in 1933-34.

Difficulties in the transfer of waste by river and rail were also identified. In the case of river transport it was found that many of the wharves were inadequately equipped and there was a problem of uncovered barges. The rail sidings used were often unsatisfactory in both their construction and condition, and local authorities were in some difficulty in attempting to make improvements to Railway Companies' property. The 1934 Ministry of Health Report also recommended that many of the incineration plants should now be closed down on health and safety grounds because of their production of smoke and dust, and that no further facilities should be located in densely populated areas. The 1930s also saw, perhaps for the first time, official concerns from within the waste management profession, over the conditions and long term employment prospects of belt pickers at London's incineration plants. The 1937 Conference of the Municipal and County Engineers reported that in some boroughs, juvenile labour was being used to pick refuse, who were laid off after a few years and not offered re-employment in other work for the local authorities (Tee, 1937).

However, the Metropolitan Boroughs rejected most of the Ministry of Health's criticisms, and published their own reports under the Cleansing Sub-Committee of the Metropolitan Boroughs' Standing Joint Committee. Robson (1939) described how their Report of July 1934 showed 'a degree of satisfaction bordering on complacency' in asserting that there had been a continuous amelioration in the situation (Robson, 1939 p. 210). The Metropolitan Boroughs' Report of January 1937 claimed that their collection and disposal services would bear favourable comparison with those services in any other part of the country and especially in comparison with local authorities in outer London (Robson, 1939). Yet, on economic grounds alone, a survey for the Institute of Municipal Treasurers, had found that unit costs for waste collection and disposal in 1937-38 were markedly more expensive in London, than in Birmingham, Liverpool or Manchester, and that the costs of waste collection and disposal in the LCC area were nearly double those in the outer London Urban Districts and Non-County Boroughs, as shown in Table 3.2.

Table 3.2: Expenditure on waste collection and disposal in the year 1937-38

Net cost of waste collection and disposal per ton

	s	d
Urban Districts (average)	8	9
Non-County Boroughs (average)	11	8
County Boroughs (average)	12	10
Birmingham	12	10
Liverpool	14	11
Manchester	17	10
London County Council	19	7

Source: Lloyd and Humphries (1944)

By the late 1930s, few if any of the Ministry of Health's recommendations had been acted upon and at a conference on London Cleansing held by the Institution of Municipal and County Engineers in 1937, the Borough Engineer for Woolwich, Mr H.W. Tee argued that:

The basic factor of the ever-increasing complaints of London's disposal methods, culminating in a series of investigations spread over the last 12 years or so, can be attributed to the indiscriminate dumping of the refuse of one local authority in the area administered by another. (Tee, 1937 p. 240).

Tee noted the on-going problem of boroughs not accepting outside waste from other boroughs for their own incineration and transfer facilities, and that there was a pervasive attitude of no further responsibility for disposal when it had been handed over to a private contractor. He also reiterated Dawes' concerns over waste collection, because of the absence of satisfactory dustbin provision which was discussed in the 1937 Report of the Ministry of Health Cleansing Committee:

The present multiplicity of the types and sizes of containers in use is a definite drawback and is unsatisfactory and uneconomic...The containers should be the property of the council, there should be a uniform charge throughout London, together with a standard form of hire agreement. (Tee, 1937 p. 259).

The 1937 conference also found that the problems of waste collection had been made more difficult by the trends in public housing design, which necessitated the use of chutes and shared paladins. The Borough Engineer for Shoreditch, Mr C.T. Fulcher, noted that:

...in my Borough east of the City, we have one of the most densely populated areas of Great Britain, and the tendency today in rehousing the population is to put them in five storey human packing cases. One of the most remarkable results of this intensive housing, which is resulting in my Borough in 245 persons per acre, is the peculiar difficulty and costliness of getting not only refuse but street cleansing properly and adequately dealt with...My experience has been that the chute question, apart from its sanitary angle of consideration, is a definitely more expensive method of collection. (Fulcher, 1937 quoted in Tee, 1937 p. 275).

The 1937 Ministry of Health Report also noted that the cost of collection was rising because the waste stream was becoming lighter and bulkier and this was attributed to the growing proportion of packaging materials in the waste stream, as illustrated in Figure 3.5. Above all, Tee expressed exasperation at the lack of progress in the implementation of the central recommendation of the Dawes Report for a central body to co-ordinate waste management for London:

> ...either the task of centralisation is insuperable, or the present administrative system of London will not permit of a satisfactory scheme being evolved, or the Boroughs lack the goodwill to co-operate. (Tee, 1937 p. 263).

Progress in realising Tee's plea for greater co-operation between the boroughs proved to be painfully slow. In 1947 after considering these proposals for 15 years, the Metropolitan Borough Councils introduced a scheme for combining into groups for disposal purposes, but by 1960 only two of the ten groups which had been set up were still operating. Additionally, only the Metropolitan Borough of Southwark and the City Corporation had exercised their statutory powers to acquire tipping sites (Vick and Flintoff, 1966) and by 1952 only the Metropolitan Boroughs of Woolwich and Fulham relied on incineration for waste disposal, as shown in Figure 3.6.

Figure 3.5: The changing composition of household waste in London

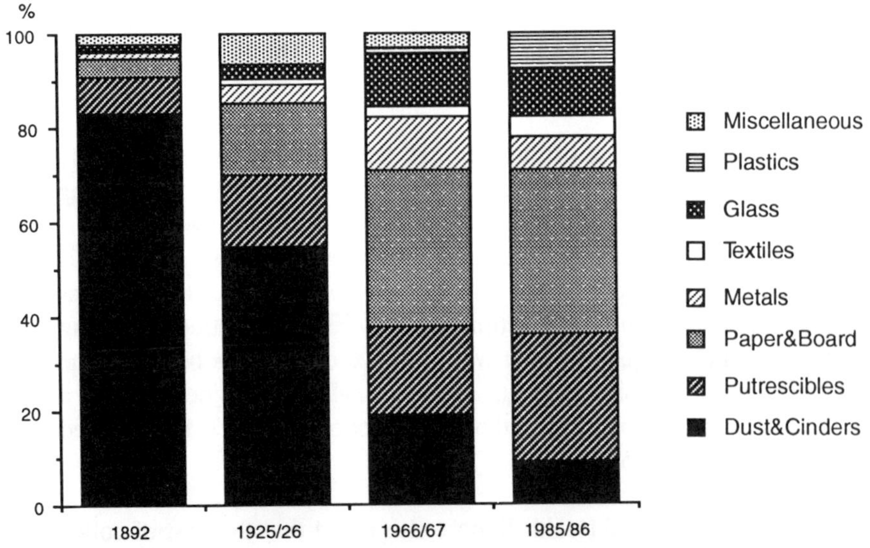

Source : LCC (1893); Ministry of Health (1929); GLC (1967; 1986b)

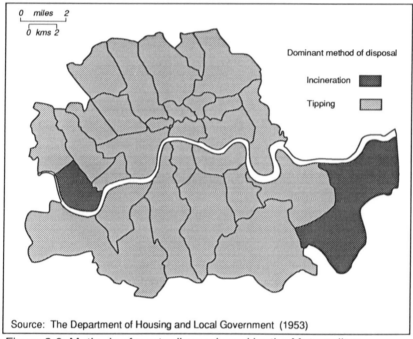

Source: The Department of Housing and Local Government (1953)

Figure 3.6: Methods of waste disposal used by the Metropolitan Boroughs in 1952-53

In the 1950s the increasing quantities of waste arising from the London area were perceived as a matter of urgency by the adjoining County Councils because of the exhaustion of landfill sites and growing recognition of the environmental consequences of poorly monitored waste disposal practices. By the late 1950s new environmental concerns over waste disposal were emerging. For example, the environmental impact of landfill by the pollution of ground water was beginning to attract attention from central government. An investigation by the Ministry of Housing and Local Government found that 'the matter has proved exceedingly complex', and that there was an urgent need for further research to overcome the difficulties many local authorities were experiencing in finding suitable sites for refuse disposal (Ministry of Housing and Local Government, 1961).

In summary, the period of the London County Council from 1889 to 1965 was marked by a growing recognition of the administrative inadequacies of the existing system of waste management to cope with the needs of public health and economic efficiency for the management of London's growing waste stream. The material presented in the next section suggests that no improvements were to be achieved until the wider movement for local government reform swept aside the opposition of individual Metropolitan Boroughs to the centralised co-ordination of waste management in London.

The creation of the GLC Public Health Engineering Department

In 1960 the Royal Commission on Local Government in Greater London published its report (Herbert Commission, 1960) and concluded that the organisation and practice of waste management in London was unsatisfactory:

> The whole situation is in our opinion, unhealthy from the point of view of good local government, unbusinesslike, and wasteful in land use. The system has grown up haphazardly and piecemeal. (Herbert Commission 1960 p. 171-172).

During the period of the London County Council from 1889 to 1965 each of the ninety five local authorities in the Greater London area had carried out the task of both refuse collection and disposal and the LCC had no operational responsibility for waste management. Under the London Government Act of 1963 responsibility for waste disposal was for the first time to be separated from that for waste collection. The disposal of London's waste became the responsibility of the new GLC Public Health Engineering Department, the largest Waste Disposal Authority in Europe, and the collection of waste and street cleansing remained with the now thirty two London Boroughs and the City of London Corporation, illustrated in Figure 3.7. Public Health Engineering was to be one of seventeen departments in the GLC, and in addition to refuse disposal, it was also responsible for main drainage, sewage purification and trade effluent control, along with land drainage, river pollution control and Thames flood prevention. It therefore not only represented an integrated authority for the disposal of all solid municipal waste, but also provided London with a strategic organisational framework for the management of all London's waste. However, the responsibility for water was to be taken away in 1973-4 with the creation of the unelected Thames Water Authority, and this marked an important early reversal in the strategic GLC role for public service provision in the capital (Mukhopadhyay, 1975).

Figure 3.7: The new administrative boundaries for London in 1965

The establishment of the GLC role in waste management

After the appointment of the Director of Public Health Engineering in July 1965, a skeleton establishment of technical and administrative posts had been approved by the Council, and a phased transfer to the GLC of borough responsibilities for waste disposal was to be completed by March 1967 (Vick and Flintoff, 1966). Five operational areas for waste disposal were established, as shown in Figure 3.8, and a comprehensive rationalisation of facilities and arrangements for refuse transportation was undertaken.

At the formation of the GLC and the London Boroughs on March 31st 1965, there was an annual municipal solid waste stream of 2,877,000 tonnes of refuse to be handled. The GLC Public Health Engineering Department had inherited a diverse array of plant and equipment from the ninety five local authorities in the Greater London area: 14 incinerators in use; 1 composting plant; 17 wharves (river transfer stations); 3 rail transfer stations; 25 road transfer stations, and 43 tipping sites (16 operated by the local authorities and

81

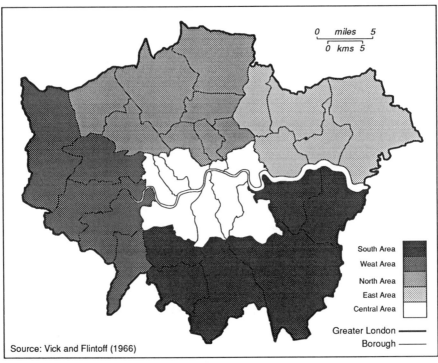

0   *miles*   5

0   *kms*   5

South Area

Weat Area

North Area

East Area

Central Area

Greater London ———

Borough ———

Figure 3.8: The regional divisions of the GLC Public Health Engineering Department

27 by contractors), as illustrated in Figure 3.9. In the first full year of GLC operation, 90 per cent of the municipal waste stream was sent to landfill, with the remainder mostly sent to incineration plants, showing that the contribution of incineration had declined substantially since its heyday in the Edwardian period, and that landfill was to be the overwhelming means of waste disposal for the GLC Public Health Engineering Department. In terms of methods used for the transportation of waste to landfill sites, 71 per cent of the waste was transported by road, 22 per cent by barges on the Thames, and 7 per cent by rail (Vick and Flintoff, 1966).

The newly-formed GLC also inherited a range of difficulties: there was scant information on the quantities and types of waste (weighbridge facilities were absent from many transfer stations and there was a need to determine how waste content varied between inner and outer London); there was no comprehensive or co-ordinated plan; there were numerous transport and disposal contracts of varying duration; employees were transferred with a wide range of salaries, wages, and protected conditions of service; the

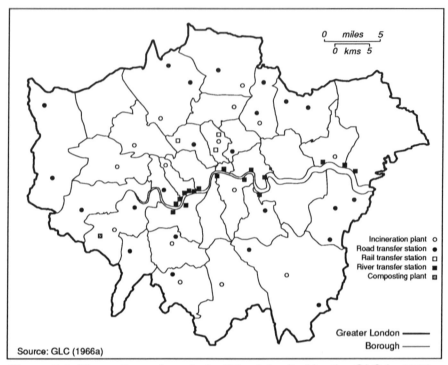

Figure 3.9: The pattern of waste facilities inherited by the GLC in 1965

inventory of mobile and fixed plant was old and inadequately maintained because of impending re-organisation; there were ill-defined sites and areas of land on which to operate; and there was a simultaneous reorganisation of local government resulting in the reduction of administrative areas from ninety five to thirty three, leaving the new London Boroughs to face similar problems to those being faced by the GLC (Townend, 1982). A key anomaly, was that some boroughs had disposal facilities close to their collection areas, whilst others were having to transport their refuse in the collection vehicles for up to 30 miles. Chelsea, for example, was sending refuse by road to Stone in Kent, whereas Lambeth was sending refuse to Gerrards Cross in Buckinghamshire, the collection vehicles passing each other on Battersea Bridge. Consequently, refuse was often not going to the nearest transfer station or disposal site, or travelling by the most convenient route (Vick and Flintoff, 1966). As a result of these diverse and uncoordinated arrangements, the cost of waste disposal in 1963 varied from 12/7d to 44/11d per tonne in the GLC area, with an average figure of some

26/-d at the year ending 31st March 1965 (Vick and Flintoff, 1966).

A number of problems were identified with the 17 incineration plants inherited by the GLC: there was inadequate storage capacity for waste on the cramped sites; many relied on unpleasant manual tasks such as belt picking, manual stoking and manual clinkering (removal of ash), and this large labour requirement was very expensive; there was atmospheric pollution by dust, flue-gases and flue grit; many plants had down-rated capacities, sometimes only half that of the design capacity, owing to changes in the composition of refuse leading to its lower density and increased calorific value, as shown in Figure 3.5; and the clinker produced was useless with a high metal and organic content. It was resolved, therefore, to build new and technically superior incineration plants and the old generation of plants were gradually phased out, with the last closure at Auckland Road, Leyton, in 1980 (Cooper, 1981).

The existing practices of controlled tipping were equally found to be unsatisfactory: the ever-increasing content of paper and plastic made it impossible to avoid extensive wind-borne littering of the tip and its environment, only controllable with ugly open-mesh fencing; the lower cinder and ash content (especially since the 1956 Clean Air Act) had rendered the waste more pungent and lighter in colour (less putrescibles and paper were now burnt in the home with the rise of gas and electric heating systems); the greater compaction from new mechanical as opposed to manual handling methods on the tips had resulted in a general failure of the waste to reach a high enough temperature to decompose aerobically to the extent of destroying hazardous pathogens; the top soil from the sites was often sold or re-used too quickly, resulting in the sites being covered with more refuse; there was failure to win support from the Ministry of Agriculture over the programme of land reclamation; and finally, the practice of tipping was increasingly unpopular with the public, at a time of growing environmental concern (Vick and Flintoff, 1966).

A first priority of the GLC, as foreshadowed in the Report of the Herbert Commission, was to improve the data on London's waste stream and carry out research into possible alternatives, so as to enable effective planning for the future. An initial aim of the new Design Development Division within the GLC's Public Health Engineering Department was therefore to determine the composition and seasonal fluctuation of London's waste. The GLC chairman and vice-chairman, along with officers of the Public Health Services Committee, also went on a number of fact finding trips to incineration plants at Lyons, Stuttgart, Hamburg, and Rotterdam. Technical improvements noted within a year of the formation of the GLC, were the use of pulverisation technology at transfer stations to facilitate controlled tipping by reducing the volume of waste and to increase the safety of waste handling (Vick and

Flintoff, 1966). An early piece of research was into the use of a mechanical screen to improve the safety and economic efficiency of crude refuse sorting for the Barking incinerator, where there were increasing difficulties experienced with cans, bottles, plastic containers and some textiles:

> Screening refuse into sizes suitable for further treatment is both effective and reliable. The process will separate objects unacceptable to hammer mills and will therefore eliminate the need for hand picking. The costs of the screen over the life of the plant is more than off-set by the wages of the manual labour it replaces. (GLC 1966b p. 11).

The first planned waste management strategy for London developed by the GLC, was the construction of a new ring of incineration plants for the intermediate areas of London, which lacked either access to the river wharves or to nearby tips (GLC, 1966a; Vick and Flintoff, 1966). As a result, the 1965 GLC Waste Management Plan had three main elements:

> i) The treatment of the Thames, as high up as practicable, as the main highway for the disposal of refuse from the riparian boroughs.
>
> ii) The arrangement of direct delivery to controlled tips by those local authorities, particularly on the outskirts, for which this will be the most economical course.
>
> iii) The Provision of a ring of incinerators at a radius of eight to ten miles from Charing Cross which would receive all refuse which would otherwise require to be transferred to bulk haulage vehicles.
>
> (GLC, 1966a p. 28)

The effective choice at this time, was therefore seen as either incineration or landfill, with no major contribution envisaged from either waste reduction or recycling activities until the re-emergence of environmental concern in the 1980s.

The development of waste management under the GLC

Early appraisals of the GLC's role in waste management were enthusiastic about the new arrangements, and the potential for strategically planned and capital intensive forms of waste disposal:

The GLC's responsibility for refuse disposal is producing a rationalised and more effective system, symbolised in the building (at a cost of £10 million), of a new refuse incineration plant, which will supersede the individual and somewhat haphazard arrangements which existed previously. (Rhodes and Ruck, 1970 p. 175).

The 1971 Sumner Report into waste management for the Department of the Environment, concluded that the disposal of solid wastes of all types should be co-ordinated and controlled over reasonably large areas by strategic Waste Disposal Authorities on the GLC model (DoE, 1971). The report found that there was a lack of comprehensive statutory responsibility or control for the disposal of wastes in the UK, with operators tending to find the cheapest and easiest methods, with no regard for the environmental consequences. Likewise, a DoE Consultation Document on Waste Disposal also stated that London was now the model for national waste policy: the pattern of separating waste disposal from waste collection was subsequently to be repeated throughout Britain under the provisions of the Local Government Act of 1972, with waste disposal becoming the responsibility of County Councils and waste collection remaining with the smaller District Councils:

This division of functions between counties and districts will correspond to that which is already successfully established in London between the GLC and the London Boroughs. (DoE, 1973b p. 7).

The initial optimism of the late 1960s was to be countered, however, by the difficulties in fulfilling the three components of the first strategic plan: the construction of a ring of new incinerators for inner London; the increased use of the river for central London; and the usage of nearby landfill capacity by outer London.

The use of landfill was more difficult than anticipated. The access to nearby landfill capacity for London was rapidly exhausted because of the growth of London's waste stream since 1965 (GLC, 1980a) and because of new legislative controls, principally from the 1974 Control of Pollution Act, as a response to the increasing political salience of environmental concern. As a result of these developments, the waste had to be transported over progressively greater distances. Furthermore, only one of the five planned incinerators was ever built. The serious technical and financial difficulties which were experienced with the Edmonton plant, effectively precluded the possibility of any more incineration plants being built by the GLC:

Completed in 1971 at a cost of £13 million, the incinerator experienced numerous teething problems which took years to remedy and at a cost which probably doubled the original price. The main fault was severe corrosion and erosion of the boiler tubes by acidic gases produced by plastic materials and within a short time all five boilers had to be replaced. Its first full year of operation was 1975/76, and even then it was restricted to about 75 per cent of its design load, so that only about 22 MW of electricity was exported. (Cooper, 1981 p. 10).

There were also problems with utilising river transfer for a large proportion of inner London's waste in order to 'reclaim' low-lying land and reduce the reliance on road haulage. Much of London's waste was generated some miles from the river and there were limitations imposed by the location and capacity of the existing river transfer stations. There was unwillingness on the part of contractors to undertake large capital investments in new barges and there were physical constraints on the more intensive use of the river, with a finite availability of disposal sites close to the river. There were high costs incurred in site preparations to receive waste, and there was a relative lack of flexibility in the use of river transport, necessitating the use of road transport in the event of any operational breakdown (SCLSERP, 1978).

Following the problems in implementing the first GLC waste plan, a new strategy emerged during the 1970s based around the increased use of landfill at more remote sites, using bulk transfer by rail rather than road to transport the waste. There were major new investment programmes instituted, which resulted in the construction of new rail transfer stations from 1977, at Hendon in Barnet and Brentford in Hounslow, each with a daily 800 tonne capacity (Cooper, 1981). As a result of these developments, the GLC was the only UK Waste Disposal Authority to make substantial use of rail transfer of waste with its environmental advantages over road haulage (GLC, 1980a). The Brentford Rail Transfer Station was the first of its kind to be constructed and served as an integrated rail transfer system for waste disposal (GLC, 1979). Both Brentford and Hendon were superior on both economic and public health grounds to the three rail transfer stations inherited by the GLC in 1965, which had used open top wagons with both loading and discharging occurred in the open (GLC, 1977). By the late-1970s the GLC had undertaken a complete rationalisation of its waste management infrastructure, which now consisted of 18 road transfer stations, 5 river transfer stations and 3 rail transfer stations and there was a co-ordination of waste disposal facilities in order to maximise economic efficiency in the transfer of waste.

A number of national legislative developments during the period of the GLC affected waste management in London. The first relates to the problem

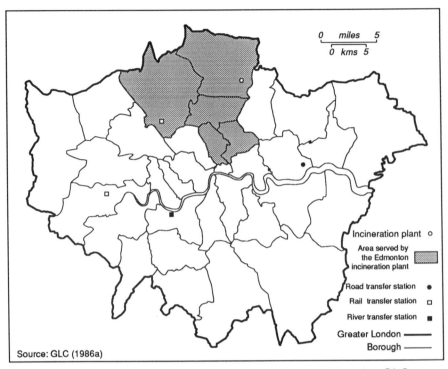

Source: GLC (1986a)

Incineration plant ○

Area served by
the Edmonton
incineration plant

Road transfer station ●

Rail transfer station □

River transfer station ■

Greater London ━━━━

Borough ───

0   miles   5

0   kms   5

Figure 3.10: Major new investments undertaken by the GLC

of disposing of bulky household waste, and in particular of unwanted cars, a problem which was recognised as needing urgent attention by the GLC in 1966 (GLC, 1967). The problems arising from the fly-tipping (illegal tipping) of these kinds of waste led to Duncan Sandys' Private Member's Bill of 1966, later to become the 1967 Civic Amenities Act, amended as the 1978 Refuse Disposal (Amenities) Act (Civic Trust, 1967; Coggins et al., 1989a). This legislation gave local authorities the responsibility of providing civic amenity facilities where the public could bring items of bulky waste free of charge. By the early 1980s, some 14 per cent of the municipal waste stream in London was derived from 38 civic amenity sites, and their use by the public had grown by over 12 per cent annually since their creation in 1967 (GLC, 1986a; Townend, 1982). These civic amenity sites were later to become an integral focus of recycling activity as multi-material recycling centres with the advent of on-street collection facilities for recyclable materials during the 1980s.

Further legislative developments concerned the inadequacies of waste regulation and the disposal of hazardous and toxic wastes. The Key Committee was set up by central Government in 1970 to report on the disposal of toxic waste, and recommended that the GLC should be the authorising body for toxic waste regulation and disposal, as the strategic local authority for London (DoE, 1971). These concerns were later to be incorporated into the 1972 Deposit of Poisonous Wastes Act and Section Two of the 1974 Control of Pollution Act, and became part of the GLC's new site licensing and monitoring responsibilities for landfill sites. The 1974 Control of Pollution Act saw the introduction of three main changes for UK waste management: the formal recognition of strategic policy making in waste disposal; the duty of Waste Disposal Authorities to produce plans; and the introduction of a licensing system for waste disposal sites. It was noted in 1975, however, that the implementation of the 1974 Act was already being delayed because of the need to restrict local authority expenditure (GLC, 1975c).

By 1985, as a result of the improvements in London's transfer stations, all waste carried by road, rail or river was fully containerised. The GLC had been able to realise substantial investment programmes in major new transfer facilities, which enabled the long term co-ordination of economic efficiency, the improvement of environmental standards, and the utilisation of state of the art technologies in public health. The role of the GLC had evolved from simply being the Waste Disposal Authority for the 3 million tonnes of municipal waste in London, into a wider regulatory role for 17 million tonnes of industrial, construction and other wastes in the London area, involving the handling of toxic and hazardous wastes:

> Since 1965 the role of the disposal authority has changed from purely co-ordinating and operating a disposal service for the collection authorities to that of controlling all waste produced in the council's area through statutory planning, exercising control over the disposal system of both public and private sectors, and the detailed control of collection, transport and disposal of special (toxic) wastes. (Townend, 1982 p. 235).

The development of recycling in London

The salvage of materials from London's waste stream

A report by the Local Government Board in 1915 found that there was widespread sorting of refuse after its collection to salvage useful materials.

Whereas in the nineteenth century, the main salvage activities had been for horse manure and other valuable items derived from street cleansing, the extension of waste collection to individual households had two main effects: firstly, the size of the waste stream for disposal began to grow rapidly, as increasing numbers of households were incorporated into the collection rounds; and secondly, the nature of the waste stream began to change, as shown in Figure 3.5, bringing in increasing quantities of potentially useful items, such as glass bottles and metals cans. The rationale for the reclamation of materials now extended beyond the economic value of the materials, to the perceived need to reduce the waste stream and to improve the operational efficiency of incineration plants, which could not dispose of the increasing quantities of incombustible glass and metals:

> Before the refuse is disposed of it is frequently subjected to a sorting process, which often brings in a small revenue, and which enables the Council to get rid of a part of it, and especially of that part - old tins, glass and other material - which is most difficult to deal with satisfactorily. (Local Government Board, 1915 p. xi).

Examples are given in Croydon, Enfield, Barking Town and Acton, of 'contractors paying a weekly sum for the privilege of sorting over the refuse and taking out materials which can be sold' (op cit p. xi). Elsewhere, materials were often removed by hand picking from a moving belt at refuse transfer stations. A detailed description of a model plant in the early 1920s shows that a long travelling belt was used, from which the following articles were saved: tin cans, waste paper, refuse of meat and fish markets (used to make manure for gardens), grease from waste meat (used for candle making and lubricating oils), and butcher's refuse and waste food (used for pig swill and poultry feed) (Metropolitan Borough of Shoreditch, 1925).

The case was also made for the effective separation of re-usable fractions of waste by householders before they entered the waste stream. In 1925, for example, the Borough Electrical Engineer for Shoreditch, C. Newton Russel, noted that:

> In order to make the best use of refuse from a salving point of view, it is desirable that the various items, viz.: ashes, paper, straw, scraps of food, vegetables, bones etc., should be put into separate receptacles by the householder ready for the dustmen. (Metropolitan Borough of Shoreditch, 1926 p. 4)

During the period of the London County Council and the Metropolitan Boroughs, the 'salvage' of materials was generally carried out for economical and technical reasons, which is in marked contrast to the environmental rationale behind recycling today, and the scope and extent of recycling activity was only significantly extended in wartime as part of the national war effort. There is evidence that both the 1914-1918 and the 1939-45 wars were instrumental in increasing, albeit temporarily, the level of waste reclamation or 'salvage' for a wide range of materials. During wartime, wastes were viewed completely differently, as an essential part of the war effort (Temple, 1943). In wartime Enfield, for example, there were collection points on every street corner, where six different waste fractions were left by householders: kitchen waste (without tea leaves) for pig swill, old bottles, cans, bones, rags and newspapers[1]. The Metropolitan Borough of Paddington ran its own pig farm profitably during the war, using locally collected kitchen waste (Flintoff, 1950).

Wartime fears over food shortages, the agricultural depression of the 1930s, and the Attlee Government's strategic Agriculture Act of 1947, gave impetus to the promotion of composting as a means of helping the production of food. In the 1950s, many local authorities ran separate collections services for paper and waste food. Composting was seen by many commentators as superior to both the use of incineration and controlled tipping, and its widespread promotion was portrayed as feasible on both economic and technical grounds (see Burke, 1949; Davies, 1961). Davies (1961) predicted that the use of composting would inevitably rise as a result of the mounting economic and environmental difficulties associated with alternative means of waste disposal:

Controlled tipping must have at least reached its peak, even if not yet in decline, due mainly to adverse space and haulage considerations...Incineration costs, especially in relation to new plants, are now fairly high and the method lacks favour for a number of reasons, not least of which is the requirements of clean air policy. (Davies, 1961 p. 191).

Attitudes towards the handling of refuse were also different in the immediate post-war period. As late as the 1950s hand picking of refuse was seen as unproblematic because it was necessary anyway for the operation of the older generation of incineration plants. Isaac (1953) showed that 'where the refuse is to be incinerated, it is almost essential to separate the refuse first, since it can contain up to 50 per cent dust and other material of low calorific value' (p. 212). In comparison with the 1920s and 1930s hand picking in the 1950s was often combined with a number of mechanical sorting devices: magnetic separation for ferrous metals and a system of screens for dust (used for brick making and fertilisers) and cinders (for fuel). The remaining

Table 3.3: Materials recovered from London's waste stream during different periods

1800-1914	Ash for brickmaking; Horse manure; Pig swill
1914-1919	All materials as part of national war-effort
1919-1939	Glass and metals at incineration plants; Pig swill
1939-1945	All materials as part of national war-effort
1945-1965	Metals; Glass; Paper; Textiles; Pig swill
1965-1977	Metals; Paper
1977-1982	Metals; Glass (launch of bottle bank scheme)
1982-1990	Metals; Glass; Paper; Textiles; CFCs; Waste Oil

Source: Gandy (1992a)

fractions of paper, re-usable bottles, glass cullet, non-ferrous metals and rags (used for paper making, linoleum and industrial wiping cloths) were recovered by belt picking where '40 feet per minute is regarded as a maximum speed for efficient hand-sorting' (Isaac, 1953 p. 212). In contrast, other commentators such as Morrison, noted in his review of London government that recycling was no alternative to the existing means of waste disposal for London's ever growing waste stream:

> The London refuse problem is immense. Pigs benefit considerably from the food refuse, and paper is now available as a valuable salvage. But the hard core of tins and bottles, ashes and clinker have to be got rid of. Some is dealt with in borough destructors; but most of it is still barged down the Thames or taken away by rail. (Morrison, 1949 p. 92)

Technical and economic barriers to recycling in the 1970s

By 1970 after the new GLC waste management arrangements had been in operation for five years, recycling activity was focused on paper along with some ferrous metals, including scrap from unwanted cars (GLC, 1971). The one composting plant which the GLC inherited was based at Sunbury-on-

Thames and had been run by a consortium of three local authorities (Sunbury-on-Thames; Staines; and Twickenham). It was found that the plant's compost was seriously contaminated with heavy metals, mainly lead and zinc, and the plant was shut down. No more composting plants were commissioned during the period of the GLC.

When the local government system for London was reorganised in 1965, twenty five of the new London Boroughs had inherited separate collections of waste paper within all or part of their area, as shown Figure 3.11, and the earliest recorded kerbside paper collection scheme run by a local authority in London was started by Westminster in 1929[2]. The GLC recognised that since the former local authorities in the London area had been responsible for both the collection and disposal of waste, there had been significant benefits in waste transport and disposal costs where authorities were able to divert tonnages of recyclable materials from the waste stream. When the GLC took over the responsibility for waste disposal they introduced a rebate to the boroughs for their waste paper collections based on the marginal cost savings for waste transport and disposal, calculated on a separate basis for the individual boroughs. Consequently, the boroughs in inner London which used waste transfer stations and incurred high costs of transport in addition to their tipping fees, received higher levels of rebate than the boroughs in outer London which delivered their waste directly to landfill sites with their own collection vehicles (Cooper 1990a). The GLC also carried out price negotiations on behalf of the London Boroughs with Thames Board Mills and Merton Paper Mills.

In spite of the GLC rebate and negotiated price contracts, the quantity of paper collected by the London Boroughs declined steadily during the early 1970s, as shown in Figure 3.12, and by 1975 the number of boroughs running kerbside collection schemes for waste paper had fallen to sixteen. In Newham, for example, there were weekly collections of paper from households in pink plastic bags by a fleet of ten specially adapted electric vehicles[3] and an earlier scheme in Newham had operated continuously from 1946 to 1970[4]. The main reason for this decline in kerbside paper collections by local authorities was attributed to the increasing labour costs of collection and the weakness of the secondary materials market for paper. It was also suggested that the separation of the waste collection and disposal functions of the former Metropolitan Boroughs with the creation of the GLC had contributed to the declining economic viability of paper collections by the new London Boroughs responsible only for the collection of waste (GLC, 1975d).

During the early 1970s there was an upsurge of interest in waste reclamation, associated with the 'limits to growth' period of environmental concern described in Chapter One and there was a proliferation of not only

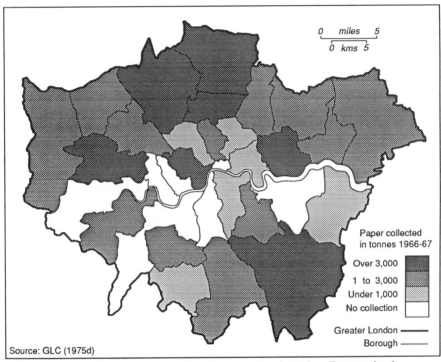

Figure 3.11: Waste paper collections by the London Boroughs in 1966-67

Figure 3.12: Declining waste paper collections by the London Boroughs

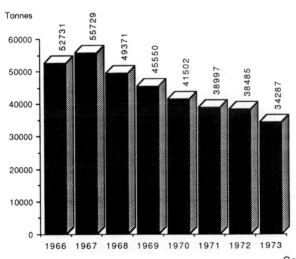

local authority, but also voluntary sector schemes, particularly kerbside collection schemes for waste paper. In 1974, the newly formed Camden Friends of the Earth presented proposals for a comprehensive paper recycling initiative for the entire borough, involving the purchase of a fleet of eight specially adapted vehicles and the construction of a paper baling plant to handle 5,200 tonnes of paper per annum. The proposed scheme, conceived in 'an era of shortages', claimed that 'apart from the positive beneficial environmental effects, such a scheme will show an average net profit of £9,000 per annum, and a discounted actual rate of return of 11.5 per cent, for an investment of £149,000' (Camden FoE, 1974 p. 2). In the event, the Camden scheme never materialised because of the repeated fluctuations and weaknesses of the waste paper market, which undermined the central assumption of the proposed scheme, that the predicted resource scarcity of the 1970s would be certain to bring about a sustained increase in the price of waste paper.

There is evidence that fluctuations in the price of waste paper have adversely affected waste paper schemes in previous periods. In Barking and Dagenham, for example, financial losses were sustained on a new paper baling plant which had been constructed by the authority in 1965[5] and many schemes in London collapsed as a result of the 1966-67 decline in demand for waste paper (LAMSAC, 1971). Similarly, the borough of Enfield suffered considerable loss on a baling plant built in 1970 to serve Enfield, Haringey and Waltham Forest[6]. The collapse of many established recycling schemes in the early 1970s led to intense debate over the role of central government in maintaining recycling schemes in the national interest. The Labour MP Brynmor John, for example, called for a publicly owned recycling industry, since 'private enterprise has failed, except in scrap metal, to a get a recycling industry into being on its own account' (John, 1974 p. 60). John argued for a massive input of government money in relation to the existing recycling budget of just £98,000 for 1974, and suggested that the best solution would be the construction of twenty regional centralised sorting plants, to be owned and operated in the public sector. In September 1974 the minority Labour government published its White Paper *War on Waste: A Policy for Reclamation* (DoE/DTI, 1974). It appeared that central Government was moving towards a nationally based waste reclamation strategy, which recognised the potential difficulties facing individual local authorities, voluntary groups and firms handling the collected materials. The Waste Management Advisory Council was set up, concerning itself initially with the problem of packaging and the need for standardised returnable containers. As early as 1973, the Paper and Board Federation had been lobbying central government to undertake intervention buying in order to stabilise the waste paper market (Townsend, 1975). The Government responded in 1974 by

95

setting up an Advisory Group on Waste Paper Recycling and there were discussions over the possibility of introducing joint government and industry schemes, as already successfully established in Japan and the Netherlands, but these never materialised (Meacher, 1975).

In December 1974, the economic slowdown heralded a rapid collapse in the waste paper market, and the industry called for £10 million of state aid under Section Eight of the 1972 Industry Act (Townsend, 1975). By early 1975 the GLC was calling for urgent government assistance to prevent the collapse of paper collection services in the London Boroughs (*Municipal Engineering*, 13th June 1975) and the GLC Public Services Committee reported on the 10th June that Thames Board Mills were refusing to accept any more paper because of their huge stockpile (GLC, 1975d). Just two days later, for example, Hounslow council made an emergency decision to stop its waste paper collection service with immediate effect (*Brentford and Chiswick Times*, 12th June 1975). Yet at this critical moment in 1975, as a consequence of mounting political and economic problems and ministerial reshuffles, recycling quickly slipped down the public policy agenda.

The deteriorating situation had led to the landfill of collected paper and urgent investigations into ways of reducing the cost of waste paper collections. The mid-1970s saw calls for the voluntary sector involvement in collection to be quickly expanded in order to cut the labour costs of local authority run services (*Materials Reclamation Weekly*, August 28th 1976) and the cessation of schemes created furious local rows over the loss of 'trailer money' for drivers with waste paper trailers behind the dustcarts (*Barking and Dagenham Post*, 14th April 1976). The new emphasis on the role of the voluntary sector was reflected in a joint DTI/DoE publication in 1977, which stated that 'voluntary organisations are the vital link in the recycling industry between householders who can provide the right materials and the reclamation industry which can use them in manufacture' (DTI/DoE, 1977 p. 1). In addition to calls for greater voluntary sector involvement, there were proposals to examine alternative and cheaper means of collecting paper by encouraging the public to bring paper to civic amenity sites[7]. The harnessing of the potential for public participation was later to form the basis of 'on-street collection facilities' such as bottle banks and multi-material recycling centres.

The recycling of glass also faced difficulties during the 1970s, but this was for technical and economic reasons, rather than a result of the weakness in the secondary materials market. The recovery of glass from post-consumer waste had declined because of the high labour costs of hand picking at transfer facilities and incineration plants and the absence of investment in new mechanical recovery plants for London (GLC, 1984g). Many of London's transfer stations were on cramped sites where the introduction of conveyor belts for the manual or mechanical sorting of waste would be impractical. The proportion of packaging derived from returnable glass bottles had declined sharply since the 1960s as other containers which were lighter, cheaper and easier to stack and transport had entered the market (GLC, 1985a) and this decline in the use of returnable containers led to direct criticism of the glass industry by the Chair of the GLC Public Services Committee:

> The re-use of glass bottles and jars is a field in which we have gone backwards over recent years because of a deliberate policy of industry, namely, designing for scrapping. (Edwards, 1974 p. 67).

In 1975 the Director of the GLC Public Health Engineering Department received a letter from the Glass Manufacturers Confederation, acknowledging the authority's wish to see an increase in standardised returnable containers, but highlighting the costs involved and outlining new research into the re-use of glass[8]. There is evidence that the glass industry had been carrying out research into re-using glass cullet (broken glass) since 1973 but had not yet devised an economically viable scheme for the separate collection of glass (Townsend, 1974). In 1975 there were discussions between the GLC and United Glass at Harlow, over the possibility of encouraging the public to deliver used bottles to civic amenity sites since it was concluded that any system reliant on local authorities to collect, sort and clean bottles would be too expensive. It was not until the introduction of the bottle bank scheme in 1977 that an economically viable solution to the diversion of glass from the waste stream was devised. This can be interpreted as a response to criticism of the glass industry throughout the 1970s over the declining use of returnable bottles and pressure from the EC over the problem of beverage containers. It is of interest that in 1978, the United Nations Environment Programme published a report *The State of the Environment*, urging the mandatory use of returnable glass containers, yet the glass and packaging industry lobbied against the mandatory use of returnables throughout the 1970s (UN, 1978). Despite the introduction of bottle banks, the argument over the use of returnable containers remains an enduring element within many alternative non-market based strategies to increase recycling and reduce the production of waste at source.

In the 1970s there was also interest in making better use of transfer stations for the post-consumer recovery of ferrous metals and glass, along with the production of refuse derived fuel (RDF). Attention was drawn to the joint DoE and local authority funded centralised recovery plants at Doncaster and Newcastle as possible models for the region (see Ayres, 1979; Cointreau et al., 1984; Cooper, 1981; Gulley, 1979; SCLSERP, 1978). In February 1979, the Parliamentary Under Secretary for the Environment, Ken Marks, announced the Labour Government's intention to carry out centralised sorting and RDF production for 20 per cent of the UK municipal waste stream by the early 1980s (*Hansard*, 13th February 1979). The GLC invited tenders for the production of RDF at the Cringle Dock river transfer station in Wandsworth and anticipated major revenue savings from such a project (GLC, 1984m). The increased production of electricity from waste was considered too expensive an option unless government subsidy could be made available (Schomburgk, 1975) and the economic viability of RDF as a coal substitute was consistently seen as better than incineration for the London region (see Bidwell and Mason, 1975).

Table 3.4: The extent of recycling in London in the mid-1970s

Material	Method of recovery
Paper	Collapse of Kerbside collection by London boroughs and the voluntary sector
Glass	No satisfactory system
Plastics	No satisfactory system
Metals	Magnetic recovery at Edmonton incineration plant and Cringle Dock river transfer station Scrap from abandoned vehicles Totting at civic amenity sites etc.
Textiles	Some recovery by totting and activities of the voluntary sector
Putrescibles	No satisfactory system (demise of pigswill collections)

Source: Various including GLC (1975a); SCLSRP (1978)

In the 1980s, there was renewed interest in recycling in London, as elsewhere in the UK, as a reflection of the re-emergence of environmental concern described in Chapter One. Unlike the 1970s, however, where the emphasis was on the kerbside collection of paper, recycling in the 1980s was marked by the use of on-street collection facilities for glass and other materials and the conversion of civic amenity sites into multi-material recycling centres.

The move towards the use of a 'bring' system has been made possible because of unprecedented environmental concern and levels of public participation to an extent not seen since war-time reclamation activities. This growing emphasis on public participation can be interpreted as an example of the 'partial self-provisioning' thesis and the reduction of the labour costs of service provision by reducing the operational role of the public sector and increasing the role of individual households and the voluntary sector (Gershuny and Miles, 1983; Pinch, 1989). In 1982, for example, Brent Friends of the Earth lobbied the GLC for money in recognition of their free labour and the savings in waste collection and disposal costs for the public sector.

The shift from the 1970s methods of recycling to the 1980s use of 'bring' systems dependent on public participation can best be illustrated through the case of glass. The emergence of the widespread use of on-street collection facilities for glass can be traced to the launch of the bottle bank scheme by the Glass Manufacturers Federation in 1977, which was strongly supported by both the London Boroughs Association and the GLC. The first bottle banks were used in Brent in 1979, and by 1982 15 boroughs were participating in the scheme (LBA, 1982) and the tonnage of glass recycled in London grew steadily, as suggested by Figure 3.13. The London Boroughs Association aimed to see 10 per cent of London's glass recycled within a few years and argued that glass recycling was beneficial on a number of economic and environmental grounds:

> Glass recycling through the bottle banks scheme benefits the environment, local authorities and the glass industry...It offers collection authorities the chance of some income, while making possible some reduction in collection costs. It provides a direct saving for disposal authorities on transport and landfill costs and space. It enables the glass industry to save raw materials and the energy used in the original manufacture of glass. And in the case of the consumers, it enables them to make a direct contribution to the conservation of the environment, energy and raw materials. (LBA, 1982 p. 1).

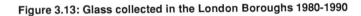

Figure 3.13: Glass collected in the London Boroughs 1980-1990

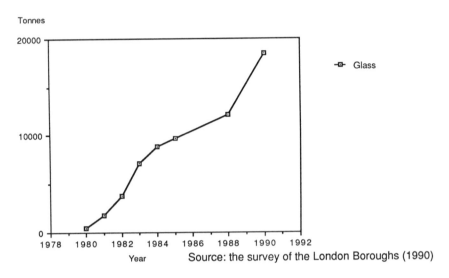

Tonnes

Source: the survey of the London Boroughs (1990)

The early 1980s saw four other developments which increased the potential for the success of the bottle banks scheme: firstly, the introduction of smaller fibreglass modular units, which were less aesthetically intrusive, could be conveniently emptied on site, and also allow an extension of the bottle bank scheme into places with restricted access, such as smaller shopping centres and 'out-of-town' situations with lower collection rates; secondly, from 1982 the GLC offered a rebate of £7 per tonne to the London Boroughs for the recovery of glass, in recognition of the savings in marginal waste disposal costs; thirdly, the glass industry now provided a guaranteed market for colour-separated glass, provided that any contamination was kept to specified minimum levels; and finally, and most importantly, a major new plant was opened by United Glass at Harlow, which improved the transport economics for the collected glass cullet. Prior to 1982, all but one of the London Boroughs had sent their glass by bulk haul to the Rockware Reclamation plant at Knottingley in West Yorkshire, which had led the London Boroughs Association to argue that the absence of a glass recycling plant in the South East had held back the widespread development of the bottle bank scheme (LBA, 1982).

The other major development during the 1980s, in addition to the use of on-street collection facilities was the transformation of the role of civic

100

amenity sites into multi-material recycling centres. In 1982, the first GLC recycling centre was opened at the Victoria Road civic amenity site in Hillingdon, handling glass, paper, cans, scrap metals, oil and textiles brought in by the general public. By 1984, a further 10 of the 40 GLC run civic amenity sites had been converted into recycling centres, as part of a major investment programme (Castle, 1986; GLC 1984g, 1985c). Yet, despite the introduction of the bottle banks scheme and the creation of recycling centres, the recycling rate stood at only 1.8 per cent of the municipal waste stream in the early 1980s (GLC, 1986a), a figure which was to rise only slightly to 2.1 per cent by the end of the decade, as described in the next chapter.

Radical waste management under the GLC 1981-1986

At the GLC *Talking Rubbish* conference held in 1980, a revised strategy for waste management in London was outlined, containing four main elements: a new focus on both energy and materials recovery, in recognition of renewed environmental concern, using centralised recovery, RDF and CHP technologies and the re-establishment of paper recovery schemes by the London Boroughs; a continuing need for a unified organisation to enable economic efficiency, research and policy development, and the co-ordination of available landfill space with demand; the improvement of data sources on wastes produced in the private sector, and now the regulatory responsibility of the GLC under the 1974 Control of Pollution Act; and a new generation of rail transfer stations was to be built in order to reduce the environmental impact of road haulage. It was envisaged that the financing of new waste management infrastructure would be primarily by a partnership of local and central government (GLC, 1980a). This echoed Gulley (1979) and other contemporary waste management literature, where the public sector was seen as taking the leading role in both policy development and also the construction and operation of waste management facilities.

The radical shift in direction of policy under the GLC, in recognition of environmental concern, was given added impetus by the election of a 'new left' GLC administration in 1981 (Gyford, 1985). An Environmental Panel was formed by elected members, and this quickly sought a strategic policy making role in both recycling and waste management. As an early initiative in January 1982, the GLC sent a letter to all the London Boroughs emphasising 'the need for the GLC to move the emphasis away from disposal of waste towards the maximum useful extraction of waste materials' and asked for the boroughs' response to this change in policy. However, the response from some boroughs was sceptical, and several emphasised their disastrous recent experience with paper recycling (Croydon, Enfield, Lewisham and Kensington and Chelsea). The chief executive of Merton,

W.A. McKee, noted that 'recycling will never be a surrogate for a positive and effective waste disposal policy...the amount of recoverable waste in a domestic dustbin forms a very small percentage of the whole and could scarcely make a significant contribution to the problem'[9].

An initial policy initiative was the emphasis on the employment creation potential of recycling. In November 1984 the *Recycling for Employment* conference was held at County Hall and it was reported that some 200 jobs in London were provided by recycling activities. These included employees in recycling workshops, the voluntary sector, and also licensed totters at civic amenity sites (GLC, 1984l). The GLC promoted recycling workshops by the provision of financial assistance and the granting of access to the waste stream at civic amenity sites for six inner London recycling workshops established across London in 1981 (one of which was specifically set up for the employment of people with disabilities). These recycling workshops also received funding from the Community Programme of the Manpower services Commission, charities and the London Boroughs, and the longer term aim was to fully integrate their activities with the recycling centres and civic amenity sites (GLC, 1984f).

With the submission of the GLC's Waste Management Plan *No Time to Waste* in November 1983, some indication was given of how the new commitments to materials and energy recovery were to be achieved. The new strategy would be based on the expansion of the 'bring' system of on-street collection facilities and improved environmental standards in waste disposal assisted by 'high technology' recovery of the energy value of waste from incineration and from landfill gas, which had been carried out at the Aveley landfill site in Essex since 1982 (GLC, 1983a; 1983d). The GLC recognised that the provision of on-street collection facilities and recycling centres could not allow the recycling of the major fraction of municipal waste derived from putrescibles. This was seen as best achieved either through the encouragement of households with gardens to carry out composting or as an energy source from landfill gas (GLC, 1983a; 1983d). Yet it was recognised that there were important limitations for a recycling policy reliant on householders to carry out their own composting:

> In practice the (disposal) savings will be somewhat lower because the scope for composting is greater in the outer London Boroughs which have generally lower disposal costs. The inner London Boroughs with their higher density flat and maisonette dwellings offer less potential for composting by households. (GLC, 1983c p. 1).

The 1983 GLC Waste Management Plan emphasised the need to tackle the production of waste at source, with a nationally oriented waste management strategy. This marked a phase of lobbying by the GLC of both Whitehall and the European Commission, to put greater emphasis on the reduction of waste at source:

> As a longer term goal the rationalisation of packaging and the increased repair and re-use of goods represent means of reducing the burden of waste disposal faced by the community. Society must consider ways in which it can reduce the volume of waste it creates. (GLC, 1983d p. 9).

Examples of the lobbying role of the GLC include the evidence presented to the Royal Commission on Environmental Pollution in 1984 and the European Commission in 1985, where the GLC called for the reduction and control of packaging and the increased use of returnable and reusable beverage containers based around a national beverage containers deposit scheme to be introduced by the Government (GLC, 1984i; 1985i). In 1984, the House of Commons Trade and Industry Committee held an inquiry into waste recycling to which the following recommendations were submitted by the GLC:

- The need for one government department to overcome the split of responsibility between the DEn, the DoE and the DTI.

- The appointment of a minister for recycling.

- The relaxation of capital controls and provision of financial assistance to the funding of recycling facilities.

- The need for government funding for community recycling initiatives and employment generation.

- National level co-ordination between local authorities and the recycling industry.

- The introduction of a national policy with clear recycling targets.

- The use of fiscal measures such as 'green taxes' on non-recyclable products.

- A new emphasis on municipal composting.

- The extension of the 'polluter pays principle' to waste producers.

- An extension of the waste disposal rebates scheme run under section 20 of the 1974 Control of Pollution Act.

- Financial support for the high running costs of kerbside collection schemes.

- The creation of markets for recycled products, including the use of public purchasing policy.

(GLC, 1984g)

In the event, the only change in central Government policy was the appointment of a minister for recycling, and no other significant changes to recycling policy at a national level were made until the enactment of the 1990 Environmental Protection Act (see Chapter Five).

During the 1980s there was a divergence of views in the UK over the future direction of waste management policy. In 1979, the new Conservative administration began to change the emphasis of waste management policy away from the public sector: there was a reduction in funding for pollution control agencies; the nationally based Waste Management Advisory Council set up in 1974 was abolished; the enactment of Section Two of the 1974 Control of Pollution Act was postponed; there was a progressively more market oriented approach to waste management in the UK; and increasingly stringent controls on local government expenditure limited the potential for new locally funded waste management initiatives (Macrory and Withers, 1989; Turner and Thomas, 1982).

In contrast to national developments, Townend (1982) argued that London needed a strengthening in the powers of the GLC Public Health Engineering Department, in order to gain greater control over the activities of the collection authorities and ensure the further overall integration of waste management policy. In particular he suggested that an improvement would be the submission of detailed plans by the collection authorities of their operations to the GLC. The closer integration of waste collection and disposal at a strategic level was also identified by Davidson and MacEwan (1983), as a key element behind any strategy to increase levels of materials recovery in urban areas. The GLC recognised that an integrated system of waste collection and disposal, as in Wales and Scotland, would make resource recovery easier to co-ordinate (GLC, 1985c). The suggested modifications to the waste management framework established for London in 1965 were, however, to be overtaken by wider political events.

The abolition of the GLC Public Health Engineering Department

In June 1983 the Thatcher government was re-elected with an increased Commons majority to its second term in office. A late and little-discussed commitment in its manifesto had been the proposed abolition of the Greater London Council and the six Metropolitan County Councils. In October 1983, the Government produced its White Paper, *Streamlining the Cities*, which outlined how the manifesto commitment would be achieved. In Chapter Two of the White Paper, paragraphs 11 and 12 proposed the disbandonment of the GLC Public Health Engineering Department and the redistribution of its functions:

> The responsibilities of the GLC and the MCCs for waste regulation and disposal will be transferred to the borough and district councils. The Government will wish to see that, in the setting up of the new arrangements for disposal, the maximum encouragement is given to increasing private sector participation. (DoE, 1983a p. 7).

The GLC abolition debate and waste management in London

According to a study in 1985, the White Paper was unique in that 'the proposed reform of local government is unlike previous ones; it has emerged without detailed analysis of the present system and the possible alternatives' (Flynn et al., 1985 p. ix). The wider rationale for GLC abolition set out in the White Paper, rested on four arguments: firstly, the upper tier authorities had been created in an era when there was 'a certain fashion for strategic planning' (op cit. p.1); secondly, the existing system was too expensive and the proposed arrangements would be cheaper; thirdly, the upper tier had too few service delivery functions and this caused them to search for a wider strategic role and 'promote policies which conflict with national policies which are the responsibility of central government' (op cit. p.1); and finally, the White Paper claimed that the proposals would 'provide a system which is simpler for the public to understand' (op cit. p.1).

In terms of waste disposal, these four arguments can be considered in turn. Firstly, the perception that strategic planning was no longer relevant or appropriate, clearly contradicted almost all the arguments over the advances made under the GLC, and the need to plan for the future of London's waste:

> The Government ignores the body of evidence from objective studies that reiterates the need for the interrelated problems of the major conurbations to be handled in a comprehensive and strategic manner. (Metropolitan Counties, 1984, quoted in Flynn et al., 1985 p. 49)

Table 3.5: The costs of waste disposal in England 1986-87

Net cost per tonne

Non-Metropolitan Counties	£5.64
Metropolitan Counties	£12.12
Greater London Council	£18.43

Source: CIPFA

Secondly, it was certainly true that the GLC's waste disposal expenditure was higher per capita than elsewhere, as indicated by Table 3.5, but this can be attributed to the intrinsic differences between urban and non-urban waste management: the per capita rate of waste generation is higher in urban areas therefore raising overall disposal costs and the distances to landfill sites are greater, involving the use of transfer stations and complex haulage arrangements, as shown in Table 3.6. London has seen a substantial rise in the overall net cost of waste disposal per tonne since the formation of the GLC, rising from £1.47 in 1966/67 to £12.12 in 1980/81, representing an increase of 80 per cent after allowing for inflation (Townend, 1982).

Table 3.6: Methods of waste disposal in England and Wales 1986-87

	GLC	England and Wales
Direct to landfill...........................	28%	62%
Transfer without treatment.........	30%	16%
Transfer with treatment (compacting, shredding and baling)	28%	13%
Incineration..............................	14%	9%

Source: CIPFA (1987)

However, this can be attributed to a number of factors: the rise in the debt charges arising from the construction of new plants; the fact that in 1967 some 30 per cent of the waste was delivered direct to landfill in the collection vehicles, compared with under 10 per cent in 1985, as illustrated in Figure 3.14; the growing distance to landfill sites for secondary road, rail and river transport from the transfer stations, as shown in Figure 3.15; and the fact that the service was run down before re-organisation in 1965 resulting in the need for urgent replacement of much of the fixed and mobile plant and vehicles.

106

Further significant factors include the cost of complying with higher environmental standards imposed by planning, licensing and water authorities at transfer stations and landfill sites; the extensive investment by the GLC in modern transfer and disposal facilities since 1965; and the need to renew contracts negotiated at historically low prices, in the context of new EC regulations on drivers' hours and rising labour costs (GLC, 1980a).

Figure 3.14: The proportion of waste delivered directly to landfill sites

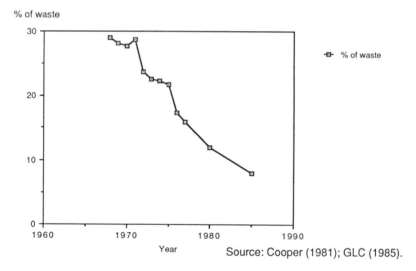

Source: Cooper (1981); GLC (1985).

Figure 3.15: Average length of haul to landfill sites for London's waste 1968-77

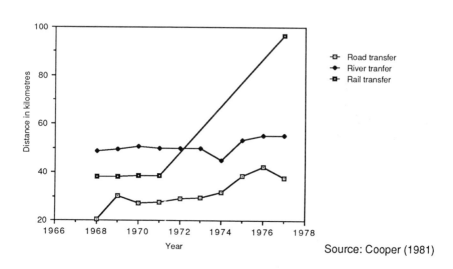

Source: Cooper (1981)

Thirdly, waste disposal was a clear example of a strategic service delivery role which was carried out by the GLC and the MCCs. It involved a combination of strategic planning, along with functional and resource allocation roles, and was a cornerstone of the rationale for the creation of the GLC. Indeed, public health (including the fire service) accounted for the third largest share of the GLC budget after transport and housing.

And finally, the GLC's Public Health Engineering Department was replaced by a system of waste management for London which rather than simplifying arrangements, replaced one London wide Waste Disposal Authority with sixteen others. Four of these Waste Disposal Authorities were to be statutory, whilst the remaining twelve Waste Disposal Authorities were individual boroughs. Eleven of these boroughs formed three voluntary waste disposal groups, whilst Bexley in south east London formed an arrangement with Kent County Council for its waste disposal.

On the 5th June 1984, the Secretary of State, Patrick Jenkin, told the Institute of Wastes Management Conference, that cost-effective solutions 'must involve a major extension of private sector participation and investment...The private sector must grasp the opportunity with imagination and flair...I want our proposals for reorganisation to be seen as a major opportunity to secure the real advantages that competition brings' (quoted in Flynn et al, 1985 p. 6). Yet, few were convinced of the Government's case for the abolition of the GLC Public Health Engineering Department, and extensive use of the private sector was already made in the operational aspects of waste haulage. Indeed, opposition to the Government's proposals was expressed by almost every organisation involved in the management of London's waste in both the private and public sector, including the CBI, the Civic Trust, the Hazardous Wastes Inspectorate, the Institution of Civil Engineers, the Institution of Public Health Engineers, the Institute of Wastes Management, the Federation of British Aggregate Construction Materials Industries, the National Association of Waste Disposal Contractors, the Royal Town Planning Institute, the Sand and Gravel Association Limited, the Town and Country Planning Association, the regional planning forum SERPLAN, and the Waste Disposal Engineers Association (GLC, 1984h). The response of the GLC Conservative Group to the White Paper remarked that:

> The GLC's record in the area of waste disposal has been a credit to local government, and its considerable advances over the years since the system was unified and streamlined have been due to economies of scale, to considerable capital investment, to a fruitful partnership with the private sector and to the expertise of its skilled and innovative professional staff...Nowhere in the Consultation Paper is

there the slightest criticism of waste disposal arrangements in London...Devolution of waste disposal responsibilities is simply a consequence of abolition and not one of the reasons for it. (GLC, 1984b pp. 38-39).

The new administrative framework established for waste management in 1986

The Government's aim of having a satisfactory scheme for each part of London, agreed by the relevant local authorities before December 1984, was not realised. When the provisions of the White Paper, were eventually enacted in the 1985 Local Government Act, the Secretary of State, Patrick Jenkin, had to use his reserve powers to set up four statutory waste disposal authorities for the twenty one boroughs which had not yet agreed on arrangements for their waste disposal, as shown in Figure 3.16.

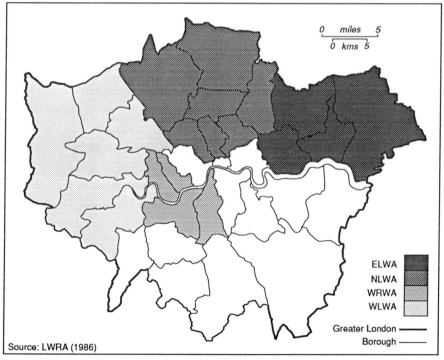

Figure 3.16: The four statutory Waste Disposal Authorities set up in 1986

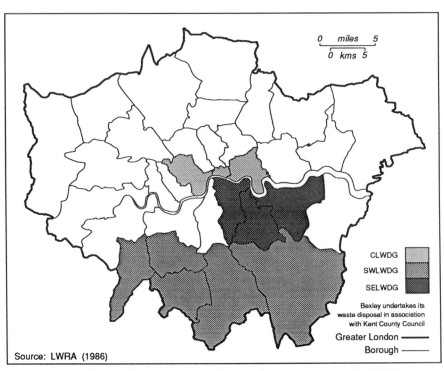

Source: LWRA (1986)

Figure 3.17: The voluntary waste disposal groups set up in 1986

Further difficulties lay in the area of toxic waste management and the fulfilment of waste regulation responsibilities under the 1974 Control of Pollution Act. The need for regional planning in the field of hazardous waste disposal and the regulation of waste disposal was reiterated in the Gregson Report of 1981, which noted the lack of scientific skills and capacity for regional planning in smaller local authorities (House of Lords Select Committee on Science and Technology, 1981) After sustained lobbying of the 1985 Local Government Bill, the regulatory functions of the GLC under the 1974 Control of Pollution Act and responsibilities for toxic waste disposal remained intact at a London-wide level, and were passed to the London Waste Regulation Authority (LWRA). The LWRA is in effect, therefore, a continuation of the former GLC Hazardous Waste Unit as a surviving fragment of the Public Health Engineering Department.

The main difference between the statutory joint Waste Disposal Authorities and the voluntary groups, as illustrated in Figures 3.16 and 3.17, is that staff and facilities in the former are entirely separate from the individual members. Income is raised mainly by a levy on each member borough. Within

110

voluntary groups each individual council maintains its own staff and facilities with arrangements for contracting services from neighbouring councils and the co-ordination of certain functions, such as negotiation of contracts with private firms. The membership of both the statutory joint Waste Disposal Authorities and the joint committees overseeing voluntary groups is composed of two elected members nominated from each borough council, and the new Waste Disposal Authorities now operate within the London-wide planning and regulatory framework provided by the London Waste Regulation Authority (Hebbert and Travers, 1988). The London Boroughs continued in their role as Waste Collection Authorities, but were now responsible for running all the 40 civic amenity sites and recycling centres formerly under the control of the GLC. In effect, the current pattern of waste management in London, particularly among the 16 boroughs outside the statutory waste disposal authorities is very similar to that under the Metropolitan Boroughs before 1965, and it is the pattern of materials recycling in the London Boroughs under this post-1986 administrative framework which is examined in the next chapter.

Conclusion

Once the connection between dirt and disease had been clearly made in the mid-nineteenth century, the subsequent history of waste management in London was one of finding a satisfactory organisational solution to the problem of street cleansing, which eventually led to the need for the collection and disposal of wastes collected from individual households. The evidence suggests that major improvements in the management of London's waste were not achieved until the findings of the 1929 Dawes report were realised with the centralisation of waste disposal under the GLC Public Health Engineering Department in 1965. The question of improvements for waste management in London has been inseparable from the wider arguments for the reform of the administrative and organisational structure of local government - an issue which is returned to in Chapter Seven in the context of the contemporary debate over the future of London's government.

The choice of different means of waste disposal since the late nineteenth century has been consistently affected by the relative costs and environmental impact of different options, which were rarely evaluated with much degree of accuracy. Throughout the period of the London County Council, the main methods of disposal were either by the use of small incinerators or the transfer of wastes along the Thames to suitable tipping sites. Local authorities outside the County of London, had tended to rely on either incineration or the direct tipping of refuse into the surrounding countryside, often into areas administered by other local authorities. The period from the Dawes Report of 1929 to the Herbert Commission of 1960 was marked by the failure of Chamberlain and successive administrations to legislate, and the failure of the Metropolitan Boroughs to co-operate in order to raise standards in waste management.

The strategic public sector role in waste management under the GLC emerged for a combination of reasons: the need to raise economic efficiency and environmental standards in the handling of London's growing waste stream; the need to replace the local government structure, which had proved inadequate and chaotic for urban waste management; and the replacement of numerous private sector contractors who were unable or unwilling to raise standards. The creation of a unified structure for waste management in London was made possible by wider political developments since 1945 which legitimated an expanded role for strategic planning and municipal government in public policy (just as the abolition of the GLC was enabled by the opposite process of the political marginalisation of the role of the public sector in policy making).

During the period of the GLC after 1965, the use of landfill quickly emerged as the cheapest and most convenient option, even when the construction and operation of new bulk transfer facilities for more distant and carefully licensed sites were taken into account. The promotion of incineration during the GLC period proved an expensive failure, and there were also difficulties in realising the use of river transport to its full potential. The arguments for other means of waste disposal, principally composting, recycling, and waste reduction, were often made, but have only ever made a very small contribution to the overall management of London's waste, except during wartime. In the 1990s as in the past, London is still faced with immense difficulties in its waste management arising from the increasing scarcity of landfill and rising cost of operations. During the 1970s and 1980s, a new challenge emerged based around the need to integrate waste management policy and environmental policy in order to pursue globally oriented policy aims through the promotion of recycling.

The nadir in recycling activities occurred during the mid-1970s, as a combination of technical problems with centralised sorting, the escalating costs of local authority kerbside schemes and problems with the secondary materials market for paper. This led to a new phase of recycling activity based around the promotion of the 'bottle banks scheme' as a reflection of the new emphasis on public participation and the voluntary sector in order to cut the costs of recycling activity. In the next chapter the success of this innovatory organisational solution to the earlier difficulties facing recycling is evaluated, to determine whether the economic and technical barriers to recycling have been satisfactorily resolved.

Notes

1   Interview with the Assistant Cleansing Manager for the London Borough of Enfield, Peter Joyce, 12th June 1990.

2   Interview with the Policy Development Officer for the City of Westminster, Donna Clarke, 20th November 1989.

3   Interview with the Assistant Cleansing Manager for the London Borough of Enfield, Peter Joyce, 12th June 1990.

4   Interview with the Special Projects Officer for the London Borough of Newham, Peter Anderson, 16th May 1990.

5   Interview with the Highways and Cleansing Manager for the London Borough of Barking and Dagenham, Terry Mirams, 7th June 1990.

6   Letter from the Chief Executive of the London Borough of Enfield, W.D. Day, to the GLC dated 16th February 1982.

7   Letter from the Controller of Operational Services to the GLC Public Health Engineering Department, 22nd May 1974.

8   Letter from the Glass Manufacturers Federation to D. Ayres of the GLC Public Health Engineering Department, dated 9th September 1975.

9   Letter from the Chief Executive of the London Borough of Merton, W.A. McKee, to the GLC, dated 26th February 1982.

4 The recycling of household waste in London

In this chapter the contemporary pattern of household waste recycling and materials recovery policy in London is examined under the administrative and legislative framework established for London in 1986. I show that the level of recycling in the London Boroughs is very low in relation to the Government's stated target of 25 per cent recycling by the year 2,000 (DoE, 1990b). The chapter begins by examining the pattern of policy and the rationale for recycling, followed by an analysis of the different factors accounting for the low and varied rates of recycling in London. In order to examine the underlying factors behind low levels of recycling activity it is necessary to consider the specific difficulties facing the recovery of different fractions of the waste stream. This involves an examination of the interaction between locally operating constraints and wider factors affecting the promotion of recycling across all the London Boroughs.

Recycling policy in London

The pressures for the development of recycling policy

Chapter Two described how recycling has moved up the political agenda since the early 1970s and has now become an integral element in environmental policy. In this section the pressure on the London Boroughs to carry out recycling is evaluated and the strength of the political pressure from public concern is considered. The survey of the London Boroughs[1] examined the impact of a range of different factors on the development of recycling. Table 4.1 suggests that the most important factors affecting the development of recycling policy in London are public pressure, the enthusiasm of local government officers, the commitment of the administration and elected

Figure 4.1: The composition of municipal waste in London in 1985

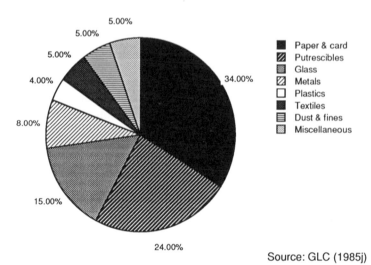

- Paper & card
- Putrescibles
- Glass
- Metals
- Plastics
- Textiles
- Dust & fines
- Miscellaneous

Source: GLC (1985j)

Table 4.1: Factors stimulating the development of recycling in London

	Important or very important		Not Important		Not known or data witheld	
	%	Boroughs	%	Boroughs	%	Boroughs
Public pressure...............................	87.5	28	6.3	2	6.3	2
Enthusiasm of officers within the local authority...	75.0	24	9.4	3	15.6	5
Activities of a few elected members....	68.8	22	15.6	5	15.6	5
Examples set by other local authorities in the UK...	68.8	22	18.8	6	12.5	4
The commitment of the 1986-1990 administration...................................	65.6	21	18.8	6	15.6	5
Media interest.................................	46.9	15	21.9	7	31.3	10
Central government.........................	43.8	14	46.9	15	9.4	3
Examples set by other authorities outside the UK.................................	28.1	9	50.0	16	21.9	7
The pressure of party activists on the elected members............................	25.0	8	28.1	9	46.9	15

Source: The survey of the London Boroughs (1990)

115

members, and the example of other local authorities. A clear majority of the interviewees felt these factors were significant in encouraging the recycling activities of their local authority. In particular, public pressure was identified as an important factor in twenty eight boroughs, confirming the impact of rising environmental concern in stimulating the development of recycling initiatives. However, it appears that the growth of public pressure for recycling has been somewhat uneven across London, with prosperous outer London Boroughs such as Richmond and Sutton experiencing a growth in public concern since the early 1980s, whereas in east London, it was reported that there had been no substantial rise in environmental concern before the summer of 1989 and media coverage surrounding the elections to the European Parliament[2].

The objectives of recycling in London

I found that there was a political consensus in all the London Boroughs and in all political parties for the expansion of recycling. This confirms the view that not only has environmental policy making now taken a key position within the public policy agenda, but that it is also ostensibly not identifiable with any particular political perspective. This in turn reflects the fact that environmental concern encompasses a wide spectrum of political views, and has been integrated into a number of disparate ideological conceptions of society and public policy making as part of the 'greening' of mainstream politics described in Chapter One. Behind this apparent consensus, however, there are significant variations in the degree of priority which local authorities felt should be afforded to the policy, and also to different potential objectives of the policy. The consensus that exists over the promotion of recycling does not, therefore, extend to the way in which it can be most effectively developed or over the precise objectives of the different initiatives.

In Chapter Two it was shown how the variety of different arguments for recycling mirrored the diversity of environmentalist thought: the rationale for recycling ranged from geo-political security and reduced waste disposal expenditure to the generation of employment and the creation of alternative types of societies based around decentralised forms of social and economic organisation. In the survey of the London Boroughs, nine objectives for recycling were examined spanning a range of different justifications put forward in the literature: the conservation of natural resources; the saving of energy in the production process; the control of pollution; the promotion of environmental education; the encouragement of public participation; the fostering of goodwill in the community; the reduction of expenditure on waste disposal; the lowering of costs for industry; and the creation of employment.

In evaluating the environmental objectives of recycling in the London Boroughs, as shown in Table 4.2, it is interesting to note that many local authorities are now promoting global environmental policy objectives for perhaps the first time, contrasting with the more local and regional concerns for greater economic efficiency and improved standards in public health demanded by the Dawes Report and the Herbert Commission. Indeed, these new global environmental objectives for municipal waste management policy are widely perceived as essential for the mobilisation of public concern and the maintenance of public participation in the use of on-street collection facilities.

Table 4.2: The objectives of recycling policy in London

	Important or very important		Not Important		Not Known or data witheld	
	%	Boroughs	%	Boroughs	%	Boroughs
The encouragement of public participation.........	84.4	27	3.1	1	12.5	4
The education of the public about environmental problems..	81.3	26	3.1	1	15.6	5
The combating of environmental pollution...........	81.3	26	6.3	2	12.5	4
The conservation of natural resources................	78.1	25	9.4	3	12.5	4
The reduction of the costs of waste disposal.......	78.1	25	12.5	4	9.4	3
The increase of goodwill in the community..........	75.0	24	9.4	3	15.6	5
The saving of energy in the production process..	65.6	21	21.9	7	12.5	4
The lowering of costs for British industry.............	28.1	9	46.9	15	25.0	8
The creation of employment................................	15.6	5	68.8	22	15.6	5

Source: The survey of the London Boroughs (1990)

Table 4.2 suggests that five objectives were clearly identified as central to recycling policy in twenty five boroughs: the reduction of the costs of waste disposal; the conservation of natural resources; the control of pollution; the encouragement of public participation; and the promotion of environmental education. Note in Table 4.2 that three objectives for recycling were not selected as important in a majority of boroughs: the saving of energy, the reduction of industrial costs, and employment creation. Whilst the reduction of industrial costs is an argument less often put forward in the literature, both employment creation and particularly energy saving have formed an integral part of the justification for recycling, as described in Chapter Two. It is of particular interest that employment creation appears to be by far the least important objective of recycling revealed by the questionnaire survey. The results of the survey indicate that the linking of recycling to locally-based job creation and economic regeneration is now a very low priority in London, despite persistently high unemployment since the late 1970s. Only two authorities, Labour controlled Hackney and Waltham Forest, considered employment creation to be an important aim of recycling, with financial support available for backing locally-based recycling enterprises, such as waste paper handling co-operatives[3] (see Sheridan, 1990). In Chapter Two I described how the job creation potential of recycling formed an element within the red/green type arguments for a form of environmental Keynesianism in the mid-1980s. The lack of priority afforded to this aspect of recycling in London suggests that there has been a decline in policy strategies which seek to link employment creation with environmental protection, and that employment creation is now increasingly seen as 'beyond the brief' of recycling and waste management policy in local government. This may be related to the absence of a more radical strategic level of government, which had existed briefly in the early 1980s under the GLC, as described in the last chapter, where the linking of employment generation and recycling policy was undertaken in London.

The economic viability of recycling

A consideration of the economic aspects of recycling in London is important, because a key reason for the promotion of recycling is frequently argued to be the potential of schemes to generate a profit from the sales of materials and the creation of savings in waste disposal costs, as illustrated in Table 4.2. The reduction of the costs of waste disposal is also integral to market-based conceptions of recycling policy described in Chapter Two whereby the elimination of 'market failure' in waste disposal is argued to lead to increased levels of recycling. The economic viability of recycling in London is derived from three main elements: the financial aspects of recycling policies, in terms of the capacity of schemes to generate an income for local authorities; the generation of any savings in the costs of waste disposal, and their recognition through rebates or credits; and finally, the profitability of the recycling industry, which is dependent on the secondary materials market and the demand for recycled products. The question of rebates and the secondary materials market is discussed later in this chapter, but it is necessary first to consider the potential 'profitability' of recycling schemes and whether they can generate a net income for local authorities.

Figure 4.2 shows that in the case of bottle banks for glass, the net income derived from recycling activities depends on expenditure on capital equipment

Figure 4.2: Factors affecting the economic viability of glass recycling using on-street collection facilities

Income

Sales of glass cullet

    Quantity of glass
    Two or three colour separation
    Degree of contamination
    Secondary materials market

Waste disposal rebate

    Level of rebate (if any) granted by the
    WDAs to the London Boroughs
    as WCAs.

Other income

    Private sector sponsorship
    Supplementary credit from
    central government.

Expenditure

Operational costs

    Capital cost of bottle banks
    Emptying costs
    Tranport costs
    Storage costs

Site maintenance

    Fly-posting
    Fly-tipping and litter
    Site monitoring and liaison
      with collection agency

Publicity material

Other overheads

    Running costs of civic amenity
    sites
    Joint sites with transfer stations

Staff wages

i) Direct involvement of
   recycling officers and other staff.
ii) Indirect involvement of
   administrative, maintenance
   and cleansing staff etc.

Strategies for reducing costs

Use of private contractors

Increased reliance on the role
  of the voluntary sector and
  public participation.

Creative accountancy and masking
  of overheads.

Source: The survey of the London Boroughs (1990)

and operational costs such as the emptying and transportation of facilities, coupled with the income from sales of materials and receipt of rebates from waste disposal savings. Many boroughs have seen a rise in their income from sales of materials over the 1980s, reflecting a greater range and larger quantity of materials recovered and sold, but the range of associated overheads and other costs has also risen. Yet these hidden costs and overheads render the calculation of recycling expenditure much more difficult than that of income derived from either the sales of materials or rebates from the Waste Disposal Authority (WDA)[4]. A key question concerns the distribution of costs, such as labour and capital equipment between the recycling budget and the cleansing budget as a whole[5]. In the case of expenditure, local authorities do not normally separately calculate all the costs involved, beyond specific items such as capital investment in new facilities and the salaries of recycling officers, though even this information is increasingly restricted from the public as a result of compulsory competitive tendering (CCT). Indeed, even senior consultants within the waste management industry concede that costings are both subjective and contingent (on interest rates, legislative change and other factors) and that calculations simply reinforce existing preconceptions through the selection and method of calculation for the innumerable different potential costs and benefits[6].

This difficulty in determining the net income from recycling is important, because this informs the rationale for further expanding the policy on purely economic grounds, whether this be in terms of reducing the costs of waste disposal or the promotion of recycling to make a net profit for local authorities. If it can be demonstrated that a local authority's recycling activities have resulted in a net profit, as some local authorities claim, then a rationale for the policy becomes an additional source of income to the local authority. However, the ability of some local authorities to claim substantial profits for recycling in comparison with other boroughs was widely questioned during the survey, and a number of hidden costs were identified: the existence of specially arranged rates with their own workforce to carry out operational activities such as the cleaning of sites and removal of fly-posters[7]; the exclusion of certain overheads within the overall waste management budget[8]; the fact that the civic amenity sites are run through the cleansing budget, yet the income from the sales of materials and the rebate is in some instances placed solely in the recycling budget[9]; and finally, the transport of collected materials, raising the question of the need for the costings of greater energy usage and transport costs involved in the haulage of separated fractions of the waste stream, for which no locally based recycling industry exists to handle the collected materials[10]. In Richmond, for example, the maintenance of on-street collection facilities was also carried out by the voluntary sector or by part-time 'managers', often pensioners or young mothers, earning £100-£120 a month, in exchange for daily tidying of the site and informing the local authority when the site is full (Pollock, 1990). These arrangements illustrate how the use of extensive voluntary sector and public involvement in the running of 'bring' collection systems allow an escape for local authorities from the dilemma of high labour costs for recycling, which were a key factor behind the collapse of local authority kerbside collection schemes for paper in the 1970s described in the last chapter.

A further dimension to the question of net expenditure and income concerns the abolition of the GLC. Until 1986, much of the essential capital expenditure on new and improved facilities and the promotion of activities in London was carried out by the GLC. The abolition of the GLC led to an erratic distribution of recycling assets across London, serving to assist some boroughs in making their recycling efforts appear profitable, whilst disadvantaging others. The borough of Camden, for example, fared especially badly out of the redistribution of GLC assets and also receives no waste disposal rebate from the North London Waste Authority, making it very difficult for the local authority to realise a net income on its recycling activities. For Camden's recycling development officer, the attempts to generate a net income from recycling were simply a political attempt to conform to the 'intrinsic cost-efficiency' arguments, which have been so pervasive in public policy since the 1980s[11].

It appears that recycling in the London Boroughs is only doubtfully a net source of income for local authorities: the claims by some local authorities that recycling is making substantial profits is more a product of creative accountancy and the masking of overheads than the efficacy of policy. Indeed, the 'profitability' for local authorities can only be assured when the policy is focused on valuable materials collected and transported with minimal capital and labour costs and buoyed by favourable contractual arrangements for the sale of materials.

The pattern of recycling in the London Boroughs

The measure of recycling used as the basis for the analysis is the percentage recycling rate. This is calculated from the total tonnage of materials recovered from the municipal waste stream by recycling activities in the London Boroughs[12]. In addition to the recycling of materials, it is important to note that the recovery of energy from the waste stream is also undertaken for the seven boroughs served by the Edmonton incineration plant operated by the North London Waste Authority (Barnet, Camden, Enfield, Hackney, Haringey, Islington, and Waltham Forest). In the year 1989-90, I found that the recycling rate for the municipal waste stream varied from 0.1 per cent in the socio-economically diverse inner London Borough of Kensington and Chelsea and nil in the Corporation of London (where there was no recycling activity) to 8.2 per cent and 8.8 per cent in the largely prosperous and residential outer London Boroughs of Richmond and Havering, as shown in Figure 4.3. Apart from Havering, only four other boroughs achieved a recycling rate in excess of 4 per cent (Harrow, Hillingdon, Merton and Richmond), and all these boroughs are located in outer London. As for those boroughs, whose recycling rate was 0.5 per cent or less (Hackney, Kensington and Chelsea, Newham, Southwark, and Wandsworth), these were all located in inner London. The average recycling rate for all the London Boroughs was 2.1 per cent, which is slightly less than the 2.3 to 2.6 per cent recycling figures calculated for the UK municipal waste stream at a national level (DoE, 1990a; FoE, 1991), and far below the Government's target of 25 per cent recycling by the year 2,000 (DoE, 1990b).

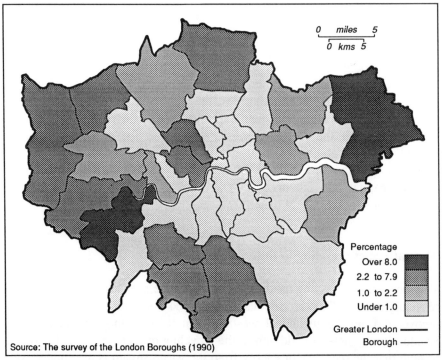

Figure 4.3: The level of recycling in the London Boroughs 1989-1990

Table 4.3: Methods of materials recovery used for household waste in London

Method of recovery	Materials recovered
Kerbside collection	Paper (Havering only) Textiles (mainly second hand clothes and items for jumbles sales etc.)
On-street collection facilities	Glass Paper (lower grades) Steel and aluminium cans Plastics (pilot schemes only)
'Bring' facilities at civic amenity sites and recycling centres	Glass Paper (mixed grades and card) Plastics (pilot schemes only) CFCs in aerosols (Camden only) Steel and aluminium cans Oil Textiles
Centralised recovery at the Edmonton incineration plant	Ferrous scrap
Centralised recovery at civic amenity sites and recycling centres	CFCs and refrigerator components
Licensed totting at civic amenity sites and recycling centres	Ferrous scrap Non-ferrous scrap

Source: The survey of the London Boroughs (1990)

The borough recycling rates can be further differentiated by examining the relative tonnages of different materials recovered and the different methods employed to separate the materials from the waste stream. It emerges that the dominant three materials recovered in tonnage terms are glass, paper and scrap metals, as shown in Figure 4.3, and the main means by which materials are separated from the waste stream is by the 'bring' system of recycling. The 'bring' system in London is comprised of on-street collection facilities (mainly for glass, paper and metal cans) and civic amenity type facilities used as recycling centres for a wider range of recyclable materials, as set out in Table 4.3. There were only a few exceptions to the use of the 'bring' system in London: a kerbside collection scheme for paper in Havering; voluntary sector kerbside collections of clothes and other unwanted household goods in most boroughs; the recovery of ferrous metals by magnetic separation at the Edmonton incineration plant; the declining activities of 'rag and bone' type collections; and the informal scavenging of waste for valuable non-ferrous scrap and re-usable consumer durables.

Exploratory analysis of recycling in the London Boroughs

The next stage of the data analysis was to identify the factors behind the low level of recycling in London and also the wide variations observed between individual boroughs. Note that the recycling rate is mainly a function of the effectiveness of the 'bring' collection system based around the use of on-street collection facilities and recycling centres in all boroughs, with the only major exception being Havering with its comprehensive kerbside collection scheme for paper. An initial research finding was that the pattern of recycling cannot be satisfactorily accounted for by differences in the political control of the 1986-1990 borough administrations (13 Conservative, 15 Labour, 3 Liberal Democrat, and 1 no overall control). The only political pattern begins to emerge where the administrations are further differentiated in terms of a characterisation of local government politics from 'new right' authorities to 'new left' authorities. The survey suggests that the 'radical liberal' boroughs of Richmond and Sutton, stand out as achieving relatively high rates of recycling, whereas the 'old left'[13] authorities such as Newham and Southwark, appear to have consistently lower rates of recycling. Yet, there are a number of interrelated factors which could account for these differences, not least of which is the relationship between the socio-economic complexion of local authorities and the characteristics of their administrations (see Gandy, 1988; Gyford, 1985 and King, 1989, on the socio-economic factors generating 'old' and 'new' left authorities in London). The question of interest is whether the socio-economic and political profile of local authorities is a significant factor in determining levels of recycling.

The quantitative data on recycling in the London Boroughs was examined in relation to a range of different potential explanatory variables shown in Table 4.4 and the first stage in the analysis was the use of correlation analysis[14] to explore the strength of any possible relationships, illustrated in Table 4.5. Note that there are three factors which are not statistically significant: the level of waste disposal rebate; the sophistication of recycling policy; and the level of education.

Table 4.4: Explanatory variables used for the statistical analysis

Variable selected and source	Potential explanatory role in the data analysis
Housing structure The proportion of total dwellings which are flats, maisonettes or rooms. Source: DoE (1979)	A measure of the amount of space within the home for storing recyclable materials; the presence of gardens and the scope for home composting; the extent of usage of paladins and shared waste collection facilties.
Population density Population per hectare. Source: Registrar General (1988)	A measure of the degree of urban congestion and available space for the location of on-street collection facilities and competition over land use.
Level of socio-economic deprivation Composite Z-score derived from eight indicators: level of unemployment; level of overcrowding; % single parent households; % pensioners living alone; % of households lacking basic amenities; % of households where head of the household was born in the New Commonwealth or Pakistan; % population decline1971-1981; and the standardised mortality rate 1980. Source: 1981 Census and other data compiled by the DoE Inner Cities Directorate	The potential impact of levels of socio-economic deprivation as suggested by analysis of the socio-economic characteristics of recyclers and factors affecting levels of public participation. Possible links with policy making at a local level in terms of the priority attached to recycling in comparison with other social and economic needs.
Level of education The proportion of the population with higher or further educational qualifications. Source: 1981 Census	The idea of middle class environmentalism and the connection between levels of education and public participation in recycling.
Population per bottle bank site The population per each bottle bank site. Source: British Glass and the Survey of the London Boroughs (1990)	The influence of the density of facilities on the likelihood of the public to participate in recycling, through shorter average distances to on-street collection facilities.
Proportion of civic amenity site derived waste % of the municipal waste stream derived from civic amenity sites. Source: The survey of the London Boroughs (1990)	The extent of recycling infrastructure allowing the public to bring a wide variety of materials, including oil, scrap metals, CFCs and other materials which are not easily collected by on-street facilities.
Level of waste disposal rebates Level of rebate passed from WDAs to WCAs. Source: The survey of the London Boroughs (1990).	The main market-based policy instrument advocated by Government, allowing an evaluation of the efficacy of MBIs to raise levels of materials recycling.
Scope of recycling policy in the London Boroughs Composite Policy Index of the following components of recycling policy: the presence of a recycling officer; the operation of a recycling sub-committee or working party; and the degree of support for recycling from elected members and local government officers. Source: The survey of the London Boroughs (1990).	The scope and sophistication of recycling policy at a local level within the London Boroughs, allowing a consideration of how far local level policy may affect levels of recycling.

Gandy (1992a)

Table 4.5: Correlation analysis of levels of recycling in London

	% recycling rate
Proportion of households living in flats, maisonettes or rooms...	- .524 **
Population density..	- .586 **
Level of socio-economic deprivation (Z-score of four indicators)	- .585 **
Level of higher and further educational qualifications................	+ .170
Population per bottle bank site...	- .367 **
Proportion of waste derived from civic amenity sites...............	+ .526 **
Level of waste disposal rebate..	+ .271
Sophistication of recycling policy (Policy Index measure)..........	+ .286

All coefficients refer to log data

Significance levels

0.05 *
0.01 **

Source: The survey of the London Boroughs (1990)

Table 4.6: Multiple regression analysis of recycling in the London Boroughs

Adjusted R-squared = .541   Durbin-Watson statistic = 1.95   F-test = 5.572

	t-Value	Probability	Partial F-test
% Flats, maisonettes or rooms	.129	.9	0.017
Population density	1.538	.14	2.364
Z-score of socio-economic deprivation	.207	.84	.043
Level of educational qualifications	1.219	.24	1.486
Population per bottle bank site	2.807 **	.01	7.881 **
% Civic amenity derived waste	.912	.37	.832
Level of waste disposal rebate	1.059	.30	1.123
Policy Index of recycling policy development	.936	.36	.877

Significance levels

0.01 **

Source: The survey of the London Boroughs (1990)

The statistical analysis of the quantitative data was taken further using multiple and step-wise regressions[15]. The regression results are summarised in Tables 4.6 and 4.7. Note that the coefficient of multiple determination or R-squared tests the goodness of fit of the regression in explaining the variation in the per cent recycling rate. The adjusted R-squared (reworked to take account of the reduction in the degrees of freedom with additional explanatory variables) of .541 estimates a fairly good statistical fit of the model in accounting for variations in the rate of recycling. However, the F statistic (testing the overall significance of the regression with the ratio of explained to unexplained variance) of 5.57 does not exceed the critical value of 7.50 for significance at the 0.01 level of probability. Indeed, Table 4.6 shows that the partial F-statistic is only exceeded by the measure of the density of bottle bank facilities, with an F value of 7.88.

The regression was then re-calculated using a stepwise multiple regression. Under the stepwise regression, shown in Table 4.7, both population density and housing structure were eliminated from the model, since they were strongly correlated with the Z-score measure of socio-economic deprivation (which includes a measure of overcrowding)[16] and the degree of multicollinearity[17] between the different variables is illustrated in Table 4.9. Interestingly, both the Policy Index measure of policy development within the boroughs (see below) and the level of education were now included in the model, as having some explanatory significance, even though they were not found to be statistically significant in the correlation analysis. However, the level of waste disposal rebate, the central element in the Government's market-based recycling strategy, remains statistically insignificant under the new model, despite a higher adjusted R-squared of .71 and a much improved F value of 14.69.

The stepwise multiple regression model in Table 4.7 suggests that the differences in the rate of recycling in the London Boroughs can be satisfactorily accounted for by five variables: the population per bottle bank site; the Z-score for socio-economic deprivation; the percentage of civic amenity derived waste; the Policy Index; and the percentage of the population with further or higher educational qualifications. The very high adjusted R-squared value suggests that 71 per cent of the variation in the recycling rate in the London Boroughs can be accounted for by the selected variables. However, this high R-squared value should be treated with caution, since this may suggest that the dependent and independent variables within the model are themselves correlated together with one or more underlying factors excluded from the analysis, and the direction and nature of causality for the variations in recycling is not clearly specified. It is important to note that these models refer to data collected in one year and in one city only. It is

Table 4.7: Stepwise multiple regression analysis of recycling in the London Boroughs

Adjusted R-squared = .71   *Durbin-Watson statistic = 2.45*   *F-test = 14.686*

Variables in equation	F to remove	Beta value
Population per bottle bank site	9.163	-.633
Z-score of socio-economic deprivation	6.559	-1.445
% Civic amenity derived waste	8.171	.259
Policy index of recycling policy development	5.083	.809
Level of educational qualifications	6.374	.716

Variables not in equation	F to enter	Beta value
Level of waste disposal rebate	2.684	.317
% Flats, maisonettes or rooms	1.593	-.260
Population density	.011	-.022

Intercept = 2.314   Standard error = .233

Source: The survey of the London Boroughs (1990)

Table 4.8: Correlation between the explanatory variables

	X1	X2	X3	X4	X5	X6	X7	X8
X1 Housing structure	1							
X2 Pop. density	.092 **	1						
X3 Z-score	.811 **	.837 **	1					
X4 Level of education	.301	.211	-.007	1				
X5 Pop. per site	-.06	-.128	.084	-.105	1			
X6 % CA Waste	-.712 **	-.697 **	-.625 **	-.352	-.042	1		
X7 Level of rebate	.078	-.015	-.058	-.008	-.31	.22	1	
X8 Policy Index	-.082	-.139	-.036	.317	-.006	.083	.054	1

<u>Significance level</u>

0.01 **

Source: The survey of the London Boroughs (1990)

likely that in other urban areas and in different historical circumstances, that the parameters of the model could change. In particular, a number of dynamic factors can be expected to have an impact: the changing impetus in the growth of environmentalism; the restructuring within the waste management industry; the evolving legislative framework, as regards national controls on packaging, for example; and the changing relationship between key agencies, notably between the private and public sectors in the provision of environmental services. These and other contextual developments are examined in the next chapter. There are also difficulties in the collection of accurate data on waste, which must be taken into account when interpreting the results of the survey analysis. In particular, this raises difficulties in extending quantitative research beyond that of exploratory data analysis into the realm of predictive modelling for policy making purposes.

Housing structure, population density and urban morphology

An important influence on recycling which emerged from this study was the influence of housing structure, population density, and urban morphology on the levels of recycling. Figure 4.5 shows how the proportion of dwellings which are flats, maisonettes or rooms, ranges from under 25 per cent in five outer London Boroughs, to over 75 per cent in nine inner London Boroughs. The influence of housing density and population density on rates of recycling, could be interpreted in two main ways. Firstly, the higher housing and population densities are correlated with greater degrees of socio-economic deprivation, as shown in Table 4.8. This could result in lower levels of recycling through a variety of mechanisms, such as a lower policy priority on the part of the local authority and more limited public interest or participation in recycling. However, Table 4.5 shows that the degree of socio-economic deprivation (as measured by the Z-score of eight indicators) was barely correlated with the Policy Index measure of the sophistication of recycling policy with a correlation coefficient of only -.036 and there was only limited evidence of socio-economic barriers to public participation (see below). The second and more usual explanation for the influence of higher population and housing densities is that the congested inner London Boroughs face a morphological barrier to recycling in terms of the lack of space along highways and in common areas for the location of collection facilities. For example, in the inner London Boroughs of Islington, Kensington and Chelsea, Tower Hamlets and Westminster, it was maintained that lack of space was the main constraint on recycling, marked by the high proportion of waste collected down chutes into communal paladins, as shown in Figure 4.6. Physical congestion both in the smaller homes and flats, combined with

Figure 4.4: The proportion of different materials recycled 1989-90

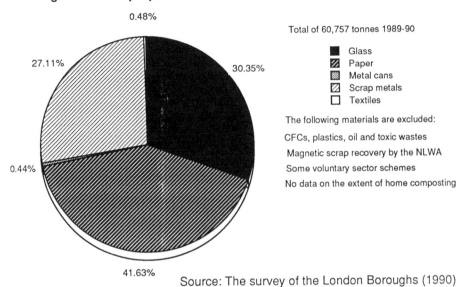

0.48%

27.11%

30.35%

0.44%

41.63%

Total of 60,757 tonnes 1989-90

- ■ Glass
- ▨ Paper
- ▨ Metal cans
- ▨ Scrap metals
- □ Textiles

The following materials are excluded:

CFCs, plastics, oil and toxic wastes

Magnetic scrap recovery by the NLWA

Some voluntary sector schemes

No data on the extent of home composting

Source: The survey of the London Boroughs (1990)

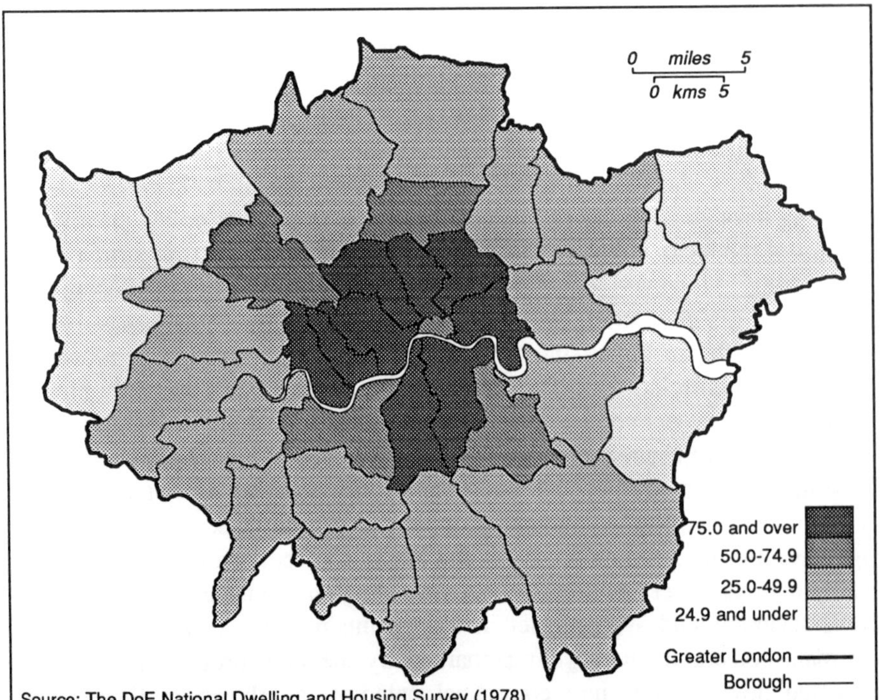

0   miles   5

0   kms   5

75.0 and over
50.0-74.9
25.0-49.9
24.9 and under

Greater London ———
Borough ———

Source: The DoE National Dwelling and Housing Survey (1978)

Figure 4.5: The proportion of households living in flats, maisonettes or rooms in London

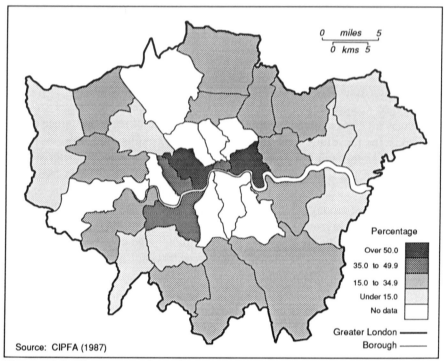

Percentage

Over 50.0

35.0 to 49.9

15.0 to 34.9

Under 15.0

No data

Greater London ——

Borough ——

Source: CIPFA (1987)

Figure 4.6: The proportion of dwellings served by paladins in London

cramped common areas and pavements, made the introduction of more on-street collection facilities extremely difficult and made the introduction of multiple bin systems and kerbside schemes impracticable[18]. The lack of any recycling facilities provided by the Corporation of London was attributed solely to the problems of lack of space and urban congestion[19].

The impact of socio-economic deprivation

There is a statistically significant negative correlation of -.585 between the multivariate Z-score of socio-economic deprivation and the level of recycling, but the nature of the causal relationship remains unclear, because of the mixture of morphological and socio-economic factors affecting levels of recycling, which can be separated conceptually but not quantitatively. It is important to note, however, that these borough level figures disguise important ward level variations, such that the ten most deprived wards in

131

London include Colborne in Kensington and Chelsea and White City in Hammersmith and Fulham, and that within some boroughs, notably Brent, Croydon and Greenwich, there are very wide ward level disparities in the level of socio-economic deprivation (see Townsend et al., 1987).

The pattern of public pressure described earlier, could theoretically be related to the socio-economic complexion of different boroughs, in line with the thesis of middle class environmentalism and the demands for 'positional' goods (see Cotgrove and Duff, 1980, 1981; Inglehardt, 1977). However, there was no clear evidence of this affecting the rate of recycling, since public demands for recycling were important in all boroughs, and only in Tower Hamlets was there any suggestion that the socio-economic characteristics of residents had led to a low demand for recycling facilities[20]. It is frequently argued that environmental 'awareness' and participation in environmental action is higher among people who have post school leaving age educational qualifications (Cotgrove and Duff, 1980; Hülsberg, 1988), though there is some contrary evidence of the socio-economic characteristics of participants in recycling from surveys of individual recyclers and non-recyclers (Vining and Ebreo, 1990). The indicator examined here, was the percentage of people who had higher or further educational qualifications, and was based on the 10 per cent sample in the 1981 census. The proportion of people who have passed through higher or further education varied from 3.6 per cent in Barking and Dagenham, to over 25 per cent in Camden and Richmond. The correlation coefficient with the level of recycling of +.170 was statistically insignificant, though the variable was just selected in the stepwise regression model shown in Table 4.7. It appears, therefore, that the analysis of recycling in London does not provide any clear support for the middle class environmentalism thesis, in terms of aggregate levels of participation in recycling.

The density of on-street collection facilities

The ratio of population to bottle bank site varied from under six thousand people per site in Westminster to over sixty thousand per site in Barnet, and the variations across London are illustrated in Figure 4.7. Both the correlation and regression analysis showed that the density of bottle bank facilities has a clear impact on the overall recycling rate, since glass is the most important material recovered in tonnage terms for eighteen boroughs, and bottle bank sites are often combined with other facilities for the collection of waste paper; metal cans, and other materials. Table 4.5 shows that there was a statistically significant correlation of -.367 between the population per bottle bank site and the rate of recycling. This can be explained by the longer

132

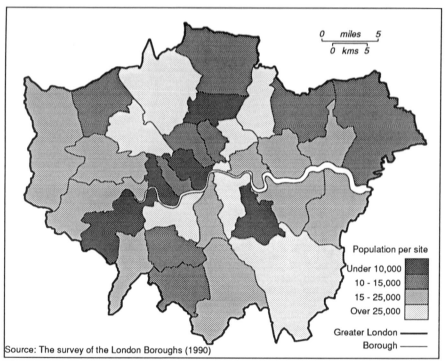

Source: The survey of the London Boroughs (1990)

Figure 4.7: The population per bottle bank site in the London Boroughs

average distances that must be travelled to collection sites, where the ratio of population to site is higher. It might be expected from the analysis of bottle bank density and the rates of glass recovery in other European cities, that there would be an S-shaped double logarithmic relationship whereby beyond a certain level of provision, it becomes increasingly difficult to raise the levels of materials recovery any further, and obtain the participation of the 'lazy' recyclers[21]. If such a relationship held for the London data, it would be expected that the Logit transformation of the data, which incorporates a bounded dependent variable after a threshold value for the independent variable is achieved, would have provided a better regression model in terms of the F-value and R-squared measure. It is arguable, however, that the failure of the Logit transformation to provide a better fit than the Log-log model is attributable to the fact that none of the London Boroughs have a similar density of facilities to the other European cities where this relationship has thus far been observed (GEWOS, 1987a; ITU, 1989). In other words, none of the observations for London, are likely to be near the threshold value for bottle bank density at which the increase in the rate of recycling becomes constrained, leading to the observed shape of the relationship in other studies.

Figure 4.8: The recycling rate and the population per bottle bank site

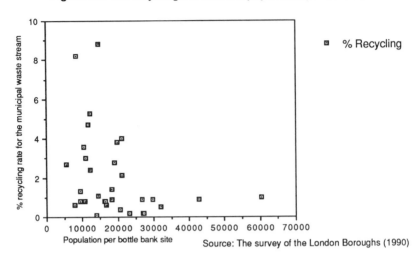

Source: The survey of the London Boroughs (1990)

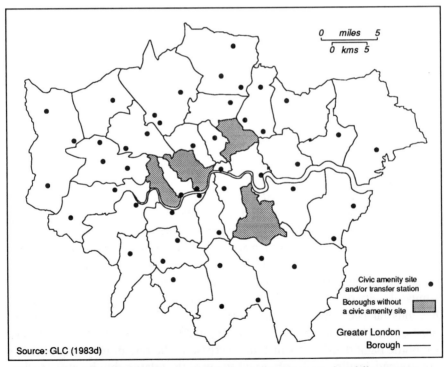

Figure 4.9: The distribution of civic amenity sites and public sector transfer stations

The distribution of civic amenity facilities is shown in Figures 4.9. This provides a clear indication of the extent of waste management infrastructure in individual boroughs, and in particular the scope for expanding civic amenity sites into multi-material recycling centres, which began with the conversion of the Victoria Road civic amenity site in Hillingdon in 1982 (see Chapter Three). Inner London Boroughs such as Hammersmith and Fulham, for example, do not have any civic amenity sites, which in many other boroughs have been successfully turned into multi-material recycling centres, recovering scrap metals, oil, textiles, CFCs from refrigerators and many other items. The role of civic amenity sites is reflected in Table 4.5 by a statistically significant positive correlation of +.526 between the proportion of civic amenity derived site waste and the level of recycling. The importance of civic amenity sites used as recycling centres is also suggested by Figure 4.10 showing the range of materials brought by the public to the Jamestown Road recycling centre and civic amenity site in Camden. Figure 4.11 illustrates how the range of materials recovered from the waste stream varied from under four materials in some inner London Boroughs such as Hackney and Southwark, to over ten different kinds of materials in the better equipped boroughs, with recycling centres and a wider range of on-street collection facilities available. The absence of much waste management and recycling infrastructure in inner London, was considered to be due to high land values which inevitably led to other forms of land-use yielding higher rates of return[22]. Indeed, in one inner London Borough, it was alleged that a former joint Conservative and Liberal administration from 1982 to 1986, had decided to use land previously designated for a civic amenity site for property development instead. In the next chapter the question of recycling and waste management infrastructure is examined further with the privatisation of the operational aspects of waste management whereby waste management facilities are being sold to the private sector. These developments have important implications for the continued development of land uses with a low rate of return since recycling centres are essentially a loss-making public service when the full range of overheads and other expenses are taken into consideration.

What limited recycling infrastructure that is available is currently very heavily used in London. Indeed, the rapid rise in public demand for recycling facilities and their increased usage has overwhelmed some local authorities' capacity to respond. In Camden, for example, the Jamestown Road recycling centre shares a cramped site with a road transfer station, and saw a fourfold increase in public usage in the period 1986-1989, handling over 40,000 visits

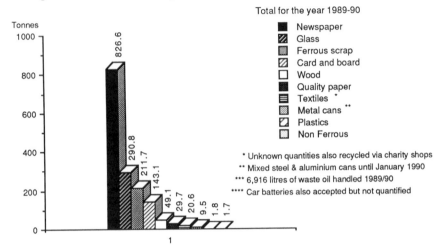

Figure 4.10: Materials brought to Jamestown Road recycling centre in Camden

Total for the year 1989-90

Tonnes

Key	
■	Newspaper
▨	Glass
▨	Ferrous scrap
▨	Card and board
☐	Wood
■	Quality paper
☰	Textiles *
▨	Metal cans **
▨	Plastics
☐	Non Ferrous

* Unknown quantities also recycled via charity shops
** Mixed steel & aluminium cans until January 1990
*** 6,916 litres of waste oil handled 1989/90
**** Car batteries also accepted but not quantified

Bar values: 826.6, 290.8, 211.7, 143.1, 49.1, 29.7, 20.6, 9.5, 1.8, 1.7

Source: The survey of the London Boroughs (1990)

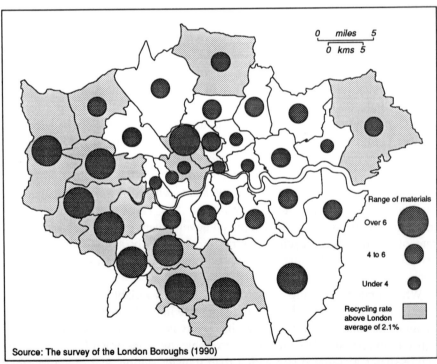

Figure 4.11: The range of different materials recycled in the London Boroughs 1989 -1990

136

by the public in the year 1988-89 alone. The original staff of three in 1986 had been reduced to two as a cost cutting measure, and the site was closed on three occasions during 1988-89 because of safety fears for staff and public due to overwhelming numbers of people using the site (Camden Borough Council, 1989). It is conceivable that Camden's higher than average recycling rate for inner London, is approaching the maximum level achievable without the provision of new recycling centres and the use of different (and more expensive) methods of separation for recyclable materials.

A further point of interest is the question of accessibility to recycling centres, since facilities in inner London have been found to be used by a higher proportion of women, the elderly, and households without cars. For example, a study of the users of two recycling centres, one in Harrow in outer London, and the other in Camden in inner London, found that over 70 per cent of people surveyed had arrived by car, and 50 per cent had claimed to have made a special journey to use the facilities. The pattern of usage in the two recycling centres differed in several respects: the proportion of women respondents was 49 per cent in Camden compared with just 14 per cent in Harrow; in Camden, more recyclables as opposed to discarded household items were brought; and Camden saw more local residents arriving on foot with smaller quantities of materials (Coggins et al., 1988). This raises important distributional issues over the potential for different groups in society to participate in recycling if they wish to do so.

The impact of waste disposal rebates

The provision of rebates or credits for recycling activities, calculated from the costs that would otherwise have been incurred from the disposal of the materials as waste, has become an important element in the recycling policy debate. The practice of granting rebates was legally recognised in the 1974 Control of Pollution Act, and has been extended as the mandatory introduction of 'recycling credits' in the 1990 Environmental Protection Act. Waste disposal rebates were first introduced by the GLC in 1971 for waste paper collections by local authorities and from 1982 for glass following the increasing participation of the London Boroughs in the Bottle Banks Scheme launched in 1977. With the abolition of the GLC in 1986, three of the four statutory Waste Disposal Authorities, have been granting rebates to their Waste Collection Authorities and the calculation of waste disposal savings has also been carried out by most boroughs within the voluntary waste disposal groups, as shown in Figure 4.12.

With the 1990 Environmental Protection Act, rebates or 'recycling credits' now form the key element in the Government's market-based strategy to raise

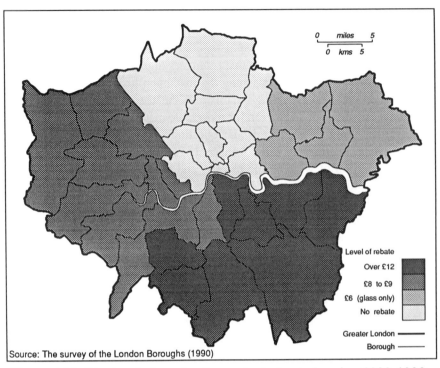

Figure 4.12: The level of waste disposal rebates in London 1989-1990

the level of recycling by the internalisation of the costs of waste disposal. However, Table 4.5 suggests that the level of rebates appears to have no clear impact on the extent of recycling activities in the London Boroughs with a statistically insignificant correlation coefficient of +.271, and the variable was also eliminated from the stepwise regression on account of its low explanatory value. If the levels of recycling in individual boroughs under the same statutory WDA, with the same levels of rebate are compared, it can be seen that there is little direct relationship between the levels of rebate and differences in recycling. For example, within the West London Waste Authority, with a rebate of £8 per tonne in the year 1989-90, the recycling rate varied from 0.8 per cent to 8.2 per cent among the six constituent boroughs, suggesting that there are other important factors involved in determining levels of recycling.

One possible explanation for the low impact of rebates is the limited extent to which income derived from rebates and sales of materials was actually ploughed back into recycling activities. The study found that the incorporation of the waste disposal savings into the expenditure on recycling activities, was undertaken in just six boroughs, whereas in the other boroughs the rebate simply enters the general rate fund with less direct impact on recycling activities. A further explanation is that the policy focus on 'market failure' derived from the absence of cost internalisation for alternative means of waste disposal neglects a number of other potential sources of 'market failure' in the secondary materials market and elsewhere. Certainly, the analysis of the perceived barriers to recycling shown in Table 4.9 suggests that the low cost of waste disposal is not viewed as a key factor in limiting the potential for materials recovery.

The influence of policy organisation within the boroughs

The study found that whilst most local authorities rely on the use of on-street collection facilities and recycling centres, there are important differences in the way recycling policy is organised. The London Boroughs can be differentiated on the basis of a number of administrative and organisational features in their recycling policy: the presence or absence of one or more full-time recycling officers; the existence of a recycling or environment sub-committee; the presence of relevant working parties or policy forums; the extent of formal monitoring procedures and systematic data gathering on the impact of recycling initiatives; the extent of involvement by senior officers and elected members in policy promotion and development; and the degree of integration for recycling initiatives with other areas of activity within the authority as a whole (illustrated through purchasing policy). It is of interest, for example, that twelve boroughs were not operating a policy for the promotion of recycled paper use within the authority, which is integral to any attempt to improve the secondary materials market for waste paper. These different components from the survey material have been combined together to produce a Policy Index measure of the organisational scope and sophistication of recycling policy for the statistical analysis. It emerges that the average Policy Index score is 10.1, ranging from 5 in Southwark to 29 in Richmond. Only six other boroughs had a Policy Index score of over twenty (Brent, Camden, Ealing, Hillingdon, Hounslow and Sutton), and all these boroughs, with the exception of Camden, are situated in outer London, as shown in Figure 4.13. Note in Table 4.5, that if the Policy Index is compared with the recycling rate, there is a statistically insignificant correlation coefficient. The weakness of the relationship between the level of recycling and policy development at a borough level can be explained by a consideration of the perceived obstacles to raising levels of recycling illustrated in Table 4.9. It is apparent that the most important barriers to

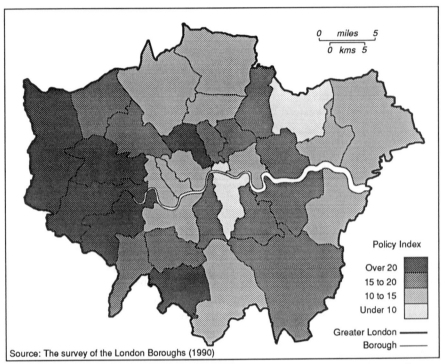

Source: The survey of the London Boroughs (1990)

Figure 4.13: The scope of recycling policy in the London Boroughs

recycling are the lack of resources in investment in kerbside collection schemes, the weakness of the secondary materials market, and need for greater control over packaging and other materials in the waste stream, which all lie effectively outside local authority control.

Much of the current discussion of recycling policy in London is marked by an over-emphasis on individual boroughs as if differences in recycling simply reflect the degree of commitment of administrations to environmental policy (see Breckon, 1990, for example). The use of a 'league table' borough level focus of policy evaluation can be criticised as ignoring the socio-economic disparities between boroughs, and the greater prosperity and less pressing social and economic problems facing outer London Boroughs, in comparison with deprived inner London Boroughs. This picture of relative disadvantage is amplified further when the distribution of recycling infrastructure, car ownership and availability of suitable locations for on-street collection facilities is taken into consideration.

The main policy innovation in the London Boroughs noted as having a direct input into recycling was the appointment of a specialist full-time recycling officer, the first of which was appointed by Richmond in 1984. There are a number of potential advantages that have been identified from the appointment of recycling officers: the initiation of waste reduction policies throughout the local authority; the participation in environmental auditing and recommendations on purchasing policy; the development and management of recycling schemes; and the education of the general public, schools and the authority's own workforce. In the year 1989-90, only nine boroughs had full-time recycling officers and of the twenty three boroughs which lacked this post, sixteen saw the lack of a recycling officer as an important constraint on the expansion of recycling in their area, as shown in Table 4.9. In the absence of a full-time recycling officer, responsibility for recycling normally fell to one specific cleansing officer, in either a senior managerial position, as in Merton and Wandsworth, or a more junior position, as in Hammersmith and Fulham and in Southwark. Some boroughs stated that they could not afford to employ a full-time recycling officer, a problem which was exacerbated in Tower Hamlets by the presence of seven separate Waste Collection Authorities following local government decentralisation in 1986[23]. It was also reported in two boroughs, that there were difficulties in recruiting and retaining recycling officers as a result of the low morale and unsatisfactory career structure within the local authority. The problems had been worsened by the role of early retirements in diluting the experience of staff[24] and the financial crisis facing local government had left some authorities, such as Tower Hamlets, with a vacancy level affecting the adequate discharge of statutory duties[25]. The situation led the beleaguered principal engineer for Waltham Forest with responsibility for recycling, to claim that 'morale is not just low, but rock bottom in local government'[26].

The role of recycling officers has also created tension between the technical engineering based public health traditions in municipal waste management and the new environmental activist type appointments (many recycling officers were previously employed in the voluntary sector and environmental pressure groups rather than in public cleansing departments). It was suggested in one borough that the increasing appointment of recycling officers was creating growing potential conflict with some established professionals from within waste management, who preferred to restrict wider public debate and involvement in the existing technical basis of decision making within public health engineering. From this perspective, the recent popularisation of recycling was seen as 'just a fad', accompanied by the increasing intrusion of relatively naive environmental activists into the complex technical world of efficient and safe waste management[27].

Table 4.9: Obstacles to raising levels of recycling in the London Boroughs

	Important or very important		Not Important		Not Known or data witheld	
	%	No. of Boroughs	%	No. of Boroughs	%	No. of Boroughs
The weakness of the secondary materials market..	84.4	27	3.1	1	12.5	4
The need for more on-street collection facilities...	78.1	25	6.3	2	15.6	5
Restrictions on local government expenditure.	71.9	23	3.1	1	25.0	8
The high labour costs of kerbside collection....	71.9	23	6.3	2	21.9	7
The need for legislation to control the packaging industry......................................	71.9	23	6.3	2	21.9	7
The high capital costs of kerbside collection	71.9	23	9.4	3	18.8	6
The need for legislation to ensure production of recyclable and durable products.............	71.9	23	9.4	3	18.8	6
The need for more recycling centres.............	68.8	22	6.3	2	25.0	8
The lack of coherence in the Government's overall strategy to increase recycling........	65.6	21	6.3	2	28.1	9
The need for more recycling officers.............	62.5	20	15.6	5	21.9	7
The capital costs of centralised recovery.......	59.4	19	12.5	4	28.1	9
The need for more environmental education....	59.4	19	12.5	4	28.1	9
Lack of public knowledge of available facilities	56.3	18	25.0	8	18.8	6
The need for a strategic authority for London.	53.1	17	18.8	6	28.1	9
The impact of the Community Charge.............	46.9	15	9.4	3	43.8	14
Limited partnership with voluntary sector.....	46.9	15	21.9	7	31.3	10
The impact of CCT in waste collection............	46.9	15	21.9	7	31.3	10
The need for staff training and expertise........	46.9	15	31.3	10	21.9	7
The potential impact of the Environmental Protection Act..	43.8	14	9.4	3	46.9	15
The need for legislation to ensure that householders segregate their waste..............	43.8	14	25.0	8	31.3	10
The technical barriers to recycling...............	43.8	14	28.1	9	28.1	9
The need for greater usage of CA sites...........	43.8	14	31.3	10	25.0	8
The impact of high interest rates on costs and investment programmes........................	40.6	13	18.8	6	40.6	13
The low cost of landfill.................................	40.6	13	31.3	10	28.1	9
The lack of support from other officers..........	37.5	12	28.1	9	34.4	11
The lack of support from elected members.....	37.5	12	34.4	11	28.1	9
Workforce resistance to new policies.............	34.4	11	34.4	11	31.3	10
Limited public participation...........................	34.4	11	43.8	14	21.9	7
The abolition of the Community Programme....	15.6	5	43.8	14	40.6	13

Source: The survey of the London Boroughs (1990)

The recovery of different materials from the waste stream

In the previous sections, it was suggested that differences in the level for recycling in the London Boroughs could be explained by the interaction between a number of local factors, principally population density, housing structure, the level of socio-economic deprivation, the density of on-street collection facilities, and the proportion of the waste stream derived from civic amenity sites. In this section, the impact of factors operating at a local and national level is integrated with an examination of the practical difficulties experienced in the recycling of different fractions of the waste stream, with particular emphasis on the three largest fractions of London's municipal waste by weight - paper, putrescibles, and glass.

Paper

In six boroughs, paper was the main material recovered from the waste stream (Bromley; Enfield; Harrow; Havering; Camden and Westminster). There were three reasons for the dominance of paper in some boroughs: firstly, some paper recovery schemes were covered by favourable contractual arrangements drawn up before the late 1980s collapse in the price of waste paper (as in Westminster); secondly, some authorities, notably Westminster, undertook collections of higher grade paper from commercial premises which were not so adversely affected by the fluctuations in the secondary materials market; and thirdly, in one case, that of Havering, there was a long established local authority run kerbside collection scheme for waste paper operating, as a last survivor of the schemes run in most boroughs in the 1970s and earlier.

Paper is a diverse component of waste, with over 60 different grades recognised by the British Waste Paper Association. This is reflected by the existence in many boroughs, of several different paper reclamation schemes operating simultaneously and using different merchants and mills. As a result, markedly different incomes arise for the local authorities, emerging from contractual arrangements with different merchants and mills, drawn up at different times, for different grades of paper and card. The diversity of paper in the waste stream is also reflected within London, with inner London having a larger proportion of paper (particularly higher grades) within the waste stream, as a result of differences in the commercial waste component of the municipal waste stream. In the borough of Richmond in outer London, for example, there were five different schemes in operation: firstly, a network of on-street collection facilities for newspapers and magazines, which were transported to Ellesmere Port, by a sub-contractor; secondly, a higher grade collection scheme focused on commercial premises and run by a contractor; thirdly, the operation of a skip for the collection of card and board by the voluntary sector; fourthly, a second skip for card and board, run by a contractor; and finally, the authority's own in-house collection scheme for higher grade office paper[28].

The fluctuations in the price of paper since the mid-1980s, as shown in Figure 2.6, have particularly badly affected the recycling of paper from household waste, in comparison with collections of paper from commercial premises. This can be attributed to four main factors: firstly, household waste paper consists of predominantly lower grades, such as newspapers, yet demand is strongest for higher grades of office and computer paper; secondly, household waste paper is frequently a mixture of different kinds of paper and card, which are difficult to sort and command a lower price than sorted grades; thirdly, the paper is often contaminated by laminates and other materials; and finally, the period since 1988 has seen a rapid increase in the collection of waste paper by households, swamping an already fragile market for mixed and low grade paper. A key problem has been an accumulated glut of 800,000 tonnes in UK waste paper, the flooding of the market with cheap imports from North America following the implementation of mandatory paper recycling legislation and the suspension of plans to build two new paper mills at Aylesford in Kent and Gartcosh in Scotland, because of high interest rates and unfavourable macro-economic conditions for investment in new plants (the Aylesford plant may now proceed following the award of an EC approved £20 million government grant). The period since 1988, has seen the disappearance of many schemes run by local authorities, the private sector, and the voluntary sector. An example is in the borough of Lambeth, where the mixed paper collection facility at the Norwood civic amenity site had been discontinued, because no paper merchants were willing to even collect the materials[29]. The laissez-faire approach to recycling by central government was clearly illustrated in January 1990, when the government minister with responsibility for recycling, David Heathcoat-Amory, stated that there were no plans to assist charities and other organisations thrown into financial difficulties by the fall in the waste paper prices (*Materials Reclamation Weekly*, 13th January 1990).

The only local authority kerbside collection scheme for paper still operating in London was based in Havering in outer London, and had become a financial disaster since 1988. This was the largest paper recycling initiative in London and covered most of the residential areas in the borough, with a household participation rate of 25 per cent. The paper was collected fortnightly, baled within the borough, and then transported to the Davidsons mill at Purfleet. Despite the collection of 4,500 tonnes in 1989-90, the scheme had been making an annual loss of £140,000, which dwarfed all other recycling income in the borough from other materials, including glass and scrap metals[30]. In an attempt to cut costs, the collections were reduced from fortnightly to monthly, but the amount collected had also fallen, simply exacerbating the financial difficulties of the scheme.

The recovery of low grade paper from households illustrates that factors outside the control of local authorities, such as the state of the secondary materials market and the absence of sufficient capacity in the paper recycling industry, are far more significant obstacles to paper recovery than the willingness of the public to participate. The collapse in the price of paper has had a major impact on the potential expansion of paper recycling, and this aspect of recycling activity has in many boroughs become a net loss or a zero source of income. The problems with paper recycling have created confusion and disillusion on the part of the public, and exasperation on the part of local government officers inundated with public demands for paper recycling facilities. So serious has the impact of the slump in the waste paper market been, that this has now become one of the justifications behind the expansion of the burning of municipal waste to produce electricity described in the next chapter.

Putrescibles

A consideration of the recycling of putrescibles is central to the discussion because putrescibles represent the main fraction of municipal waste after paper in London, as shown in Figure 4.1, and any comprehensive recycling strategy would necessarily extend to kitchen and garden wastes. There exist two main possibilities for the recycling of putrescible waste: the production of pig swill and animal feed; or the production of compost. As recently as the 1960s, food wastes were routinely recovered separately in most boroughs for use as pig swill. The only recent examples of this kind of activity are the occasional collections of food wastes for London's eighteen city farms, each of which has its own policy on what food wastes are accepted and used as animal feed. For example, The Hackney city farm in Haggerston currently only uses bread and fresh vegetables for feeding poultry, carrots for rabbits, and stale bread collected from bakers for pigs. In the past, the farm has made use of mixed food wastes from households for animal feed, but this practice is now largely discontinued for a number of reasons: the food is often in an advanced state of decay by the time it is received; the organising of regular collections is not cost-effective; and the nature of food wastes is too variable and irregular to be a constant element in animal diets. A further factor behind the ending of the practice of using household derived pig swill, is the legislative control over pig swill that has had any contact with meat, reflecting of tighter agricultural regulations from the EC. The key piece of legislation is the 1975 Movement and Sale of Pigs Order incorporated into the 1981 Animal Health Act[31].

There are now no major schemes for the recovery of putrescibles from household waste in London and in many boroughs composting was not viewed as an important aspect of recycling. The question of composting was considered by the GLC in 1985, but the centralised production of compost was ruled out for two main reasons: there was doubt over its cost-effectiveness; and there was no satisfactory operational experience under the GLC. As a result of these uncertainties it was concluded that the best option would be the promotion of home composting activities (GLC, 1985e). The decline in the practice of composting waste originates from the increasing presence of heavy metals derived from the growing proportion of toxics in the municipal waste stream and this was the reason behind the closure of the Sunbury-on-Thames composting plant inherited by the GLC in 1965. In 1984 the GLC had investigated the possibility of a centralised composting plant making saleable products from sewage sludge and household waste as a privately funded joint venture between the GLC, the Thames Water Authority and Taylor Woodrow Resource and Recovery Ltd. The plant was to be built at the site of the Beckton Gas Works using refuse passing through the Jenkins Lane road transfer station in Newham, but the scheme never materialised (GLC, 1984a). In Richmond and Sutton, the potential for composting has been closely examined by the recycling sub-committees and working parties[32]. A number of boroughs have sought to encourage households with gardens to carry out their own composting activities, but there is no direct involvement of local authorities in the form of separate organic waste collection services or the provision of centralised composting facilities. In 1991, the North London Waste Authority began a scheme for the composting of waste from parks, but this has not been extended to collections from individual households[33].

Glass

Chapter Three described how the emergence of glass recycling epitomised the expansion of recycling in the 1980s and has only been made possible by the introduction of on-street collection facilities known as bottle banks with their cheaper costs in comparison with kerbside collection or centralised recovery technologies. In the year 1989-90 the level of glass recycling in London was 4.6 per cent and only in Richmond in outer London did the rate exceed 15 per cent. Glass is the only material which was recovered in every single local authority in London (with the exception of the Corporation of London). Indeed, in 18 boroughs glass emerged as the most important material recovered from the waste stream in tonnage terms during the year 1989-90, yet glass accounts for no more than 15 per cent of London's municipal waste stream (GLC, 1986a), and glass recycling is of relatively low environmental significance, as suggested by Table 2.4.

The arrangements for the emptying and transportation of the cullet were of three main types: eighteen boroughs used a private contractor for both the emptying of facilities and the transportation of glass cullet; seven boroughs emptied the facilities themselves, and then made use of private contractors for the transportation of the glass from transfer stations; and finally, six boroughs carried out the emptying and transportation of cullet under arrangement with the borough of Newham, which had inherited two specialised glass haulage vehicles and storage space for mixed and clear glass at the Jenkins Lane road transfer station, after the abolition of the GLC in 1986. In addition to the Newham scheme, there are other examples of boroughs entering into arrangements with each other, as in the case of Hammersmith and Fulham paying to make use of storage facilities in Richmond[34]. In twenty boroughs the high capital cost of providing new facilities was considered an important obstacle to the expansion of glass recycling.

The need for planning permission for bottle bank sites was found to be a difficulty in six mainly affluent boroughs: Bromley; Hammersmith and Fulham; Kensington and Chelsea; Redbridge; Richmond; and Wandsworth. In Wandsworth, it was reported that there were greater planning restrictions on locating facilities in more affluent middle class areas, such as Putney and Roehampton, because of sustained and effective opposition from the local residents[35]. In some boroughs there has been a legacy of bad experiences with bottle banks as far back as the late 1970s, and in the case of Kensington and Chelsea this was given as a reason for the current administration's reluctance to greatly expand the minimal number of sites for new facilities[36]. In inner London, there were difficulties in locating a sufficient density of facilities in congested boroughs with very low levels of car ownership, such as Tower Hamlets, where in most wards over two thirds of households do not have a car[37] (Townsend et al., 1987). In contrast, in outer London Boroughs such as Bromley, there was the difficulty of low population densities creating problems in terms of providing sufficient access to facilities and reaching site usage targets[38]. In addition to the influence on the level of recycling, shown in Table 4.5, the number and location of facilities has a number of further impacts: the proportion of materials brought by car or on foot; the degree of local congestion and the impact of local environmental problems; the degree of opposition to the location of facilities in residential areas; and the implications of making of special trips to use the facilities as opposed to combining journeys with other activities for energy consumption and traffic congestion (Boustead, 1989; GLC, 1983b).

During the period of the study, some eighteen boroughs undertook three colour separation, whilst five boroughs provided facilities for mixed or clear glass only. In the remaining nine boroughs there were collections for both two and three colour separated glass, which in some cases reflected the existence of commercial and public glass collection schemes operating simultaneously or the limitations posed by the design of existing collection facilities[39]. The collection and transportation of mixed cullet instead of green and brown cullet was clearly more efficient, but would require expensive post-consumer separation if it was to be integrated within a three-colour glass recovery scheme[40]. A further anomaly found in the case of Haringey and Lambeth, was the fact that three-colour separated glass, which was collected by the London borough of Newham in an agreement following GLC abolition, was being mixed together in the collection vehicles because of the limited storage capacity for glass cullet at Jenkins Lane road transfer station in Newham[41]. A difficulty noted with the operation of bottle banks was the contamination of glass at the collection points. The main sources of contamination were the mixing of different colours, especially clear with green glass, since the colour contamination thresholds are higher for clear glass in comparison with green glass (*WARMER Bulletin*, January 1990). The price of mixed or poorly segregated materials also fluctuated more than high quality materials, which is an economic as well as a technical reason for ensuring that levels of contamination are kept as low as possible[42]. In the case of Westminster, the degree of contamination with other materials had led to the extensive dumping of glass from bottle banks at landfill sites[43]. The problem in Westminster derived in particular, from the presence of broken crockery from hotels, restaurants and other establishments and is therefore related to the high proportion of commercial waste within the borough's municipal waste stream.

The adoption of either two or three colour separation systems for public glass collection facilities is becoming an increasingly important consideration because of growing difficulties arising from the potential saturation of the market for green and mixed glass, illustrated in Table 4.10. An important difficulty for glass recovery is that green and mixed glass forms the dominant fraction of recovered cullet, yet the demand is strongest for clear and brown glass in the glass industry. It emerged that United Glass at Harlow, is becoming increasingly reluctant to take any more mixed glass, because their furnace for mixed and green glass was nearing capacity[44]. As a result of this, the company had begun to ship green glass from London up to its other plant

148

Table 4.10: The pattern of glass consumption and glass recycling in the UK

	Clear	Brown	Green
Glass consumption in tonnes.	1,250,000	250,000	280,000
	68.5 %	15.3 %	16.2 %

	Clear	Brown	Green *
Glass recycled from post-consumer waste in tonnes......	47,300	11,300	129,300
	25.1 %	6.0 %	68.8 %

* The green category
includes mixed glass

Source: British Glass and DoE (1991a)

in Ayr, southern Scotland[45]. This development raises three issues: firstly, the question of energy consumption and the transport costs involved; secondly, the potential conflict over the use of the plant when Strathclyde's newly instituted recycling programme becomes fully established; and thirdly, the question of whether a 'market barrier' is being approached for green and mixed glass which could drive down prices. One possible solution is the use of a mixed glass colour for all glass containers, in order to remove this potential hindrance to further recycling, but this would require national and EC level legislation and would be strongly opposed by the glass industry.

The operation of bottle banks in London reveals that there is an environmental trade-off between the global environmental goals of recycling policy identified in Chapter Two and the local environmental impact of their operation. Table 4.11 shows that the operation of bottle banks in London has been associated with a number of problems including the noise from their usage and emptying at unsocial hours, and the over-flowing of broken glass onto the street. Further difficulties identified were visual intrusion (particularly from the older metal containers); the encouragement of litter and fly-tipping in the vicinity; and the periodic traffic congestion created by people using the facilities and the collection vehicles. The operation of bottle banks has been subject to mounting criticism from the public, along with critical coverage within the London Press (*What's On*, 17th January 1990; *Time Out*, 1st January 1991). Table 4.11 shows that twenty four boroughs had experienced complaints from local residents (usually over noise and litter) and that twenty two boroughs were faced with the periodic overflowing of

Table 4.11: Problems experienced with the operation of bottle banks in London

	Important Very Important		Not Important		Not Known or data witheld	
	%	Boroughs	%	Boroughs	%	Boroughs
Complaints from local residents..................	75.0	24	15.6	5	9.4	3
Periodic overflowing of glass onto the street...	68.8	22	15.6	5	15.6	5
Capital costs of providing facilities.............	62.5	20	25.0	8	12.5	4
Unreliability of cullet collection...................	50.0	16	37.5	12	12.5	4
Organisational and logistical problems.........	46.9	15	31.3	10	21.9	7
Limited public participation.........................	34.4	11	46.9	15	18.8	6
Lower market value of green and mixed glass cullet..	15.6	5	34.4	11	43.8	14
Gaining of planning permission...................	15.6	5	65.6	21	18.8	6

Source: The survey of the London Boroughs (1990)

glass onto the street. There was a particular concentration of local environmental problems around bank holidays, when there is greater use of the facilities, yet the usual emptying routine is frequently disrupted. In Camden, it was argued that the inefficiency of glass collections was not only causing a loss of public confidence in the policy, but also an appreciable loss of income from the sale of the lost glass through overflowing at the borough's fifteen bottle bank sites[46].

Table 4.11 also reveals that the problem of unreliability in collection of glass cullet showed a marked disparity in responses, with almost a half of the boroughs experiencing serious difficulties, whilst a significant minority of a third, were not experiencing any problems with the reliability of cullet collections. When the pattern of responses is compared with the different arrangements for the emptying of facilities and the transportation of cullet, a clear distinction emerges: in the eighteen boroughs dependent on a private contractor, fourteen had experienced problems with the reliability of cullet collection; none of the boroughs served by the London Borough of Newham had recorded important difficulties in this area, and six out of seven of the local authorities who undertook their own emptying had experienced no problems of this kind. An explanation of the cause of the difficulties with the main private contractor, H. Marks and Son, is that they had bought out their main rival Cleanaways, shortly before the rapid rise in environmental concern

150

in 1988, and subsequently found themselves overwhelmed by the rapid rise in bottle bank usage[47]. A number of authorities expressed the view that they would prefer to take on the operation of facilities themselves if they could afford the necessary equipment and additional labour costs, and showed exasperation at their overflowing banks and irregular collections[48].

The local environmental problems and constraints on further use of on-street collection facilities, were identified as being particularly acute in the congested inner London Boroughs of Hammersmith and Fulham; Haringey; Islington; Kensington and Chelsea; Wandsworth; and Westminster[49]. The prospects for increased glass recycling with on-street collection facilities will be dependent on a number of factors: the environmental impact and operational problems of 'bring' facilities in congested inner urban areas; the degree of contamination with different cullet colours and materials; the long term potential for stability in the market for green glass, in the absence of any national legislation on the colour of glass containers; and the uncertainty surrounding long-term public motivation to use the facilities, in view of the negative local impacts of bottle banks and the growing uncertainties over their potential benefits (apart from for the glass industry)[50].

Other materials

The remaining fractions of the household waste stream make up around 25 per cent of the total household waste stream by weight, and are therefore less important in terms of the overall goal of reducing the size of the waste stream. However, there are a number of materials, notably textiles, scrap metals and oil, which are significant as an established component of recycling activity in the London Boroughs.

i) *Car components* There are no satisfactory facilities in London for the disposal of car batteries and tyres. Indeed, the fly tipping of tyres, for which no adequate disposal arrangements exist, emerged as a serious problem, especially in boroughs with large areas of derelict land such as Tower Hamlets[51]. During the study period, Croydon was considering investing in a tyre reclamation plant as a joint venture with a number of other boroughs[52]. A development during 1990 was the proposal for a national tyre recovery plant at Wolverhampton, which if completed would burn half the UK's annual production of waste tyres to produce energy under contract to Midland Electricity and would be eligible for government support under a levy called the Non Fossil Fuel Obligation (NFFO), examined further in Chapter Five (Cheesewright, 1990; Sychrava, 1990).

ii) *Chlorofluorocarbons (CFCs)* The recovery of CFCs from refrigerators, though a toxic waste disposal service rather than an aspect of materials reclamation, was being carried out by nineteen boroughs as part of their recycling activities. The usual arrangements were that the old refrigerators are either brought by the public to recycling centres and civic amenity sites, or the refrigerators are collected by local authorities from households. The recovery of CFCs was undertaken for purely environmental reasons, and not as a potential source of income[53]. The lack of a strategic authority following GLC abolition had made CFC recovery more difficult: there was a multiplicity of half measures and schemes launched at different times; there was duplication of capital investment in equipment[54]; and there was lack of co-ordination of the provision of storage space[55]. The separate collection of CFC propelled aerosols was only carried out in Camden, where these items were collected separately at the Jamestown Road Recycling Centre on an experimental basis[56].

iii) *Plastics* The recovery of plastics is at a rudimentary stage in London, with the highest total of 1.8 tonnes recorded for Camden in 1989-90. This reflected the interaction of a number of unfavourable factors: the lack of collection facilities; the poor economies of scale for individual boroughs; the difficulties for the public in distinguishing between different polymers, leading to contamination of collections[57]; the difficulties in collecting enough of a particular polymer to make its collection economically worthwhile; and the transport costs for London were high, because most firms capable of handling the collected materials are located in the North of England[58]. The only forms of plastics recovery found in the survey were the experimental collection of PET and mixed plastics in Camden, Hounslow and Richmond, and the recovery of the calorific value of plastics at the Edmonton incineration plant run by the North London Waste Authority. There have, however, been operational difficulties at the Edmonton plant, as a result of the incineration of polymers such as polyvinyl chlorides (PVCs), which also form an important source of emission concerns from dioxins[59] (WEN, 1989). In Richmond, an on-street collection facility for mixed plastics was run on an experimental basis by BXL (a subsidiary of BP) but transport costs of £50 a tonne exceeded the value of the materials because of the high volume to weight ratio (Richmond Borough Council, 1990; Taylor-Brown, 1990). Plastics recovery in London is now also being hampered by the import of materials from Germany as a result of collections arising from the new packaging regulations exceeding the capacity of the German plastics recycling industry (see Chapter Six).

iv) *Scrap metals* Scrap metals are the main fraction of London's domestic waste stream to be recovered by post-consumer separation, and unlike glass and paper, invariably include a large proportion of materials of high value. London has a well developed secondary materials industry for scrap metals, and rates of metals recovery for the UK as a whole compare favourably with other developed economies (Hockley et al., 1989). Most scrap metal recovery takes place at civic amenity sites, where metals are recovered from bulky household waste. In the borough of Ealing in outer London, for example, most scrap metals are derived from discarded electrical goods and other household items, deposited at the borough's three intensively used civic amenity sites. The recovery of scrap metals from household waste in Ealing has increased steadily in the 1990s for two reasons: firstly, in 1991 the authority introduced a new bonus scheme for the in-house totting of metals by staff at the civic amenity sites/recycling centres; and secondly, the rapidly expanding CFC recovery scheme has provided an additional source of scrap metals from the disposal of old refrigerators[60]. Significant quantities of valuable non-ferrous metals are also removed from the waste stream in London by unlicensed totting[61]. Factors involved here include labour practices in waste collection and the degree of supervision at civic amenity sites and waste transfer stations. However, non-ferrous scrap normally accounted for a very small proportion of metals recovered by licensed totting at civic amenity sites, when compared with ferrous metals. In Camden, for example, 97.6 per cent of recovered metals were ferrous and just 2.4 per cent non-ferrous in the year 1989-90.

v) *Steel and aluminium cans* Steel and aluminium cans were collected in fifteen boroughs, and were normally collected together in skips or purpose built banks, as part of the national Save-a-Can Scheme launched by the Can Makers Federation in 1979, and they could subsequently be separated magnetically. The potential for the recovery of aluminium cans has been greatly improved by the new British Alcan aluminium recycling plant opened at Warrington in December 1991. This plant will now handle pure aluminium scrap much more efficiently than the old plant, and a set price of £700 tonne for baled and pelletised cans is being offered[62]. In 1989 links were established between the Aluminium Can Recycling Association (ACRA) and 16 scrap metal merchants in the London area as the first stage in the separate collection of aluminium, in preparation for the opening of the new British Alcan recovery plant base at Warrington (ACRA, 1989). The UK can industry have lobbied for source separation schemes with on-street collection facilities rather than the use of reverse vending machines or compulsory deposit systems and a pilot aluminium can scheme was launched in Richmond in 1990, to evaluate public usage of on-street collection facilities for aluminium. Richmond, was chosen as a 'green borough', because of its extensive community and voluntary sector networks for recycling. The role of the local authority was seen as a purely enabling role by ACRA, for the provision of sites, contacts, and the co-ordinating of the link between local residents and the recycling industry (Brown, 1990). Similarly, in Bromley, the local authority acted simply as an introductory agent between scrap merchants and the voluntary sector for the schools based 'Tidyman's Canpaign' for aluminium cans[63] (Ellender, 1990).

vi) *Textiles* Textiles represent a small but important aspect of the recycling activities in the London Boroughs. There were collection facilities for textiles in 17 boroughs at their civic amenity sites, usually owned and run by private sector rag merchants, with over forty tonnes of textiles collected in Enfield, Richmond and Sutton in the year 1989-90. The other main type of collection is charitable collections run by the voluntary sector (normally for better quality textiles and second hand clothes), for which no comparable figures are collected by the Waste Collection Authorities.

vii) *Waste oil* The recovery of waste oil was undertaken at recycling centres and civic amenity sites in 25 boroughs in 1989-90, and was done for two main reasons: the environmental impact of its direct disposal into the sewerage system; and its potential to generate income for the local authorities. Many of the oil recovery schemes were set up under the GLC, and have since been continued at formerly GLC controlled civic amenity sites, such as Greenford in Ealing[64]. The recovery of oil was particularly difficult for those inner London Boroughs, which lack civic amenity sites and the space for oil storage.

The underlying barriers to recycling in London

This chapter has demonstrated that there is a limit to an explanation of recycling based simply on the analysis of variations between different boroughs on the basis of local factors. A fuller picture of the prospects for increasing the level of recycling in London towards the Government's stated objective of 25 per cent can be obtained by an examination of the perceived barriers to higher levels of recycling in the London Boroughs. Table 4.9 shows that the most important barriers to recycling can be divided into three groups: the weakness of the secondary materials market; the cost of new recycling facilities and kerbside schemes, in the context of restrictions on local government expenditure; and the need for greater controls over products and processes, particularly the 35 per cent by weight of waste, constituted by packaging. The limits to materials recycling can consequently be argued to lie largely outside the control of individual London Boroughs, which helps to explain why the Policy Index measure of policy development in the boroughs is so weakly correlated with the level of recycling, as illustrated in Table 4.5. Table 4.9 shows that limited public participation is perceived as the least important factor affecting recycling, with the exception of the abolition of the Community Programme, which adversely affected some voluntary sector initiatives (see FoE, 1989). Other factors emerging as of little importance, include the need for greater usage of civic amenity sites (clearly a function of public participation). The role of technical barriers to recycling is also of limited importance, reiterating the fact that present rates of recycling do not approach the technical barriers to materials reclamation. It is also of interest that the low cost of landfill is not selected as a significant barrier to recycling, since this is identified in much of the literature and also in official government documents as the primary source of 'market failure' which has hindered the development of recycling (see DoE, 1990b; FoE, 1992; Pollock, 1987; Turner, 1990, 1992).

A preliminary conclusion to emerge from the London analysis is that the widely discussed influence of limited public participation and cheap landfill costs are negligible barriers to higher levels of materials recycling. On the basis of the perceived barriers to recycling identified in Table 4.9, a recycling rate of 25 per cent in London would require increased state intervention in the production process to control packaging and other components of the waste stream, the extension of fiscal and other measures to the secondary materials market and recycling industry, and also higher public expenditure in order to finance comprehensive kerbside collection schemes. The concern over the cost of kerbside collection schemes is also reflected nationally, with a recent survey suggesting that 84 per cent of local authorities had no intention of introducing kerbside collection schemes because of the costs involved (FoE, 1991), yet most research suggests that recycling rates in excess of around 20 per cent cannot be achieved without some form of kerbside collection scheme in operation because of limited rates of materials recovery with 'bring' systems.

The survey found that the pattern of recovery for different materials varied in a number of key respects: the contribution of different agencies; the use of different recovery methods; and the justification for their recovery (charitable, economic, or environmental). Figure 4.4 shows that although the largest fractions of municipal waste are paper and putrescibles, the main fractions of materials recovered are paper, glass and metals, reflecting their ease of

Table 4.12: Difficulties with materials recycling in London

Glass	Local environmental impact of collection facilities (Noise, litter, fly-posting, congestion etc.) Contamination of glass (colour contamination and other materials, particularly crockery) Potential saturation of the green glass market
Paper	Weakness of secondary materials market for lower grade waste paper Local operational problems with collection facilities
Putrescibles	No recent operational experience of separate collection schemes Uncertainties over marketing compost
Scrap Metals	Difficulties for boroughs lacking civic amenity type facilities
Metal cans	Rudimentary network of 'bring' facilities and low rates of recovery
Textiles	Lack of data on voluntary sector activities Weakness of secondary materials market for mixed and synthetic fibres
Oil	Difficulties for boroughs lacking civic amenity type facilities
CFCs	Difficulties for boroughs lacking civic amenity type facilities
Plastics	Separate collection found to be economically unviable Lack of secondary materials market for mixed plastics Problems of achieving economies of scale and transporting the collected materials Swamping of UK plastics recycling industry with German imports resulting from the DSD system since 1991

Source: Gandy (1992a)

separation and collection, along with the state of the established secondary materials markets. These differences between materials are summarised in Table 4.12, which highlights the main barriers to the recycling of specific materials. It appears that the role of the voluntary sector is only significant for materials with a high intrinsic value, such as higher grade paper, aluminium cans and second hand clothing. The private sector was similarly only directly involved in recovery schemes for which it judged there could be a reasonable rate of return. In contrast, the role of the London Boroughs, in their capacity as Waste Collection Authorities, varied from that of a purely enabling role, in the provision of sites for on-street collection facilities to a more active operational involvement in inherently loss making environmental services such as CFC recovery from old refrigerators. It can be concluded that the extent of local authority involvement in relation to the private and voluntary sectors, is inversely related to the value of the materials and the logistical and economic difficulties in recovering the materials from the waste stream.

The logic of individual borough organising the collection of each material in its area was widely questioned. It was claimed, for example, that the successful Newham glass scheme (with one borough undertaking operational activities for a number of other boroughs), could be applied to other materials[65]. This would also help to achieve scale economies for a wider range of recoverable materials, and also avoid the problems which had been experienced with the unreliability of private contractors. Local authorities could potentially play an important role in improving the economies of scale for materials of low value such as waste paper, by bulking them up to the point where a merchant or mill might take an interest. The widespread recycling of CFCs, plastics, and centralised composting of putrescibles would also require better resourced and strategically co-ordinated local government, to extend recovery beyond a purely experimental basis, as at present, and is therefore a question related to the wider issue of local government reform for London.

Conclusion

This chapter began by confirming the importance of public pressure in stimulating the development of recycling as a political response to environmental concern. It was demonstrated, however, that contemporary recycling is also undertaken for economic as well as environmental reasons in order to reduce the costs of waste disposal. There is also a view in some authorities that recycling should generate a net income or at least break even, but local authority recycling budgets do not include the full range of expenditure on recycling, and in some cases mask overheads in order to justify a public service on narrowly conceived economic grounds.

The level of recycling in London was found to be below the average for the UK as a whole and well below technically achievable levels. The wide variations in the level of recycling across London could be accounted for primarily by the distribution of recycling facilities, which was in turn a function of urban congestion, land values and the distribution of recycling infrastructure inherited by the London Boroughs from the GLC in 1986. The data analysis suggested that three variables widely mooted in the literature are of limited explanatory value: firstly, the socio-economic characteristics of the population could only be weakly related to recycling activity; secondly, the role of waste disposal rebates, as the key market-based policy instrument to raise levels of recycling, was found to be statistically insignificant and was considered of limited importance by the boroughs themselves; and finally, the weak impact of the scope of recycling policy within the London Boroughs suggested that the underlying factors affecting recycling lie largely outside local government control. The survey identified the underlying factors as the weakness in the secondary materials market, the limited resources of local government to implement comprehensive recycling systems, and the need for greater control over different fractions of the waste stream.

The analysis of the recycling of individual materials served to clarify the interaction between different factors in accounting for the low and uneven rate of recycling across London. A number of other difficulties were also noted including the question of a trade-off between the wider environmental goals of recycling and local environmental impact of on-street collection facilities used in the 'bring' system of materials recovery. The survey findings suggest that the Government target of 25 per cent recycling would not be achieved without a fundamental change in recycling and waste management policy at a national level, underlining the need to examine the changing legislative framework and policy context in greater detail.

In the next chapter, I show how the political and economic policy context for recycling is shifting as a result of a combination of processes which have been neglected in most existing studies of recycling. In particular I suggest that the demunicipalisation of waste management has important and far reaching consequences for the integration of waste management with environmental policy.

Notes

1   The questionnaire survey of the London Boroughs was carried out in 1990 and involved the collection of a range of quantitative and qualitative data from each of the London Boroughs (see notes to Introductory Chapter).

2   Interview with the Highways and Cleansing Manager for the London Borough of Barking and Dagenham, Terry Mirams, 7th June 1990. Interview with the Senior Planner for the London Borough of Sutton, Graham Dean, on the 10th January 1990.

3   Interview with the Client Services Manager for the London Borough of Hackney, Alan Emery, on the 8th May 1990. Interview with the Principal Engineer (services) for the London Borough of Waltham Forest, Barry Higgs, 22nd May 1990.

4   Interview with the Project Officer (cleansing) for the City of Westminster, Caesar Voûte, 15th May 1990.

5   Interview with the Senior Planner for the London Borough of Sutton, Graham Dean, on the 10th January 1990.

6   Personal communication with Derek Bargh of GEC Alsthom, 1991.

7   Interview with the Recycling Officer for the London Borough of Hounslow, Andrea Davies, 24th May 1990.

8   Interview with the Highways and Cleansing Manager for the London Borough of Barking and Dagenham, Terry Mirams, 7th June 1990.

9   Interview with the Recycling Development Officer for the London Borough of Camden, Mike Newport, 15th June 1990.

10 Interview with the Cleansing Officer for the London Borough of Lambeth, Bob King, 17th May 1990.

11 Interview with the Recycling Development Officer for the London Borough of Camden, Mike Newport, 15th June 1990.

12 The extent of quantitative data availability varied between the

boroughs, depending on whether quantities of materials had been systematically recorded at weighbridge facilities. Furthermore, some materials included in the survey such as car batteries were not normally recorded separately and some valuable materials such as non-ferrous metals disappeared from the waste stream by unlicensed totting, sometimes by the refuse collectors themselves. Another difficulty in assessing the borough recycling rates is that sites are sometimes used by residents from neighbouring boroughs, particularly where they are located near the local authority boundary with other authorities which lack similar facilities. Finally, some materials handled by the voluntary sector, particularly textiles, will have been underestimated in the survey, but textiles make up only a small fraction of municipal waste, and much of the voluntary sector textiles recovery is focused on re-use rather than materials recovery within the hierarchy of recycling options illustrated in Figure 2.4.

13   The category 'old left' refers to those Labour controlled London Boroughs such as Barking and Dagenham where the so-called 'New Urban Left' has had comparatively little impact (see Boddy and Fudge, 1984; Gyford, 1985).

14   An initial difficulty with the use of the parametric Pearson's product moment coefficient of correlation for the statistical analysis was the non normality of the raw data, which was measured using the Bowman Shanton test for kurtosis and skewness (see Harvey, 1989). A further concern was that most of the eight explanatory variables, as shown in Table 4.4, and the dependent variable (the recycling rate in the boroughs) consisted of closed number systems of percentage data. An additional complexity was that the non-linear relationships between the variables revealed in the raw data plots and in the non-random scatter of residuals. In order to satisfy the mathematical and statistical assumptions behind the use of parametric analysis, both dependent and independent variables were therefore log transformed to give a log-log model for the analysis (see Johnson, 1984). The correlation analysis, as shown in Table 4.5, was also re-examined using a non-parametric measure, to see whether the strength of any of the relationships would be significantly altered. The Kendall's Tau was used instead of the Spearman's Rank, because it is considered to be a more powerful test when used on non-normal data in small samples (Neave and Worthington, 1988). Unlike the parametric Pearson's measure, which examines the existence of a linear association, the non-parametric

Kendall's Tau test measures the strength of any monotonic association between the variables, whether linear or curvilinear, which is helpful at the exploratory sage of the analysis. The results of the Kendall's Tau analysis confirmed the strength and the signs of the correlation observed with the parametric analysis.

15   The statistical analysis was extended using regression analysis of the log transformed data. An initial finding was that the adjusted R-squared measure and F-test were higher with the log transformed data than with the raw data. The multiple regression analysis suggested that the density of on-street collection facilities was by far the most significant explanatory factors within the model, as shown in Table 4.6. In order to extend the analysis further, a stepwise multiple regression was used in order to identify the effect of collinearity between the different variables and also to eliminate those variables which were of low statistical significance, as illustrated in Table 4.7. For the stepwise regression, the F-ratios chosen for the model were 4.24 for the inclusion of variables, based on the procedure outlined by Shaw and Wheeler (1985), and a default F-ratio of 3.99 was used for the exclusion of variables from the model.

16   The Z-score of multiple deprivation derived from eight indicators: level of unemployment; level of overcrowding; per cent single parent households; per cent pensioners living alone; per cent of households lacking basic amenities; per cent of households where head of household was born in the New Commonwealth or Pakistan; per cent population decline 1971-1981; and the standardised mortality rate 1980. Source: 1981 Census and other data compiled by the DoE Inner Cities Directorate.

17   Multicollinearity refers to a situation where independent variables exhibit correlation with each other (see Shaw and Wheeler, 1985).

18   Interview with the Cleansing Manager for the London Borough of Islington, Bob Lapsley, 18th April 1990. Interview with the Cleansing Officer for the London Borough of Kensington and Chelsea, Moira Billinge, 16th May 1990. Interviews with the Environmental Development Manager, Peter Brooker, and the Cleansing Officer, David Masters, for Globe Town Neighbourhood, London Borough of Tower Hamlets, 20th June 1990. Interview with the Project Officer (cleansing) for the City of Westminster, Caesar Voûte, 15th May 1990.

19   Personal communication with Roger Parker, the Corporation of London, 1990.

20   Interview with the Cleansing Officer for Bow Neighbourhood, Gary King, for the London Borough of Tower Hamlets, 8th June 1990.

21   Interview with Fr. Wiebke Sager, Amt für Entsorgungsplanung, Hamburg, 17th September 1990.

22   Interview with the Recycling Development Officer for the London Borough of Camden, Mike Newport, 15th June 1990. Interview with Technical Services Officer for the London Borough of Hammersmith and Fulham, Tony Talman, 15th May 1990. Interview with the Project Officer (cleansing) for the City of Westminster, Caesar Voûte, 15th May 1990.

23   Interview with the Cleansing Officer for Bow Neighbourhood, Gary King, for the London Borough of Tower Hamlets, 8th June 1990. Interviews with the Environmental Development Manager, Peter Brooker, and the Cleansing Officer, David Masters, for Globe Town Neighbourhood, London Borough of Tower Hamlets, 20th June 1990. Interview with the Highways and Cleansing Officer for Bethnal Green Neighbourhood, Gery McCleary, London Borough of Tower Hamlets, 11th July 1990.

24   Interview with the Recycling Officer for the London Borough of Brent, Betty Morton, 17th May 1990. Interview with the Assistant Cleansing Manager for the London Borough of Enfield, Peter Joyce, 12th June 1990. Interview with the Cleansing Officer for the London Borough of Lambeth, Bob King, 17th May 1990. Interview with the Principal Engineer (services) for the London Borough of Waltham Forest, Barry Higgs, 22nd May 1990.

25   Interview with the Cleansing Officer for Bow Neighbourhood, Gary King, for the London Borough of Tower Hamlets, 8th June 1990.

26   Interview with the Principal Engineer (services) for the London Borough of Waltham Forest, Barry Higgs, 22nd May 1990.

27   Interview with the Recycling Development Officer for the London Borough of Camden, Mike Newport, 15th June 1990.

28   Interview with the Assistant Recycling Officer for the London Borough of Richmond, Sally Lawes, 19th June 1990.

29   Interview with the Cleansing Officer for the London Borough of Lambeth, Bob King, 17th May 1990.

30   Interview with the Waste Disposal Manager for the London Borough of Havering, Ralph Johnson, 13th June 1990.

31   Personal communication with Lindsey Proctor of the Hackney City Farm, 1991.

32   Interview with the Assistant Recycling Officer for the London Borough of Richmond, Sally Lawes, 19th June 1990.

33   Interview with Waste Planning Officer for the East London Waste Authority, Tom Butterfield, 14th June 1990. Personal communication with Tony Parnham of the NLWA, 1992.

34   Interview with the Assistant Recycling Officer for the London Borough of Richmond, Sally Lawes, 19th June 1990.

35   Interview with the Principal Services Officer for the London Borough of Wandsworth, Alan Barrett, 1990.

36   Interview with the Cleansing Officer for the London Borough of Kensington and Chelsea, Moira Billinge, 16th May 1990

37   Interviews with the Environmental Development Manager, Peter Brooker, and the Cleansing Officer, David Masters, for Globe Town Neighbourhood, London Borough of Tower Hamlets, 20th June 1990.

38   Interview with the Environment Promotions Officer for the London Borough of Bromley, Simon Bussel, 18th May 1990.

39   Interview with the Senior Planner for the London Borough of Sutton, Graham Dean, on the 10th January 1990.

40   Interview with the Technical Officer for the London Borough of Haringey, Tim Marshall, 25th April 1990. Interview with the Cleansing Officer for the London Borough of Lambeth, Bob King, 17th May 1990.

41   Interview with the Recycling Development Officer for the London Borough of Camden, Mike Newport, 15th June 1990.

42   Interview with the Recycling Development Officer for the London Borough of Camden, Mike Newport, 15th June 1990. Interview with the Project Officer (cleansing) for the City of Westminster, Caesar Voûte, 15th May 1990.

43   Wide coverage of the issue in the London press (e.g. *What's On*, 17th January 1990).

44   Interview with the Cleansing Officer for the London Borough of Lambeth, Bob King, 17th May 1990.

45   Interview with the Recycling Development Officer for the London Borough of Camden, Mike Newport, 15th June 1990.

46   Interview with the Recycling Development Officer for the London Borough of Camden, Mike Newport, 15th June 1990.

47   Interview with the Cleansing manger for the London Borough of Islington, Bob Lapsley, 18th April 1990.

48   Interview with the Assistant Cleansing Manager for the London Borough of Enfield, Peter Joyce, 12th June 1990.

49   Interview with Technical Services Officer for the London Borough of Hammersmith and Fulham, Tony Talman, 15th May 1990; Interview with the Technical Officer for the London Borough of Haringey, Tim Marshall, 25th April 1990; Interview with the Cleansing manger for the London Borough of Islington, Bob Lapsley, 18th April 1990; Interview with the Cleansing Officer for the London Borough of Kensington and Chelsea, Moira Billinge, 16th May 1990. Interview with the Principal Services Officer for the London Borough of Wandsworth, Alan Barrett, January 1990. Interview with the Project Officer (cleansing) for the City of Westminster, Caesar Voûte, 1990.

50   Interviews with the Recycling Marketing Officer, John Hefferman and the Research Officer (environmental services) for the London Borough of Ealing, 12th June 1990.   Interview with the Project Officer (cleansing) for the City of Westminster, Caesar Voûte, 15th May 1990.

51   Interviews with the Environmental Development Manager, Peter Brooker, and the Cleansing Officer, David Masters, for Globe Town Neighbourhood, London Borough of Tower Hamlets, 20th June 1990.

52   Interview with the Public Cleansing Manager, Peter Hooper, for the London Borough of Croydon, 11th May 1990.

53   Interview with the Recycling Development Officer for the London Borough of Camden, Mike Newport, 15th June 1990. Interviews with the Recycling Marketing Officer, John Hefferman and the Research Officer (environmental services), Tina Sutherland, for the London Borough of Ealing, 12th June 1990. Interview with the Senior Planner for the London Borough of Sutton, Graham Dean, on the 10th January 1990.

54   Interview with the Recycling Officer for the London Borough of Brent, Betty Morton, 17th May 1990.

55   Interview with the Environment Promotions Officer for the London Borough of Bromley, Simon Bussel, 18th May 1990.   Interview with the Cleansing Officer for Bow Neighbourhood, Gary King, for the London Borough of Tower Hamlets, 8th June 1990.

56   Interview with the Recycling Development Officer for the London Borough of Camden, Mike Newport, 15th June 1990.

57   Interview with the Recycling Development Officer for the London Borough of Camden, Mike Newport, 15th June 1990.

58   Interview with Technical Services Officer for the London Borough of Hammersmith and Fulham, Tony Talman, 15th May 1990.

59   Aluminium Can Recycling Association, personal communication 1991.

60   Interview with the Recycling Marketing Officer for the London Borough of Ealing, John Hefferman, 21st May 1991.

61   Interview with the Technical Officer for the London Borough of Haringey, Tim Marshall, 25th April 1990; Interview with the Cleansing Officer for the London Borough of Kensington and Chelsea, Moira Billinge, 16th May 1990.

62   Aluminium Can Recycling Association, personal communication 1991

63   Interview with the Environment Promotions Officer for the London Borough of Bromley, Simon Bussel, 18th May 1990. Interview with the Recycling Marketing Officer for the London Borough of Ealing, John Hefferman, 21st May 1991. Interview with the Assistant Cleansing Manager for the London Borough of Enfield, Peter Joyce, 12th June 1990.

64   Interview with the Recycling Marketing Officer for the London Borough of Ealing, John Hefferman, 21st May 1991

65   Interview with the Highways and Cleansing Manager for the London Borough of Barking and Dagenham, Terry Mirams, 7th June 1990.

5 The changing policy context for recycling in London

The last chapter established that the explanation for low rates of recycling lies beyond locally operating factors in the London Boroughs, and rests on wider political and economic aspects of waste management and recycling policy at a national level. In this chapter this policy context for recycling is examined in greater detail, with particular emphasis on changes in the legislative framework, as illustrated in Figure 5.1. It is suggested that a narrow focus simply on recycling in the London Boroughs will overlook the general pattern of developments within urban waste management, and as a result, misinterpret the prospects for increasing levels of recycling as an alternative means of waste disposal. The last decade has seen a number of political and legislative developments which are fundamentally altering the policy making context for recycling and waste management in London. A key dimension is the process of demunicipalisation, whereby the operational aspects of waste collection and disposal are being increasingly carried out by the private sector.

The impact of GLC abolition

A key question following GLC abolition is whether there is a continuing need for a strategic waste disposal authority for London, as recommended in the Herbert Commission of 1960. There are four main areas of interest to be considered: the arguments over the cost and economic efficiency of the new arrangements for waste disposal; the question of improved accountability and flexibility in relation to local needs; the maintenance of environmental standards in waste management under the new regulatory framework; and the impact of GLC abolition on recycling in London.

An initial question concerns the economic efficiency of the waste disposal

Figure 5.1: The administrative structure of waste management in London 1889-1991

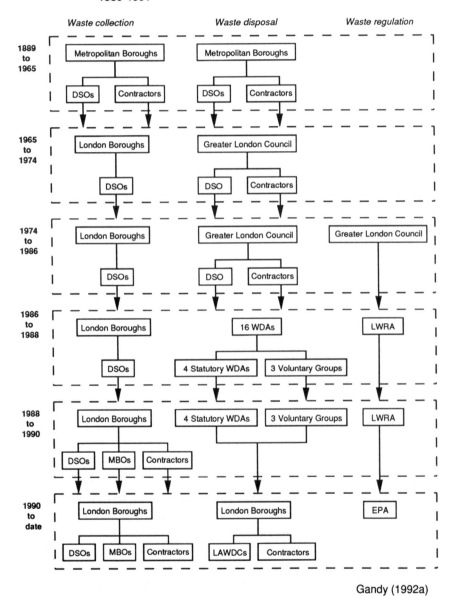

Gandy (1992a)

arrangements set up to take over from the GLC Public Health Engineering Department in 1986, since one of the Government's primary objectives had been to reduce the costs of waste disposal and increase the role of the private sector (see Chapter Three). An early evaluation by the Director of Public Services for Croydon, within the South West London Waste Disposal Group (SWLWDG), which includes the outer London Boroughs of Bromley, Croydon, Kingston-upon-Thames, Merton and Sutton, suggested that the Government's stated objectives in terms of cost savings and improved services were being met. It was argued that within two years of the new arrangements, there was a range of opportunities for rationalisation, efficiency and cost-savings; and additional local services had been introduced. It was also claimed that the operating WDAs had become more manageable in size, with local operations allowing greater day to day managerial control, and improved local responsiveness and accountability in comparison with the remote GLC County Hall. In particular, it was claimed that the South West London Waste Disposal Group (SWLWDG) had experienced substantial cost-savings (£300,000 per annum in Croydon alone); and that the recycling rate had increased as a result of greater local operational control over waste management and increased provision of on-street collection facilities (Ollier, 1988). In contrast, the view from a Waste Collection Authority within the statutory North London Waste Authority (NLWA) was very different. It was maintained that there have been no substantial cost savings and there has been a collapse in the waste management career structure across London, with a haemorrhage of experienced officers from the public sector[1].

At the time of GLC abolition, the Government had argued that the localisation of waste disposal costs would be an incentive to cut costs through increased local accountability for expenditure, yet this failed to recognise that there were intrinsic differences in the costs of waste disposal across London, particularly between inner and outer London (GLC, 1986a). The GLC correctly predicted that the main consequence of abolition for waste disposal costs would be a divergence rather than an overall reduction in costs for London:

> Superficial savings occur when a London wide system is devolved to groups. Some outer London Boroughs were understood to favour the Government's abolition proposals for waste disposal because costs of disposal of their waste could be reduced if they were enabled to run their own individual operation. Outer boroughs producing largely household waste and with good transport access to relatively close landfill facilities enjoy a cost advantage over inner boroughs because

of the shorter distances involved and lower level of traffic congestion. (GLC, 1986a p. 8).

This helps to explain why some outer London Boroughs such as Croydon welcomed the 'decentralisation' of waste disposal and have been able to claim substantial cost savings. It is not in the narrowly-conceived financial interests of outer London Boroughs to share in the costs of waste management for inner London, and the support of the abolition of the GLC Public Health Engineering Department by some outer London Boroughs represented a political demand for fiscal independence from the high waste management costs facing inner London. The Recycling Development Officer for Camden claimed that GLC abolition had been at best an irrelevance to waste management in London, since the decentralised structure of waste disposal existed anyway with the five regional divisions operating under the GLC Public Health Engineering Department, as shown in Figure 3.8. It was also suggested that with the 1980s rise in environmental concern the level of recycling had been increasing with the larger quantities of materials brought by the public to on-street collection facilities and recycling centres irrespective of GLC abolition[2].

A number of criticisms have been levelled at the four statutory Waste Disposal Authorities in London, which were imposed on twenty one boroughs by the Secretary of State in 1986: there has been conflict amongst the constituent Waste Collection Authorities over questions of policy[3]; they have suffered from the low calibre and poor attendance of elected members at their meetings[4]; they employ very few people and have a rudimentary career structure in comparison with the GLC Public Health Engineering Department[5]; and they have a weak management structure, failing to deliver in policy terms[6]. As might be expected, there is a pattern of more effective co-operation among the voluntary waste disposal groupings, as in the plans for an incineration plant for the South East London Waste Disposal Group (SELWDG), which is a continuation of proposals contained in the GLC Waste Management Plan drawn up in 1983 (GLC, 1983d).

The capacity of the London Waste Regulation Authority (LWRA), which took over the waste regulation function of the GLC, to regulate and monitor waste disposal has also been questioned on a number of counts. In some local authorities, the LWRA specified tonnages to be handled at civic amenity sites and transfer stations are being regularly exceeded. Previous to the regulatory role of the GLC established in the early 1970s, the Summers Lane transfer facility in Barnet, for example, had been receiving some 600 tonnes of unmonitored wastes a week from trade and other sources. Under GLC supervision this had fallen to under 250 tonnes per week, but had risen rapidly since 1986, with increasing proportions of illicit trade wastes and other unknown wastes[7]. It was also suggested that the problem of fly-tipping (estimated to be 1 million tonnes a year by the GLC in 1984) appears to be worsening in some areas[8]. The Association of London Authorities have maintained that the LWRA can have little impact on controlling the activities of unknown waste producers and illegal disposal activities, when their capacity to monitor known operations is severely limited by lack of resources (ALA, 1987). In the case of toxic 'special' wastes, as defined under the Control of Pollution (Special Wastes) Regulations, 1980, there are more than 1,000 known producers of special wastes in the Greater London area. The initial staff allocation of 79 at the LWRA has meant that between only 30 and 40 per cent of these special wastes producers can be visited annually (ALA, 1987). In the year 1989-90 the LWRA made 17,266 site visits and carried out 94 prosecutions covering a range of offences: the contravention of licence conditions; the operation of an unlicensed site; non-compliance with section 93 of the 1974 Control of Pollution Act (provision of information); and fly-tipping. The annual number of prosecutions has risen steadily, from 20 in 1986-87 to 94 in 1989-90, and this raises the question of whether the rising number of prosecutions indicates growing vigilance in waste regulation in London, or a decline in environmental standards since GLC abolition (LWRA, 1987; 1988; 1989; 1990).

An important question is the evaluation of the potential for strategic policy making in waste management in the absence of a elected strategic authority. Six London Boroughs had a recycling sub-committee, specifically devoted to the promotion of recycling, as described in the last Chapter. These committees could examine longer term policy options including the promotion of composting; undertake detailed data analysis of waste management in the borough; and closely monitor the effectiveness of policy. In June 1990 London was left with only five recycling sub-committees: following the May 1990 local elections the incoming Conservative administration for Hillingdon, abolished the recycling sub-committee as a cost cutting measure[9]. In addition, seventeen boroughs had working groups or policy forums where recycling was considered along with other aspects of waste management and environmental policy. What continuity in London wide waste management since 1986 that does exist through forums such as the Waste in London Joint Officers Group (WILJOG) and the London Recycling Forum, have been very heavily used by the London Boroughs. In the case of the London Recycling Forum, this was a joint arrangement created by the GLC in 1984 now held under the auspices of the London Waste Regulation Authority, and the survey found that twenty eight boroughs regularly attend.

In the absence of the GLC, a number of important aspects of recycling policy have disappeared for a mix of political and organisational reasons: the promotion of recycling employment as part of a wider industrial strategy for London; the national and international lobbying role over the 1984 DTI *Wealth of Waste* report and the 1985 EC Directive on packaging; and the provision of financial assistance to charities and others involved in recycling activities. Perhaps the greatest overall impact of GLC abolition is in terms of direct democratic control over the available options for long-term waste management. In the absence of a regional Waste Disposal Authority with a sufficiently large budget, the London WDAs can only afford to embark on major capital intensive projects such as new incineration plants, composting plants or refuse derived fuel plants, by relying on either central government (which can be ruled out in present circumstances) or the private sector.

The interviews in the London Boroughs revealed that the case for the re-establishment of a strategic authority for waste management in London rested on a wide range of different concerns: the on-going need for a combination of strategic transport and land use planning[10]; the construction of a new rail link to facilitate the transport of waste from south London to available landfill sites north of the Thames, which could not be carried out with the current radial system of rail connections[11]; and the minimisation of waste flows through the co-ordination of transfer facilities to reduce transport costs[12]. A number of specific advantages for recycling were also identified: the dissemination of relevant information to all boroughs and the avoidance of unnecessary duplication and effort on the part of officers in policy analysis and production of publicity material[13]; the effective development of London wide collections, for materials such as plastics, for which it was difficult for individual Waste Collection Authorities to achieve economies of scale[14]; and the introduction of loss making collection schemes on purely environmental grounds for CFCs, putrescibles and other materials, not adequately handled in the private or voluntary sectors[15].

The introduction of competitive tendering for waste collection

The political challenge to municipal waste collection

In Chapter Two the political challenge to municipal waste management and its links to the wider agenda of reducing public expenditure on local government services was introduced. With the 1978-79 'winter of discontent', and piles of uncollected refuse in the streets, a spotlight was thrown on the problems of managing refuse collection by local authority DSOs (Direct Services Organisations) and there is evidence of a long history of labour relations problems in waste collection for some local authorities (Clisham, 1969; GLC, 1971). The problems with labour practices such as bonus schemes which reduce productivity can be traced to the 1960s, when there were serious labour shortages for the collection of waste during periods of full employment. The existence of low productivity and high costs in waste collection can therefore be related to the difficulties of retaining staff, in what has for many years been regarded as an unpleasant form of employment with low status within the public sector (Roberts, 1965).

In a 1984 study, the Audit Commission found that waste collection in England and Wales was costing in excess of £500 million a year, making it one of the most expensive local government services, despite substantial improvements in productivity of 15 per cent since 1978. They found, however, that there were wide variations in the cost of waste collection between very similar local authorities in terms of geography and collection methods. The Audit Commission found that waste collection was some 17 per cent more expensive than expected in the London Boroughs, on the basis of the ROSS (Refuse Operations Systems Simulation) used to estimate expected costs in different local authorities. They estimated that savings in the order of £50 million were achievable in England and Wales by further improvements in labour and vehicle productivity (Audit Commission, 1984). A report commissioned by the Department of the Environment in 1981 singled out the London Borough of Islington as an example of a local authority faced by gross waste collection costs of £28.44p per tonne in 1978-79 and reliant on a 'task and finish' system of waste collection:

'Task and finish' is a system of collection entailing variable hours of work by the manual workers employed. As soon as the 'task' (i.e. the collection round) is complete the employees are free to leave. This can be as early as mid-day, resulting in some employees working for only 25-30 hours per week. It is common for such employees to hold other part-time jobs (not with the authority), so that there is resistance to changing the system to one where standard days are worked. (Coopers and Lybrand, 1981 p. 55).

The Audit Commission recommended that cost savings could be achieved by a variety of measures: the elimination of existing time standards, such as 'task and finish' practices and ineffective bonus schemes, constituting up to 30 per cent of labour costs); changing vehicle and crew levels; changing collection methods for faster and easier collection of dustbins from households; improving vehicle utilisation rates and maintenance; and the introduction of competitive tendering for refuse collection. In the early

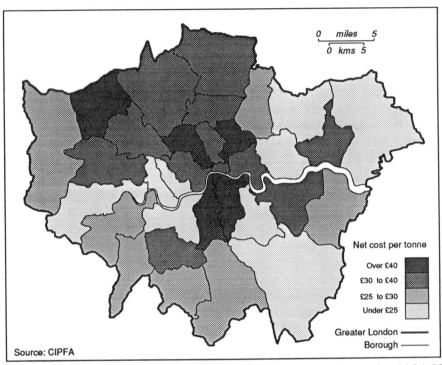

Figure 5.2: The cost of waste collection in the London Boroughs 1984-85

1980s, competitive tendering began to emerge as something of a panacea to the New Right and there was increasing interest in extending the role of the private sector into waste collection, based on the comparative experience of refuse collection in Europe and especially the US (DoE, 1981; Savas 1979). Competitive tendering enabled a reduction in local government expenditure; a diminution in the entrenched role of public sector unions, which had become so unpopular during the 1970s; and an opportunity to increase the role of the private sector (Coopers and Lybrand, 1981; Forsyth, 1980; Green, 1987; Walsh, 1989). With the 1980 Local Government Planning and Land Act, compulsory competitive tendering (CCT) was introduced for building works and highways maintenance and there was evidence that tendering resulted in savings of 20 per cent or more in contract prices, irrespective of whether work had been won by the private sector or by the authorities' own workforce (Audit Commission, 1989). All local authorities which had put refuse out to tender voluntarily during the 1980s had experienced cost savings (Audit Commission, 1984; 1989).

In summary, the political challenge to municipal waste collection since the early 1980s can be traced within the general development of conflict between central and local government. Waste collection proved especially vulnerable to these changes because there was already a well established private sector role in waste collection; the work itself is not complex; and waste collection has emerged as a financial burden for local authorities (Walsh, 1989). With the enactment of the 1988 Local Government Act, central government sought to radically restructure waste collection in order to reduce the operational role of the public sector in waste management, as part of its wider political and economic agenda for UK local government.

The introduction of compulsory competitive tendering

Under the 1988 Local Government Act, compulsory competitive tendering was extended to a range of local government services including catering, leisure management and waste collection for the first time, releasing £30 billion of potential business to the private sector, should they win the contracts (Evans, 1991). This has forced the London Boroughs to adopt a client-side role in the provision of services and a complete overhaul in managerial practice (Jackson and Robson, 1990). The result is a growing split within the structure of local authorities between their client side and operational side, composed of either a local authority DSO; an outside contractor from the private sector; or a management buy-out, as illustrated in Figure 5.1. The private sector has tendered successfully for a growing number of refuse collection and street cleansing contracts, and many European companies are trying to get a foothold on the lucrative and long-term market in municipal service provision in the capital.

In Westminster, for example, following a management buy-out, all waste collection and street cleansing responsibilities passed to MRS Environmental Services Ltd in February 1989 as a £12 million a year contract with 756 staff redundancies in the largest contracting out yet undertaken in the UK at the time[16]. However, there has been disquiet over public sector professionals using their privileged knowledge of the market in order to command private sector salaries through the creation of management buy-outs for local government services, since they owe their position to expertise derived from publicly funded salaries, training, and research trips (Miller, 1990). The client/contractor split within local government is also reflected in a growing polarisation within the workforce between the increasing proportion of white collar workers and the decreasing proportion of indirectly employed routine manual staff, with poorer pay and conditions (Walsh, 1989) and it is these demoralised manual workers who would be the key labour force for any comprehensive kerbside schemes or dual bin systems for recycling in London. In some London Boroughs the manual workers not re-employed after the new waste collection arrangements have tried to find their own niche within waste management, an example being the NUPE Ex-Dustmen's Co-op tendering for totting rights at the Feathers Wharf civic amenity site in Wandsworth in the early 1980s[17].

Nowhere has the implementation of CCT in waste collection been more complex than in the Borough of Tower Hamlets, which following the election of a new Liberal Democrat administration in May 1986, split into seven separate neighbourhoods. Waste collection was one of the last services to be decentralised in August 1989, with waste disposal operations continuing to be run centrally from the Northumberland Wharf river transfer station. The CCT contracts for Tower Hamlets were awarded on the basis of three spatial groupings, based on Bethnal Green; Bow; and the other five smaller neighbourhoods, linked together as a single entity. The contracts were offered as a threefold functional package covering street cleansing; market cleansing and refuse collection. In the event, the contracts for Bow and the grouping of five neighbourhoods, were won by their own DSOs, but in Bethnal Green, the contract went to the Anglo-French Cory Onyx (which has also won contracts in Bromley and Camden), creating dismay within the DSO workforce's union NUPE[18]. In 1990 Cory Onyx split into two companies, Cory Environmental now collecting waste for Bromley and Bethnal Green, and Onyx UK with waste collection contracts for the Corporation of London, Brent and Camden. Onyx UK is a wholly owned subsidiary of Compagnie Generale d'Enterprises Automobiles, a branch of Compagnie Generale des Eaux (CGE), Frances's fifth largest company. The European companies have a number of identifiable advantages for tendering in the UK: they have established experience in tendering for contracts; they have financial backing from larger parent companies taking a longer term view than their UK competitors; and they have built up a high degree of technical expertise in the field of municipal services, in not only waste management but also areas as diverse as water, energy, leisure management, homes for the elderly and mortuaries (*The Economist*, 14th October, 1989; Evans, 1991).

Most of the London Boroughs considered that the introduction of CCT would have a mixed impact on waste collection and recycling activities. On the question of cost reduction in waste collection, the evaluation of the cheapest option was argued to be a complex question involving consideration of a range of wider ostensibly non-economic factors, not examined in the ROSS (Refuse Operation Systems Simulation) procedure used by the Audit Commission: the costs of waste storage and sharing of facilities[19]; the potential cost of staff redundancies[20]; the health and safety of the workforce[21]; the potential increase in bureaucratic complexity on the client side[22]; and the limits to the implementation of kerbside recycling schemes or the collection of difficult materials such as plastics and toxic household waste. It was widely held that the immediate impact of CCT on recycling would depend on the extent of environmental criteria included in the tender specifications, the cost of which could potentially affect the basic purpose of CCT in ensuring lower expenditure by local authorities. For example, loss-making collection schemes would not be attempted under CCT, wherever the primary concern on the client side, was the fiduciary responsibilities to the community charge and rate payers.

In summary, the process of competitive tendering is changing the policy context for waste collection by accelerating a number of organisational and technical developments. It is altering the relationship between the different agencies involved in the provision of services, and has important implications for the manner in which policies are developed and implemented. Its significance for recycling is somewhat paradoxical, since it has introduced the possibility for change in waste collection but simultaneously increased the pressure to reduce costs. Its impact on policy is arguably a narrowing of the terms of reference to criteria of economic efficiency and also a diminution in the legitimate scope of public policy, as the planning for operational aspects of waste collection is increasingly handled by large private sector companies on a profit basis:

> The competitive tendering principle, which now drives local government, is based on the assumption that the public are consumers only. Their sole legitimate interest is in the quality and price of services. They are not supposed to have any stake in those services, or any control over how they are provided, who is employed, or on what terms. (Miller, 1990 p. 21).

The 1990 Environmental Protection Act

The 1990 Environmental Protection Act is the most important piece of environmental legislation that has been passed in the UK since the 1974 Control of Pollution Act, and was the result of pressure from diverse sources, including the Royal Commission on Environmental Pollution, the European Community, the environmental lobby, industry, and public concern[23]. The Environmental Protection Act will, according to the former Secretary of State for the Environment, Chris Patten, 'set out the environmental agenda for the rest of this century' (quoted in the *WARMER Bulletin*, August 1990 p. 12).

However, the EPA as it finally emerged has been widely criticised within the environmental movement as a belated response to new EC directives and the critical reports of the Environment Select Committee of the House of Commons and there are doubts whether the HMIP and other bodies have adequate staff and resources to enforce it effectively[24].

It is important to note that other aspects of the EPA ostensibly not aimed at recycling may also have an impact on the overall resources available for waste management. A small but politically significant fraction of the municipal waste stream is derived from street cleansing. This aspect of local authority cleansing responsibilities will be affected by new measures under Section Four of EPA to tackle the problem of litter, which has been shown to be a serious nuisance in inner London by a number of studies (Breckon, 1990; Hillman, 1989). Under Section Four of the Environmental Protection Act a new system of street zoning and fines will be introduced to tackle litter. The consequences of this new system, if fully implemented, will be to substantially increase the costs of street cleansing by 60 to 100 per cent on some estimates[25] (AMA, 1991a). If there is no overall increase in the local authority cleansing budget, there could be a diversion of resources away from recycling as a form of 'zero-sum environmental policy'[26]. A further effect might be the reluctance to use more on-street collection facilities because of their local impact on litter and fly-tipping. It is conceivable, therefore, that the Environmental Protection Act will have a greater impact on litter than on recycling, and that the measures to control litter could indirectly affect recycling to a greater extent than the parts of the legislation specifically intended to encourage recycling[27].

Part 2 of EPA covering waste management, will replace part 1 (sections 12-14) of the 1974 Control of Pollution Act, which has yet to be fully implemented because of lack of resources[28]. The waste management legislation includes nine main elements: the formation of 'arms length' Local Authority Waste Disposal Companies (LAWDCs) from the operational aspects of Waste Disposal Authorities; a new *Duty of Care* from waste production to final disposal, thereby reinforcing the trend towards higher costs for waste management, which will apply to 800,000 businesses in the UK; improvements to the waste management licensing system; new powers over receptacles for waste collection; the production of recycling plans by Waste Collection Authorities; modifications to the production of waste disposal plans; the introduction of recycling credits; and the clarification of the recycling powers of Waste Collection Authorities and Waste Disposal Authorities.

As a result of the Environmental Protection Act, recycling has been given statutory recognition as a potential alternative means of waste disposal.

Under Section 46, powers are given to Waste Collection Authorities to require householders to separate waste and place it in separate containers or compartments and under Section 49 the Waste Collection Authorities are obliged to set out in their recycling plans how they intend to reach the Government's stated target of 25 per cent recycling for household waste by the year 2,000. The key question of interest here is whether the different measures included in this legislation will have a positive or negative impact on the prospects for raising levels of recycling in London. In the next sections, three specific elements in the legislation of potential significance for recycling are examined: the extension of the principles of CCT to the disposal of waste with the formation of LAWDCs; the introduction of mandatory recycling credits, as a formal extension of the practice of granting waste disposal rebates; and the new obligation on Waste Collection Authorities to produce recycling plans.

The formation of Local Authority Waste Disposal Companies

The origin of the formation of LAWDCs (Local Authority Waste Disposal Companies) can be traced to the early 1980s debate over the use of compulsory competitive tendering to extend the private sector role in waste management to not only the collection but also the disposal of waste. A study commissioned by the DoE in 1981, concluded that the costs of municipal waste management could be significantly reduced by the forming of joint venture companies to handle all or part of the waste disposal functions of local government. In particular it was suggested that the greatest cost savings might be achieved by contracting out both waste collection and waste disposal simultaneously to the same contractor (Coopers and Lybrand, 1981). Though the rationale for reducing the public sector role in waste disposal was being clearly established by central government, there remained a number of uncertainties over whether the private sector had the capacity to take on a major operational role in waste management, particularly for large urban areas. It was also recognised that waste disposal could not be fully privatised because of the regulatory and licensing aspects of waste management, so that attention was focused on the operational alternatives for service delivery. In January 1989 the Government produced a White Paper entitled *The Role and Function of Waste Disposal Authorities*, as the result of a wide-ranging review of waste management policy in England and Wales, initiated by the then Secretary of State for the Environment, Nicholas Ridley, in September 1986. The White Paper argued that local authorities should be divested of their operational role on the premise that the dual operational and regulatory role of local authorities was not in the best interests of high environmental standards.

These proposals were incorporated into Part 2 of the 1990 Environmental Protection Act, by placing the operational aspects of Waste Disposal Authorities into an 'arms length' local authority waste disposal company, called a LAWDC. However, the legislation failed to take into account the different structure of waste management in London, where the regulatory and operational functions were already separated between the LWRA and the sixteen WDAs, following the abolition of the GLC in 1986, since the separation of the operational and regulatory sides of waste disposal is clearly aimed at County Councils currently performing both functions[29]. As a result of this legislation, the four statutory WDAs in London will be abolished in their current form and the operational side of their activities will form 'arms length' Local Authority Waste Disposal Companies (LAWDCs), whose shareholders will be the constituent boroughs[30]. The WDAs will remain as a purely client side organisation, seeking tenders from the newly formed LAWDCs in competition with private sector waste disposal companies, for not only the disposal of waste but also other operational activities including the running of civic amenity sites and waste transfer stations. The opposition to the formation of LAWDCs has been particularly strong in the four statutory Waste Disposal Authorities. The new LAWDCs structure, as 'arms length' local authority companies, was set out in Part Five of the 1989 Local Government and Housing Act, placing waste disposal expenditure by LAWDCs in competition with spending on other areas such as education and social services:

> Any capital which is borrowed by the LAWDC will be treated as if it is capital borrowed by the local authority for capital spending and will, consequently, be subject to current restrictions as set out in the Local Government and Housing Act 1989. (Lambert and Laurence, 1990 p. 199).

For Lambert and Laurence, the creation of LAWDCs is either a form of 'back door' privatisation for waste disposal or a result of a fundamental misconception on the part of government, since the structure of the LAWDCs will make it impossible for them to raise the necessary capital in order to improve facilities and raise environmental standards. The structure of LAWDCs will render them at a competitive disadvantage in relation to larger private sector waste disposal companies with greater resources available. Not surprisingly, the private sector waste disposal industry represented through the National Association of Waste Disposal Contractors (NAWDC) has welcomed the formation of LAWDCs (Wakeford, 1990).

Following the formation of LAWDCs the running of transfer stations may be problematic, since some 50 public sector stations will be in competition with over 100 licensed private sector transfer facilities in the London area. Most of London's public sector transfer stations are complex capital intensive stations, built or upgraded by the GLC to improve standards in the handling of municipal waste. These stations are expensive to operate and maintain, and have little capacity for private sector wastes from construction and other sources. In contrast, the private sector transfer stations in London, with the exception of a few joint GLC-private sector ventures, were established around the skip industry and are designed to handle a mixture of wastes as cheaply as possible. Few feature dust extraction and sealed containers for transport, and many are simply open air operations. As licensed transfer stations they can operate much more cheaply than their competitors in the public sector. If existing public sector sites remain significantly more expensive than legal private sites working to lower standards, then it is conceivable that WDAs under financial stress will choose the cheaper option. The level of standards in waste regulation would affect the prospects for WDAs or LAWDCs to invest in environmentally sound capital projects in the face of legal competition from environmentally inferior alternatives. As a result of these concerns, some WDAs have argued for the need for higher standards to be imposed by the already under-staffed London Waste Regulation Authority for the operation and design of all private sector waste disposal facilities. This could be undertaken by restrictions on new sites and progressive upgrading of existing licenses to enable fair competition between the public and the private sector, and also prevent decline in standards for the handling of municipal waste as a result of the 1990 Environmental Protection Act. The key issue here is who will pay for the new investment in waste transfer facilities and how the more effective regulatory regime will be financed to ensure that improvements are made.

Eleven boroughs expressed concern over the potential loss of local authority control of civic amenity sites and recycling centres, when these are put out to tender. This is understandable, since for many London Boroughs, the civic amenity sites form a major focus of recycling activities and also provide a source of income to local authorities from the sale of materials such as valuable scrap metals[31]. It seems probable that the better equipped and better run civic amenity sites, which gain more income from the sales of materials, will be especially susceptible to outside tendering bids. This places local authorities in a dilemma, since if they spend money to develop good civic amenity sites with new plant and equipment and then lose control of the site, they will still have to pay for the disposal of materials collected there, but without any income from the sale of materials[32]. The prospects for civic amenity sites and recycling centres may be especially poor in inner London for two main reasons. Firstly, many inner London sites handle larger proportions of low value commodities such as paper, the value of which is less than their notional savings in waste disposal. These would no longer apply if a waste disposal company was running both civic amenity sites and waste disposal[33]. Secondly, it is difficult to conceive how civic amenity type services with a low rate of return could survive in the face of high land values, and private sector pressures for other land uses with a higher rate of return[34].

In summary, it is likely that the introduction of competitive tendering in waste disposal will be far more complex and uncertain in outcome, than for waste collection. Indeed, the creation of LAWDCs can be viewed as simply a phased privatisation of waste management in the UK, as the LAWDCs are displaced by larger competitors in the private sector. These concerns are borne out by more recent evidence, suggesting that many UK local authorities are not forming LAWDCs, but are simply selling off their assets to the private sector amid continuing confusion over the arrangements for capital investment (Financial Times Survey, 1991b). This is the case in the voluntary South West London Waste Disposal Group, where the boroughs of Bromley, Croydon, Kingston, Merton and Sutton have opted simply for the privatisation option, and will not be setting up a LAWDC. This is also the case with Southwark, formerly within the South East London Waste Disposal Group. The public sector is likely to retain its regulatory role (though in an uncertain form) but the decline of the operational role of the public sector will have important effects on a range of recycling and waste management activities currently undertaken by local authorities, such as the operation of civic amenity sites, recycling centres and transfer stations.

Credits, rebates and market-based recycling policy

It is of particular interest that the level of waste disposal rebate, the key element in the Government's market-based strategy to raise levels of recycling, is not a key factor determining levels of recycling in London, as discussed in the last chapter. The use of rebates began under the GLC in 1971 and involves the payment of money from Waste Disposal Authorities (the GLC in the period 1965 to 1986) to Waste Collection Authorities (the London Boroughs) in recognition of financial savings stemming from the removal of recyclable materials from the waste stream. However, doubt over the efficacy of rebates is provided by the historical evidence of the decline in local authority waste paper collections in the 1970s despite the introduction of a rebate in 1971 (GLC, 1975d). The decline in waste paper recycling through local authority collections in the 1970s was a result of associated labour costs and a deteriorating secondary materials market for low grade paper, irrespective of the operation of a rebate.

In the case of London, the level of rebates in the late 1980s varied from nil in the seven boroughs under the North London Waste Authority to £30 in the borough of Merton within the voluntary South West London Waste Disposal Group, where this high figure represented the direct equivalent of gross waste disposal costs and assumed that the removal of materials from the waste stream involves no net costs but only financial savings. In the period since the formation of the statutory and voluntary WDAs for London in 1986, not only the quantity but also the range of materials recycled has increased. In the West London Waste Authority (WLWA), for example, the rebates to its seven constituent Waste Collection Authorities have been extended to not only glass, paper and cans, but also scrap metals, and have been paid out retrospectively back to its year of creation in 1986. However, waste oil has been excluded from the rebate, because the WLWA have argued that oil brought to civic amenity sites would normally be put into the sewerage system and therefore never enters the municipal waste stream. Consequently, the WLWA has argued that it is under no obligation to recognise disposal savings from oil by its constituent Waste Collection Authorities[35]. The exclusion of waste oil from rebates raises important difficulties in terms of the practical application of the 'polluter pays principle' and the internalising of environmental costs in waste management, where solid waste management is administratively separate from water supply and the sewerage system.

The market-based approach to raise levels of recycling is focused on the need to internalise the full range of environmental externalities associated with the costs of alternative means of waste disposal. The focus of contemporary market-based policy has been on the internalisation of the costs of waste disposal through the UK government's mandatory introduction of recycling credits under the 1990 Environmental Protection Act replacing the existing voluntary system of rebates recognised under the 1974 Control of Pollution Act:

> Market forces are the best way to deliver a sustainable approach for waste and recycling for the long term...Recycling credits are payments by local authorities to those who collect materials for recycling...The credits will provide a market incentive to recycle waste. (DoE, 1991c p. 149).

It is claimed that the current trend towards increasing waste disposal costs operates as an economic incentive to recycle in the sense that low landfill costs have previously acted as a disincentive to expand recycling. This argument is now often found within a wide spectrum of environmentalist literature and by mainstream policy makers, where it is assumed that recycling will prove progressively more attractive as improved environmental standards in waste management force up the cost of waste disposal. The Government's main strategy for increased recycling is echoed by the analysis of the prospects for recycling by R.Kerry Turner, a leading advocate of the use of MBIs in waste management, who argues that the extent of recycling will rise as a consequence of the rising costs of landfill in response to the implementation of higher environmental standards within the EC legislative framework:

> Legislative pressure at the EC level will reinforce the cost escalation trend for land-based disposal...The cost rise, reflecting the true social costs of waste disposal, will have important positive ramifications for waste minimisation and waste recycling...Current disposal options are under-priced by the market and government intervention is required to correct for market failure. (Turner, 1990 p. 4-12).

Turner's assumptions over the relationship between rising landfill costs and higher levels of recycling are flawed on three grounds. Firstly, the experience of London both in the 1980s and earlier suggests that rebates and credits to reflect waste disposal savings are not a very effective policy tool for raising levels of recycling. Secondly, there has been an overemphasis on 'market failure' in the costs of waste disposal to the relative exclusion of an examination of other potential sources of market failure, such as the virgin raw materials market. Finally, the cost of high levels of materials recycling is systematically underestimated in relation to more profitable alternatives such as the generation of electricity from landfill gas and municipal waste incineration, described later in this chapter. The results of the survey of perceived obstacles to recycling shown in Table 4.9 suggest that contrary to the assumptions of market-based recycling strategies, the low cost of waste disposal by landfill is seen as one of the least important factors in hindering the expansion of recycling, yet the literature has consistently underestimated the cost of comprehensive recycling programmes in relation to either landfill or incineration, even after tighter environmental regulations have been introduced.

There is also the problem of who should pay the credits or rebates, and whether the money should be derived from the community via rates or charges, or from the original producers of waste in the packaging sector and other industries (Flood, 1991a). In other words, rebates and credits could be conceived as simply an 'end of pipe' attempt to introduce the 'polluter pays principle' into waste management. For some commentators (see Cooper, 1990a), the role of credits and rebates has been overemphasised, because the money is simply circulating between local authorities, and may not even enter recycling budgets or lower community charge or council tax bills as a form of incentive. The survey of the London Boroughs supported this position, since the income derived from recycling activities was passed back into the recycling budget in only six cases in the year 1989-90 and there was no identifiable relationship between the presence and level of rebates and the recycling rates in the London Boroughs, as indicated in Table 4.5. The evidence in London suggests that the use of rebates or credits both now and in the past has been a relatively ineffectual policy tool in comparison with the need to strengthen the secondary materials market and fund the provision and operation of recycling facilities. It is of interest that the non market-based economic instrument represented by the introduction of the Non Fossil Fuel Obligation (NFFO) subsidy for non fossil-fuel sources of electricity is already having a much more significant role in waste management than rebates have ever had, and the impact is not leading to higher levels of materials recycling but towards increased energy recovery from waste, as discussed in the next chapter. In Hamburg, the issue of rebates did not arise, because the same tier of local government is responsible for both the collection and disposal of waste, and any savings in the costs of waste management accrue directly to one overall budget for waste management (though the evidence from Hamburg suggests that recycling seldom if ever saves money anyway). This suggests that the issue of rebates is simply an anomaly arising out of the administrative separation of waste collection and disposal. This is borne out by the fact that the legislation on recycling credits will not apply to Scotland and Wales, where the same tier of local government carries out both the collection and disposal of waste.

The introduction of recycling plans

It was established in the last chapter, that the key underlying factors affecting levels of recycling lie largely outside local authority control. It is not surprising, therefore, that the main criticism levelled at the production of plans by the London Boroughs was that these would be increasingly irrelevant as the operational aspects of waste management are progressively removed from local authority control as a result of the formation of LAWDCs and the process of demunicipalisation. A recent SERPLAN report has indicated that privately run civic amenity sites would lead to a loss of data, particularly for valuable tottable items for which there is already an extensive black market (SERPLAN, 1988c). In future, the already incomplete official CIPFA statistics on waste disposal will have to come either from the LAWDCs or the private sector, yet there is the argument that data could only be improved by putting both the collection and the disposal of waste under a single authority, as was suggested as a reform of the GLC Public Health Engineering Department in the early 1980s (Townend, 1982).

The impetus of current trends in the administrative framework for waste management is likely to increase the complexity of data gathering and co-ordination between different local authorities, particularly as the operational aspects of waste management are increasingly handled in a multiplicity of private sector companies. A further development is the Government's proposal to create a National Environment Agency which would remove local authorities from the role of waste regulation coupled with uncertainty over the possible replacement of counties and districts with new unitary authorities. The reason for the proposed abolition of the LWRA and the regulatory functions of the County Councils appears to rest on their lack of qualified staff and expertise coupled with doubts over the implementation of national standards:

> As the standards and techniques of waste management become increasingly sophisticated, it is becoming more difficult for individual waste regulation authorities either to provide the necessary expertise, or to co-ordinate policies and standards over a wide enough area. (DoE, 1991d para. 14).

In the absence of the statutory WDAs and the LWRA, the prospects for the planning and co-ordination of recycling policy in London would seem to become more remote, in spite of the new responsibilities for the production of recycling plans. Indeed, London wide data availability for municipal waste management is probably worse now than at any time since the early 1960s, with no detailed data available on the composition of the waste stream in individual boroughs and a lack of analysis of different policy options.

Recycling policy at a national level

A basic criticism to emerge of the Environmental Protection Act, is that there is still no coherent policy for recycling and waste management at a national level, addressing the full range of barriers to higher levels of materials recycling. Indeed, Table 4.9 shows that the need for a coherent national waste management and recycling policy, was identified by twenty one boroughs as necessary for increasing levels of recycling. Yet the concept of a national waste management policy or plan has been explicitly rejected by the Government. For example, the junior Environment Minister, Lord Hesketh, in replying to the Lords debate calling for a national environmental waste policy, stated that waste policy must be market-based and that waste minimisation and recycling had to succeed on the basis of economic viability, effectively precluding anything but the use of on-street collection facilities for London:

> What the waste disposal industry and the country do not need is anything like a national plan for waste disposal, which might attempt to specify what should happen to which sort of waste and where...It is the Government's job to set the standard and for the local authorities to enforce it, but within that regulatory regime it should be perfectly possible for the market to determine the answer for particular wastes...We do not want to lower the cost of recycling by subsidy. Undeserved subsidies are not a long-term solution to encouraging environmentally friendly routes. (Lord Hesketh, *Hansard*, 10th May 1990)

A number of developments since the passage of the EPA, suggest that the Government has begun to modify earlier resistance to any national level state involvement in recycling policy. Examples include the promotion of a voluntary 'green levy' on tyre producers; pressure on newspaper publishers to raise the level of recycled fibre usage to 40 per cent by the year 2,000; and the setting up of a new Advisory Committee on Business and the Environment to investigate the creation of markets for recycled products (DoE, 1991c). A further development was the announcement in the 1990 Autumn Statement that some £40 million 'supplementary credit' approvals for local government in the period up to 1994 would be made available as an extra borrowing allowance within their Basic Credit Approval, and 17 boroughs along with the NLWA benefited from this extra capital investment in the year 1991-92. In a sense, this drift towards some form of financial assistance and limited intervention brings national recycling policy back full circle, to where it was in 1974 with the publication of the *War on Waste* Green Paper and the first tentative attempts to build a national recycling and waste management strategy described in Chapter Three.

Emerging trends in London's waste management

In this section the main trends in waste management for London are examined, and a number of the themes and issues identified in previous sections are brought together. Evidence of a shift towards energy rather than materials recovery is presented as the outcome of the demunicipalisation of waste management and the reliance on market-based policy instruments focused on the internalisation of the costs of waste disposal.

The future of landfill

Some of the Waste Disposal Authorities and larger private sector waste management companies have their own landfill sites which they will continue to use for at least another ten years. Landfill is, therefore, likely to remain the dominant form of waste disposal at least until the year 2,000 and the end of current contractual arrangements. The main strategic policy forum for waste management in London, the South East Regional Planning Conference, has produced four reports on waste since the abolition of the GLC. The main findings of these reports are that there will be a generalised shortage of landfill space in the South East before the year 2,000 (SERPLAN, 1987; 1988a; 1988b; 1988c). SERPLAN estimate that eight counties in the South East will be facing a shortfall of landfill space for all wastes by, or shortly after the year 2,000: Berkshire, East Sussex, Essex, the Greater London area, Hampshire, Isle of Wight, Kent and Surrey[36]. However, for household waste it is predicted that in the year 2,000, nearly half the region may be facing a shortage of landfill space; another third will have nearly exhausted available space; and the only significant volumes of landfill space will be in the outer north-west part of the region, principally in Bedfordshire, Buckinghamshire and Oxfordshire, as shown in Table 5.1 and the current pattern of landfill destinations will change, with less quantities of waste disposed of in Essex, Kent, Hertfordshire and Bedfordshire.

In addition to the predicted future shortages of landfill, there have been a number of operational and technical changes in the use of landfill for waste disposal. For technical control reasons, in order to raise environmental standards, there is a trend towards larger landfill sites. As a consequence, these sites are being operated by fewer and larger private contractors, with a gradual diminution of the direct operational activities of the Waste Disposal Authorities. In this respect, the formation of LAWDCs in the Environmental Protection Act will accelerate this trend already underway in waste management (Financial Times Survey, 1991).

One development is the systematic extraction of landfill gas as a fuel

Table 5.1: Remaining landfill capacity in the South East by the year 2,000

	All Waste, Types A,B & C	Type C Waste
Bedfordshire	25.9 %	19.0 %
Berkshire	9.2 %	0.0 %
Buckinghamshire	17.9 %	11.9 %
Essex	0.0 %	0.0 %
Greater London	11.9 %	0.0 %
Hampshire	4.9 %	0.0 %
Hertfordshire	0.0 %	0.1 %
Isle of Wight	0.0 %	0.0 %
Kent	19.4 %	0.0 %
Oxfordshire	28.9 %	2.6 %
Surrey	18.9 %	0.0 %
Sussex	0.0 %	0.0 %

Source: SERPLAN (1988b)

source from landfill sites, now integral to the Government's market-led strategy to raise the proportion of electricity generated from non fossil-fuel sources to 24 per cent by the year 2025 (DoE, 1990b; Thomas, 1990b). Energy production from landfill gas has been carried out since 1982 at the former GLC Aveley landfill site in Essex, which is now operated by the East London Waste Authority. Aveley Methane Ltd, a joint venture between ELWA and Coal Products Ltd., sells fuel gas to Thames Board Ltd at Purfleet for use in the production of steam in paper making[37] (ELWA, 1989b; GLC, 1983a). The trend towards landfill gas extraction from the larger landfill sites serving London, appears to be continuing. In the summer of 1990, Cory Environmental Ltd announced that it would be generating 3.7 MW of electricity from late 1991 at its vast landfill site at Mucking, Essex, and has signed a deal with Eastern Electricity (*WARMER Bulletin*, August 1991). In the UK as a whole, the extraction of landfill gas has increased steadily during the 1980s, for a number of reasons: the larger landfill sites in use in the 1980s have improved the economics of bio-gas recovery: the higher cost of landfill has encouraged operators to control pollution profitably; the design and engineering of new landfill sites is facilitating the recovery of gas; following electricity privatisation, the Non Fossil Fuel Obligation (NFFO) was introduced in 1990, which instituted a levy on fossil sources, thereby improving the financial viability of renewable and non-fossil sources; and there is the potential to integrate gas recovery into schemes for the anaerobic fermentation of putrescible waste and the recycling of sewage sludge, which may expand following the privatisation of water and the stricter controls on dumping of sewage at sea following the 1990 Conference on the North Sea and new EC directives (*WARMER Bulletin*, August 1991).

It can be concluded that the landfill of London's waste is set to remain both environmentally and economically competitive with other forms of waste disposal for some years. As a result of the Environmental Protection Act and the privatisation of electricity, the operational and advanced technical aspects such as the extraction of landfill gas will be increasingly handled in large private sector concerns specialising in waste management and the provision of other municipal services. The critical long-term issue is what will happen to waste management in London after many of the current landfill sites are exhausted or too distant for economic use. The next section suggests that rather than an inevitable increase in efforts to recycle or reduce the waste stream, as is assumed in much of the literature, the most likely development will be an increase in the profitable burning of waste with electricity generation.

The re-emergence of incineration

The use of incineration as a waste disposal option in London is now re-emerging for the first time in over twenty years. This can be attributed to four main developments: the rising cost and future uncertainty of landfill, especially for inner and south London[38]; the improved profitability of the former GLC Edmonton incineration plant[39]; the arrangements for the privatisation of electricity in 1989, with the introduction of the NFFO subsidy for non fossil-fuel sources of energy; and finally, the price collapse in the waste paper market and other difficulties with materials recycling, forcing a re-evaluation of different recycling options[40]. In the 1970s, the cost of incineration was consistently seen as higher than other alternatives to landfill for London, such as the production of refuse derived fuel (see Bidwell and Mason, 1975; Gulley, 1979). The economic and technical problems with the GLC Edmonton incineration plant had acted as a disincentive to build new incineration plants in London[41], but the North London Waste Authority have experienced improved profitability at the Edmonton plant during the 1980s from the sale of electricity[42], as shown by Table 5.2. A recent paper compared the waste disposal costs at Edmonton of £12 per tonne with £25 per tonne for long distance rail transfer to landfill sites 50 miles outside London (Porteus, 1990), and this disparity has widened still further since the introduction of the NFFO levy. The Edmonton plant was also successfully modified during this period to comply with the EC emissions directive (89/369), which had threatened many other UK plants with closure (Holmes, 1989).

Table 5.2: Improved profitability of the Edmonton incineration plant

Year	Tonnes of refuse	Total Export MWh	Total Income
1977-78	420,000	187,692	£1,520,000
1980-81	399,000	184,053	£2,592,000
1986-87	364,560	148,858	£4,257,395
1987-88	388,162	157,748	£4,164,334
1988-89	344,159	144,744	£3,938,320

Source: WARMER Bulletin, January 1991

The privatisation of electricity has made it easier for new consortia to sell electricity to the national grid from non fossil-fuel sources. The potential economic viability of incineration plants has been enhanced by the introduction of the Non Fossil Fuel Obligation (NFFO) included in the electricity privatisation legislation, which will last until 1998 under agreement with the European Commission, though there has been lobbying of the EC by the Government to continue the levy for renewable energy after 1998 (Aubrey, 1992; Thomas, 1990b). Table 5.3 shows that in 1990, some 82 per cent of electricity generating capacity supported by the NFFO levy was made up of energy from waste schemes, including the Edmonton incineration plant. However, the underlying rationale of the NFFO is to subsidize the nuclear industry and some 98 per cent of the NFFO has been spent on nuclear energy and 2 per cent on renewables. This imbalance in financial support between nuclear energy and renewable sources has been criticised by a variety of different sources, including the Commons Select Committee on Energy, Friends of the Earth, the Conservative Bow Group, and the Association of Independent Electricity Producers (Sychrava, 1991).

The increased use of non fossil-fuel sources of energy from municipal waste has been identified by the Watt Committee on Energy as a key element in their proposed strategy to tackle global warming, consisting of energy conservation, afforestation, wind power, and the production of electricity from municipal waste incineration (Watt Committee on Energy, 1990).

Studies have suggested that the burning of 40 per cent of the UK municipal waste stream in incineration plants could result in the environmental impact of a reduced consumption of 65 million tonnes of coal equivalent from the production of heat and electricity, coupled with the reduced emissions of methane at landfill sites (Porteus, 1990). There is now a policy consensus forming for the use of energy from waste as a component of global warming policy. A pledge at the 1990 Labour conference was a commitment to meet the IPCC (Intergovernmental Panel on Climatic Change) target for a 60 per cent reduction in carbon emissions, and this was to be achieved by a variety of measures including the use of electricity generation from municipal waste (*Financial Times*, 4th October, 1990). Likewise, the Government's 1990 White Paper *This Common Inheritance* sets a target of 1,000 MW for renewables by the year 2,000, constituting around 2 per cent of total UK energy needs (DoE, 1990b).

Table 5.3: Projects supported by the renewables price levy

Form of energy	Number	Capacity (%)
Hydro power	26	11
Landfill gas and bio-gas	33	36
Waste incineration with energy recovery	7	46
Wind power	9	7

Source: Office of Electricity Regulation (1990)

The first incineration scheme to emerge for London has been put forward by the South East London Waste Disposal Group (SELWDG), involving the construction of a new incineration plant on derelict land in New Cross, in preference to long distance landfill. This will be the first incineration plant to be built in the UK since 1976, 'ushering in a new era in waste management'[43].

The project is managed by the South East London Combined Heat and Power Consortium (SELCHP) comprising AEP (Associated Energy Projects), the London Borough of Lewisham, the London Power Company (a subsidiary of London Electricity), the Laing Technology Group, and ISS Mainmet (*WARMER Bulletin*, February 1992). Its construction and operation will be in the private sector, and the plant will handle 400,000 tonnes of municipal waste a year when fully commissioned. The plant, as originally proposed in the GLC waste strategy of 1983, was designed to strike a balance between available funding and the possibilities for high environmental standards and enhanced technical flexibility in combining a DH (district heating) winter component for 10,000 homes in Southwark, with a summer focus on electricity generation for the national grid[44] (GLC, 1983d). However, the design emphasis of the £395 million plant has shifted to potential electricity sales to London Electricity in response to the NFFO levy (Flood, 1991b). Interestingly, the public announcement of the scheme met with little local opposition, and there has been support for the project from all political parties in Greenwich and Lewisham, though in Southwark, the administration chose to withdraw from the scheme in order to focus on recycling[45].

Other examples of incineration plants are at an earlier stage of planning and consultation. Both Merton and Sutton within the South West London Waste Disposal Committee (SWLWDG) have been approached by private consortia interested in building further incineration plants. A plant with a 500,000 tonne capacity has been submitted for planning approval by Capital Power & Waste Ltd, based on the conversion of the derelict Battersea Power Station within the catchment of the Western Riverside Waste Authority (*WARMER Bulletin*, August 1990). A further proposal has been put forward by the waste management firm Cory Environmental Ltd for an 80 MW to 100 MW plant in south east London at Belvedere in Bexley, which if constructed would be among the world's largest incineration plants and handle a third of London's municipal waste stream, equivalent to some 1 million tonnes a year (*The Financial Times*, August 6th 1990). Unlike the Deptford plant, the Belvedere proposal has met with opposition from Bexley council, which has called for a public inquiry into the public health (there are homes within 40 metres of the site) and traffic implications of the project. Concern has also been expressed over the plant's impact on business investment and other developments in the vicinity (*Planning*, 16th August 1991). The newly created private electricity utility National Power is currently investigating the feasibility of burning 10 per cent of the UK municipal waste stream. It is calculated that some 60 per cent of the income will be derived from waste disposal fees paid by local authorities and the remaining 40 per cent from sales of electricity (Brown, 1991). National power has now applied for planning permission to construct a major new incineration plant at Gravesend in Kent using waste from the South East London and Kent area[46]. The Royal Commission on Environmental Pollution has also endorsed incineration as the most environmentally acceptable approach to waste management it its report *Incineration of Waste* published in May 1993 (RCEP, 1993).

The development of incineration and energy from waste schemes in London serves as a refutation of simplistic arguments seeking to show that higher landfill costs will necessarily lead to higher levels of materials recycling. It seems clear that the waste disposal pattern of the late 1990s and beyond in London is likely to have a growing component of incineration, as suggested by Figure 5.3, particularly as landfill space is exhausted after the year 2000. In this respect the future path of waste management in London will begin to mirror more closely developments elsewhere in Europe, where there have been long established economic, political and environmental disincentives to rely on landfill.

Figure 5.3: The location of new incineration plants for municipal waste

Conclusion

The analysis of the changing political, economic and legislative context for recycling demonstrates that recycling cannot be understood separately from wider developments in waste management. I argue that the process of demunicipalisation in waste management is leading to policy being increasingly determined by the relative profitability of different options for the private sector waste management industry. This will favour energy recovery over materials recovery, principally through the generation of electricity from landfill gas and the incineration of municipal waste. In contrast, a recycling policy centred on materials recovery and waste reduction at source would require a national waste management policy, a better resourced and co-ordinated system of local government, and greater degrees of state intervention in production and consumption. This would involve greater strategic planning over waste management than was established under the GLC Public Health Engineering Department. This chapter has therefore reiterated the findings of the historical analysis, that the pattern of waste management in London is inseparable from the wider question of the role and function of local government.

In the next chapter the key themes and issues identified in London are taken further with a comparative case study based on the city of Hamburg. The economic and political aspects of recycling and waste management are examined in a city where there has been a greater politicisation of waste management than in London and a higher rate of materials recycling has been achieved.

Notes

1   Interview with the Recycling Development Officer for the London Borough of Camden, Mike Newport, 15th June 1990.

2   Interview with the Recycling Development Officer for the London Borough of Camden, Mike Newport, 15th June 1990.

3   Interview with the Cleansing Officer for the London Borough of Kensington and Chelsea, Moira Billinge, 16th May 1990.

4   Interview the Special Projects Officer for the London Borough of Newham, Peter Anderson, 16th May 1990.

5   Interview with the Waste Disposal Manager for the London Borough of Havering, Ralph Johnson, 13th June 1990.

6   Interview with the Waste Disposal Manager for the London Borough of Havering, Ralph Johnson, 13th June 1990.

7   Interview with the Recycling Development Officer for the London Borough of Camden, Mike Newport, 15th June 1990. Interview with the Principal Engineer (services) for the London Borough of Waltham Forest, Barry Higgs, 22nd May 1990.

8   Interview with the Environmental Development Manager, Peter Brooker, and the Cleansing Officer, David Masters, for the Globe Town Neighbourhood, London Borough of Tower Hamlets, 20th June 1990

9   Interview with the Environmental Operations Manager for the London Borough of Hillingdon, Bob Summers, 9th May 1990.

10   Interview with the Project Officer (Cleansing) for the City of Westminster, Ceasar Voûte, 15th May 1990.

11   Interview with the Waste Reduction Officer for the London Waste Regulation Authority, Jeff Cooper, 20th March 1991.

12   Interview with the Waste Planning Officer for the East London Waste Authority, Tom Butterfield, 13th June 1990.

13   Interview with the Recycling Development Officer for the London Borough of Camden, Mike Newport, 15th June 1990.

14   Interview with the Highways and Cleansing Manager for the London Borough of Barking and Dagenham, 7th June 1990. Interview with the Technical Services Officer for the London Borough of Hammersmith and Fulham, Terry Mirams, 7th June 1990.

15   Interview with the Recycling Development Officer for the London Borough of Camden, Mike Newport, 15th June 1990. Interview with the Senior Planner for   the London Borough of Sutton, Graham Dean, 10th January 1990.

16   Interview with the Project Officer (Cleansing) for the City of Westminster, Ceasar Voûte, 15th May 1990. *The Guardian*, 5th October 1988.

17   Letter to the Chair of the GLC Environmental Panel, May 12th 1983.

18   Interview with the Highways and Cleansing Officer for Bethnal Green Neighbourhood, London Borough of Tower Hamlets, Gery McCleary, 11th July 1990.

19   Interview with the Highways and Cleansing Manager for the London Borough of Barking and Dagenham, 7th June 1990.

20   Interview with the Cleansing Officer for Bow Neighbourhood, London Borough of Tower Hamlets, Gary King, 8th June 1990.

21   Interview with the Environmental Development Manager, Peter Brooker, and the Cleansing Officer, David Masters, for the Globe Town Neighbourhood, London Borough of Tower Hamlets, 20th June 1990

22   Interview with the Highways and Cleansing Officer for Bethnal Green Neighbourhood, London Borough of Tower Hamlets, Gery McCleary, 11th July 1990.

23   Personal communication with Cathy MacKenzie, Institution of Environmental Health Officers, 1990.

24   Personal communication with Steve Clark of the Land Wastes Division of the Department of the Environment, 1992.

25   Interview with the Cleansing Officer for Bow Neighbourhood, London Borough of Tower Hamlets, Gary King, 8th June 1990.

26   Interview with the Cleansing Officer for the London Borough of Lambeth, Bob King, 17th May 1990.

27   Interview with the Cleansing Officer for the London Borough of Southwark, Mr M. Vijay, 1st July 1990.

28   Interview with the Assistant Cleansing Manager for the London Borough of Enfield, Peter Joyce, 12th June 1990. Personal communication with Steve Clark of the Land Wastes Division of the Department of the Environment, 1992.

29   Interview with the Principal Engineer (Services) in the London Borough of Waltham Forest, Barry Higgs, 22nd May 1990.

30   Personal communication with Steve Clark of the Land Wastes Division of the Department of the Environment, 1992.

31   Interview with the Assistant Cleansing Manager for the London Borough of Enfield, Peter Joyce, 12th June 1990. Interview with the Principal Engineer (Services) in the London Borough of Waltham Forest, Barry Higgs, 22nd May 1990.

32   Interview with the Recycling Development Officer for the London Borough of Camden, Mike Newport, 15th June 1990.

33   Interview with the Recycling Development Officer for the London Borough of Camden, Mike Newport, 15th June 1990.

34   Interview with the Highways and Cleansing Officer for Bethnal Green Neighbourhood, London Borough of Tower Hamlets, Gery McCleary, 11th July 1990.

35   Interview with the Senior Assistant Manager for the West London Waste Authority, Ray Brown, 16th February 1990.

36 Waste can be categorised in terms of its environmental impact at landfill sites. Type A includes material for which the environmental impact of decomposition is less than, or comparable with that of topsoil (ash, clinker, glass). Type B includes material which may decompose slowly, but in its deposited form is only slightly soluble in water (plastics, textiles, metals). Type C includes material which may decompose rapidly and may contain soluble matter which could cause pollution if allowed to enter ground or surface water systems (putrescibles and paper) (ELWA, 1989).

37 Personal communication with the Aluminium Can Recycling Association, 1991.

38 Interview with the Assistant Cleansing Manager for the London Borough of Lewisham, Malcolm Kendall, 7th February 1990.

39 Interview with the Waste Reduction Officer for the London Waste Regulation Authority, Jeff Cooper, 20th March 1991.

40 Personal communication with Derek Bargh of GEC Alsthom, 1991.

41 Interview with the Environment Promotions Officer for the London Borough of Bromley, Simon Bussel, 18th May 1990.

42 Interview with the Waste Reduction Officer for the London Waste Regulation Authority, Jeff Cooper, 20th March 1991.

43 Interview with the Waste Reduction Officer for the London Waste Regulation Authority, Jeff Cooper, 20th March 1991.

44 Questionnaire survey return from the Head of Client Services in the London Borough of Greenwich, Bill Tombs, 1990. Interview the Assistant Cleansing Manager for the London Borough of Lewisham, Malcolm Kendall, 7th February 1990. Interview with the Cleansing Officer for the London Borough of Southwark Mr M. Vijay, 1st July 1990.

45 Interview with the Waste Reduction Officer for the London Waste Regulation Authority, Jeff Cooper, 28th September 1992.

46 Personal communication with Derek Bargh of GEC Alsthom, 1991.

6 The case of Hamburg

In this chapter, I present a comparative case study of the city of Hamburg, enabling a clarification of the underlying political and economic barriers to recycling under a market economy. The first theme of interest is the higher rate of recycling of 13 per cent achieved in Hamburg, in comparison with the 2 per cent average figure for the London Boroughs. This contrast is examined in terms of the impact of differences in the organisational structure of waste management and local government, the extent of available recycling facilities, and the degree of politicisation of waste management.

I argue that Hamburg is faced by a crisis in its waste management, leading to a conflict between two main policy positions. On the one hand, a focus on the need to control expenditure on waste management but respond adequately to public demands for recycling. On the other hand, an alternative environmentalist position seeking to maximise levels of recycling and waste reduction at source, coupled with a clear rejection of the growing private sector role in waste management, and the demunicipalisation process identified in London.

Government and policy making in Hamburg

The city of Hamburg lies on the mouth of the river Elbe in northern Germany and is the second largest city in the federal republic. In 1988 Hamburg had a population of some 1,576,000 and its population has begun to grow slightly, after a long period of decline since its peak of 1,850,000 in 1965 (Dangschat and Ossenbrügge, 1990). Administratively, the city has special status, as a federal *Land* in its own right, and is therefore represented in the powerful *Bundesrat* second chamber, as are the cities of Bremen and Berlin. Figure 6.1 shows that the city of Hamburg is sub-divided into 104 districts (*Stadtteile*) and seven *Bezirke*, similar in size but with a weaker service

Figure 6.1: The administrative boundaries for the city of Hamburg

Source: Hamburg City Planning Department

delivery role than the London Boroughs. Only the Bezirk Bergedorf and Harburg in the south of the city assume more wide ranging responsibilities for the provision of local government services, which is an historical anomaly arising from local government reorganisation in 1937 extending the city boundaries into more autonomous outlying areas (Hartwich, 1990).

In contrast to the unitary state structure of the UK, there is a federal system of 'decentralised centralisation' in Germany. The sixteen regional *Länder* (eleven before October 1990) enjoy very extensive powers under the Basic Law of 1949. According to Article 30 of the Basic Law, executive and legislative competence exists in the federal republic at *Bund* level nationally, and also at the level of the *Länder*. At a national level, the *Bundesrat*, composed of representatives from the *Länder*, is closely involved in the passage of legislation by the federal government, elected to the *Bundestag* parliament in Bonn, on an alternative member system of proportional representation.

With the exception of a brief interval from 1953 to 1957, the Hamburg administration or Senate, has been controlled during the post-war period by the *Sozialdemokratische Partei Deutschlands* (SPD), broadly equivalent to the British Labour Party. On failing to gain an absolute majority, the SPD has formed coalitions with the smaller centre party, the *Freie Demokratische Partei* (FDP), as was the case from 1986 to 1990 (Mintzel and Oberreuter, 1990). The right of centre *Christliche Demokratische Union* (CDU), constitutes the main opposition party, along with *Die Grünen/Grüne Alternative Liste (GAL)*, which have been represented in the Senate since 1982, as shown in Table 6.1. By 1986 there were 13 Green members of the Hamburg Senate, and by 1989 there were some 3,000 elected representatives in federal, state and local parliaments across Germany (Goodhart, 1989; Mintzel and Oberreuter, 1990). By contrast, none of the local government elections held in London have ever used systems of proportional representation enabling the representation of environmentalist political parties.

It was described in Chapter One how the diversity of views within the environmental movement is reflected in the German Greens with their stark internal differences since their inception in 1980. The main division has been between the grassroots dominated *Fundis* faction and the pragmatic *Realos* faction dominant in the *Bundestag*, the Party leadership, and among elected councillors (Hülsberg, 1988). This *Fundis/Realos* split is also reflected geographically, such that the radical *Fundis* are dominant in urban centres such as Hamburg and the former West Berlin (Müller-Rommel and Poguntke, 1990).

Though the 1970s was a period of relative prosperity for Hamburg, the 1980s was marked by a process of intense economic restructuring away from

Table 6.1: Elections to the Hamburg Senate 1974-1991

	CDU	SPD	FDP	Greens
1974	40.6%	44.9%	10.9%	-
1978	37.6%	*51.5%	4.8%	**4.5%
1982a	43.2%	42.8%	4.8%	7.7%
1982b	38.6%	*51.3%	2.6%	6.8%
1986	41.9%	41.8%	4.8%	10.4%
1987	39.3%	46.5%	6.0%	7.1%
1991	35.1%	*48.0%	5.4%	7.2%

*   This SPD gained an overall majority of the seats in the Senate

** This figure includes 3.5% for the BLW (Rainbow Slate) and 1.0%
for the GLU (Environmentalist Green Slate)

Source: Hulsberg (1988) and the German Embassy, London.

traditional industries such as shipbuilding and raw materials processing. The city experienced steadily rising unemployment until the late 1980s, and ran into a fiscal deficit for the first time in 1984[1]. The response of the SPD city administration has been a move away from demand-side state intervention policies in locally based traditional industries, towards a 'neo-liberal' supply-side approach, based on selective investment in key high return sectors such as information technology (Dangschat and Ossenbrügge, 1990; Ossenbrügge, 1989)[2]. As a consequence, there has been increased political friction over the levels of state expenditure in different areas, such as education, housing, and environmental protection, which has been exacerbated by the recent influx of immigrants from poorer European countries and from the former East Germany. The political and economic restructuring in Hamburg since the late 1970s, along with the upheaval associated with German reunification and the collapse of state socialism in eastern Europe, has shifted the policy making context for municipal waste management and recycling towards increasingly tight control over state expenditure.

The organisation of waste management in Hamburg

In this section the key components of the administrative and organisational structure of waste management in Hamburg are outlined. Note in particular that the city is reliant on incineration for the disposal of a greater proportion

203

of the waste stream than in London. Note also that there is a unified administrative structure for the collection and disposal of waste across the city and that waste management is primarily financed by means of a flat rate direct charge to households called the *Müllgebühr*.

The emergence of municipal waste management

By 1900, the population of Hamburg approached 800,000, and the city had become the fourth most important seaport in the world, after London, New York, and Liverpool. The city faced a worse threat to public health than in London, with no less than fourteen cholera epidemics occurring between 1831 and 1873. In 1892 there was a major cholera epidemic traced to polluted drinking water from the river Elbe, in which over eight thousand people died and the city administration was transformed as a result, constructing a water purification plant and setting up a municipal sanitary institute in 1893:

> The cholera epidemic of 1892 highlighted - and symbolized - the helplessness of the politics of notables in the face of the challenge posed by the social and environmental consequences of rapid industrial and urban growth. (Evans, 1991 p. 566).

The progress towards better standards in public health for Hamburg appears to have been faster than in London. It was noted as early as 1909, in a major review of street cleansing in twenty different world cities, that Hamburg had already developed 'a peculiar and very satisfactory form of municipal government...the streets are, many of them, handsomely built, well paved, and very well kept' (Soper, 1909 p. 121). The work of the city's street-cleansing department included the cleaning of all public streets and pavements, the watering of streets to reduce dust, the removal of snow and ice, supervision over the removal of street and house refuse, removal of refuse from the docks and city parks, and the cleaning and maintaining of 'public comfort stations' (op cit.). The key feature of interest, is that since the reform of local government in Hamburg in the 1890s, both the collection and the disposal of waste have been consistently handled by one tier of local government under centralised democratic control, unlike London, where these functions have never been combined at a city wide level.

In the early part of this century the city of Hamburg was served by one large incinerator at Ballerdeich, constructed between 1893 and 1896. This Horsfall type destructor, with its one hundred workers, was said to be among the best and largest of the time, incorporating a number of novel technical and operational features: the works were situated on the outskirts of the city and appeared 'to produce little offence on account of odour' (op cit. p. 129); there were weighbridge facilities, collecting data concerning the quantity of the refuse which was handled by the works; a high labour efficiency was reported for the stoking process; and a high temperature incineration process was used to reduce emissions, and the remaining ash and clinker were cooled and sifted to remove metals, which were then sold. The dust and clinker was used as raw materials for building purposes, and it was noted that, 'at times the work of building is so active that the production of ground clinker scarcely meets half of the demand' (op cit. p. 132). The steam raised from the four boilers was used both for the running of the machinery necessary for the operation of the plant, and also for the production of electricity, which was transported and consumed in other parts of the city (Meyer, 1901). By contrast, none of the 'dust destructors' in London matched the size of the Ballerdeich plant, because they were constructed only to serve the catchment area of individual Metropolitan Boroughs, rather than the strategic needs of a whole city, as described in Chapter Three.

The emergence and predominance of incineration as the solution to municipal waste management in Hamburg, in the early part of the twentieth century, suggests that both Hamburg and London initially followed a similar path of development. In the 1930s, however, their development began to diverge, with the emphasis in London moving increasingly towards the use of cheap and accessible landfill rather than incineration. Yet Hamburg was never been able to develop a virtual reliance on landfill because of administrative and political restrictions imposed by the neighbouring local government administrations to accepting large quantities of waste, resulting in the need to focus waste disposal within the city boundaries.

The present spatial and organisational structure of waste management in Hamburg was established in 1949 with the creation of a new city cleansing department, the *Stadtreinigung*, handling the collection and disposal of all municipal waste. In the period 1949 to 1985, the volume of household waste grew by 86 per cent to some 5.4 million cubic metres, and over the thirty year period 1952 to 1982, the density of the waste fell by 71 per cent, primarily reflecting the reduced use of coal for heating purposes and the increasing quantity of packaging materials entering the waste stream. In response to the growth of the waste stream, there was an extensive programme of investment in new incineration capacity in the 1960s and 1970s, and the contemporary waste management infrastructure for incineration was fully operational by 1979 (ITU, 1989).

As in the US and the UK, there were political and economic pressures since the mid-1970s to control the rising costs of municipal waste management. If the overall costs for waste management are examined, it is apparent that waste collection and transport costs accounted for 71 per cent of the total in 1982, with waste disposal costs making up the remaining 29 per cent (ITU, 1989). The concern over the rising cost of waste management was resolved at least temporarily in Hamburg, by the splitting of the operational side of waste management off from the *Baubehörde* (Public Works Department) in 1988 to form a public corporation owned by the city of Hamburg, called the *Landesbetrieb Hamburger Stadtreinigung*, handling both the collection and the disposal of waste. This process of 'semi-privatisation' is different from the process of demunicipalisation in London in a number of respects: there remains a unified strategic structure for the collection and disposal of waste; there is no CCT process enabling an operational role for outside companies; and there are no capital controls on investment comparable with those faced by the LAWDCs under the 1989 Local Government and Finance Act. The LB-HSR remains under political control of the elected city Senate, which has a 100 per cent shareholding and strategic policy decisions are made by elected politicians in the Senate[3].

The contemporary legislative and administrative framework

Federal administration for the environment is very small, although a federal Ministry for Environmental and Nature Protection and Nuclear Safety, was created by the Kohl Administration in April 1986, incorporating all the environmental functions of the Ministry for the Interior. Since the *Bund* has no territorial administration of its own, it is dependent on the *Länder* for the implementation of policy, which further strengthens the political role of regional and local government.

The core of German waste management policy is contained within the 1972 Waste Management Act and with the exception of provisions for nuclear waste, the obligations for waste management are handled by regional and local government in Germany. In the city based *Länder*, such as Hamburg and Bremen, the responsibility for both waste collection and waste disposal is passed to the city Senate (Kromarek, 1986). Under the fourth amendment to the 1972 Waste Management Act, which came into force in November 1986, there is now a focus on recycling and waste reduction as an integral element in waste management (Hedlund, 1988). Other important legislative developments include the TA Abfall technical regulations for waste management initiated in 1984, concerning higher environmental standards in waste disposal with a particular emphasis on incineration emissions and the more recent legislative controls on packaging introduced in June 1991 discussed later in this chapter.

The city of Hamburg carries out the collection and disposal of all its municipal waste. Figure 6.2 shows that the planning and client side of waste management is the responsibility of the city's public works department, the

Figure 6.2: The organisational structure of waste management in Hamburg

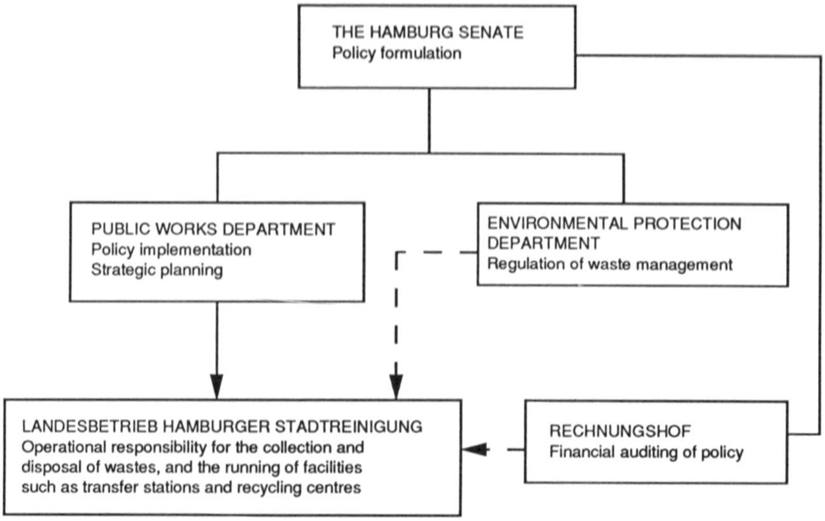

Source: Freie und Hansestadt Hamburg (1989)

Baubehörde, and the operational side of waste management is handled by its former department, now the *Landesbetrieb Hamburger Stadtreinigung*. The public works department is one of eleven different departments, as shown in Figure 6.3, and the environmental regulation of waste management activities is handled separately by the environment department, the *Umweltbehörde*. The city's environment department is, for example, responsible for monitoring the problems of contaminated ground and surface water, and the emissions of noxious gas from former landfill sites. In addition to the environmental regulation of waste management, there is also an independent financial auditing office within the Senate called the *Rechnungshof*, as shown in Figure 6.2.

The collection of municipal waste

Beneath the Hamburg Senate, are the seven smaller local government units, the *Bezirke*, which have no direct role in waste collection, except for Bezirk Harburg and Bergedorf. These two *Bezirke* collect household waste and carry out street cleansing, but are not responsible for the collection of bulky

Figure 6.3: The administrative structure of local government in Hamburg

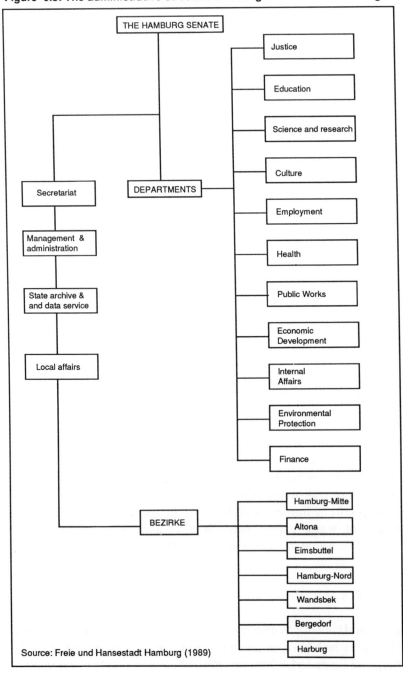

Source: Freie und Hansestadt Hamburg (1989)

household waste or the final disposal of the wastes collected, and resemble the role of London Boroughs during the period of the GLC Public Health Engineering Department from 1965 to 1986 (see Chapter Three). In the other five *Bezirke* (Altona, Eimsbüttel, Hamburg-Mitte, Hamburg-Nord, and Wandsbek), the *Landesbetrieb Hamburger Stadtreinigung* is responsible for all waste collection and disposal. For bulky household waste (*Sperrmüll*), Hamburg is divided into sixty zones, from which the *Landesbetrieb Hamburger Stadtreinigung* carries out a quarterly kerbside collection. There is also a network of nine civic amenity sites, as shown in Figure 6.6, all now operating as multi-material recycling centres known as *Recyclinghöfe*, in addition to toxic waste handling and employment creation functions.

For the purposes of waste management planning, the whole city is divided at street level, into six different categories on the basis of the physical characteristics of the buildings. These *Siedlungstruktur* categories ranged from detached and semi-detached dwellings with gardens, dominant in wealthy residential areas in outer Hamburg, to high multi-occupied dwellings with narrow streets, in the old inner areas of the city. The organisation of waste collection and provision of recycling facilities, was closely related to the distribution of these six categories, enabling detailed evaluation of the potential impact of changes in waste management policy[4]. A charge called the *Müllgebühr* was levied for the collection of household waste by the *Landesbetrieb Hamburger Stadtreinigung*, and this charge had risen by 17 per cent, to 280 DM per year, for a 120 litre bin during 1990, which made it the highest *Müllgebühr* charge in Germany[5]. It should be noted that of the 860,000 households in Hamburg, only 140,000 were charged *Gebühr* separately and individually by the city, since the charge is normally incorporated into rent in the non owner-occupied housing tenures.

The disposal of municipal waste

Hamburg is currently served by four incineration plants and four landfill sites, as shown in Figure 6.5. Two of the incineration plants are owned by the city of Hamburg at Borsigstraße and Stellinger Moor; a third at Stapelfeld in the neighbouring *Land* of Schleswig-Holstein, is 80 per cent owned by Hamburg and 20 per cent owned by the local government *Krise* (broadly equivalent to a County Council in the UK); and the fourth, is a small privately-owned specialised plant, the *Abfallverwertungsgesellschaft m.b.H* (AVG) also at Borsigstraße, used primarily for the high temperature incineration of toxic and hazardous waste. An average charge of 120 DM a tonne has been imposed for the city's incineration capacity, to avoid private sector waste swamping the cheapest plant at Stapelfeld, which had federal assistance in its construction[6].

Figure 6.4: Methods of waste disposal in London and Hamburg

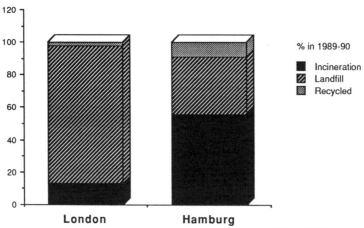

Source: LB-HSR (1990) and survey data

Table 6.2: Waste disposal costs in London and Hamburg 1990

	Sterling or equivalent	D Mark or equivalent
London		
Incineration (NLWA Edmonton plant with NFFO levy)	£7	21 DM
Incineration (NLWA Edmonton plant without NFFO levy)	£10-12	30-36 DM
Landfill (ELWA direct to landfill)	£8	24 DM
Landfill (CLWDG river transfer)	£30	90 DM
Landfill (NLWA rail transfer)	£30	90 DM
Landfill (SWLWDG and SELWDG road transfer)	£20	60 DM
Hamburg		
Landfill (Schonberg in the DDR)	£23	70 DM
Incineration (Average figure for the three MVA plants)	£40	120 DM

Source: LB-HSR (1990) and various interview data

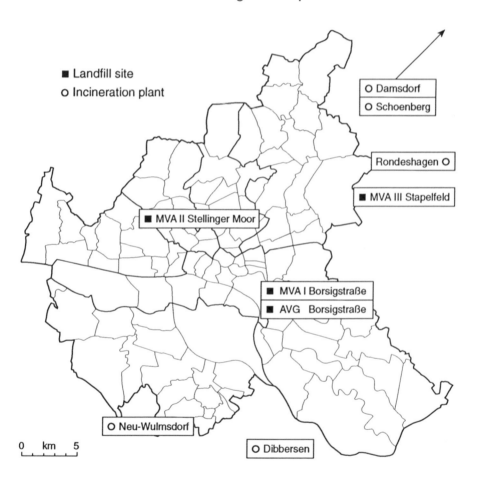

Figure 6.5: The location of incineration plants and landfill sites for Hamburg's municipal waste

■ Landfill site
○ Incineration plant

○ Damsdorf
○ Schoenberg

Rondeshagen ○

■ MVA III Stapelfeld

■ MVA II Stellinger Moor

■ MVA I Borsigstraße
■ AVG Borsigstraße

○ Neu-Wulmsdorf

0   km   5

○ Dibbersen

Source: Freie und Hansestadt Hamburg (1989c)

During the late 1980s, the incineration option for Hamburg faced increasing difficulties: firstly, there was pressure from the neighbouring *Land* of Schleswig-Holstein to have exclusive use of the Stapelfeld incineration plant because the Land had decided to stop sending its waste to landfill in the former East Germany; secondly, the large and old Borsigstraße incineration plant, will have ended its working life by 1994, substantially reducing Hamburg's incineration capacity; and finally, the Hamburg Senate had decided in 1986 to phase out the use of the important Schönberg landfill site in the former East Germany, a decision which has been given added impetus by German reunification and concern over environmental standards in eastern Germany[7]. A replacement incineration plant capable of handling 400,000 tonnes of waste a year would cost in excess of 300 million DM - well beyond the scope of the City's present finances[8]. In the case of waste management, federal funding from central government is normally only available towards research and development costs, therefore putting the onus on local government to find the money to fulfil their statutory waste management duties.

The use of landfill, whilst cheaper than incineration, as shown in Table 6.2, has been faced with intense political restrictions from the powerful system of local government and strong local opposition to new sites since the early 1970s: the last remaining site within the city area having been exhausted in October 1986. As a result of these constraints, there has been intense political pressure on Hamburg to solve its waste management difficulties within the city boundaries. The only new landfill sites in the city area under consideration in the 1980s were on the edge of the city at Duvenstedter Brook, Hummelsbüttel, and Rahlstedt, and all presented serious difficulties in terms of land use planning and potential opposition from local residents[9]. The neighbouring *Länder* of Schleswig-Holstein and Lower Saxony have shown increasing resistance to taking any of Hamburg's waste for landfill, which explains the emergence of the former East Germany as the main recipient of waste, where there were lower levels of public resistance to landfill and the need for hard currency. In the period 1986-1990 between 213,800 and 538,400 tonnes of waste that could not be burnt, were transported annually 120km by road, to be landfilled at Schönberg in the Mecklenberg region of eastern Germany, along with 230,000 tonnes of sewage sludge and 90,000 tonnes of hazardous waste.

The limited landfill that was carried out within the neighbouring *Länder*, rather than in the former East Germany, was subject to strict controls and often complex political negotiations. Some 50,000 tonnes of sewage sludge, for example, was transported annually in the 1980s to Norderstedt in Schleswig-Holstein, as part of a deal with the City of Hamburg, which involved the construction of an extension of the city public transport network to the town of Norderstedt. Similarly, there has been negotiation with the neighbouring *Land* of Lower Saxony over the construction of a motorway link through a section of outer Hamburg, in exchange for potential landfill capacity in the semi-rural areas outside the city boundary[10].

In summary, incineration has been consistently the main waste disposal option for the city for a combination of political and organisational reasons stemming from the administrative structure of local government. The powerful federal regional government structure imposed greater political and economic constraints on the use of landfill than in London, and helps to explain the predominance of incineration for waste disposal. Unlike London, therefore, Hamburg was faced with finding, as far as possible, a satisfactory solution to its waste disposal problem within its own administrative boundaries. This in turn, accounts for the relatively high cost of waste management in Hamburg in comparison with London, as shown in Table 6.2, and the resulting political difficulties in finding a cost-effective and environmentally acceptable waste management strategy for the city. In addition to the predominance of incineration and the higher cost in Hamburg in comparison with London, the policy making context was different in three distinct ways: firstly, the collection and disposal of waste is under unified centralised control by local government; secondly, there has been greater pressure for environmentally superior forms of waste management, primarily as a result of the direct lobbying role of the powerful environmentalist movement via the representation of the Green Party on the Hamburg Senate; and finally, the use of a direct charge, the *Müllgebühr*, for the city's waste management service, places intense political and economic pressure on the Senate to ensure that they provide an economically efficient and politically acceptable system of waste management. The combination of these political pressures and local difficulties in waste management has led to an increasing policy emphasis in the 1980s on recycling and measures to reduce the size of the waste stream in Hamburg.

The pattern of recycling activity in Hamburg

In this section, the extent and pattern of recycling activity is considered in order to account for the differences between London and Hamburg in terms of the variation in the recycling rate, the organisation of recycling activity, and the rationale for recycling policy. The essential differences in comparison with London are that the objectives of recycling are predominantly environmental rather than economic, and that a higher rate of recycling is achieved through a more intensive use of the 'bring' system of collection in conjunction with a variety of pilot projects extending to the centralised production of composting using a dual-bin system in Bezirk Harburg.

The rationale for recycling

The 1989 Waste Management Plan, approved by the Hamburg Senate, argued for an expansion of incineration rather than an increased use of landfill, whilst recognising that neither option was wholly satisfactory in environmental terms. It was envisaged that by 1995, out of a larger total of some 2.6 million tonnes of waste generated by the city from all sources, only negligible quantities would be landfilled. The plan aimed to recycle over 50 per cent of all waste, including construction waste and sewage sludge, necessitating only a modest overall expansion in incineration at present levels but involving the construction of a new incineration plant on derelict land at the Borsigstraße site in the Hamburg docks. In terms of household waste recycling, it was planned that 30 per cent of household waste would be recycled within five years, based on a dramatic improvement on existing rates of materials recovery of 13 per cent (Freie und Hansestadt Hamburg, 1989d).

The development of recycling in Hamburg has been associated with four main arguments: the historical promotion of recycling for economic reasons, illustrated in the exchange of waste materials between different firms in the Chamber of Commerce; the recycling of materials for social and charitable purposes, as in Red Cross collections of paper and textiles; the emergence of environmentalist recycling from the urban based environmental movement, shown by student groups at the University of Hamburg in the 1970s sending aluminium to Berlin for reprocessing; and finally, the emergence of recycling in the 1980s, as an important element in municipal waste management in response to declining landfill availability and the environmental opposition to incineration. In the contemporary context, the recycling of household waste in Hamburg is seen as an environmental service, and not as an additional source of income or a means of reducing the costs of waste management for the Hamburg Senate[11]. Indeed, the limited income that was to be made from the recycling of glass, and to a lesser extent paper, accrued almost wholly to the private sector, who undertook operations under contract to the *Landesbetrieb Hamburger Stadtreinigung*[12]. This contrasts with London where it was found that the economic objectives of recycling were very widespread, as illustrated in Table 4.2.

The organisational approach to recycling

Contemporary recycling in Hamburg is carried out principally by four agents: the *Landesbetrieb Hamburger Stadtreinigung*; the private sector; the citizens of Hamburg; and the voluntary sector. The voluntary sector role was focused

Table 6.3: Methods of materials recovery used for household waste in Hamburg

Method of recovery	Materials recovered
Kerbside collection	Dual-bin system for putrescible waste in Bezirk Harburg Voluntary sector collections of paper
On-street collection facilities	Paper Glass Dry-cell batteries Textiles
Recycling centres (Recyclinghofe)	Paper Glass Textiles Ferrous scrap Non-ferrous scrap Bulky waste items for renovation and repair CFCs and refrigerators Oil Toxic household wastes (e.g. paints, bleach, pesticides etc.)
Centralised recovery by magnetic separation at incineration plants	Ferrous scrap
Recycling workshops	Renovation and repair of bulky household waste CFCs and refrigerator components Ferrous scrap Non-ferrous scrap

Source: Gandy (1992a)

on employment creation and the social objectives of recycling[13]. Four voluntary sector schemes employ long-term unemployed labour (with financial support from the Hamburg employment office) and carried out a variety of work including the removal of CFCs from refrigerators, and the renovation of items such as old bicycles and discarded furniture. There is also the Hamburg branch of the federal *Bund für Umwelt-and Naturschutz* (BUND), which has an important national lobbying role, similar to Friends of the Earth in the UK. A further aspect of voluntary sector involvement are the collections of paper carried out in some areas on behalf of the Red Cross. In contrast to London, the voluntary sector role is focused on the social rather than environmental objectives of recycling, especially the potential for employment creation from the renovation and repair of items in the waste stream.

Table 6.3 shows the different methods of materials recovery used in Hamburg. Note the predominance of the 'bring' system as in London, and the restriction of kerbside collection to some voluntary sector collections and the use of the pilot dual-bin system for putrescible waste in Bezirk Harburg. The density of the glass banks varies from 1,800 to 4,000 inhabitants per site in the Bezirke, whilst in London there is a range of 2,600 to 60,000 inhabitants per bottle bank site (Freie und Hansestadt Hamburg, 1989d)[14]. Given that there is a clear relationship between the density of collection facilities and the rate of materials recovery (see Chapter Four), this helps to explain the higher level of recycling in Hamburg.

In addition to the network of on-street collection facilities there is a well developed system of combined recycling centres and civic amenity type facilities across the city. Figure 6.6 shows that the catchment areas of the nine recycling centres (*Recyclinghöfe*) run by the *Landesbetrieb Hamburger Stadtreinigung* cover most of the city. Each of these centres has at least two full-time qualified staff, and they handle the whole range of recyclable materials brought by the public. In addition to the recovery of materials, the centres perform an important advisory and educational role, particularly for toxic wastes, and there are plans to open a further five facilities by 1994 (Freie und Hansestadt Hamburg, 1989a). The *Landesbetrieb Hamburger Stadtreinigung* also provides a 'recycling bus', making five special stops across the city every two weeks, to which the public can bring any toxic household items to *Landesbetrieb Hamburger Stadtreinigung* staff. However, the planned expansion of this service has faced difficulties because of the associated labour costs[15].

The level of recycling in Hamburg

The recycling rate for municipal waste in Hamburg for the period 1988-1990

Figure 6.6: Recycling centres in Hamburg

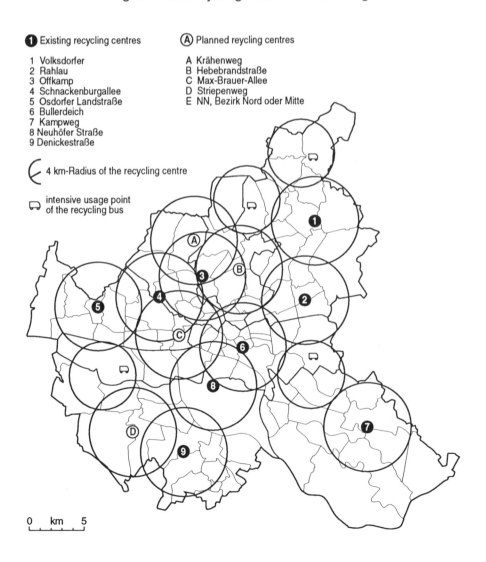

● Existing recycling centres

1 Volksdorfer
2 Rahlau
3 Offkamp
4 Schnackenburgallee
5 Osdorfer Landstraße
6 Bullerdeich
7 Kampweg
8 Neuhöfer Straße
9 Denickestraße

Ⓐ Planned reycling centres

A Krähenweg
B Hebebrandstraße
C Max-Brauer-Allee
D Striepenweg
E NN, Bezirk Nord oder Mitte

⊂ 4 km-Radius of the recycling centre

intensive usage point
of the recycling bus

0   km   5

Source: Freie und Hansestadt Hamburg (1989d)

is estimated by the *Landesbetrieb Hamburger Stadtreinigung* to be 13 per cent (Bürgerschaft der Freien Hansestadt Hamburg, 1989; LB-HSR, 1990). Some additional calculations have also been made for individual *Bezirke*, with a 13 per cent figure given for Bezirk Eimsbüttel, which includes a wide range of the *Siedlungstruktur* housing types[16], and a 20 per cent rate is estimated for Bezirk Harburg[17], which lies predominantly in outer Hamburg. These figures may be compared with an average recycling rate of 2.1 per cent for the London Boroughs in 1989-90, and a range from 0.1 per cent to 8.8 per cent in individual boroughs (see Chapter Four). In the case of Bezirk Harburg, widely considered to have the highest rate of recycling in the city of 20 per cent, the recycling was organised around a number of different initiatives: a 'bring' system of on-street collection facilities for glass and paper; a kerbside 'collect' system for paper; the collection of a wide range of materials at the Harburg Recyclingzentrum (a major civic amenity type facility with four full-time staff); collections of textiles, paper and glass at schools and offices; and a dual-bin scheme to remove putrescibles for the centralised production of compost[18].

However, there are difficulties in estimating the level of recycling in Hamburg for a variety of reasons: the *Landesbetrieb Hamburger Stadtreinigung* considered that the figures provided by the private sector for glass and paper collections should be treated with caution[19]; the figures for materials collected from on-street collection facilities were not broken down spatially for the different Bezirke[20]; some aspects of recycling present special difficulties, such as textiles recovery by the voluntary sector, for which only limited information was readily available[21], as is the case in London; and unknown amounts of waste are also removed through the composting of putrescibles by households with gardens, independently of the *Eigenkompostierung* programme to promote composting by households themselves in outer Hamburg.

The lack of direct comparison of rates of recycling between the different Bezirke, was due to their diversity in terms of housing structure, and the belief that differences in the rate of recycling do not reflect differing commitments of Bezirke level administrations, which in any case do not have any major role in waste management. What variations that do exist, are attributed to general constraints on the development of recycling, which operate in a similar fashion throughout the city[22], and the influence of local variations in housing type. In London, by contrast, there was a degree of direct competition between local authorities, as if variations in recycling were simply a result of the levels of commitment of individual administrations to environmental policy making, yet the analysis of recycling in the London Boroughs suggested that policy variations at a local level were of only minor explanatory significance, as described in Chapter Four.

Figure 6.7: The composition of household waste in Hamburg 1986

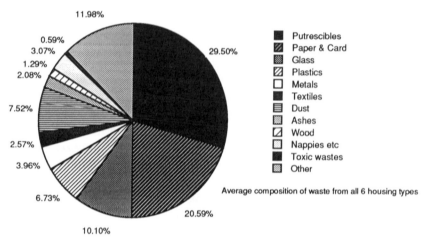

11.98%
0.59%
3.07%
1.29%
2.08%
7.52%
2.57%
3.96%
6.73%
10.10%
29.50%
20.59%

Putrescibles
Paper & Card
Glass
Plastics
Metals
Textiles
Dust
Ashes
Wood
Nappies etc
Toxic wastes
Other

Average composition of waste from all 6 housing types

Source: Data adapted from ITU (1989)

Table 6.4: Waste composition and housing structure in Hamburg

	Siedlungstruktur 1-2	Siedlungstruktur 3-4	Siedlungstruktur 5-6
	Detached or semi-detached	Terraces or maisonettes	High rise appartments
Putrescibles	36.0%	31.0%	25.9%
Paper and card	22.8%	19.2%	22.7%
Glass	6.3%	10.0%	13.0%
Metals	2.4%	3.3%	5.5%
Plastics	7.3%	5.9%	6.8%

Source: Freie und Hansestadt Hamburg (1989a)

The recovery of different materials from the waste stream

In the rest of this section the recovery of different fractions of the waste stream is examined in greater detail. This allows a closer examination of the experience of recycling in Hamburg, and helps to elaborate on some of the conclusions drawn from the analysis of recycling in London.

Paper

Paper is mostly collected under contract by two private firms, using collection points across the city for lower grade materials, particularly newspapers, most of which are taken to the Temming mill at Gluckstadt, 50km outside the city. New contracts were under negotiation at the time of the study, but there had been considerable difficulties since the 1987 collapse in the price of waste paper, which had forced the *Landesbetrieb Hamburger Stadtreinigung* to take over many loss making waste paper collections, to avoid a political backlash from the powerful recycling electorate[23]. As in the case of glass (see below), there had been disagreements between the *Landesbetrieb Hamburger Stadtreinigung* and the private sector concerning the interpretation of the clause in the contract concerning responsibility for the maintenance and upkeep of the collection sites, which could incur major labour costs, potentially greater than the current value of the waste paper in the collection facilities. These operational difficulties paralleled the problems experienced with the use of on-street collection facilities in London, set out in Table 4.11.

Putrescibles

The main impetus for the promotion of composting has come from the Hamburg Senate, who have demanded a radical expansion of this option in response to political pressure from all political parties, as part of a wider strategy to reduce the reliance on landfill and incineration and also to reduce methane emissions and other environmental impacts of putrescibles. The expansion of composting can be seen as a policy initiative arising from the elected politicians in the Senate, rather than a policy promoted for conventional technical or economic reasons, as part of the routine waste management responsibilities of the *Baubehörde* and the *Landesbetrieb Hamburger Stadtreinigung*.

The composting of putrescible waste was identified as the key component of a comprehensive recycling programme for the city capable of raising levels of recycling towards the 30 per cent target in the 1989 Waste Management Plan. The significance of composting is that some 29 per cent of the household waste in Hamburg is derived from putrescibles, as shown in Figure 6.7, yet there would be a need to devise a system of composting for households without gardens. It was envisaged in the 1989 Waste Management Plan, therefore, that higher rates of composting would be met by two main means: firstly, the city's promotion of composting by households themselves with access to a garden, as part of the *Eigenkompostierung* programme; and secondly, the development of a dual-bin system for the separate collection and centralised production of compost, from households without gardens. The 1989 Waste Management Plan expected that by 1995, up to 80,000 tonnes of waste per year would be handled by four composting facilities, located in Bezirk Altona, Bergedorf and Harburg, and just outside the city boundary in the neighbouring *Land* of Schleswig-Holstein. It was assumed that these plants would be joint ventures between the *Landesbetrieb Hamburger Stadtreinigung* and the private sector.

The first element in the Hamburg composting strategy, the production of compost by households with gardens in the *Eigenkompostierung* programme, has been promoted since 1985 using the incentive of free provision of composting units which would have normally retailed at 20 DM each[24]. The objective was to enable households to need a smaller bin for their routine waste collections and hence incur a lower *Gebühr* charge, so as to stimulate recycling activity. Figure 6.9 shows how the potential for households to carry out their own composting is closely related to housing structure and the number of households with gardens. In theory, the incentive scheme was possible because the *Gebühr* charge is made on the basis of bin size. In practice, however, this objective has proved problematic, since the 17 per cent increase in the *Gebühr* in 1990, incorporated a 2 per cent rise for larger bins, and a 40 per cent rise for smaller bins. This had followed demands from the City's audit commission, the *Rechnungshof*, that the existing anomaly, whereby the larger bins were effectively subsidizing the smaller bins, be redressed[25].

The second element in the composting programme, was the separate collection of putrescibles for the centralised production of compost. This aspect of policy is being carried out by a major pilot scheme running in Bezirk Harburg, and involving 5,200 households (12,500 people), in a wide range of housing types. The scheme uses a dual-bin system for wet (i.e. putrescible) and dry waste, the putrescibles being collected either weekly or fortnightly and taken to the centralised composting facility nearby. The aerobic composting process takes six to eight months, and involves the employment of the long-term unemployed at the plant (with state subsidy for the labour costs). The scheme was a free service, with no increase in the *Gebühr* until October 1990, after which a 30 per cent rise in the *Gebühr* charge was introduced to cover the extra cost of the scheme, the effects of

Figure 6.8: The composition of recycled materials in Hamburg 1988

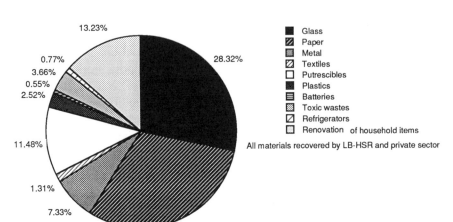

- Glass
- Paper
- Metal
- Textiles
- Putrescibles
- Plastics
- Batteries
- Toxic wastes
- Refrigerators
- Renovation of household items

All materials recovered by LB-HSR and private sector

Source: LB-HSR (1990)

which had yet to be monitored over a long period. The project has also been run on a voluntary basis, contrasting with mandatory schemes in operation in some other German cities[26].

A number of specific issues were to be examined in the Harburg pilot project: the level of public participation and the degree of contamination of collections associated with different housing types; the technical and economic aspects of the collection and production process in comparison with alternative means of waste disposal; and the potential for successful marketing of the final product in competition with commercial garden peat. The analysis of the Harburg project found that the main contamination problem was from the presence of non-putrescible waste, such as metals and plastics, the proportion varying from 0.2 per cent to 7 per cent depending on the housing structure. The highest levels of non-putrescible contamination were found in shared bins serving high rise public sector housing and this necessitated the cleaning of the compost with sieves before sale, though small fragments of metal and plastic always remained[27].

The levels of public participation varied from 55 to 80 per cent of the households in the catchment study, depending on the housing type, with the highest levels of participation in larger detached and semi-detached homes. The explanation for the lower participation rates and higher levels of compost

222

Figure 6.9: The extent of potential composting by households as part of the *Eigenkompostierung* programme

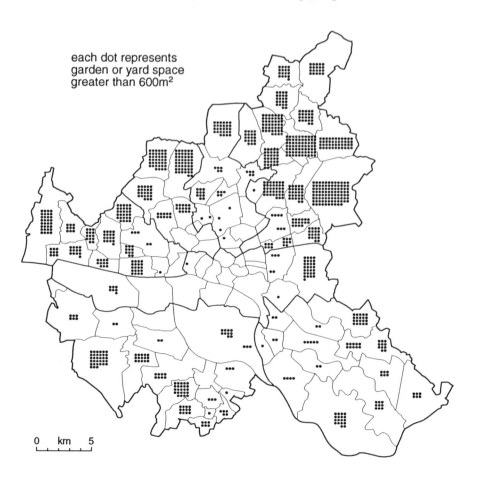

each dot represents
garden or yard space
greater than 600m²

0   km   5

Source: Freie und Hansestadt Hamburg (1989d)

contamination in high rise housing was thought to rest on three main factors: firstly, the relative social anonymity of communal bins, as a psychological encouragement to contamination with non-putrescible waste and lack of care in waste separation; secondly, householders without gardens were less acquainted with gardening and the potential use of organic wastes; and thirdly, the influence of higher levels of socio-economic disadvantage on participation in environmental policy[28]. The Turkish form the main ethnic minority in Hamburg and are concentrated in high rise accommodation. Some Turkish households may have had difficulty reading the public information leaflets in German (only the Berlin cleansing department is known to produce public information leaflets in Turkish)[29].

The main economic obstacle to centralised composting appeared to be the higher cost compared with other waste disposal options, as suggested by Table 6.5. Calculations for the Harburg project put the cost at some 430 DM per tonne, compared with between 242 and 290 DM for waste collection and disposal by incineration and around 240 DM for landfill[30]. One possible way of reducing the cost to 380 DM per tonne was through fortnightly rather than weekly collections to cut labour costs, but this presented new sets of problems in terms of the increased smell, especially in summer, and the associated lower levels of public participation, which have also been observed in other pilot projects elsewhere in Germany (ITU, 1989). The problem of smell in Hamburg was also greater for the high rise collections, where the putrescibles were dominated by wetter kitchen waste, decomposing faster than garden waste[31].

A further difficulty included the space requirements of the composting facilities in competition with other more profitable urban land uses. There is also a need to site the facility at least 500 metres from a residential area, because of the local environmental complaints created by the smell of putrescibles in the early stages of composting, though there were plans in future to utilise anaerobic methods, which whilst more expensive, would be quicker, require less space, and produce a less pungent smell, with the added advantage of being integrated into bio-gas energy recovery schemes. Despite the low levels of heavy metal contamination for the compost[32], the strength of the market for the final product in competition with commercially marketed peat (a non-renewable resource) is not yet fully known, and is a key factor influencing the overall economics of an expansion in composting[33].

The example of composting in Hamburg, illustrates that the achievement of very high rates of urban recycling would necessarily involve the use of putrescible waste from households without gardens. The results of the Harburg project suggest that composting of household waste is more difficult than is widely appreciated in the literature (see Brown et al., 1990; Pollock, 1987), and that considerable uncertainties over the cost and long-term public participation in such schemes remain. Analysis of the projected costs of different recycling strategies suggests that the use of a comprehensive dual-bin system as part of a programme to raise levels of recycling to 30 per cent would raise the costs of waste management by between 89 and 144 DM per tonne, depending on the combination of different methods of materials recovery and whether the separate collections of putrescibles were weekly or fortnightly (Bürgerschaft der Freien und Hansestadt Hamburg, 1989). The implications are that the extension of recycling to the environmentally significant waste fraction of putrescibles (in terms of methane emissions and protection of wetland ecosystems, along with the overall goal of waste reduction) is significantly more expensive than routine waste disposal by landfill or incineration, and may have socially regressive and politically unpopular consequences through a forced increase in the flat rate *Gebühr* charge to individual households for the collection and disposal of their waste.

Glass

The glass from bottle banks is collected mainly by two firms under contract from the *Landesbetrieb Hamburger Stadtreinigung*, which provide the collection facilities and take the glass cullet to the Nienbergen Glashütte processing plant, 150km outside the city for 60 DM a tonne under contract[34]. Collection facilities are provided for white and coloured (mixed) glass, since the cullet is used to make only white and green glass. Separation of brown glass is unnecessary for the making of green glass, but not for the manufacture of brown glass, which explains its separate collection in southern Germany, where it is used for the manufacture of wine and beer bottles. As in London, there is concern over the possible saturation of the market for green and mixed glass at a national level since 50 per cent of domestic glass production is for clear glass and the level of glass recycling is higher than in the UK (Hedlund, 1988; von Schönberg, 1990). The main local difficulties reported for glass recycling were similar to those in London, being principally the impact of noise and broken glass in the vicinity of the collection points; and there was also periodic contamination of white glass with coloured glass, necessitating expensive further sorting of the glass cullet[35]. A growing problem between the *Landesbetrieb Hamburger Stadtreinigung* and the private sector emerged during 1990, concerning the interpretation of the contractual obligation for site maintenance and cleansing, and also over demands from the private sector for a special subsidy, to help cover their losses created by increasing price instability in the glass market[36].

Figure 6.7 shows that some 60 per cent of the Hamburg waste stream is derived from paper, glass and putrescibles. The remaining 40 per cent of the waste stream is composed of a diverse array of different materials, many of which pose a range of logistical and economic difficulties for their effective recovery, as shown in Table 6.6. These difficulties are reflected in the pattern of materials recycled shown in Figure 6.8, showing that glass and paper account for 59 per cent of recovered materials, and a further 32 per cent consisted of metals, putrescibles and renovated items of bulky household waste.

Batteries and household toxic wastes A range of toxic wastes are handled at the *Recyclinghöfe* and by the special 'recycling bus' rounds. The removal of toxic materials from the domestic waste stream was hampered by the absence of any federal legislation concerning what may, or may not be, thrown into household refuse. The handling of toxic waste was not, however, considered of great relevance to the policy goals of recycling and waste reduction, because the quantities amount to just 0.59 per cent of the total waste stream, as shown in Figure 6.7. There is a growing network of on-street collection facilities for dry-cell batteries but this represents a development in toxic waste management rather than a part of the recycling programme.

Plastics The recovery of plastics in Hamburg by local government had been virtually abandoned for a combination of economic and technical reasons. This was largely a result of the experiences of a number of pilot projects in Bezirk Bergedorf, Eimsbüttel and Harburg. In the case of the Bergedorf collection scheme for mixed plastics from 1984 to 1987, the scheme foundered not through lack of public participation (there was on-going public demand for plastics to be collected separately), but because of the unresolved question of what to do with the collected materials: the capacity of the pyrolysis plant at Ebenhausen in Bavaria was quickly exceeded in 1987. Table 6.5 shows that the costs of the Bergedorf project were estimated to be about 1,000 DM per tonne for the kerbside plastics and 500 DM per tonne for the plastics taken by the public to on-street collection facilities and it was concluded that the recycling of plastics was too expensive to justify as part of the city's waste management services. An additional consideration in relation to plastics, is their role in maintaining the calorific value of waste for the production of energy from waste, yet they are also largely responsible for emissions concerns from the burning of PVCs and the production of dioxins. The problem of plastics was perceived to lie beyond the practical capacity of regional waste management and attempts by the city to recycle plastics were viewed as an expensive and politically embarrassing failure. The reduction of the amount of plastics entering the waste stream is critically dependent on the need for federal legislation to control the packaging industry, and the problem of plastics has been an integral part of the rationale for the new Töpfer regulations on packaging which came into force in June 1991[37](see below).

Metals and the renovation of household goods In addition to the magnetic recovery of ferrous metals at the city's incineration plants, both ferrous and non-ferrous metals were handled at the recycling centres in conjunction with the state supported *Abfallverwertungsgesellschaft* (AVG), which provided employment for the long-term unemployed. The AVG, which worked in partnership with the *Recyclinghöfe* for the recovery of metals, also worked with the *Landesbetrieb Hamburger Stadtreinigung* for the safe removal of CFCs from old refrigerators.   Other joint state and voluntary sector organisations for metal recovery and renovation of discarded household items include the *Beschäftigungs Gesellschäfte* for Hamburg West and Hamburg Nord, and the *Ottensen Sperrmüll Hof*. The Hamburg West *Beschäftigungs Gesellschaft* (HAB Altona) handles some 30,000 refrigerators a year, involving not only the removal of CFCs, but also the separation of metals, plastics, glass and wood. This complex and expensive operation is carried out by the long-term unemployed in a joint venture between the voluntary sector and the Hamburg labour office, thereby reducing the labour costs of recycling and also creating employment[38]. Unlike London, this employment creation aspect of recycling forms an integral part of the rationale for material recovery and renovation of household goods, as an example of re-use within the hierarchy of recycling options shown in Figure 2.4, and it can be argued that environmental Keynesianism persists in Hamburg as part of the wider strategic goals of recycling activity.

Textiles In Hamburg, on-street collection facilities for textiles and clothes, are serviced by a private contractor on behalf of the Red Cross. The best quality clothes are distributed to refugees from Eastern Europe and to social security claimants.   Poorer quality clothes are exported to developing countries and also to areas of disaster relief, the remaining fraction of low grade textiles used for industrial rag manufacture and cloth making[39]. A small proportion of old clothes is also recycled via the network of second-hand shops in Hamburg. The 1989 Waste Management Plan noted that there exist no reliable data, both in Hamburg and for Germany as a whole, on the quantities of textiles and old clothes being recycled outside public sector schemes, but as Figure 6.7 shows, textiles accounted for less than 3 per cent of the household waste stream.

Waste oil and tyres   In 1986, the fourth amendment to the 1972 Waste Management Act included special provisions for waste oil. These required any retailer to take in the same quantity of waste oil from a customer that they had sold to the same customer, and not charge any fees for this service. In practice, however, retailers in Hamburg have not been accepting oil without a receipt as proof of purchase. Because of the difficulties which have arisen out of these arrangements, the *Landesbetrieb Hamburger Stadtreinigung* decided to take in waste oil at its nine *Recyclinghöfe*, illustrated in Figure 6.6, at a charge of 5 DM for every 6 litres[40]. Tyres were similarly covered by arrangements between retailers and their customers, but this again necessitated the role of the *Recyclinghöfe* to take in additional tyres. The collected tyres were then passed to the recycling industry, principally for pyrolysis, but the problems of fly-tipping had not been eliminated[41].

The closing circle of policy options for Hamburg

Hamburg is faced with a potential crisis in its waste management from four main sources: intense political pressure to increase the level of recycling, led principally by the Greens in the Hamburg Senate; a high and rising *Gebühr* charge to individual households for waste management services; the decision to cease landfill operations at the major Schönberg site in the former East Germany; and the imminent decommissioning of the oldest and largest of the city's three incineration plants at Borsigstraße. The scale of the contemporary difficulties facing Hamburg can be illustrated by the fact that the Schönberg landfill site and the Borsigstraße incineration plant currently handle between them, over half of Hamburg's municipal waste stream.

   Hamburg's difficulties are further heightened by the inability of the city to finance new incineration capacity itself. The cost of waste management in Hamburg has become increasingly contentious in the Senate, in the face of growing fiscal difficulties, and this situation has created an intense political debate within the ruling SPD administration over the appropriate role for the private sector in waste management[42].   The left of the ruling SPD administration, had pushed for a major waste reduction and recycling strategy coupled with new landfill sites, in order to reduce the need for incineration. However, the newly ascendant centre-right of the SPD along with their FDP coalition partners has since 1987, largely abandoned this approach because of the cost implications for waste management, and has shifted the policy emphasis towards the goal of reduced waste management expenditure by the city[43].

   The political difficulties facing the SPD controlled Senate's waste management policies have been heightened by fluctuations in their share of the vote since the early seventies, as indicated by Table 6.1, forcing them into coalition with the centrist FDP in order to gain an absolute majority in the Senate. In contrast to the SPD, the FDP have wanted to see most waste management handled in the private sector, in order to cut costs[44]. The FDP proposed the experimental privatisation of waste collection in Bezirk Bergedorf and Harburg, as the first step towards complete privatisation of waste management, called for by the CDU opposition in the Senate (CDU, 1990a; 1990b; FDP, 1989).

Table 6.5: Comparative costs of waste management options in Hamburg

Waste management options 1988-1989	Cost per tonne DM
Provision, emptying and transport of glass and paper from on-street collection facilities (Average price under contract)	60
Waste collection and disposal by landfill (Schoenberg site in the former DDR)	240
Waste collection and disposal by incineration (Average cost at the city's three plants)	290
Fortnightly collection of putrescible waste and centralised production of compost (Bezirk Harburg pilot project for dual-bin system)	380
Weekly collection of putrescible waste and centralised production of compost (Bezirk Harburg pilot project for dual-bin system)	430
Bring system of plastics collection including sorting and transport costs (Bezirk Bergedorf pilot project)	500
Kerbside collection of mixed plastics including sorting and transport costs (Bezirk Bergedorf pilot project)	1,000

Source: Various interview material.

The Greens, represented by the radical *Fundis* wing in Hamburg, are opposed to any role for the private sector in waste management, and have advocated the elimination of incineration as an option, coupled with the maximum technically achievable increase in recycling and waste reduction at source[45]. After the 1987 elections, there were negotiations in Hamburg over the possibility of forming a coalition between the Greens and the SPD, as was the case in West Berlin creating a 'red-green' coalition (SPD, 1989). However, the policy gulf between the Fundis dominated Greens and the traditional centrist orientated SPD proved unbridgeable, and the SPD eventually formed an administration with the FDP, as it has always done in the past, on failing to gain an absolute majority in the Senate (Mintzel and Oberreuter, 1990).

The FDP within the 1987 to 1991 SPD/FDP coalition agreed to a compromise over the privatisation of waste management, insisting only on the eventual privatisation of individual services provided by the *Landesbetrieb Hamburger Stadtreinigung*, such as bulky refuse collection and street cleansing, and the continued dominance of the private sector in the provision and operation of on-street collection facilities for glass and paper[46]. The opposition CDU in the Hamburg Senate has come down in favour of the increased use of incineration, and in the early 1980s, joined with the Greens in opposition to a proposed landfill facility in a nature reserve (Duvenstedter Brook) within the city boundaries. The CDU arguments against landfill rested on three main elements: its contribution to global warming from methane emissions (CDU, 1988b); the expense of future decontamination and land reclamation of former landfill sites at Tegelweg and especially at the major Georgeswerder site (CDU, 1988a); and finally, the belief that Hamburg should handle its own waste within the city boundaries, without relying on complex and expensive negotiations with the neighbouring *Länder* of Schleswig-Holstein and Lower Saxony[47].

The proposed solution to Hamburg's waste disposal crisis, following heated debate within the SPD city administration, was to give the go-ahead to a joint private venture between the Hamburg based electricity utility, Hamburger Electricitätswerke AG (HEW), and the national VEBA Kraftwerke Ruhr AG (VKR), to build one of the largest incineration plants in Germany on derelict land on the Borsigstraße site in the Hamburg docks. During the 1980s, there has been widespread diversification within the German energy industry, as state owned utilities such as AVG in Nord-Rhine Westfalen, and other private sector concerns including Babcock; Preußen Electra; Siemens and VEBA move out of nuclear energy (which has been in decline since the late 1970s), and into energy recovery schemes based on the incineration of municipal waste[48]. The new Borsigstraße incineration plant is planned to be operational from 1994, and the *Landesbetrieb Hamburger Stadtreinigung* will be under contract to supply it with at least 40 per cent of Hamburg's municipal waste stream per year. In addition to receiving a guaranteed income from waste disposal at the site, the operators will also make substantial profit from the utilisation of waste heat and the sales of electricity generated (Marten, 1990b).

Table 6.6: Difficulties with the recycling of different materials

Paper	Weakness of the secondary materials market
	Contamination problems
	Demands from contractors for financial assistance to cover their losses
	Disagreements with contractors over the contractual obligations for the maintenance of collection sites
Putrescibles	Expense of the dual-bin system for households without gardens
	Smell from composting plants and fortnightly collections
	Competition over land use for composting plants
	Uncertainty over markets for final product
Glass	Green and mixed glass market close to saturation
	Disagreements with contractors over the contractual obligations for the maintenance of collection sites
Plastics	The expense of separate collection, transport and sorting
	Potential conflict over the maintenance of the calorific vaue of waste under contract to the new Borsigstrasse incineration plant.
Metals	High labour costs of separation of metals from consumer durables
Textiles	Lack of data on voluntary sector activities for planning purposes
Oil	Non compliance of retailers with the 4th amendment to the 1972 Waste Management Act

Source: Various interview material

The 1989 Waste Management Plan drawn up by the Baubehörde and approved by the Hamburg senate, brought to a head the political conflict over the future of waste management in Hamburg, and in September 1989, there was a major street demonstration against the plan. The main groups involved in the demonstration were workers from the *Landesbetrieb Hamburger Stadtreinigung*, represented by their union Öffentlicher Dienste, Transport und Verkehr (ÖTV), campaigning against further privatisation plans, along with numerous environmentalist and citizens' action groups, campaigning against the construction of the new incineration plant planned for Borsigstraße, and the associated risks from dioxin emissions[49]. The opposition to the 1989 Plan was marked by the production of an alternative plan, the *Müllkonzept*, drawn up by the Hamburg Green Party (GAL), environmentalist groups and a Hamburg based environmental consultancy Ökopol GmbH. The basic elements in the alternative plan, as illustrated in Table 6.7, focused on the cancellation of the Borsigstraße project, which they argued could be made possible by a combination of greatly increased recycling and waste reduction at source; the adaptation of existing incineration capacity at Stapelfelt and Stellingermoor to take more waste; and the use of new landfill sites outside Hamburg, based on full public planning and consultation procedures (Ahrens et al., 1989).

Table 6.7: The main alternative policy positions in Hamburg

The 1989 Waste Management Plan approved by the Hamburg Senate	The Alternative 'Mullkonzept'
Construction of a new incineration plant by a private sector joint venture between HEW and VKR to handle 40% of Hamburg's municipal waste. Moderate expansion of dual-bin system for putrescible waste Increased density of 'bring' facilities and recycling centres.	Cancellation of order for new incineration plant New landfill sites based on full public planning and consultation procedures. No increased role for the private sector in waste management. Comprehensive expansion of dual-bin system for putrescible waste. Increased density of 'bring' facilities and recycling centres. Emphasis on reducing the size of the waste stream by waste reduction and prevention at source, both within the home and within the production process

Source: Ahrens et al. (1990); Freie und Hansestadt Hamburg (1989d)

The Hamburg Greens have campaigned for the separate collection of putrescible waste throughout the city as an extension of the Harburg pilot project, except where this is impracticable, or where households with gardens can carry out their own composting, as part of the *Eigenkompostierung* programme[50], the scope for which is illustrated in Figure 6.9. The Borsigstraße incineration project, approved by the Senate, was argued in the alternative plan to be the most expensive option in comparison with increased recycling and landfill (though this is disputed in other analyses, see ITU, 1989; Thiel, 1988 and Table 6.5). Most importantly, however, its construction was seen as a disincentive to expand recycling and waste

232

reduction because of the contractual controls which would be instituted over the waste management activities of the *Landesbetrieb Hamburger Stadtreinigung*. In particular, they draw attention to the contractual obligation on the *Landesbetrieb Hamburger Stadtreinigung* to provide 40 per cent of the municipal waste stream in Hamburg for the Borsigstraße incineration plant[51]. This, they argue, would ease the pressure to expand recycling and waste reduction, since the successful operation of incineration plants does not rely on waste reduction, and a larger waste stream would simply present greater opportunities to build more incineration capacity in the future:

> Its construction would be a signal to industry that changes in the production process to increase waste reduction and recycling are not essential. (Ahrens et al., 1990 p. 6 in translation).

If the supply of waste in total tonnage terms to the plant was reduced below the minimum specified by recycling and waste reduction measures, the cost per tonne for waste disposal would rise accordingly. This would be in effect, a financial disincentive for widespread recycling and waste reduction, a point which was forcefully argued in the alternative waste management plan (Ahrens et al., 1990). Further concerns centred on the obligation to maintain the calorific value of the waste stream which could be interpreted as a contractual veto on the widespread recycling of plastics. With the construction of the new incineration plant at Borsigstraße, the city would be under contract to supply waste with a calorific value of between 6,500 KJ/Kg - 8,000 KJ/Kg (Bürgerschaft der Freien und Hansestadt Hamburg, 1990). Indeed, the specificity of the proposed contract arose from the fact, that changes in the composition of the waste stream, could entail expensive adaptations to the incineration plant[52].

Theoretically, however, the Hamburg Senate would still have some control over the plant, through their majority share holding in the city's electricity company, *Hamburger Elektricitäts Werke* (HEW) (the partner with VKR in the joint construction venture). Yet local authorities in Germany are increasingly selling off their share holdings in such utilities, both for ideological reasons, in terms of extending privatisation, and also as an additional source of income[53]. Indeed, there was speculation during 1990, that the SPD administration might sell off the *Landesbetrieb Hamburger Stadtreinigung*, either as a whole, or split up into different areas spatially[54], and an offer for the *Landesbetrieb Hamburger Stadtreinigung* had already been received from a French waste management firm[55]. If carried out, this would in effect be a complete privatisation of all operational aspects of waste management in the city, as is currently taking place in the voluntary WDAs in

London opting for outright privatisation rather than the formation of LAWDCs, as described in the last chapter. The SPD administration faces the difficulty of having to pursue a waste management policy which fulfils its statutory responsibility for waste collection and disposal in the most efficient and cost-effective manner possible, without alienating the left wing of the party, which are sympathetic to the alternative *Müllkonzept*. The 1989 Waste Management Plan can be interpreted as a compromise between political expediency (in the face of environmental lobbying) and economic constraints (principally from the city budget deficit and the need to control the *Gebühr* charge). A large expansion of recycling by the *Landesbetrieb Hamburger Stadtreinigung* would necessarily entail a further and politically unpopular rise in the *Müllgebühr* charge.

In summary, the Hamburg Senate is faced with a complex set of political and economic dilemmas in resolving its future arrangements for waste management. This situation had arisen for a combination of logistical, economic and political reasons, mainly beyond the effective control of the Hamburg Senate. The increasing dominance of incineration in the future could paradoxically lead to a lessening of the pressure to expand recycling, despite the stated objectives to expand recycling in the 1989 Waste Management Plan. This and other fears, made the planned Borsigstraße plant the central focus of conflict over the future of waste management for the city, between the two main strategies: the 1989 Waste Management Plan put forward by the Senate, involving increased incineration in the private sector; and the alternative *Müllkonzept* based around the maximum promotion of recycling and waste reduction at source.

The Töpfer law and new forms of state intervention

An investigation into recycling and waste management in Hamburg would not be complete without mention of important recent developments within national waste legislation in Germany. The increased political pressure during the 1980s for the recycling of waste has not been confined to local government, indeed the representation of *Die Grünen* in the *Bundestag* from 1983 to 1991 and the 'greening' of the other political parties has had a profound impact on national legislative developments (Mintzel and Oberreuter, 1990).

The political pressure for higher rates of recycling and the difficulties faced by local government in recycling the diverse and growing component of waste derived from packaging, coupled with public opposition to new incineration plants, has led to radical new legislation at a national level in Germany[56]. A total of some 48 incineration plants in Germany now burn around 30 per cent of the municipal waste stream but have met with sustained public opposition (Akkre, 1991; Friedrich, 1989; Spill and Wingert, 1990). The issue of waste and recycling has assumed an important place on the national policy agenda, in part through growing frustration with the seemingly ineffectual attempts to control waste at a local level (Drösser, 1990). The new packaging law, widely referred to as the Töpfer law after the environment minister Professor Klaus Töpfer, was passed by the *Bundesrat* upper house in April 1991, and sets out stringent requirements for the collection and recycling of packaging. Retailers and manufacturers are now obliged to take back the packaging materials used in their products. By July 1st 1995, 80 per cent of packaging waste must be collected, and at least 90 per cent of glass and metals must be recycled and 80 per cent of the paper, board, plastics and laminates. The legislation specifically rules out the recovery of energy from incineration as a form of recycling (Akkre, 1991; Thornhill, 1991).

The Töpfer law has instituted a 'dual waste system' (DSD), where industry must organise the reclamation of re-usable packaging waste and local authorities will continue to handle the collection and disposal of the remaining *Restmüll* from routine waste management and carry out their own recycling activities. The *Duales System Deutschland* (DSD) has been set up by 400 companies in the private sector in order to comply with the new legislation. Products in the scheme carry a green dot showing that their packaging can be recycled and qualifies for collection under the DSD scheme and firms within the scheme pay a levy for the operation of the scheme (Newham and Knight, 1991). It is estimated that an average of 2 pfennig has been placed on each item of packaging, the cost of which is passed on to the consumer, in order to finance the 7 million DM investment in 200 regional sorting facilities for the recyclable materials collected from retailers. It is anticipated that the legislation will reduce the quantity of packaging by 25 per cent within five years and also force changes in the packaging materials used: there are already indications that plastics manufacturers are seeing reduced profits whereas aluminium appears to have benefited slightly from the scheme (Goodhart, 1991).

The Töpfer law has been fiercely criticised by two main interest groups: German industry and the radical wing of the environmentalist movement. German industry and economic interest groups within government regard the new packaging controls as an unnecessary intrusion of the state and a threat to economic competitiveness (*Die Welt*, 27th August 1990). The UK based INCPEN representing 60 international companies from all sections of the packaging sector has lodged an official complaint with the European Commission. They claim that the law will distort trade between the EC member states and also threaten recycling industries in other countries. Their belief is that German industry will be unable to cope with the collected materials, leading to dumping in other countries and a general collapse in recycling activities, as a result of a general depression of the secondary materials market (Hibbeln, 1992). This is already the case with plastics and the UK government lodged an official complaint with the EC in May 1993, since the UK plastics recycling sector was receiving German material at zero cost and delivered free of charge, or in some cases with an incentive payment of up to £200 per tonne (Carvel, 1993; Lean, 1993). Further concerns include the discovery of DSD green dot packaging materials dumped at landfill sites in France and Indonesia (Genillard, 1993).

INCPEN have argued that recycling should be driven by the market rather than legislation and claim that recycling for 'its own sake' makes no commercial or environmental sense (Goodhart, 1991). Likewise, the European Recycling and Recovery Association (ERRA), funded by 27 companies with interests in packaging, presented a case to the EC Environment Commissioner Carl Ripa de Meana in June 1991, criticising the focus on a narrow definition of recycling based around returnables, and ERRA has been financing its own pilot voluntary recycling projects in six EC countries as the basis of an alternative approach to recycling policy.

The packaging lobby clearly fear the influence of the German legislation on a new packaging directive being drawn up by the EC and have been pushing for an extension of the definition of recycling to include energy recovery (Akkre, 1991; Goodhart, 1991; Rassmussen, 1991). There are already signs that new legislation in France, Austria and the Netherlands is being modelled on the Töpfer law, and the first draft of the EC packaging directive in October 1991, called for a halt in the growth of the municipal waste stream to 150 kg per head and the recovery of 90 per cent of packaging waste within ten years (EC, 1991a).

The legislation has also been attacked by the *Fundis* wing of the Greens, who claim that the underlying rationale of waste production at source has not been addressed, and that the volume of waste may continue to rise despite a larger proportion of packaging being recycled (Newham and Knight, 1991). The Greens have taken the unusual step of backing the German Cartel Office in their claim that the legislation is a barrier to competition and will have a negligible environmental impact. There are also indications that the overall costs of waste management have been increased, and some leading German companies such as BASF are threatening to relocate their activities outside Germany to in order to maintain profitability. It is conceivable, therefore, that the political pressure for higher environmental standards may accelerate a relocation of waste producing activities outside the core economies, just as opposition to toxic waste management has given impetus to the international trade in toxic wastes and the phenomenon of 'waste colonialism'.

These legislative developments in Germany illustrate that the limits to waste management policy in local government may lead to new forms of state legislation at a national level in order to respond to political demands for higher environmental standards in waste management. Indeed, Professor Töpfer is extending the DSD principle under new legislation to consumer durables, particularly cars and white electrical goods, in order to force companies to take back and recycle as much as is technically feasible (Genillard, 1993; Goodhart, 1991). It remains to be seen whether the recycling of packaging will affect the growing contribution of incineration to waste disposal and the changes underway in municipal waste management in local government. Whilst there is a process of demunicipalisation affecting the operational aspects of waste management in local government, there are new forms of state intervention emerging at a national level in response to the perceived inadequacy of attempts by the private sector to control the waste stream. It appears that whilst the 1980s was marked by a degree of consensus over the rapid expansion of recycling using the 'bring' system of on-street collection facilities, the 1990s is seeing a period of conflict and uncertainty, with a new coalition emerging between the private sector and radical environmentalists against a seeming obsession with post-consumer materials recycling.

Conclusion

Hamburg presents a microcosm of the contemporary evolution of waste management and recycling in a developed economy where the political pressure for higher environmental standards has become more fully integrated into waste management policy than in London. The experience of recycling in the city and the variety of pilot projects have shown that comprehensive recycling strategies are clearly more expensive than routine waste disposal by either landfill or incineration. Despite the differences in the way waste management is organised in London and Hamburg, and the different rates of recycling achieved, there were a number of common obstacles to a further expansion of recycling, relevant to the wider discussion of difficulties in achieving high rates of urban recycling. The first of these shared difficulties is a chronic lack of space, particularly in the densely built up inner areas of both cities. Thus the difficulties of central London, for example, are directly paralleled in the congested inner areas of Hamburg. A second issue is the expansion of potentially profitable options, such as incineration with energy recovery. A comparison may be drawn here between the re-emergence of incineration in London described in Chapter Five, and the new Borsigstraße incineration plant under construction in Hamburg.

Notes

1   Interview with Dr Manfred Körner in the research department of the Hamburg branch of the Sozialdemokratische Partei Deutschlands (SPD), 4th July 1990.

2   Interview with Dr Jürgen Ossenbrügge at the Universität Hamburg, 5th September 1990.

3   Interview with Wiebke Sager in the Amt für Entsorgungsplanung, Hamburg Baubehörde, 10th July 1990.

4   Interview with Wiebke Sager in the Amt für Entsorgungsplanung, Hamburg Baubehörde, 17th September 1990.

5   Interview with Dr Joachim Wüttke in the Umweltbundesamt, Berlin, 18th September 1990.

6   Interview with Wiebke Sager in the Amt für Entsorgungsplanung, Hamburg Baubehörde, 17th September 1990.

7   Interview with Wiebke Sager in the Amt für Entsorgungsplanung, Hamburg Baubehörde, 17th September 1990.

8   Interview with Dr Manfred Körner in the research department of the Hamburg branch of the Sozialdemokratische Partei Deutschlands (SPD), 4th July 1990.

9   Interview with Wiebke Sager in the Amt für Entsorgungsplanung, Hamburg Baubehörde, 17th September 1990.

10   Interview with Wiebke Sager in the Amt für Entsorgungsplanung, Hamburg Baubehörde, 17th September 1990.

11   Interview with Martis Okekke in the Recycling Zentrum Harburg, 6th September 1990.

12   Interview with Gerd Eich in the Landesbetrieb Hamburger Stadtreinigung (LB-HSR), 5th September 1990.

13   Interview with Olaf Stüdt in Nutzmüll e.V., 10th September 1990

14   Interview with Wiebke Sager in the Amt für Entsorgungsplanung, Hamburg Baubehörde, 17th September 1990.

15   Interview with Wiebke Sager in the Amt für Entsorgungsplanung, Hamburg Baubehörde, 10th July 1990.

16   Interview with Dr Manfred Körner in the research department of the Hamburg branch of the Sozialdemokratische Partei Deutschlands (SPD), 4th July 1990.

17   Interview with Wiebke Sager, Amt für Entsorgungsplanung, Hamburg Baubehörde, 17th September 1990. Interview with Martis Okekke in the Recycling Zentrum Harburg, 6th September 1990.

18   Interview with Dr Ingo Wittern, Grüne Naßmüll Project Harburg, 6th September 1990. Interview with Martis Okekke, Recycling Zentrum Harburg, 6th September 1990.

19   Interview with Gerd Eich in the Landesbetrieb Hamburger Stadtreinigung (LB-HSR), 6th July 1990.

20   Interview with Wiebke Sager, Amt für Entsorgungsplanung, Hamburg Baubehörde, 17th September 1990.

21   Interview with Wiebke Sager, Amt für Entsorgungsplanung, Hamburg Baubehörde, 17th September 1990.

22   Interview with Wiebke Sager, Amt für Entsorgungsplanung, Hamburg Baubehörde, 17th September 1990.

23   Interview with Gerd Eich in the Landesbetrieb Hamburger Stadtreinigung (LB-HSR), 5th September 1990.

24   Interview with Gerd Eich in the Landesbetrieb Hamburger Stadtreinigung (LB-HSR), 6th July 1990.

25   Interview with Wiebke Sager, Amt für Entsorgungsplanung, Hamburg Baubehörde, 17th September 1990.

26   Interview with Martis Okekke, Recycling Zentrum Harburg, 6th September 1990.

27   Interview with Dr Ingo Wittern, Grüne Naßmüll Project Harburg, 6th September 1990.

28   Interview with Dr Ingo Wittern, Grüne Naßmüll Project Harburg, 6th September 1990.

29   Interview with Michaela Moser, Institut für ökologisches Recycling, 20th September 1990.

30   Interview with Wiebke Sager, Amt für Entsorgungsplanung, Hamburg Baubehörde, 17th September 1990.

31   Interview with Wiebke Sager, Amt für Entsorgungsplanung, Hamburg Baubehörde, 17th September 1990.

32   Interview with Dr Ingo Wittern, Grüne Naßmüll Project Harburg, 6th September 1990.

33   Interview with Gerd Eich in the Landesbetrieb Hamburger Stadtreinigung (LB-HSR), 5th September 1990.

34   Interview with Wiebke Sager, Amt für Entsorgungsplanung, Hamburg Baubehörde, 10th July 1990.

35   Interview with Wiebke Sager, Amt für Entsorgungsplanung, Hamburg Baubehörde, 17th September 1990.

36   Interview with Gerd Eich in the Landesbetrieb Hamburger Stadtreinigung (LB-HSR), 5th September 1990.

37   Interview with Olaf Stüdt in Nutzmüll e.V., 10th September 1990. Interview with Dr Joachim Wüttke in the Umweltbundesamt, Berlin, 18th September 1990.

38   Interview with Wiebke Sager, Amt für Entsorgungsplanung, Hamburg Baubehörde, 17th September 1990.

39   Interview with Wiebke Sager, Amt für Entsorgungsplanung, Hamburg Baubehörde, 17th September 1990.

40   Interview with Gerd Eich in the Landesbetrieb Hamburger Stadtreinigung (LB-HSR), 6th July 1990.

41   Interview with Dr Manfred Körner in the research department of the Hamburg branch of the Sozialdemokratische Partei Deutschlands (SPD), 4th July 1990.

42   Interview with Dr Manfred Körner in the research department of the Hamburg branch of the Sozialdemokratische Partei Deutschlands (SPD), 4th July 1990.

43   Interview with Gebhard Kraft, CDU Fraktion Hamburg, 13th September 1990.

44   Interview with Annette Hallerberg, FDP Fraktion Hamburg, 7th September 1990.

45   Interviews with Jürgen Hannert and Antje Möller-Bierman, Die Grünen/GAL Hamburg, 10th July 1990. Interview with Knut Sander, Ökopol GmbH, 12th September 1990.

46   Interview with Annette Hallerberg, FDP Fraktion Hamburg, 7th September 1990. Interview with Gerd Eich in the Landesbetrieb Hamburger Stadtreinigung (LB-HSR), 5th September 1990.

47   Interview with Gebhard Kraft, CDU Fraktion Hamburg, 13th September 1990.

48   Interview with Michaela Moser, Institut für ökologisches Recycling, 20th September 1990. Interview with Dr Jürgen Ossenbrügge at the Universität Hamburg, 5th September 1990.

49   Interview with Knut Sander, Ökopol GmbH, 12th September 1990.

50   Interviews with Jürgen Hannert and Antje Möller-Bierman, Die Grünen/GAL Hamburg, 10th July 1990. Interview with Knut Sander, Ökopol GmbH, 12th September 1990.

51   Interview with Knut Sander, Ökopol GmbH, 12th September 1990.

52   Interview with Knut Sander, Ökopol GmbH, 12th September 1990.

53   Interview with Dr Jürgen Ossenbrügge at the Universität Hamburg, 5th September 1990.

54   Interview with Knut Sander, Ökopol GmbH, 12th September 1990.

55   Interview with Karl-Heinz Senkpiel, A.H. Julius Rohde GmbH, 13th September 1990.

56   Interview with Gebhard Kraft, CDU Fraktion Hamburg, 13th September 1990. Interview with Knut Sander, Ökopol GmbH, 12th September 1990.   Interview with Dr Joachim Wüttke in the Umweltbundesamt, Berlin, 18th September 1990.

57   Interview with Dr Jürgen Ossenbrügge at the Universität Hamburg, 5th September 1990.

7 Conclusions

In this concluding chapter I bring together the main themes and issues to emerge from this study. I suggest that there are three critical areas neglected within the existing literature: firstly, the impact of neo-liberal policy making since the 1970s on municipal waste management; secondly, the way in which the shift towards market driven policy is leading to a growing emphasis on energy rather than materials recovery within the hierarchy of recycling options; and thirdly, the role of the administrative structure and financing of local government in facilitating the promotion of alternative non market-based waste management strategies.

The demunicipalisation of recycling and waste management

In the 1970s there were two developments of particular significance for recycling. Firstly, there was a shift of the rationale for recycling from economic well-being and the routine operation of incineration plants to the conservation of materials and energy as a reflection of rising environmental concern. Secondly, the decline in Keynesian patterns of public policy led to attempts from the mid-1970s onwards to reduce local government expenditure, particularly in expensive labour intensive areas such as municipal waste management. As a result of these twin pressures on local government, of political demands for recycling and the provision of cheaper services, the 'bring' system of recycling emerged, based on the harnessing of public concern to bring separated recyclable materials to on-street collection facilities and recycling centres.

In the case of London the rationale for extending the public sector role in waste management since the late nineteenth century until at least the mid-1970s, rested largely on the perceived inadequacy of the private sector to carry out municipal waste management in a cost-effective and environmentally acceptable way. However, the capacity of the private sector to take on operational aspects of waste management has developed substantially since the 1960s and 1970s. This has been a result of the growing size and technological sophistication of the waste management industry, with an increasing dominance of large firms, including multi-national companies specialised in the provision of municipal services. These companies are able to benefit from economies of scale and undertake research and development into profitable aspects of waste management such as bio-gas recovery and improved electricity from waste systems, increasingly beyond the operational scope and financial capacity of local government. In the UK, for example, there has been a growing involvement of energy and water utilities in municipal waste management in response to number of developments: the privatisation of public utilities; the creation of market opportunities for the provision of local government services through competitive tendering; and the decline of other less profitable sectors of technical engineering such as nuclear energy since the 1970s.

The background to this process of demunicipalisation in waste management can be considered in relation to the socio-economic restructuring debate and the periodisation in the capitalist state advanced by the neo-Marxist 'regulationist school' (see Jessop, 1988, 1991; Lipietz, 1992). The regulationists generally recognise three main periods of change in the role of the state in public policy: a phase of 'competitive regulation' spanning from the mid-nineteenth century to the 1920s; a Fordist period lasting from the 1930s until the early 1970s; and a post-Fordist period from the 1970s to date (Stoker, 1989). However, the experience of municipal waste management in London, as illustrated in Table 7.1, suggests a rather different pattern: a 'competitive regulation' period lasting at least until the 1960s with the formation of the GLC and the creation of regulatory controls over waste management; a brief Fordist municipal ethos based on strategic planning and retaining support among many London Boroughs after GLC abolition in 1986; and finally, a very recent period of post-Fordist restructuring associated with the introduction of CCT, LAWDCs and the growing role of the private sector. In Hamburg, the pattern is different with the unified Fordist phase established rather earlier and not yet completely supplanted by the formation of the *Landesbetrieb Hamburger Stadtreinigung* in 1988, though the Senate is under political and economic pressure to release operational aspects of waste management to the private sector. An important question for further research is whether these developments represent a lagged parallel of wider socio-economic changes, or whether the changes within waste management are not explicable within the categories derived from the regulationist school and the capitalist restructuring thesis.

As a result of these changes it can be seen that the process of the

Table 7.1: Schematic representation of changes in recycling and municipal waste management in London from the 1840s till the 1990s

Period	Municipal waste management	Pattern of recycling
Industrial Revolution to 1889	Period of laissez-faire non intervention by the state. Waste management focused on street cleansing and free passage along highways. Pressure for reform with the growth of the public health movement.	Economic rationale Licensed totting of horse manure Scavenging of valuable items Sales of ashes, pig swill etc.
1889 to 1965	Reforms in local government Fragmentary but powerful local government with wide ranging municipal responsibilities. Growing demands for strategic co-ordination of policy to raise environmental standards and increase economic efficiency.	Economic and Technical Rationale Metals, glass and clinker recovered as part of routine operation of incineration plants War-time salvage of wide range of materials. Local authority collection services for waste paper and pig swill.
1965 to 1986	Period of strategic policy making Separation of waste collection and disposal. Regional strategic WDA with new emphasis on data analysis and medium term planning. Major public sector investment programmme in new infrastructure.	Rise of environmental rationale Decline of existing patterns of materials recovery by local authority kerbside collections and centralised sorting. Rise of 'bring' systems dependent on public participation from the late 1970s onwards. Conversion of civic amenity sites into multi-material recycling centres from 1982 onwards. Brief period of radical policy in early 1980s linking recycling to employment creation and lobbying EC and national government for controls on packaging.
1986 to date	Period of demunicipalisation Growing operational role for the private sector. Administrative fragmentation and decline in strategic policy making.	Divergence of rationale i) Focus on waste reduction at source and state intervention in production ii) Emphasis on materials recycling and state intervention to control packaging iii) Focus on energy recovery as part of market-led programme to combat global warming.

Source: Gandy (1992a)

municipalisation of waste management from the late nineteenth century onwards, has been supplanted by a process of demunicipalisation in waste management since the early 1980s. In the case of London, the peak of municipal waste management in the 1970s in terms of its strategic scope and levels of public expenditure took some two hundred years to come about, whereas the opposite process has taken less than ten years: such is the scale and rate of change within contemporary waste management. The process of demunicipalisation has also been accompanied by a weakening of any democratic influences on strategic policy making. The choice of options for waste management is being determined increasingly by the profitability of the private sector waste management industry rather than the strategic needs of the community co-ordinated through elected local government. This process is most clearly seen in the decline of radical waste management in London since the early 1980s and the fragmentation and dissipation of the public sector role in co-ordinating and providing waste management services. This diminished democracy in waste management can also be observed in Hamburg, where there is disquiet over the contractual obligations as a result of the new private sector Borsigstraße incineration plant designed to handle some 40 per cent of Hamburg's municipal waste stream. To draw these strands together, it can be argued that the process of demunicipalisation is occurring in order to cut the costs of waste management and enable public demands for higher environmental standards to be met. This is increasing the pressure to shift the policy emphasis within the recycling hierarchy from the primary recovery of materials towards the more profitable secondary recovery of energy favoured by the private sector.

A re-evaluation of recycling policy options

The use of 'bring' systems and on-street collection facilities

Recycling since the 1980s has been shaped by the rise of individualised forms of political expression and the use of cost-effective 'bring' systems for recycling reliant on public participation. The advantages of on-street collection facilities are mainly economic and political since their provision and operation is cheaper than kerbside collections, in terms of both capital and labour costs. The role of local government can be merely an enabler for the activities of the private sector and the voluntary sector, involving a minimal cost outlay on the part of public sector. In this respect the use of on-street collection facilities is in keeping with the political and economic constraints on contemporary environmental policy in local government. Both local government and central government can therefore claim that they are responding to environmental concern, but with a minimal increase in public expenditure.

The conversion of civic amenity type facilities into multi-material recycling centres occupies a more ambiguous position within the political and economic rationale for the 'bring' system of recycling. This is because civic amenity sites and recycling centres are essentially a non-profit making public service which must compete with other urban land uses. Indeed, their role may extend to aspects of toxic waste management for the municipal waste stream; qualified staff can provide advice to the public on different aspects of household waste management; and the sites can also be combined with the renovation and repair of bulky waste items and discarded consumer durables. This last function provides the possibility for employment generation, as part of environmental Keynesianism in recycling policy, which persists in SPD controlled Hamburg but has virtually disappeared in London since the abolition of the GLC, as suggested by Table 4.2.

Since it is the operational costs associated with waste collection which constitute the greatest financial burden within waste management, as described in Chapter Two, the economic viability of recycling in relation to alternative waste management options is dependent on the degree to which the involvement of the voluntary sector, state employment and training schemes, private sector sponsorship, and the participation of the public can be used to offset the potentially high labour costs involved. In this context, the promotion of recycling schemes dependent on the active participation of individual households could be interpreted as an attempt to escape the dilemma of reducing costs whilst at the same time raising environmental standards in waste management and responding to public demands to conserve natural resources and control pollution. Yet the disadvantages of on-street collection facilities are mainly environmental: the level of recycling is lower than with the use of kerbside 'collect' systems, both in the quality and quantity of collected materials, thereby making a smaller contribution to environmental policy; the local environmental impact may outweigh the wider environmental benefits and undermine public confidence in recycling as a long-term component of municipal waste management; and the patterns of usage involve the widespread deployment of cars to transport glass, which is among the least important materials for recycling in terms of its environmental impact, as indicated by Table 2.4.

The use of comprehensive kerbside collection and dual-bin systems

The established advantages of kerbside collection systems are the higher recycling rates which are achievable and their popularity with the public. In contrast to 'bring' systems the main problems with the use of kerbside collection systems are the higher capital and labour costs for local government. These costs can only be reduced through extensive private sector sponsorship, state subsidy or voluntary sector involvement. In the case of Milton Keynes in Buckinghamshire, for example, a pilot kerbside collection scheme for glass, paper, metals and plastics has been operating since June 1990 and is claimed to have reached a recycling rate of 19 per cent by 1993. However, the scheme has needed funding from nine sources including the waste management industry, the packaging industry, the voluntary sector, Milton Keynes Development Corporation and Buckinghamshire County Council (Milton Keynes Borough Council, 1990). Most significantly, the scheme has been allocated £1.5 million under the Government's supplementary credit initiative to assist recycling (DoE, 1991c). Similarly in Adur, West Sussex, the Government's target of 25 per cent recycling is reported for a kerbside collection scheme with financial backing from the Brussels based European Recovery and Recycling Association (ERRA), representing the interests of 27 companies, including British Steel, Nestlè, Perrier and Pepsi-Cola International. ERRA is now running nine pilot projects across Europe and is also providing financial assistance for the first UK Recycling City project in Sheffield. The aim of ERRA is to prevent the development of any controls over packaging waste, and the organisation has been lobbying the European Commission not to base the new EC Packaging Directive on the new packaging regulations in Germany described in Chapter Six. An examination of the funding for these kerbside collection schemes suggests that these represent sophisticated lobbying in order to mitigate the political threat to the private sector packaging industries and also to promote voluntary recycling based on a wider definition of materials recovery, including energy from waste schemes. The private sector will only participate in these loss making schemes as part of a dual strategy to influence legislative developments for waste management and also maintain or improve their market share by demonstrating their 'green' credentials. If kerbside collection schemes are not sponsored as part of the lobbying activities of the private sector or financed by central government the costs will be borne by the local population through higher charges for their routine waste management services. In Hamburg, the higher cost would be incurred directly through an increase in the *Müllgebühr* charge, whereas in London the cost would be reflected in higher Community Charge or Council Tax bills.

Centralised sorting and capital intensive options

The use of centralised sorting rather than individual citizens as the main means of separating re-usable materials from the waste stream has had two

248

main phases of use. The first, until the early 1960s formed part of the operational aspects of waste incineration, and involved the recovery of a range of materials, usually by hand picking from a moving belt. The second phase, during the 1970s, involved the increased use of mechanical sorting of the waste stream, often with the production of refuse derived fuel (RDF). The promotion of centralised sorting plants and the production of refuse-derived fuel has steadily declined since the 1980s as a result of technical and economic difficulties combined with the advent of cheaper methods of waste separation by the use of on-street collection facilities, which have only been widely introduced since the late 1970s. The 1970s interest in RDF has also waned because the predicted shortages and price rises for primary sources of energy have not materialised, and environmental concern has shifted from the 'energy crisis' of the 1970s to a new focus on global climatic change caused by the emission of atmospheric pollutants. Since the 1980s the emphasis of centralised and capital intensive recycling and waste management has been moving towards the profitable secondary recovery of the calorific value of waste to produce electricity.

The divergence of contemporary recycling

Contemporary recycling is marked by a divergence between three main conceptions of policy, as shown in Table 7.2. The three positions can be differentiated as follows: the private sector lobbying for incineration with energy recovery as a legitimate form of recycling; national governments attempting to increase the level of materials recycling through controls on the packaging industry and other sectors of the economy, in response to the political demands of the electorate; and radical environmentalists seeking to reduce the size of the waste stream at source rather than recycling a larger proportion of a growing waste stream.

It is now widely recognised that higher levels of materials recycling would require new forms of state intervention to mandatorily increase the recycling of packaging. Yet national level policy developments such the 1991 German packaging ordinance have been criticised by radical environmentalists, the packaging industry and the private sector waste management industry. This represents a coalescence of previously opposed positions over the question of whether materials recycling in municipal waste is relatively insignificant in relation to other issues such as the generation of electricity from non fossil-fuel sources advanced by the private sector or the need to reduce waste at source, advanced by the radical environmentalists. It is claimed that increased materials recycling has a negligible or even negative environmental impact and that the rationale serves symbolic political needs rather than a reasoned

Table 7.2: The divergence of contemporary recycling policy

Policy option and proponents	Central tenets	Policy implications
Energy recovery *Waste Management Industry* *Packaging Industry*	Anti-unnecessary state intervention Focus on measurable net environmental benefits derived from different policy options Emphasis on the profitable production of electricity as a measure to reduce greenhouse gas emissions	Focus on market-based policy instruments Operational dominance of private sector waste management companies and MNCs specialised in provision of public services such as water and energy Use of cheaper 'bring' systems for recycling of some materials Low rates of materials recycling Size of waste stream and production process largely unaffected
Materials recycling *The State* *The electorate in developed economies*	Response to public demands for higher rates of materials recycling Attempt to apply the 'polluter pays principle' to the producers of waste Aim the raise recycling towards technically achievable levels Energy recovery seen as inferior policy option	Increased state intervention at a national level with legislative controls on the packaging industry Promotion of kerbside collection schemes and higher public expenditure on waste management High levels of materials recycling Use of mix of market-based and non market-based policy instruments
Waste reduction *Radical environmentalists*	Policy focus on 'waste prevention' at source Criticism of both recycling and energy recovery as 'end of pipe' responses to a growing waste stream The market economy is seen as inherently wasteful because of the need to maximise profit margins and consumption levels.	Increased state intervention at both national and local levels Reduced size of waste stream Wide ranging social, economic and political implications for other areas of public policy Reduced role of the private sector in operational aspects of waste management and state controls over products and processes

Source: Gandy (1992a)

policy response to the environmental and economic consequences of waste (Ahrens et al., 1990; Moser, 1990). This is an important claim which demands further research and analysis of the environmental impact of alternative waste management strategies. Whilst the radical environmentalists and private sector packaging and waste management industries are in agreement over the difficulties with materials recycling, they differ over the most appropriate form of waste management. Table 7.2 shows how the private sector has emphasised the use of new technologies to recover energy from waste and contribute towards global warming policy, whereas radical environmentalists are committed to the reduction of the waste stream at source and a fundamental examination of different forms of economic organisation and public policy.

The limitations to market-based recycling policies

I wish to argue that a fundamental dimension to any analysis of environmental policy in a capitalist economy is the degree and nature of state intervention in the market. The question has been widely framed within the literature in terms of the relative role of regulatory and market-based policy instruments for environmental protection, as set out in Chapter One. Indeed, the combination of these different approaches has been perceived as largely unproblematic and there has been little examination of the underlying conceptual basis for different policy instruments. I argue that there are a number of criticisms of the underlying assumptions behind market-based policy strategies to increase levels of recycling: it is assumed that low levels of recycling can be attributed simply to different forms of 'market failure', yet UK government policy and much of the literature has relied on a narrow focus on the cost externalities associated with waste disposal; there is a simplistic internalisation of 'end of pipe' externalities, rather than the application of the 'polluter pays principle' to the producers of waste at source; and there is little practical integration of recycling policy into the overall environmental objectives of waste reduction and reduced pollution emissions, as shown in the attempt to extend the definition of recycling to include energy recovery and the promotion of policies which seek merely to recycle larger quantities of materials within an ever larger waste stream.

The evidence from London suggests that the internalisation of waste disposal costs through the use of rebates and recycling credits, has had relatively little impact on the level of recycling. Under administrative structures where the same tier of local government handles both the collection and disposal of waste, and hence the same budget extends to both waste collection and disposal as in Hamburg, the attempted 'end of pipe' internalisation of costs through rebates is not recognised, since the only meaningful financial statistic is the change in unit cost for the collection, handling and disposal of each tonne of waste by the municipal authority. Under this arrangement, it is easier to compare directly the costs of recycling initiatives on a tonne for tonne basis, which may explain why environmental objectives take precedence over economic objectives in Hamburg as a justification for promoting recycling within the city. It is of interest that the NFFO levy to promote non fossil-fuel sources of electricity in the UK is clearly more effective in influencing policy, although it is a non market-based strategy to ensure the continued generation of electricity from nuclear power. The NFFO levy could also be argued to be counteracting the role of recycling credits and pressures to increase materials recycling through its support for energy from waste schemes which enhance the profitability of alternative means of waste disposal in comparison with materials recycling.

We have seen that the level of materials recycling and the policy emphasis within the hierarchy of recycling options imply different degrees of state intervention in the market, as suggested by the divergence of recycling policy illustrated in Table 7.2. The policy significance of direct state intervention in the production process, as advanced by radical environmentalists, is the possibility of reducing waste and pollution at source and gaining functional control over parts of the waste stream such as packaging, and specific materials with a high environmental impact including PET, PVC and aluminium (see Eder, 1989; Die Grünen, 1989; Lahl and Wiebe, 1989; Kreusch, 1989). In contrast, the energy recovery option requires minimal state intervention and is the favoured option by both the packaging lobby and the private sector waste management industry (see Akkre, 1991; COPAC, 1992; IGD, 1992).

The organisational dimension to policy making

An important conclusion to emerge from this study is that a narrow focus on the effectiveness of specific policy instruments may neglect the organisational aspects of policy making in terms of the administrative structure of local government. The comparison of recycling in London and Hamburg shows that there are systematic policy differences under ostensibly similar advanced capitalist economies. There is a neglected organisational dimension to the analysis of policy making in the literature, illustrated by the importance of the administrative structure of waste management and the electoral arena in Hamburg. I argue that the structure and organisation of local government is an important factor in determining the pattern of waste management policy and the level of materials recycling. The case study of Hamburg suggests that an integrated form of federal government where the collection and disposal of waste is carried out by one tier of government is more conducive to recycling than a fragmentary organisational structure where the collection and disposal of waste is carried out separately and is not accountable to one directly elected authority. The differences in the recycling rate between London and Hamburg can be accounted for in part by the different administrative structures of waste management and the degree of integration and institutionalisation of environmental policy making into waste management, aided by the direct lobbying of the Hamburg Senate by the German Green Party elected under a system of proportional representation.

The policy implications of the analysis for London are that without an extensively funded ERRA or Recycling City type initiative, a recycling rate approaching 25 per cent for London would require changes in the way in which London is governed. Yet any shift within the UK local government system towards strategic regional policy making and better resourced local government would indicate a complete reversal of recent trends in central-local relations and the balance of both political power and public expenditure between the central and local state. This question of the organisation and financing of local government is of interest to the current debate over the future of London's government, since none of the UK political parties suggest a unified administrative structure for London's waste management in their current policy documents, as illustrated in Table 7.3.

The political and economic limits to materials recycling

A conceptual distinction can be made between those processes which contribute towards the higher recycling rate in Hamburg, and the underlying factors which limit recycling in both cities under investigation. The underlying factors found to be of particular significance in this study are the constraints on local government to finance their own waste management facilities; the lack of control over the size and composition of the waste stream; and the inability of local government to tackle wider economic barriers such as the weakness in the secondary materials market. The weakness of the secondary materials market has been a key barrier to higher levels of materials recycling throughout the post-war period and earlier, and has had three main impacts on recycling activity: firstly, the periodic collapse of markets in response to increases in the amount of collected materials during periods of environmental concern; secondly, the long-term decline in some sectors, such as rubber and textiles, in response to changing patterns of production and consumption and advances in raw materials processing technology; and finally, the innate weakness of the secondary materials market, reflected in the impact of economic recession on the demand for waste paper and other commodities. These difficulties are scarcely addressed by most programmes to radically increase the level of recycling towards

Table 7.3: Waste management, recycling and London government: the competing policy positions in 1991-92

Political Party	Waste management and strategic policy framework for London	Strategy to raise levels of recycling
Conservative	No directly elected strategic authority Abolition of statutory WDAs and all operational aspects of waste disposal handled by LAWDCs or private sector. Abolition of LWRA and replacement with a national Environmental Protection Agency.	1990 Environmental Protection Act: * recycling credits * recycling plans * Internalisation of disposal costs 1990 White Paper * 25% target by year 2,000 * Supplementary credit assistance to allow borrowing for specific for specific schemes
Labour	National waste strategy under an Environmental Protection Executive Regional elected authority without service delivery role. Not elected on PR system. LWRA retained as part of new regional authority. Increased role of London Boroughs in waste management Targets and standards in waste collection	Use of public procurement policy London Boroughs to comply with "targets for recycling set by regional authorities ". Promotion of kerbside collection and extensive use of 'bring' facilities. Green taxes on unrecycled products and packaging. Voluntary use of returnables and standardised containers.
Liberal Democrat	Regional strategic authority elected under PR system No change in administrative framework for waste management	Use of public procurement policy Encouragement for kerbside collection. Environmental grants and subsidies Mandatory deposit-refund systems. Pollution tax on waste disposal
Green Party	Regional strategic authority elected under PR system No change in administrative framework for waste management	Environmental education Pressure on businesses and retailers to reduce waste Rebates to councils who reduce their waste stream "instead of the present standard charge set by the four large London waste authorities which gives no incentive for councils to recycle". Comprehensive kerbside collection of major waste fractions. Neighbourhood voluntary sector recycling schems based on the 'adoption' of banks in return for some income from the sale of materials Grants to the repair and maintenance sector

Gandy (1992a)

technically achievable levels. The problem is merely compounded by more effective collection systems such as kerbside collection or the new German DSD system in the absence of an intricately co-ordinated and planned attempt to influence the whole cycle of production and consumption. The contemporary vicious circle is a result of increasing materials collections weakening the market, and leading to the collapse of collections. This, in turn, serves to undermine public confidence in the promotion of comprehensive recycling policies, and has indirectly served to increase attention on alternatives to materials recycling such as energy from waste schemes.

The literature has tended to focus on the issue of savings in waste disposal costs and narrow conceptions of 'market failure', to the relative exclusion of not only the secondary materials market but also a coherent analysis of the overall distribution of costs within municipal waste management. Indeed, a narrowly based economic justification for recycling based simply on financial viability and reduced waste management costs, illustrated in the case of London, where most boroughs saw reduced waste disposal costs as a key rationale for recycling, as shown in Table 4.2, is certain to run into difficulties if it is extended to a comprehensive kerbside recycling scheme or a dual-bin system handling significant quantities of materials. If the justification is moved beyond a narrow economic rationale to the provision of an environmental service, as in Hamburg, the question is framed in terms of what the community is willing to pay in order to increase the level of materials recycling. There is a trade-off between the environmental and economic goals of recycling, which is not fully recognised by most proponents of materials recycling. Many advocates of materials recycling have assumed that it is a means to lower both waste collection and disposal costs (see EDF, 1987; McClaren, 1992; Pollock, 1987), but the evidence suggests that high rates of recycling are more expensive than alternative means of waste disposal. This weakens the market-based argument that higher waste disposal costs as a result of tougher environmental standards will lead to a substantial increase in the recycling of waste, because recycling becomes progressively more expensive when it is raised to levels which necessitate the use of kerbside collection schemes and the recovery of difficult fractions of the waste stream such as putrescibles and plastics.

If we establish that high rates of materials recycling are more expensive than other alternative means of waste disposal, as suggested in the last chapter, there remains the question of who will pay for the more expensive waste management system as part of environmental policy. The unresolved problem is how the higher costs will be distributed in society and the identification of the polluter if the 'polluter pays principle' is to be followed. The use of direct charges on the supposed producers of waste through the increased cost of essential environmental services such as the collection and disposal of household waste is socially regressive, as shown in concern over the *Müllgebühr* charge in Hamburg and the use of direct charges as a form of financial incentive on households to reduce their waste stream. If the expense of comprehensive materials recycling, including the recovery of environmentally significant plastics and putrescibles is imposed under a simplistic 'polluters pays' framework, this may provoke a political backlash and alienate public concern over environmental issues:

> The question of who bears the cost, is a central concern in policy design. The impact on the consumer and the tax-payer is of great importance. Too large a burden on the consumer is likely to be regressive and carries the real risk of developing consumer resistance to environmental improvements...Economists used to dismiss this objection with the argument that if the outcome is inequitable, governments can use their taxing powers to remedy this. The experience of the last decade must at least cause a pause for thought. (BANC, 1990 p. 23).

Avenues for further research

There are two main areas for further research. The first need is for more theoretically based research into the causes of environmental degradation and the relationship between people and the environment. The existing literature has a lot to say about the consequences of environmental degradation and the technical and economic evaluation of various 'end of pipe' policy responses, but rather less to say about the underlying causes of the environmental crisis. This is very much a methodological problem concerning the epistemological basis of explanation, and the weakly developed conceptual distinction between market-based and non market-based interpretations of the cause of environmental problems. The second research need, is the generation of 'radical data' providing greater insight into the measurable environmental impact of different policy options, since it is now widely held that conventional indicators of economic activity are of little value in informing policy makers of the consequences of their decisions or allowing a reasoned debate on the merits of alternative policy strategies.

The positivist and pluralist legacy

It is hoped that this study has helped to demonstrate that a positivist and ahistorical conceptual framework lacks the necessary imaginative and flexible qualities from which to further understanding of the processes of environmental degradation. Most empirical studies of recycling and waste management focus on the managerial, logistical and technical aspects of alternative waste management systems or the behavioural and socio-economic determinants of public participation, as noted in the introductory chapter. Conventional theoretical analyses have tended to adopt the positivist and neo-classical explanatory frameworks described in Chapter One. These approaches do not examine the underlying contextual political and economic factors which influence the development of policy, providing instead an 'objective' appraisal of a pre-determined set of options in relation to a pre-determined set of criteria. There has been little attempt in the existing literature to combine empirical research of recycling and waste management with wider contextual issues influencing the evolution of the legislative framework for waste management. There is at present a danger of a mono-disciplinary ascendancy of neo-classical economic based analysis within the environmental policy debate. This is worrying, because there is little evidence that market-based policy instruments are very effective in practice (except for changing limited aspects of consumer behaviour, perhaps) or that they are founded on a cogent explanation of the underlying causes of environmental problems. The contemporary emphasis on 'market failure' as the underlying cause of environmental problems is seriously flawed both empirically and theoretically, and may in time be rejected as a creature of its time, just as the 1970s neo-Malthusian conceptions of the limits to growth have now been largely discredited.

Radical data and radical policies

There is clearly a need for carefully compiled quantitative data on the net reductions in pollution emissions and usage of materials and energy associated with the recycling of different components of the waste stream throughout the whole cycle of production, consumption and final disposal, along with attempts to evaluate social and economic impacts of decision making, as illustrated in Table 7.4. Since comprehensive recycling strategies cost more than alternative forms of waste disposal, as revealed in the case of Hamburg, policy makers who wish to pursue materials recycling will need to be able to demonstrate to those opposed to increased materials recycling that the policy is worth pursuing on proven environmental grounds and that there are measurable benefits which accrue to the community. A further need is for research into urban planning and architectural design, in order to integrate both energy efficiency and the minimisation of waste. It was noted in the historical review of waste management in London, that there has been concern since the 1930s over the difficulties in waste collection from high rise

Table 7.4: The universal production matrix

9.Waste disposal	8.Transport	7.Consumption	6.Retail and marketing	5.Production	4.Transport	3.Raw materials processing	2.Transport	1. Extractive industries		
									Energy usage	Environmental impact
									Raw materials usage	
									Land usage	
									Water usage	
									Water quality	
									Waste production	
									Air pollution	
									Ground contamination	
									Pollution effluents	
									Radioactive waste	
									Flora	
									Fauna	
									Impact on countryside and green space	
									Work satisfaction	Social impact
									Health and safety at work	
									Participation in decision making	
									Cultural pluralism	
									Leisure time	
									Economic costs	Economic impact
									Macro economic effects	
									Implications for the world economy	
									North-south global dimension	
									Wealth creation and economic activity	

Source: Adapted from Teichert (1989)

housing developments. Though there has already been some research in this field (see Hahn, 1989, 1991; Kut and Hare, 1981), there is undoubtedly scope for the examination of new forms of urban planning and the practical integration of different environmental objectives into urban development through new approaches to design and data analysis accompanied by new insights into the effectiveness of different environmental policy instruments.

The consequence of the implementation of the radical waste reduction option, as depicted in Table 7.2, based around greater state controls on industrial products and processes remains uncertain. There is a need for research into the macro-economic effects, such as employment changes in different sectors of the economy and the possibility of reduced international competitiveness within the global economy. An unresolved issue is whether slower rates of economic growth from reduced production and consumption would be counter productive, since the creation of wealth provides the opportunity for investment in expensive environmental protection technologies.

Conclusion

The central question examined in this book is the identification of the underlying barriers to raising levels of materials recycling as part of sustainable policy making. I have established that levels of recycling in London and Hamburg are well below technically achievable levels, but the cause of limited recycling is not attributable to lack of public participation or 'market failure' in the costs of waste disposal. This study has indicated an important distinction between the local factors affecting the operational aspects of different recycling systems in practice, such as the extent of recycling infrastructure, and the role of general factors derived from the secondary materials market, the organisational and financial aspects of local government, and the degree of state control over the waste stream. I wish to argue that these general factors form part of the policy context for recycling, which can only be altered significantly by changes in the legislative framework and the role of the state in environmental policy. Yet this policy context for recycling is itself evolving in response to the process of demunicipalisation of waste management, caused by the combined impact of the political pressure to cut the costs of waste management and the need to respond to public demands for higher environmental standards. The result, somewhat paradoxically, is increasing pressure on recycling policy to shift the emphasis away from expensive forms of comprehensive materials recovery towards the increased use of energy recovery, thereby allowing the development of profitable 'end of pipe' private sector environmental policy compatible with the wider political and economic policy context, but ultimately paid for by consumers rather than the producers of waste at source.

The study of London and Hamburg suggests that there is a 'threshold' level of materials recycling, beyond which it is extremely difficult to raise recycling rates without two main shifts in policy: firstly, the use of progressively more expensive forms of waste management such as kerbside schemes and the dual-bin system for the production of compost; and secondly, the use of widespread state intervention in production, retailing and marketing in order to strengthen the secondary materials market and control different components of the waste stream such as packaging. The maximum level of recycling achievable without a complete transformation of waste management policy at a national level is lower in inner urban areas because of a combination of difficulties: the lack of space both in the home and in common areas for the collection and storage of recyclable materials; the need to extend the collection of putrescible waste to households without gardens; the logistical aspects of waste collection involving the use of shared paladins; and the high urban land values over which low return public service facilities such as recycling centres must compete with more profitable land uses.

It can be concluded that the recycling of materials from the municipal waste stream is not a panacea either for generalised environmental catastrophe or more localised crises in urban waste management. It does, however, present an opportunity to contribute, albeit in a small way, to higher environmental standards in waste management, particularly from the reduced impact of methane gas, ground water leachates and incineration emissions. Furthermore, it provides a unique opportunity to raise the level of environmental awareness and inform participants of the complex relationships between cause and effect that lie behind the generation of environmental problems. Indeed, this educational role for recycling forms an important justification for this book, as an exploration of contemporary environmental policy in developed economies.

Bibliography

Abert, J.G. (1985), *Municipal Waste Processing in Europe: A Status Report on Selected Materials and Energy Recovery Projects*, US, The World Bank.

Adams, J.G.U. (1974), '...And how much for your grandmother?', In *Environment and Planning A*, 6, pp. 619-626.

AGöF (Arbeitsgemeinschaft ökologische Forschungsinstitute) (1990), *Abfallvermeidung*, Raben Verlag, Munich.

Agyeman, J. (1988), 'A pressing question for green organisations', *Town and Country Planning*, February Issue, pp. 50-51.

Ahrens, A. (1989), 'Neue Regelwerke in der Abfallpolitik - ein Weg zur Abfallvermeidung', paper presented to the conference *Ökologische Abfallwirtschaft*, November 30th to 3rd December, Technische Universität Berlin..

Ahrens, A.; Gonsch, V.; Ohde, J.; Vierth, I.; Viole, J.; Vödisch, A. and Zöllner, G. (1990), *Müllkonzept*, Bund für Umwelt- und Naturschutz (BUND), Hamburg.

Akkre, E. (1991), *Thermal recovery - part of an integrated waste management strategy*, Alliance for Beverage Cartons and the Environment, London.

ALA (Association of London Authorities) (1987), *The Greater London Council: One year on - counting the cost*, ALA / London Strategic Policy Unit, London.

Alvarez, R.J. (1984), 'Energy and Materials recovered from Thermal processing of Municipal Solid Waste in the US', in Thome-Kozmiensky, K.J. (ed.) *Recycling International*, E.F. - Verlag für Umwelt und Technik, Berlin, pp. 31-37.

AMA (Association of Metropolitan Authorities) (1976), *Report on Waste Paper Collections by Local Authorities*, AMA, London.

AMA (Association of Metropolitan Authorities) (1991a), *Environmental Protection Act 1990: Litter clauses*, paper for the Central and Local Government Environment Forum, 17th October 1991.

AMA (Association of Metropolitan Authorities) (1991b), *Recycling*, paper for the Central and Local Government Environment Forum, 21st October 1991.

Ambrose, P. (1986), *Whatever happened to planning ?*, Methuen, London and New York.

Aubrey, C. (1992), Green light for energy, *The Guardian*, 20th March.

Audit Commission (1984), *Securing Further Improvements in Refuse Collection*, HMSO, London.

Audit Commission (1988), *Special Studies: DSOs and Compulsory Competitive Tendering*, Unpublished Report.

Audit Commission (1989), *Occasional Paper Number 7: Preparing for Compulsory Competition*, HMSO, London.

Ayres, D. (1979), *Waste derived fuels and the recovery of energy from domestic waste*, Churchill Memorial Trust, London.

Ayres, R. and Narkus-Kramer, M. (1976), 'An Assessment of Methodologies for Estimating National Energy Efficiency', Paper presented to the Annual Meeting of the Technology and Society Division of the *American Society of Mechanical Engineers*, 5th December 1976, New York.

Bacon, R. and Eltis, W. (1978), Too Few Producers, in Coates, D. and Hillard, J. ed. (1986), *The Economic Decline of Modern Britain*, Wheatsheaf Books Ltd., Brighton, pp. 77-91.

Badaracco, J.L. (1985), *Loading the Dice: a five country study of vinyl chloride regulation*, Harvard Business School, Boston.

Bahro, R. (1982), *Socialism and Survival*, Heretic Books, London.

Bahro, R. (1984), *From Red to Green*, Verso, London.

Bahro, R. (1986), *Building the Green Movement*, Gay Men Publishers, London.

Ball, R. (1988), 'Glass recycling by local authorities: an economic evaluation', *Resources policy*, 14, pp. 205-217.

Ballard, D.W. (1974), 'An American view of problems of Materials Reclamation', paper presented to *The Conservation of Materials Conference*, 26th-27th March, Harwell Laboratory.

BANC (British Association of Nature Conservationists) (1990), *The Conservationists' response to the Pearce Report*, BANC, London.

Barker, B. (1946), *Labour in London: A study in municipal achievement*, George Routledge, London.

Barton, A.F.M. (1979), *Resource Recovery and Recycling*, John Wiley, New York.

Barton, J.R. (1988), *Mechanical Sorting Technology for Municipal Solid Waste Reclamation*, Harwell Laboratory.

Barton, J.R. (1989) 'Recycling of packaging: source separation or centralised treatment', *Institute of Wastes Management*, one day symposium, 4th October.

Bateson, N. (1984), *Data Construction in Social Surveys*, George Allen and Unwin, London.

Beal, D. (1992), 'Recycling as part of integrated waste management: an international perspective', paper presented to the conference *Waste Reclamation Credits - Landfill vs. Recycling*, 24th September, London.

Beckerman, W. (1974), *In Defence of Economic Growth*, Jonathan Cape, London.

Bell, D. (1973), *The Coming of Post-Industrial Society*, Penguin, Harmondsworth.

Berrington, H. (1984), 'Decade of dealignment', *Political Studies*, 32, pp. 117-120.

Bernstoff, A. (1989), 'Der neue Abfallkolonialismus - Müllexporte der Industriestaaten', paper presented to the conference *Ökologische Abfallwirtschaft*, November 30th to 3rd December, Technische Universität Berlin.

Bever, M.B. (1976), *The Recycling of Metals: Ferrous Metals and Non-Ferrous Metals*, Pergamon Press, UK.

Bhaskar, R. (1989), *Reclaiming Reality: A Critical Introduction to Contemporary Philosophy*, Verso, London.

Bidwell, R. and Mason, S. (1975) 'Fuel from London's Refuse: An examination of economic viability', paper presented to the *National Conference on Conversion of Refuse to Energy*, Montreux, 3rd -5th November.

Birley, D. (1992), 'Household Waste Recycling Costs and Landfill Recycling Credits', paper presented to the conference *Waste Reclamation Credits - Landfill vs. Recycling*, 24th September, London.

Blair, I.C. (1987), 'Pulling the weight of recycling', *Beverage World*, June, pp. 28-34.

Blaikie, P. (1985), *The political economy of soil erosion in developing countries*, Longman, New York.

Blaikie, P. and Brookfield, H. (1987), *Land Degradation and Society*, Methuen, London.

Blowers, A.T.; Lowry, D.; and Soloman, B.D. (1991), *The International Politics of Nuclear Waste,* Macmillan, London.

Blowers, A.T. (1992) 'Narrowing the options: the political geography of waste disposal'. in Clark, M.; Smith, D. and Blowers, A.T. (eds.), *Waste Location: spatial aspects of waste management, hazards and disposal*, Macmillan, London, pp. 227-247.

Boddy, M. and Fudge, C. (eds.) (1984), *Local Socialism*, Macmillan, London.

Boehmer-Christensen, S. and Skea, J. (1991), *Acid Politics: Environmental and Energy Policies in Britain and Germany*, Belhaven, London.

Bojkow, E. (1984), 'Possibilities and Limitations of Waste Reduction in Beverage Packaging', in Thome-Kozmiensky, K.J. (ed.), *Recycling International*, E.F. - Verlag für Umwelt und Technik, Berlin, pp. 725-732,

Bongaerts, J. (1989), 'Das 'Blauer-Engel-Programm' soll Ökoprodukte auf EG-Ebene fördern', paper presented to the conference *Ökologische Abfallwirtschaft*, November 30th to 3rd December, Technische Universität Berlin.

Boustead, I. and Hancock, G.F. (1984), 'Energy and recycling in glass and PET beverage container systems', Thome-Kozmiensky, K.J. (ed.), *Recycling International,* E.F. - Verlag für Umwelt und Technik, Berlin, pp. 751- 757.

Boustead, I. (1989), *The Environmental Impact of Liquid Food Containers in the UK*, Open University, Milton Keynes.

Bowcott, O. (1989), 'More waste, less heed', *The Guardian*, 20th October.

Bowcott, O. (1990), 'The battle of the cans', *The Guardian*, 9th February.

Bowen, M.J. (1979), 'Scientific method - after positivism', in *Australian Geographical Studies*, 17, pp. 210-16.

Bradford, G. (1989), *How Deep is Deep Ecology?,*Times Change Press, California.

Bradley, E. (1990), *The UK Waste Management Industry,* Citicorp, London.

Bramwell, A. (1989), *Ecology in the 20th Century. A History*, Yale, New Haven and London

Brandt Commission (1980), *North-South: A Programme for Survival*, Pan Books, London.

Breckon, B. (ed.) (1990), *The Green guide to London*, Simon and Schuster, London and Sydney.

Bremme, H.C. (1984), 'Economic effects of planned governmental packaging regulations on a food chain', in Thome-Kozmiensky, K.J. (ed.), *Recycling International*, E.F. - Verlag für Umwelt und Technik, Berlin, pp. 713-718.

Brickman, R.; Jasanoff, S.; and Ilgen, T. (1985), *Controlling Chemicals: The Politics of Regulation in Europe and the United States*, Cornell University Press, Ithaca, NJ.

Brisson, I. (1992), *Packaging Waste and the Environment: Economics and Policy*, CSERGE Report 91-01, University College London and University of East Anglia.

British Plastics Federation (1979), *Technical Factors Governing the Recycling of Plastics*, British Plastics Federation, London.

Brown, A. (1990), 'British Alcan and British Aluminium Can Recycling', paper presented to the *London Recycling Forum*, 14th March.

Brown, L.R. (1991) (ed), *The Worldwatch Reader on Global Environmental Issues*, W.W. Norton, London and New York.

Brown, L.R. and Jacobson, J.L. (1987), *The Future of Urbanization: Facing the Ecological and Economic Constriants*, Worldwatch Institute, Washington.

Brown, L.R.; Flavin, C.; and Postel, S. (1990), 'Picturing a Sustainable Society', in Brown, L.R. (ed), *State of the World*, Unwin, London. pp. 173-190.

Brown, M. (1991), 'More than a load of old rubbish', *The Times*, 14th January.

Brown, P. (1989), 'Paper trade folding in recycling boom', *The Guardian*, 29th December.

Brown, P. (1993), 'Burn waste for power call', *The Guardian*, 21st May.

Brown, R.; Coggins, C.; and Cooper, D. (1990), 'Salvaging the Waste', *The*

Surveyor, 17th May, pp. 20-22.

Buekens, A. (1984), 'Opportunities in the sorting of plastic wastes', in Thome-Kozmiensky, (ed.), *Recycling International*, E.F. - Verlag für Umwelt und Technik, Berlin, pp. 531-541.

Bunyard, P. and Morgan-Grenville, F. (1987), *The Green Alternative: Guide to Good Living*, Methuen, London.

Bürgerschaft der Freien und Hansestadt Hamburg (1980), *Mitteilung des Senats an die Bürgerschaft*, Drucksache 9/2136.

Bürgerschaft der Freien und Hansestadt Hamburg (1989), *Mitteilung des Senats an die Bürgerschaft*, Drucksache 13/4091.

Bürgerschaft der Freien und Hansestadt Hamburg (1990), *Mitteilung des Senats an die Bürgerschaft*, Drucksache 13/6049.

Burgues, J.G. (1992), 'The European Commission and environmental policy', paper presented to the conference *Perspectives on the Environment: Research and Action in the 1990s*, held at the University of Leeds, 14-15th September.

Burkard, T.; Jordan, G.; and Schwensen, J. (1988), 'Ökologisches Abfallkonzept für West- Berlin: Im Vergleich zu den Auswirkungen einer geplanten Müllverbrennungsanlage', in IföR, *Abfall Vermeiden*, Fischer Taschenbuch Verlag, Frankfurt am Main, pp.145-153.

Burke, C.E. (1949), 'The Utilization of Organic Domestic Wastes', *Journal and Proceedings of the Institute of Sewage Purification*, 4, pp. 376-93.

Busck, O. (1990), *Berufliche Sicherheits- und Gesundheits- aspekte bei Zentraler Sortierung, Kompostierung und Einsammeln von Problem-Abfall*, Behörde fur Umwelt-gesundsheitsfragen, Allgemeine Dänische Nationale Arbeitergewerkschaft.

Butlin, J.A. (1977), 'Economics and Recycling', in *Journal of Resources Policy*, pp. 87-95.

Button, K.J. and Pearce, D.W. (1989), 'Improving the Urban Environment: How to Adjust National and Local Government Policy for Sustainable Urban Growth', *Progress in Planning*, 32, pp. 137-184.

Camden Borough Council (1989), *Report on recycling*, presented to the Public Health and Environment Committee, 26th September.

Camden FoE (Friends of the Earth) (1974), *Waste Not...A Report prepared for Camden Council on the Feasibility of Recycling Waste Paper*, Camden FoE, London.

Capra, F. and Spretnak, C. (1984), *Green Politics: The Global Promise*, Hutchinson, London.

Cargo, D.B. (1978), *Solid Wastes: Factors influencing generation rates*, Geography Research Paper No.174, University of Chicago.

Carson, R. (1962), *Silent Spring*, Hamilton, London.

Carvel, J. (1993), Bonn accused of littering Europe, *The Guardian*, 5th May.

Castle, K. (1986), *The Recyclers' Guide to Greater London ...& Beyond: A Handbook for Resource Recovery*, London Energy and Employment Network.

Catterall, T. (1993), 'Germany's green spot of bother', *The Observer*, 6th June.

CBI (Confederation of British Industry) (1984), *Contracting out for the Provision of Local Authority Services*, CBI, London.

CDU (Christlich-Demokratische Union) (1987), *Hamburg im Würgegriff des Müllnotstands*, Presskonferenz der CDU-Bürgerschaftsfraktion, 27th August.

CDU (Christlich-Demokratische Union) (1988a), *Mülldeponien in Hamburgs Landschaftsschutzgebieten*, Presskonferenz der CDU Bürgerschaftsfraktion, 4th October.

CDU (Christlich-Demokratische Union) (1988b), *Hamburgs Beitrag zum Schutz des Klimas*, Pressekonferenz der CDU-Bürgerschaftsfraktion, 4th November.

CDU (Christlich-Demokratische Union) (1989a), *Mit Volldampf in den Müllnotstand*, Pressekonferenz der CDU-Bürgerschaftsfraktion, 18th April.

CDU (Christlich-Demokratische Union) (1989b), *Altlast Deponie Tegelweg: Chronik der Untätigkeit*, Pressekonferenz der CDU-Bürgerschaftsfraktion, 15th November.

CDU (Christlich-Demokratische Union) (1990a), *Zum Abfallwirtschaftsplan (Hausmüll)*, Pressekonferenz der CDU-Bürgerschaftsfraktion, 25th May.

CDU (Christlich-Demokratische Union) (1990b), *Mißmanagement bei der Müllentsorgung: Millionengebühren für Hamburgs Bürger*, Pressekonferenz der CDU-Bürgerschaftsfraktion, 12th September.

Chandler, W.U. (1983), *Materials Recycling: The Virtue of Necessity*, Worldwatch Paper 56, Worldwatch Institute, Washington, DC.

Chapman, P.F. (1974), 'Energy costs of producing copper and aluminium from primary and secondary sources', paper presented to *The Conservation of Materials Conference*, 26th-27th March, Harwell.

Cheesewright, P. (1990), 'Energy from burnt rubber', *The Financial Times*, 26th October.

Chouinard, V.; Fincher, R., and Webber, M. (1984), 'Empirical research in scientific human geography', *Progress in Human Geography*, 8, pp. 347-380.

Christiansen, K. (1989), 'Substitution gefährlicher Stoffe in Haushalts- und Industrieprodukten', paper presented to the conference *Ökologische Abfallwirtschaft*, November 30th to 3rd December, Technische Universität Berlin.

Civic Trust (1967), *Disposal of Unwanted Vehicles and Bulky Refuse*, The Civic Trust, London.

Clark, M.; Smith, D. and Blowers, A.T. (eds.) (1992), *Waste location: Spatial aspects of waste management, hazards and disposal*, Routledge, London and New York.

Clawson, M. and Hall, P. (1973), *Planning and Urban Growth: An Anglo-American Comparison*, John Hopkins University Press, Baltimore, MD.

Clisham, J.W. (1968), *Reorganising a Refuse Collection Service*, Local

Government Work Study Group, London.

CLWDG (The Central London Waste Disposal Group) (1989), *Waste Disposal Plan 1989-1999*.

Coates, D. and Hillard, J. (ed.) (1986), *The Economic Decline of Modern Britain*, Wheatsheaf Books Ltd., Brighton.

Coates, D. and Hillard, J. (ed.) (1987), *The Economic Revival of Modern Britain*, Edward Elgar Publishing Ltd., Aldershot.

Coggins, P.C.; Cooper, A.D.; and Brown, R.W. (1988), *Public Use of Recycling Centres in Camden, Harrow and Wandsworth*, Civic Amenity Waste Disposal Project, Luton College of Higher Education.

Coggins, P.C.; Cooper, A.D.; and Brown, R.W. (1989a), 'Civic Amenity Waste Disposal Sites: The Cinderella of the Waste Disposal System', paper presented to *The Institute of British Geographers*, Annual Conference, Coventry Polytechnic, 5th January.

Coggins, P.C.; Cooper, A.D.; and Brown, R.W. (1989b), 'Civic Amenity Sites and Recycling Centres: Complementary or Competing Facilities', paper presented to *The Institute of Wastes Management*, Autumn Conference, 4th October.

Coggins, P.C. and Evans, G.H. (1992), 'Recycling Credits: A Waste Auditing Perspective', paper presented to the conference *Waste Reclamation Credits - Landfill vs. Recycling*, 24th September, London.

Cohen, N.; Herz, M., and Ruston, J. (1988), *Coming Full Circle: Successful Recycling Today*, Environmental Defense Fund, New York.

Cointreau, S.J.; Gunnerson, C.G.; Huls, J.M., and Seldman, N.N. (1984), *Recycling from Municipal Refuse: A State-of-the-Art Review and Annotated Bibliography*, the World Bank, US.

Cointreau, S.J. (1987), *Solid Waste Recycling: Case Studies in Developing Countries*, the World Bank, US.

Colinvaux, P.A. (1980), *Why Big Fierce Animals Are Rare*, Penguin, Harmondsworth.

Cook, S. (1990), 'The subtle art of waste disposal', *The Guardian*, 17th August, 1990.

Cooke, P. (1988), *Post-Fordism and flexible integration*, paper presented to St Catharines College Geography Society, Cambridge.

Cookson, C. (1991), 'Plastics recycling attacks new sales', *The Financial Times*, 1st May.

Cooper, J. (1981), *Rubbish: A review of the GLC's solid waste disposal plans 1965-1995*, Occasional Paper No.9, School of Geography, Kingston Polytechnic.

Cooper, J. (1985), 'How the GLC built up its waste disposal operations', *The Municipal Engineer*, 59, pp.1976-1977.

Cooper, J. (1989a), 'Recycling: Resurging in the 1990s?', paper presented at the conference, *Raising Standards in Wastes Management*, University of Lancaster, Centre for Science Studies and Science Policy, 21st September.

Cooper, J. (1989b), 'Recycling', paper presented to the SEEDS (South East Economic Development Strategy) conference *Green Plan for the South East*, Brighton, 19-20th October.

Cooper, J. (1989c), 'The Recycling Officer - New Phenomenon or Endangered Species?', *Resource and Recycling*, 13, p. 12.

Cooper, J. (1990a), 'Recycling Incentive Payments', unpublished draft paper presented to LARAC (Local Authority Recycling Advisory Committee) in October 1990.

Cooper, J. (1990b), 'Local Authority Waste Reduction', paper presented to the *DoE Regional Recycling Seminar*, 8th November.

Coopers and Lybrand Associates (1981), *Service Provision and Pricing in Local Government. Studies in Local Environmental Services*, HMSO, London.

Coopers and Lybrand Associates (1984), *Streamlining the Cities: an Analysis of the Costs Involved in the Government's Proposals*, Coopers and Lybrand, London.

COPAC (The Consortium of the Packaging Chain) (1992), *COPAC Action Plan to address UK integrated solid waste management*, INCPEN, London.

Copeman, S. (1984), 'Putting London's rubbish to use', *Port of London*, 59, pp. 57-59.

Corbridge, S. (1986), *Capitalist World Development*, MacMillan, UK.

Cornish, G. (1990), 'Superwood: Applications in the Local Authority Sector', paper presented to the *London Recycling Forum*, 26th September 1990.

Corrie, R.K. (1969), *Total Incineration - The Greater London Council's Plant at Edmonton*, Greater London Council.

Cotgrove, S. (1982), *Catastrophe or Cornucopia?*, Wiley, Chichester.

Cotgrove, S. and Duff, A. (1980), 'Environmentalism, Middle-Class Radicalism and Politics', *The Sociological Review,* 28, pp. 333-349.

Cotgrove, S. and Duff, A. (1981), 'Environmentalism, values and social change', *The British Journal of Sociology*, 32:1, pp. 92-110.

Courtney, R.G. and Sexton, D.E. (1973), *Refuse collection from houses and flats by pipelines*, DoE Building Research Establishment, Watford.

Croall, S. and Rankin, W. (1981), *Ecology for Beginners*, Writers and Readers, London.

Crowther, J. (1974), 'Substitution - For communal or sectional benefit', paper presented to *The Conservation of Materials Conference*, 26th-27th March, Harwell.

Crow, B. and Thomas, A. (1983), *The Third World Atlas*, Open University Press, Milton Keynes.

Cubbin, J.; Domberger, S.; and Meadowcroft, S. (1988), 'Competitive Tendering and Refuse Collection: Identifying the Sources of Efficiency Gains', *Fiscal Studies*, 8, pp. 49-58.

Curlee, T.R. (1986), *The economic feasibility of recycling: A case study of plastic wastes*, Praeger Publishing, New York.

Daly, H. (1977), 'The Steady State Economy: What, Why, and How?', in Pirages, D. (ed.) *The Sustainable Society: Implications for Limited Growth*, Praeger, London and New York.

Dangschat, J.S. and Ossenbrügge, J. (1990), *Crisis Management and Revitalisation in Metropolitan Areas by Social Democrats - The Case of Hamburg*, unpublished paper, Department of Geography, University of Hamburg.

Darnay, A. and Franklin, W.E. (1972), *Salvage Markets for Materials in Solid Wastes*, US Environmental Protection Agency, Washington, DC.

David Perchard Associates (1993), *EC Directive on Packaging and Packaging Waste: Compliance Cost Assessment.*, David Perchard Associates, London.

Davidson, J. and MacEwan, A. (1983), 'The livable city', in *The Conservation and Development Programme for the UK: A response to the World Conservation Strategy*, Kogan Page, London.

Davies, A.G. (1961), *Municipal Composting*, Faber and Faber, London.

De Vaus, D.A. (1986), *Surveys in Social Research*, George Allen and Unwin, London.

De Young, R. (1986), 'Some Psychological Aspects of Recycling: The Structure of Conservation Satisfactions', *Environment and Behaviour*, 18, pp. 435-449.

Dempster, A. (1968), 'The ecological impact of agricultural change', in Warren, A. and Goldsmith, F. (eds), *Conservation in Perspective*, John Wiley, London.

Derbyshire, I. (1987), *Politics in West Germany*, Chambers, London.

Derry, R. (1989), *Plastics Recycling in Europe*, Warren Spring Laboratory.

Devall, B. and Sessions, G. (1985), *Deep Ecology: Living As If Nature Mattered*, Peregrine Smith, Utah.

Die Grünen (1985), *The program of the Green Party of the Federal Republic of Germany*, Die Grünen, Bonn.

Die Grünen (1989), *Verzicht auf PVC und Chlorchemie*, Die Grünen, Bonn.

DoE (Department of the Environment) (1971), *Refuse Disposal*, HMSO, London.

DoE (Department of the Environment) (1973a), *First Report of the Standing Committee on Research into Refuse Collection, Storage and Disposal*, HMSO, London.

DoE (Department of the Environment) (1973b), *Waste Disposal: Proposals for a New Framework*, HMSO, London.

DoE/DTI (1974), *War on Waste: A Policy for Reclamation*, HMSO, London.

DoE (Department of Environment) (1981), *Service Provision and Pricing in Local Government. Studies in Local Environmental Services*, HMSO, London.

DoE (Department of the Environment) (1983a), *Streamlining the Cities*, HMSO, London.

DoE (Department of the Environment) (1983b), *Streamlining the Cities: Consultation Paper on Arrangements to be made for Waste Disposal*, HMSO, London.

DoE (Department of the Environment) (1989), *The Role and Function of Waste Disposal Authorities*, HMSO, London.

DoE (Department of the Environment) (1990a), *Government survey of local authority recycling*, unpublished survey results.

DoE (Department of the Environment) (1990b), *This Common Inheritance*, HMSO, London.

DoE (Department of the Environment) (1991a), *Waste Management Paper No.28: Recycling*.

DoE (Department of the Environment) (1991b), *The Duty of Care: A Draft Circular, A Consultation Paper and Draft Regulations under section 34 (5)*.

DoE (Department of the Environment) (1991c), *This Common Inheritance: The First Year Report*, HMSO, London.

DoE (Department of the Environment) (1991d), *Improving Environmental Quality: The Government's proposals for a new, independent environment agency*, HMSO, London.

DoE (Department of the Environment) (1992), *Digest of Environmental Statistics*, HMSO, London.

Doedens, H. (1979), 'Feasibility of the Separate Collection (Source Separation) of Recyclable Components in Refuse', paper to the *International Recycling Congress*, Berlin.

Domberger, S.; Meadowcroft, S. and Thompson, D. (1988), 'Competitive Tendering and Efficiency: The Case of Refuse Collection', *Fiscal Studies*, 7, pp. 69-87.

Donkin, R. (1989), 'The politics and profits of killing PCBs', *The Financial Times*, 19th September.

Dourado, P. (1990), 'The case against recycling the US's waste', *New Scientist*, 8th September, p. 48.

Drösser, C. (1990), 'Der Wohlstand müllt sich tot', *Geo*, 7, pp. 40-62.

DTI/DoE (1977), *Save and Recycle: A guide to voluntary waste collection*, HMSO, London.

DTI (Department of Trade and Industry) (1984), *The Wealth of Waste*, HMSO, London.

DTI (Department of Trade and Industry) (1987), *Watching Waste,* HMSO, London.

DTI (Department of Trade and Industry) (1990), *CFCs and Halons: Alternatives and the scope for recovery, recycling and destruction*, HMSO, London.

DTI/DoE (1992), *Economic Instruments and Recovery of Resources from Waste*, HMSO, London.

Dunham, K. (1974), 'Non-renewable mineral resources', paper presented to *The Conservation of Materials Conference*, 26th-27th March, Harwell.

Dunleavy, P. (1984), 'The limits to local government', in Boddy, M. and Fudge, C. (eds.), *Local Socialism*, Macmillan, London, pp. 49-83.

Dyson, B.H. (1974), 'Efficient utilisation of materials - One answer to our balance of payments problem', paper presented to *The Conservation of Materials Conference*, 26th-27th March, Harwell.

EC (European Commission) (1984), *Employment Potential of Waste Recovery and Recycling Activities and Socio-Economic Relevance of Waste Management Sector in the Community*, final report by Environment Resources Ltd. for the Directorate General for the Environment.

EC (European Commission) (1985), *The Employment Implications of Glass Re-use and Recycling*, Report by Ecotec Research and Consulting Ltd. for the Directorate General for Science, Research and Development.

EC (European Commission) (1989), *A Community Strategy for Waste Management*, SEC(89)934, European Commission, Brussels.

EC (European Commission) (1990a), *Green paper on the Urban Environment*, European Commission, Brussels.

EC (European Commission) (1990b), *Proposal for a Council Regulation (EEC) on the supervision and control of shipments of waste within into and out of the European Community*, COM(90)415, European Commission, Brussels.

EC (European Commission) (1991a), *Outline proposal for a Council Directive on Packaging*, XI/270/91, European Commission, Brussels.

EC (European Commission) (1991b), *Proposal for a Council Directive on the landfill of waste*, COM (91) 102, European Commission, Brussels.

Ecology Party (1982), 'Jobs for Keeps', in Coates, D. and Hillard, J. (eds.) (1987), *The Economic Revival of Modern Britain*, Edward Elgar Publishing Limited, Aldershot.

The Economist (1989), *Water industry: Storming the barricade*, 14th

October, pp. 45-46.

The Economist (1991), *Recycling in Germany: a wall of waste*, 30th November, p.97.

EDF (The Environmental Defense Fund) (1985), *To Burn or Not to Burn: The Economic Advantages of Recycling Over Garbage Incineration for New York City*, EDF, New York.

EDF (The Environmental Defense Fund) (1987), *Coming Full Circle: Successful Recycling Today*, EDF, New York.

Eder, G. (1989), 'Die Kunstoffproduktion von heute - ein Abfallproblem von morgen', paper presented to the conmference *Ökologische Abfallwirtschaft*, 30th November to 2nd December, Technische Universität, Berlin.

Edwards (1974), opening address by the Chair of the GLC Public Services Committee to the *Symposium on Solid Waste Disposal*, 29th October 1974.

Eedle, M. de G. (1971), 'Street Cleansing and Refuse Collection from the Sixteenth to the Nineteenth Centuries', *Surrey Archeological Society Collections*, 68, pp. 161-181.

Egerton, H.L. (1950), 'The Garchey System of Domestic Refuse Disposal', *Journal of the Institution of Sanitation Engineers*, 49, pp. 229-44.

Ehrlich, P.R. (1970), *The Population Bomb*, Ballantine Books, New York.

Ehrlich, P.R. and Ehrlich, A.H. (1970), *Population, Resources, Environment: issues in human ecology*, W.H. Freeman, San Fransisco.

Elkin, T. and McLaren, D. (1991), *Reviving the City: towards sustainable urban development*, Friends of the Earth and the Policy Studies Institute, London.

Elkington, J. (1987), *The Green Capitalists*, Victor Gollancz, London.

Elkington, J. and Hailes, J. (1988), *The Green Consumer Guide*, Victor Gollancz, London.

Ellender, P. (1990), 'Bromley's beverage can recycling scheme', paper presented to the *London Recycling Forum*, 14th March.

Elmer, A. (1990), 'Breaking the bottle bank', *The Surveyor*, 29th March, p. 7.

Elsworth, S. (1990), *A Dictionary of the Environment*, Paladin, London.

ELWA (East London Waste Authority) (1989a), *Report for 1986-1989*.

ELWA (East London Waste Authority) (1989b), *Waste Disposal Plan*.

Emel, J. and Peet, R. (1989), 'Resource managment and natural hazards', In Peet, R. and Thrift, N. (eds.) (1989), *New Models in Geography Volume One*.

Enloe, C.H. (1975), *The Politics of Pollution in a Comparative Perspective*, David McKay, New York.

Environmental Health (1991), 'The Environmental Protection Act 1990', *Environmental Health*, May, pp. ix-xii.

Esser, J. and Hirsch, J. (1987), 'The crisis of fordism and the dimensions of a 'postfordist' regional and urban structure', *International Journal of Urban and Regional Research*, 7, pp. 417-437.

Evans, R. (1991), 'French ready to pick up pieces', *The Financial Times*, 26th June.

Evans, R.J. (1991), *Death in Hamburg: Society and Politics in the Cholera Years 1830-1910*, Penguin, Harmondsworth.

Fabig, K. (1990), 'Hamburgs Müll - ein Wirtschaftsgut?', *Hamburger Tageszeitung*, 18th April.

Falk, H. (1988), 'Weissblechverpackungen: Umwelt belastungen bei der Produktion und Entsorgung', in IföR, *Abfall Vermeiden*, Fischer Taschenbuch Verlag, Frankfurt am Main, pp. 54-63.

Fay, B. (1981), 'Positivist social science and technological politics' in Potter, D. (ed.), *Society and the Social Sciences*, Routledge and Kegan Paul, London.

FDP (Freie Demokratische Partei) (1989), *Zukunft Hamburg: Liberale Ecktpunkte*, FDP, Hamburg.

Feiss, J.W. (1963), 'Minerals', in Scientific American (1963), *Technology and Economic Development*, pp. 107-118, Penguin, Harmondsworth.

Felton, R. (1990), 'The reclamation of tyres', paper presented to the *London Recycling Forum*, 20th June.

Ferguson, J. (1986), 'Tidying up the loose ends in aftermath of the GLC', *The Municipal Journal*, 6th June, pp. ix-xii.

Field, J. (1991), 'Demise of Die Grünen', *Green Line*, 84, pp. 3-4.

Fiolka, J. (1989) 'Abfallverwertung im Ballungsraum Ruhrgebiet', in Haas, H.-D. (ed.) (1989), *Müll - Untersuchungen zu Problemen der Entsorgung und des Rohstoffrecycling*, pp.19-25, Münchner Studien zur Sozial- und Wirtschaftsgeographie, Band 35, Micheal Lassleben Kallmünz, Regensberg.

Financial Times Survey (1990), *Waste Management*, September 26th.

Financial Times Survey (1991a), *Industry and the Environment*, 13th March.

Financial Times Survey (1991b), *Waste Management,* November 26th.

Financial Times Survey (1992), *Environmental Management*, November 10th.

Flintoff, F. (1950), *Municipal Cleansing Practice*, Contractors Record, London.

Flintoff, F. and Millard, R. (1969), *Public Cleansing*, McLaren & Sons, London.

Flood, M. (1991a), 'Credit where credit is due', *WARMER Bulletin*, 28, pp. 10-11.

Flood, M. (1991b), 'Waste not, want not to fuel a green future', *The Observer*, 1st December.

Flynn, N.; Leach, S., and Vielba, C. (1985), *Abolition or Reform? The GLC and the Metropolitan County Councils*, George Allen & Unwin,

London.

FoE (Friends of the Earth) (1987), *Work and the Environment*, Friends of the Earth, London.

FoE (Friends of the Earth) (1989), *Recycling projects and the employment training scheme*, UK 2000/Friends of the Earth, London.

FoE (Friends of the Earth) (1990a), *Market Barriers to Paper Recycling*, Friends of the Earth, London.

FoE (Friends of the Earth) (1990b), *Recycling: the Way Forward*, Friends of the Earth, London.

FoE (Friends of the Earth) (1990c), *Brief for the Prime Minister on Recycling*, Friends of the Earth, London.

FoE (Friends of the Earth) (1991), *A Survey of Local Authority Recycling Schemes in England and Wales*, Friends of the Earth, London.

FoE (Friends of the Earth) (1992), *Don't Throw it All Away! Friends of the Earth's Guide to Waste Reduction and Recycling*, Friends of the Earth, London.

Foley, D.L. (1972), *Governing the London Region: Reorganization and planning in the 1960s*, University of California Press, Berkeley and London.

Foley, G. (19991), *Global Warming: Who is taking the heat?*, Panos, London.

Forester, W.S. (1991), 'Municipal Solid Waste Management in the United States', paper presented to the *London Waste Regulation Authority*, Annual conference, London, 21st March.

Forrester, J.W. (1970), *World Dynamics*, Wright-Allen Press, Cambridge, Massachusetts.

Forsyth, M. (1980), *Re-Servicing Britain,* Adam Smith Institute, London.

Franck, B. and Haas, L. (1985), 'Solid Waste Handling in West Germany', BioCycle, September, pp. 35-45.

Frankel, B. (1987), *The Post-Industrial Utopians*, The Polity Press, Cambridge.

Franklin, M.N. (1985), *The Decline of Class Voting in Britain*, Clarendon, Oxford.

Freie und Hansestadt Hamburg (1988a), *Die Deponie Georgeswerder Entstehung Gefahren für die Umwelt Sanierung*, Umweltbehörde, Amt für Altlastensanierung, Hamburg.

Freie und Hansestadt Hamburg (1988b), *Ökologie-Forum 1988 - Sonderabfallplanung für Hamburg*, Umweltbehörde, Hamburg.

Freie und Hansestadt Hamburg (1989a), *Abfall Vermeiden: Aber Wie?*, Baubehörde, Amt für Entsorgungsplanung, Hamburg.

Freie und Hansestadt Hamburg (1989b), *Geshäftsbericht 1988*, Baubehörde, Landesbetrieb Hamburger Stadtreinigung, Hamburg.

Freie und Hansestadt Hamburg (1989c), *Statisticher Bericht 1986-1988*, Baubehörde, Landesbetrieb Hamburger Stadtreinigung, Hamburg.

Freie und Hansestadt Hamburg (1989d), *Abfallwirtschaftsplan*, Baubehörde, Amt für Entsorgungsplanung, Hamburg.

Freie und Hansestadt Hamburg (1990a), *Verfassung der Freien und Hansestadt Hamburg,* Landeszentrale für politische Bildung, Hamburg.

Freie und Hansestadt Hamburg (1990b), *Das Hamburger Mullentsorgungskonzept*, Baubehörde, Landesbetrieb Hamburger Stadtreinigung, Hamburg.

Freie und Hansestadt Hamburg (1990c), *Wohin mit dem Altöl?*, Umweltbehörde, Hamburg.

Fremlin, J.H. (1964), 'How many people can the world support?', In *New Scientist*, 24, pp. 285-7.

Frey, C. (1990), 'Vom Winde verweht: gift aus den Müllverbrennungsanlagen und Proteste dagegen', *Frankfurter Rundschau*, 7th July.

Friedrich, H. (1989), 'Die Müllverbrennung - eine ökologisch verantwortbare Technologie?', paper presented to the conference *Ökologische Abfallwirtschaft*, 30th November to 2nd December 1989, Technische Universität Berlin.

Galbraith, J.K. (1958), *The Affluent Society*, Penguin, Harmondsworth.

Gandy, M. (1988), *A Political Geography of Islington*, unpublished BA dissertation, Department of Geography, University of Cambridge.

Gandy, M. (1991), 'Environmental policy and local government', in McCoshan, A. and Pinto, R.R. (eds) (1991), *Local Services: Past Experiences and Possible Scenarios*, pp. 46-52, Geography Discussion Papers. New Series No.24. Graduate School of Geography, The London School of Economics.

Gandy, M. (1992a), *The recycling of household waste: urban environmental policy in London and Hamburg*. PhD thesis, London School of Economics.

Gandy, M. (1992b), *The Environmental Debate: A Critical Overview*, Research Paper 5, Department of Geography, University of Sussex.

Gandy, M. (1993), 'A critical analysis of environmental policy in developed economies: the case of recycling', in *Policies, Institutions and the Environment*, pp. 1-29, South North Centre Series Volume One, South North Centre for Environmental Policy, School of Oriental and African Studies, University of London.

Garbe-Emden, J. (1989), 'EG-Binnenmarkt - EG-Recht: Hindernis oder Chance für die Abfallvermeidung?', paper presented to the conference *Ökologische Abfallwirtschaft*, 30th November to 2nd December 1989, Technische Universität Berlin.

Gardner, D.; Peel, Q.; and Hunt, J. (1992), 'Green Germany drags Brussels into environmental arena', *The Financial Times*, 24th January.

Garnett, N. (1990), 'Power struggle', *The Financial Times*, 20th April.

Gassner, H. and Siederer, W. (1989), 'Neue wege bei der Planung von Abfallentsorgungsanlagen - 'mediation' als Vorbild aus den USA', paper presented to the conference *Ökologische Abfallwirtschaft*, 30th

November to 2nd December 1989, Technische Universität Berlin.

Gatrell, A.C. and Lovett, A.A. (1992), 'Burning questions: incineration of wastes and implications for human health', in Clark, M.; Smith, D. and Blowers, A. (eds.), *Spatial aspects of waste management, hazards and disposal*, Macmillan, London, pp. 143-158.

Gehrke, C. (1988), 'Möglichkeiten und Grenzen des abfallarmen Einkaufs', in IföR, *Abfall Vermeiden*, Fischer Taschenbuch Verlag, Frankfurt am Main, pp. 99-106.

Genillard, A. (1993), 'Bonn proposes new recycling measure, *Financial Times*, April 1st.

Genillard, A. (1993), 'Too much of a good thing', *Financial Times*, June 23rd.

Gershuny, J. (1978), *After Industrial Society: The Emerging Self-service Economy*, Macmillan, London.

Gershuny, J. and Miles, I. (1983), *The New Service Economy: The Transformation of Employment in Industrial Societies,* Frances Pinter, London.

GEWOS (Institut für Stadt-, Regional- und Wohnforschung GmbH) (1987a), *Zentral-Container-System*, GEWOS GmbH, Hamburg.

GEWOS (1987b), *Werstofferfassung in verdichteten Baugebieten: Modellversuch "Kombi-Behalter" im Bezirk Altona,* GEWOS GmbH, Hamburg.

GEWOS (1989), *Technisch-organisatorische Veranderungen in der Abfall - entsorgung, - gestaltungsbedarfe, und -möglichkeiten aus Arbeitnehmersicht*, GEWOS GmbH, Hamburg.

GEWOS (1990), *Zukunftsaufgaben im Umweltschutz und perspektiven des Öffentlichen Sektors*, GEWOS GmbH, Hamburg.

GEWOS (1991), *Erschliessung neuer Marktfelder im Umweltbereich*, GEWOS GmbH, Hamburg.

Glacken, C.J. (1967), *Traces on the Rhodian Shore*, University of California

Press, Berkeley.

GLC (Greater London Council) (1966a), *Department of Public Health Engineering: Annual Report 1965-66.*

GLC (Greater London Council) (1966b), *Tests to investigate the use of a rotating screen as a means of grading crude refuse for pulverisation and compression treatment.*

GLC (Greater London Council) (1967), *Annual Report 1966-67.*

GLC (Greater London Council) (1971), *Annual Report 1970-71.*

GLC (Greater London Council) (1975a), *Recycling of Solid Wastes*, Report of the Public Services Committee, 13th January.

GLC (Greater London Council) (1975b), *London's Refuse Disposal.*

GLC (Greater London Council) (1975c), *Review of the Solid Wastes Management Service*, report of the Public Services Committee, 14th April.

GLC (Greater London Council) (1975d), *Solid Wastes Management - Waste Paper*, Report of the Public Services Committee, 10th June.

GLC (Greater London Council) (1976a), *Solid Waste by Road: Newham, Road Transfer Station.*

GLC (Greater London Council) (1976b), *Resource recovery: Factors influencing choice of methods and equipment leading to objective assessment of trial and pilot plants*, unpublished report, GLC Public Health Engineering Department.

GLC (Greater London Council) (1977), *Solid Wastes by Rail: Hendon Rail Transfer Station.*

GLC (Greater London Council) (1979) *Solid Wastes by Rail: Transport Avenue Solid Wastes Rail Transfer Station, Brentford.*

GLC (Greater London Council) (1980a), *Talking Rubbish: The GLC's new strategy for dealing with London's waste.*

GLC (Greater London Council) (1980b), *Bottle Bank Glass Recycling Scheme*, report of the Public Services and Safety Committee, 30th April.

GLC (Greater London Council) (1983a), *Landfill sites: methane generation and recovery.*

GLC (Greater London Council) (1983b), *Proposed Measures for Increasing Glass Recycling in London*, report of the Environmental Panel, 12th May.

GLC (Greater London Council) (1983c), *Encouragement to households in London to compost domestic refuse*, report of the Environmental Panel, 5th July.

GLC (Greater London Council) (1983d), *No Time to Waste: A limited Planning Statement for Waste Regulation, Recovery and Disposal 1983-2003.*

GLC (Greater London Council) (1983e), *Waste Disposal in London - A Return to   Victorian Standards? A response to Government proposals for waste disposal in   London following publication of the White Paper 'Streamlining the Cities.*

GLC (Greater London Council) (1984a), *Progress report on composting sewage and household refuse*, report of the Environmental Panel.

GLC (Greater London Council) (1984b), *Streamlining the Cities: Response by the GLC Conservative Group.*

GLC (Greater London Council) (1984c), *Responses by GLC committees to the Government's White Paper 'Streamlining the Cities'.*

GLC (Greater London Council) (1984d), *London Recycling Forum*, Inaugural Meeting, 8th March, County Hall.

GLC (Greater London Council) (1984e), *Recycling - Financial incentives to charitable causes*, Report of the Public Services and Fire Brigade Committee, 14th March.

GLC (Greater London Council) (1984f), *Recycling - Support for recycling workshops*, report of the Public Services and Fire Brigades Committee,

14th March.

GLC (Greater London Council) (1984g), *"The Wealth of Waste": Evidence to the House of Commons Trade and Industry Committee Inquiry into Waste Recycling*, report of the Public Services and Fire Brigade Committee, 19th June.

GLC (Greater London Council) (1984h), *Preparation of the Council's case against main abolition legislation for waste disposal in London - parliamentary briefing note*, confidential paper for weekly campaign meeting on 20th August by Controller of Operational Services.

GLC (Greater London Council) (1984i), *Evidence to the Royal Commission on Environmental Pollution*, report of the Public Services and Fire Brigade Committee.

GLC (Greater London Council) (1984j), *Report of the London-wide Initiative on Fly-tipping Working Party*.

GLC (Greater London Council) (1984k), *Planning for London's Wastes*.

GLC (Greater London Council) (1984l), *Recycling for Employment Conference*, conference held at County Hall, 10th November.

GLC (Greater London Council) (1984m), *Production and Marketing of Waste Derived Fuel*, report of the Public Services and Fire Brigades Committee, 13th December.

GLC (Greater London Council) (1985a), *Recycling - A review of the recycling of beverage containers and proposals for further re-use and recycling*, report of the Public Services and Fire Brigade Committee, 31st January.

GLC (Greater London Council) (1985b), *Recycling activities - purchase of additional equipment*, report of the Public Services and Fire Brigade Committee, 31st January.

GLC (Greater London Council) (1985c), *Recycling - The Council's response to the Trade and Industry Committee's Report - "The Wealth of Waste"*, report of the Environmental Panel, 1st February 1985.

GLC (Greater London Council) (1985d), *Furniture Workshops*, report of the

Public Services and Fire Brigades Committee, 3rd March.

GLC (Greater London Council) (1985e), *Recycling - Composting at source*, report of the Public Services and Fire Brigades Committee, 7th May.

GLC (Greater London Council) (1985f), *Planning for the Future of London*, GLC Department of Public Health Engineering.

GLC (Greater London Council) (1985g), *Recycling: The Government's Response to the "Wealth of Waste" Report*, report of the Public Services and Fire Brigade Committee, 9th May.

GLC (Greater London Council) (1985h), *Recycling - The charity sponsorship scheme*, Report of the Public Services and Fire Brigade Committee, 28th June.

GLC (Greater London Council) (1985i), *European Community Environmental Policy and British Local Government*, report of the Environmental Panel, 13th September.

GLC (Greater London Council) (1985j), *The Disposal of London's Waste by Landfill*.

GLC (Greater London Council) (1986a), *The Future of London's Government Discussion Document. Public Health and Safety: Waste Disposal*.

GLC (Greater London Council) (1986b), *Recycling begins at Home: The GLC's Recycling Programme 1981-1986*.

Goddard, H.C. (1975), *Managing Solid Wastes: Economics, Technology and Institutions*, Praeger, New York.

Golding, A. (1989), 'Energieverbrauch und dessen Berechnung in vergleichenden Ökobilanzen von Getränkeverpackungen', paper presented to the conference, *Ökologische Abfallwirtschaft*, 30th November to 2nd December, Technische Universität, Berlin.

Goldsmith, E.; Allen, R.; Allaby, M.; Davoll, J.; and Lawrence, S. (1972), *Blueprint for Survival*, Penguin, Harmondsworth.

Goldsmith, E. and Hildyard, N. (eds.) (1986), *Green Britain or Industrial*

Wasteland?, Polity Press, Cambridge.

Goodhart, D. (1989), 'German Greens turn lighter shade of red', *The Financial Times*, 17th May.

Goodhart, D. (1991), 'Germany moves in front', *The Financial Times*, 14th August.

Gooding, K. (1991), 'Aluminium gets top marks for publicity', *The Financial Times*, 11th September.

Goodrich, W. (1904), *Refuse disposal and power production*, Archibald Constable and Company Ltd., London.

Gordon, J. (1987), *Waste Recycling in the Community: The Role of the Voluntary Sector in the Reclamation and Re-use of Resources*, National Council for Voluntary Organisations, London.

Gordon, J. (1988), *Sharing Resources*, LARAC/NCVO, London.

Gore, A. (1992), *Earth in the Balance: Ecology and the Human Spirit*, Plume, New York.

Gounon, J. (1984), 'Search for Optimum Energy upgrading in Paris Garbage Treatment', in Thome-Kozmiensky, K.J (ed.), *Recycling International*, EF - Verlag für Umwelt und Technik, Berlin, pp. 77-82.

Gotoh, S. and Oya, H. (1984), 'Effects of Subsidization on Civic Group Recycling', in Thome-Kozmiensky, K.J. (ed.), *Recycling International*, EF - Verlag für Umwelt und Technik, Berlin, pp. 234-239.

Gottwald, E.; Franke, M.; and Thome-Kozmiensky, K.J. (1984), 'Environmental Consequences through Beverage Packagings - methods for Systematic Assessment and Comparison, Exemplified by Beverage Packagings of Tinplate, Glass, and Laminated Cardboard', in Thome-Kozmiensky, K.J. (ed.), *Recycling International*, EF - Verlag für Umwelt und Technik, Berlin, pp. 3-750.

Grace, R.; Turner, R.K. and Walter, J. (1978), 'Secondary Materials and International Trade', *Journal of Environmental Economics and Management*, 5, pp. 172-186.

288

Graedel, T.E. and Crutzen, P.J. (1990), 'The Changing Atmosphere', in Sciemtific American, *Managing Planet Earth: readings from Scientific American*, W.H. Freeman and Company, New York.

Green, D.G. (1987), *The New Right: The counter revolution in political, economic and social thought*, Wheatsheaf Books, Brighton.

Green, D.R. (1991) 'The Metropolitan Economy: Continuity and Change 1800-1939', in Hoggart, K. and Green, D.R. (eds.), *London: A New Metropolitan Geography*, Edward Arnold, London, pp. 8-33.

Greenberg, M.R. (1976), *Solid Waste Planning in Metropolitan Regions*, Centre for Urban Policy Research, Rutgers University, New Brunswick, New Jersey.

The Green Party (1989), *Policy Pointers: Domestic Recycling*, The Green Party, London.

The Green Party (1991), *Manifesto for a sustainable London*, Federation of Green Parties, London.

Gregory, D. (1986), 'Realism', in Johnston, R.J. (ed.), *The Dictionary of Human Geography*, Basil Blackwell, Oxford.

Griesshammer, R. (1985), 'The Ecological Boomerang', in Ayrton, P.; Englehardt, T.; and Ware, V. (eds.), *World View 1985: an Economic and Political Yearbook*, Pluto Press, London and New York.

Gulley, B. (1979), 'Refuse disposal: Waste treatment systems - options for the 1980s', *Municipal Engineering*, 14th August, pp. 600-604.

Gyford, J. (1985), *The Politics of Local Socialism*, George Allen and Unwin, London.

Haas, G. (1990), 'Entgiftung durch Beschluenigung der Evolution', *Tageszeitung Hamburg*, 22nd March.

Haas, H.-D. (ed.) (1990), *Müll - Untersuchungen zur Problemen der Entsorgung und des Rohstoffrecycling*, Münchner Studien zur Sozial- und Wirtschaftsgeographie, Band 35, Verlag Michael Lassleben Kallmunz, Munich.

Haas, H.-D. and Sagawe, T. (1989), 'Kommunale und informelle Abfallwirtschaft in Santo Domingo / Dominikanische Republic', in Haas, H.-D. (ed.) (1990), *Müll - Untersuchungen zur Problemen der Entsorgung und des Rohstoffrecycling*, Münchner Studien zur Sozial- und Wirtschaftsgeographie, Band 35, Verlag Michael Lassleben Kallmunz, Munich.

Haas, H.-D. and Lempa, S. (1990), 'Müll in München: Untersuchungen zum Entsorgungsverhalten der Bevölkerung', *Geographische Rundschau*, 42, pp. 321-326.

Haas, H.-D. and Sagawe, T. (1990), 'Recycling als Entwicklungsansatz in Drittweltlandern', *Geographische Rundschau*, 42, pp. 314-319.

Hackney Borough Council (1989), *Report of the Environmental Services Committee*, 11th September.

Hadsley, N. (1990), 'The bottle to turn back the clock', *The Guardian*, 28th September.

Häfele, W. (1974), 'A systems approach to energy', *American Scientist*, 62, pp. 438-47.

Hahn, E. (1989), 'Ecological Urban Reconstruction: Urban Environmental Problems and Environmental Strategies in Different Social Systems', paper presented to the *European Colloquium 1989*, 4th-6th December 1989, Academy of the Urban Environment, Urban Ecology and Urban Open Space Planning, Berlin.

Hahn, E. (1991), *Ecological Urban Restructuring*, Wissenschaftszentrum Berlin für Sozialforschung.

Haigh, N. (1987), *EEC Environmental Policy*, (Second edition), Longman, UK.

Haigh, N. and Baldock, D. (1989), *Environmental Policy and 1992*, Institute for European Environmental Policy, London.

Hall, P. (1983), 'Patterns of Economic Policy: an Organizational Approach', in Held, D. (ed.) (1983), *States and Societies*, pp. 363-410, Martin Robinson, Oxford.

Hallbriter, G.; Brautigen, K.-R.; Katzer, H.; Braun, H.; and Vogg, H. (1984), 'Comparison of the Stack Emissions from Waste Incineration Facilities and Coal Fired Heating Power Stations', in Thome-Kozmiensky, K.J. (ed.), *Recycling International*, EF Verlag für Umwelt und Technik, Berlin, pp. 58-63.

Hannon, B.M. (1973), *System Energy and Recycling: A Study of the Beverage Industry*, Centre for Advanced Computation, University of Illinois.

Hardin, G. (1968), 'The Tragedy of the Commons', *Science*, 162, pp. 1243-8.

Hardin, G. (1974), 'Living on a lifeboat', Bioscience, 24, pp. 561-8.

Hartmann, M. and Rudolphi, M. (1989), 'Zur Frage der Akzeptanz unterschiedlicher Entsorgungssyteme im Raum München', in Haas, H.-D. (ed.) (1990), *Müll - Untersuchungen zur Problemen der Entsorgung und des Rohstoffrecycling*, Münchner Studien zur Sozial- und Wirtschaftsgeographie, Band 35, Verlag Michael Lassleben Kallmunz, Munich.

Hartwich, H.-H. (1990), *Freie und Hansestadt Hamburg: Die Zukunft des Stadtstaates*, Landeszentrale für politische Bildung, Hamburg.

Harvey, A.C. (1989), *Forecasting, structural time series models and the Kalman Filter*, Cambridge University Press, Cambridge.

Harvey, D. (1974), 'Population, resources and the ideology of science', *Economic Geography*, 50, pp. 256-277.

Harvey, D. (1989a), *The Urban Experience*, Basil Blackwell, Oxford.

Harvey, D. (1989b), *The Condition of Postmodernity*, Basil Blackwell, Oxford.

Harvey, D. (1992), 'Dialectics, Environmental and Social Change', lecture given to *The Institute for Historical Research*, 11th February, Senate House, University of London.

Hawksworth, D.L.; Coppins, B.J.; and Rose, F. (1974) 'Changes in the British Lichen Flora', in Hawksworth, D.L. (ed.) (1974), *The Changing Flora and Fauna of Britain*, Academic Press, London and New York, pp. 47-79.

Hay, A. (1979), 'Positivism in human geography: response to critics', in Herbert, D.T. and Johnston, R.J. (eds.), *Geography and the urban environment*, Volume 2, pp. 1-26, John Wiley, Chichester and New York.

Hay, A. and Wright, G. (1989), *Once is not enough*, Friends of the Earth, London.

Hay, A.; Wright, G.; and Forshaw, J. (1990), *Fashionable Waste: the make-up of a recycler,* Save Waste and Prosper Ltd., Leeds.

Hayes, D. (1978), *Repairs, Reuse, Recycling - First Steps Toward a Sustainable Society*, Worldwatch Paper 23, Worldwatch Institute, Washington DC.

Heanley, C. (1991), 'Refuse-derived fuel combustion: an overview', *WARMER Bulletin* 28, p. 8.

Hebbert, M. and Travers, T. (eds.), (1988), *The London Government Handbook*, Cassell, London.

Hecht, S. and Cockburn, A. (1989), *The Fate of the Forest*, Verso, London and New York.

Hecht, S. (1990), Guardians of the forest, *New Ground*, 24, pp. 14-15.

Hedlund, A. (1988), 'In Prosperity's Back Garden', paper presented to *Elmia waste and Recycling Conference*, 13-17th June, Jonkoping, Sweden.

Henstock, M.E. (1978), 'The Conflict Between First Cost and Recyclability in the Design of Manufactured Goods', *Resources Policy*. 4, pp. 160-165.

Henstock, M.E. (1988), *Design for Recyclability*, Institute of Metals, UK.

Herbert Commission (1960), *Report of the Royal Commission on Local Government in Greater London*, HMSO, London.

Hermes, P. (1990), 'Müllverbrennung: Ohne Glas geht hier gar nichts', *Tageszeitung*, 9th August.

292

Hershkowitz, A. and Salerni, E. (1987), *Garbage Management in Japan*, Inform, New York.

Hibbeln, K. (1992), 'The development of waste management in Hamburg', paper presented to the conference *Resource Recovery from Waste*, 21st-24th September, Imola, Sweden.

Hillman, J. (1989), *A New Look for London*, Royal Fine Art Commission, London.

Hiorns, F.R. (1956), *Town-building in History*, George G. Harrap, London.

Hirsch, F. (1977), *Social Limits to Growth*, Routledge and Kegan Paul, London.

HMIP (Her Majesty's Inspectorate of Pollution) (1989), *Waste disposal regulation and operation in the former Metropolitan Counties: a review*, DoE, London.

Hockley, G.C.; Walters, J.; and Goodall, P. (1989), *Generating Profit from Waste*, Special Report No.1182, The Economist Intelligence Unit, London.

Hoffman, R.E. (1986), Health Effects of Long-Term Exposure to 2,3,7,8 Tetrachlorodibenzo-p-Dioxin, *The Journal of the American Medical Association*, April, pp. 460-493.

Hoffmeister, S. (1988), 'Stoff- und Energiebilanzen: Ein Instrument präventiver Umweltplanung', in Ifö, *Abfall Vermeidung*, Fischer Taschenbuch Verlag, Frankfurt am Main, pp. 90-98.

Hoggart, K. and Green, D.R. (eds.) (1991), *London: A New Metropolitan Geography*, Edward Arnold, London.

Holmberg, J.; Thomson, K.; and Timberlake, L. (1993), *Facing the Future: Beyond the Earth Summit*, Institute for Environment and Development/Earthscan, London.

Holmes, J.R. (1989), *A Review of the United Kingdom Waste Industry 1989*, Centre for Extension Studies, Loughborough University of Technology.

Hooper, G. (1984), 'Possibilities of state control - development tendencies', in Thome-Kozmiensky, K.J. (ed.), *Recycling International*, EF Verlag für Umwelt and Technik, Berlin, pp. 699-701.

House of Commons Trade and Industry Committee (1985), *The Wealth of Waste*, Second Special Report from the Trade and Industry Committee Session 1984-85, HMSO, London.

House of Lords (1981), *Hazardous Waste Disposal*, Committee Report.

Howells, K. (1986), 'Mixing It: Energy, the Environment and the Unions', in Weston, J. (ed.), *Red and Green*, Pluto Press, London.

Hubbert, M.K. (1976), 'Outlook for fuel reserves', in Lapedes, D.N. (ed.), *Encyclopedia of Energy*, Mcgraw-Hill, New York.

Hughes, D. (1974), 'Towards a recycling society', *New Scientist*, 10th January, pp. 58-60.

Hülsberg, W. (1988), *The German Greens*, Verso, London and New York.

Hunt, J. (1990), 'Cowboy operators taint cleaner image', *The Financial Times*, 26th September.

Hunt, J. (1991), 'Environment agencies start to flex their muscles', *The Financial Times*, 22nd October.

IföR (Institut für ökologisches Recycling) (1988), *Abfall Vermeiden*, Fischer Taschenbuch Verlag, Frankfurt am Main.

IföR (Institut für ökologisches Recycling) (1989), *Ökologische Abfallwirtschaft: Umweltvorsage durch Abfallvermeidung*, IföR, Berlin.

IGD (Institute of Grocery Distribution), 1992 *Sustainable Waste Management: The Adur Project*, IGD, Watford.

INCPEN (The Industry Council for Packaging and the Environment) (1987), *Packaging Saves Waste*, INCPEN, London.

Inglehardt, R. (1981), 'Post-Materialism in an Environment of Insecurity', *The American Political Science Review*, 75, pp. 880-900.

Innston, H.H. (1974), 'Models of Material Consumption', paper presented to the conference *Conservation of Materials*, 26th-27th March, Harwell.

Institution of Environmental Health Officers (1989), *Landfill Gas*, 11th April, conference held at King's College, London.

IPCC (Intergovernmental Panel on Climatic Change) (1990), *Policymakers summary of the scientific assessment of climatic change*, World Meteorological Office / United Nations Environment Programme.

Irvine, J.; Miles, I., and Evans, J. (ed.) (1979), *Demystifying Social Statistics*, Pluto Press, London.

Isaac, P.C. (1953), *Public Health Engineering*, E.& F.N. Spon Ltd., London.

ITU (Ingenieurgemeinschaft Technischer Umweltschutz) (1987), *Gutachterliche Studie zur Abfallwirtschaftsplanung für die Bereiche Hausmüll, Sperrmüll und hausmüllähnliche Abfälle für die Stadt Hamburg*, Ingenieurgemeinschaft Technischer Umweltschutz, Berlin.

ITU (Ingenieurgemeinschaft Technischer Umweltschutz) (1989), *Verfahren zur Reduktion des Hausmüllaufkommens*, Ingenieurgemeinschaft Technischer Umweltschutz, Berlin.

IWM (Institute for Wastes Management) (1974), *The Treatment and Recycling of Solid Wastes*, 11th January, One-day symposium, Manchester.

IWM (Institute for Wastes Management) (1987), *A report on the status of recovery of useful materials and/or energy from household refuse*, Insitute of Wastes Management, Northampton.

IWM (Institute for Wastes Management) (1989), *The Monitoring of Landfill Gas*, Institute of Wastes Management, Northampton.

Jackson, D.W. (1980), 'Re-cycling waste in a Metropolitan Authority', paper presented to the *GLC Talking Rubbish Conference*, 30th January.

Jackson, D. and Robson, D. (1990), 'Splits in the Structure', *The Surveyor*, 1st February.

Jacobs, J. (1969), *The Economy of Cities*, Penguin Books Ltd., Middlesex.

Jager, B. (1989), *Abfallverwertung in der Bundesrepublik Deutschland*, Bundesminister für Forshung and Technologie, Bonn.

Jencks, C. (1986), *What is Post-Modernism?*, Academy Editions and St Martin's Press, London and New York.

Jensen, W.J.; Holman, J.L.; and Stephenson, J.B. (1974), 'Recycling and disposal of waste plastics', in Yen, T.F., *Recycling and Disposal of Solid Waste: Industrial, Agricultural, Domestic*, Ann Arbor Science Publishers, Michigan, US.

Jessop, B. (1988), 'Regulation Theory, Post-Fordism and the State', *Capital and Class*, 34, pp. 147-68.

Jessop, B. (1991), *Fordism and post-fordism: a critical reformulation*, Lancaster Regionalism Group, Working Paper 41, University of Lancaster.

John, B. (1974), 'Recycling politics', *New Scientist*, 10th January, pp. 60-62.

Johnson, A. (1989), 'Back to the future', *The Guardian*, 3rd November.

Johnson, J. (1984), *Econometric Methods*, McGraw-Hill Inc., US.

Johnson, J. (1990), 'Waste that no one wants', *New Scientist*, 8th September, pp. 50-55.

Johnston, R.J. (1983), *Philosophy and Human Geography*, Arnold, London.

Jordan, G. and Wessel, K. (1988), 'Papier - Baume, BILD und Altpapier', in IföR, *Abfall Vermeiden*, Fischer Taschenbuch Verlag, Frankfurt am Main, pp. 29-37.

Jordan, G. and Ranneberg, T. (1988), 'Subventionspolitik and Abfallproduktion: Wege zu einer neuen Strukturpolitik', in IföR, *Abfall Vermeiden*, Fischer Taschenbuch Verlag, Frankfurt am Main, pp. 132-144.

Keat, R. (1979), 'Positivism and Statistics in Social Science', in Irvine, J. et al. (eds.), *Demystifying Social Statistics*, Pluto Press, London.

King, D. (1989), 'The New Right, the New Left and Local Government', in Stewart, J. and Stoker, G. (eds.), *The Future of Local Government*, pp. 185-212.

Klinski, S. (1988), 'Besser als bisher - aber schlechter als nötig: Das Abfallgesetz 1986', in Institut für ökologisches Recycling, *Abfall Vermeiden*, Fischer Taschenbuch Verlag, Frankfurt am Main, pp. 123-132.

Kluge, T. and Schramm, E. (1989), 'Kriterien für eine andere Technostruktur im Abfallberiech', paper presented to the conference *Ökologische Abfallwirtschaft*, November 30th - December 3rd, Technische Universität Berlin.

Koch, T.C.; Seeberger, J.; and Petrik, H. (1986), *Ökologische Müllverwertung: Handbuch für optimale Abfallkonzepte*, C.F. Muller, Karlsruhe.

Koopowitz, H. and Kaye, H. (1990), *Plant Extinction: A Global Crisis*, Christopher Helm, London.

Kopytziok, N. (1988a), 'Grundlagen für eine umfassende Betrachtung der Abfallproblematik', in IföR, *Abfall Vermeiden*, Fischer Taschenbuch Verlag, Frankfurt am Main, pp.17-23.

Kopytziok, N. (1988b), 'Abfallvermeidung: Das praventive Element', in IföR, *Abfall Vermeiden*, Fischer Taschenbuch Verlag, Frankfurt am Main, pp. 69-74.

Kopytziok, N. and Oswald, R. (1988), 'Eine Abfall-Odysse', in IföR, *Abfall Vermeiden*, Fischer Taschenbuch Verlag, Frankfurt am Main, pp. 23-28.

Kouwenhoven, J.A. (1961), *The Beer Can by the Highway*, Doubleday, Garden City, NY.

Kreusch, J. (1989), 'Probleme der Langzeitsicherheit von Deponien - Folgerungen für eine ökologische Abfallwirtschaft', paper presented to the conference *Ökologische Abfallwirtschaft*, 30th November to 2nd December, Technische Universität, Berlin.

Kromarek, P. (1986), *European Community Environmental Policy in*

Practice. Volume 4, Federal Republic of Germany: Water and Waste. A Study of the Implementation of the EEC Directives, Graham and Trotman, London.

Kunreuther, H.C. and Linnerooth, J. (1983), *Risk Analysis and Decision Processes: the Siting of Liquefied Energy Gas Facilities in Four Countries*, Springer, Berlin.

Kut, D. and Hare, G. (1981), *Waste Recycling for Energy Conservation*, The Architectural Press, London.

Labour Party (1986), *Labour's Charter for the Environment*, The Labour Party, London.

Labour Party (1990), *An Earthly Chance: Labour's programme for a cleaner, greener Britain*, The Labour Party, London.

Labour Party (1991), *London: A World Class Capital*, The Labour Party, London.

Lahl, U. and Wiebe, A. (1989), 'Chemie im Müll - verkennen, vergessen, verdrängen', paper presented to the conference *Ökologische Abfallwirtschaft*, 30th November to 2nd December, Technische Universität, Berlin.

Lambert, E. and Laurence, D. (1990), 'Environmental Protection Bill: All Change for Waste Management', *Wastes Management*, March, pp. 187-200.

LAMSAC (Local Authorities Management Services and Computer Committee) (1971), *Waste Paper Salvage*, LAMSAC, London.

Langer, H. (1979), 'Strategies for the Use of Waste Paper Outside the Paper Industry', *Proceedings of the International Recycling Congress (Recycling Berlin '79)*, E. Freitag, Berlin.

LARAC (Local Authority Recycling Advisory Committee) (1987), *Expanding glass recycling: a LARAC guide*.

Lash, S. and Urry, J. (1987), *The End of Organized Capitalism*, Polity Press, Cambridge.

Leidner, J. (1981), *Plastics Waste: Recovery of Economic Value*, Marcel Dekker, New York.

LBA (London Boroughs Association) (1982), *Bottle Banks: Expansion of the Bottle Bank Scheme in London and the Surrounding Area.*

LB-HSR (Landesbetrieb Hamburger Stadtreinigung) (1990), *Geschäftsbericht 1989*, Umweltbehörde, Freie und Hansestadt Hamburg.

LB-HSR (Landesbetrieb Hamburger Stadtreinigung) (1992), *Geschäftsbericht 1991*, Umweltbehörde, Freie und Hansestadt Hamburg.

LCC (London County Council) (1893), *Report on Dust Destructors by the Medical Officer and the Engineer.*

Lean, G. and Ghazi, P. (1992), 'Cloak of subsidiarity is used to keep Britain polluting', *The Observer*, 6th December.

Lean, G. (1993), 'Waste tax plan offers lifeline to recyclers', *The Observer*, 16th May.

Leipert, C. and Simonis, U.E. (1990), *Environmental Damage - Environmental Expenditures: Statistical Evidence on the Federal Republic of Germany*, Wissenschaftszentrum Berlin für Sozialforschung, Berlin.

Letcher, R.C. and Shiel, M. (1986), 'Source Separation and Citizen Recycling', in Robinson, W.D., *The Solid Waste Handbook: A Practical Guide,* John Wiley and Sons, New York.

Liberal Democrats (1991), *Changing London for Good: London Region Liberal Democrat Policies for London.*

Lindberg, R.A. and Akagi, R.H. (1974), *Reclamation 1975-2000: A key to economical survival*, Dun and Bradstreet Inc., New York.

Linnerooth, J. and Kneese, A.V. (1989), 'Hazardous Waste Management: a West German Approach', *Resource,* Summer Issue, pp. 7-10.

Lipietz, A. (1992), *Towards a New Economic Order: Postfordism, Ecology and Democracy*, Polity Press, Cambridge.

Lloyd, E.J.D. and Humphries, J.H. (1944), *A survey of London Local Government*, Institute of Municipal Treasurers and Accountants, London.

Local Government Board (1915), *Return as to scavenging in Urban Districts 1914*, HMSO, London.

Lopez-Real, J. (1990), 'Composting of selected household waste', paper presented to the *London Recycling Forum*, 5th December.

Lovelock, J.E. (1979), *Gaia: A New Look at Life on Earth*, Oxford University Press, Oxford.

Lovins, A. (1977), *Soft Energy Paths*, Penguin, Harmondsworth.

Low, R.A. 1975 'Energy conversion in New York', paper presented to the *National Conference on Conversion of Refuse to Energy*, 3rd -5th November, Montreux.

Lowe, P.D. (1977), 'Amenity and equity: a review of local environmental pressure groups in Britain', *Environment and Planning A*. 9, pp. 35-58.

Lowe, P.D. and Goyder, J. (1983), *Environmental Groups in Politics*, Resource Management Series Vol.6., Allen & Unwin, London.

Lowe, P.D.; Cox, G.; MacEwan, M.; O'Riordan, T.; and Winter, M. (1986), *Countryside Conflicts: The politics of farming, forestry and conservation*, Gower, Aldershot.

Lowenthal, D. (ed.) (1965), *George Perkins Marsh: Man and Nature*, Harvard University Press, Cambridge, MA.

LPAC (London Planning Advisory Committee) (1988), *Strategic Planning Advice for London: Policies for the 1990s*.

Lubjahn, D.; Rehm, M.; and Schrimpf, M. (1988), 'Giftige Stoffe im Hausmüll Berlins: Bedrohung oder Bagatelle?', in IföR, *Abfall Vermeiden*, Fischer Taschenbuch Verlag, Frankfurt am Main, pp. 107-120.

Lukes, S. (1981), 'Fact and theory in the social sciences', in Potter, D. (ed.), *Society and the Social Sciences*, Routledge and Kegan Paul, London and Henley.

LWRA (London Waste Regulation Authority) (1986), *London's Waste Disposal System*.

LWRA (London Waste Regulation Authority) (1988), 'Making sense of rubbish', second annual conference of the *London Waste Regulation Authority*, held at the Institution of Civil Engineers, 24th March.

LWRA (London Waste Regulation Authority) (1987), *Annual Report 1986-87*.

LWRA (London Waste Regulation Authority) (1988), *Annual Report 1987-88*.

LWRA (London Waste Regulation Authority) (1989), *Annual Report 1988-89*.

LWRA (London Waste Regulation Authority) (1990), *Annual Report 1989-90*.

Mackay, L. and Thompson, M. (eds.) (1988), *Something in the Wind: Politics after Chernobyl*, Pluto Press, London.

Mackie, T. and Craig, F. (1985), *Europe Votes*, Parliamentary Research Services, London.

Mackie, T. (1990), *Europe Votes 2*, Dartmouth Publishing Company Ltd., London.

Macrory, R. and Withers, S. (1989), *Waste Management in the United Kingdom*, Wissenschaftszentrum Berlin für Sozialforschung, Berlin.

McCormick, J. (1989), *Acid Earth: The Global Threat of Acid Pollution*, Earthscan, London.

McCormick, J. (1989), *The Global Environmental Movement*, Belhaven, London.

McCormick, J. (1991), *British Politics and the Environment*, Earthscan,

London.

McGavin, B. (1991), 'Going green - but what about the workers?', *Employment Gazette*, January, pp. 11-19.

McLaren, D. (1992), 'London as Ecosystem', in Thornley, A. (ed.), *The Crisis of London*, Routledge, London and New York. pp. 56-69.

Mander, D. and Golden, J. (1991), *The London Borough of Hackney in Old Photographs 1890-1960*, Alan Sutton, Gloucestershire.

Mann, P. (1985), *Methods of Social Investigation*, Basil Blackwell, Oxford and New York.

Mansell, D. (1990), *UK 2000 Recycling City - Sheffield Kerbside Collection Project*, Friends of the Earth, London.

Marsh, D. (1991), 'Blow for Kohl as SPD wins Hamburg poll', *The Financial Times*, 3rd June.

Marsh, P. (1989), 'Muck, brass and outrage too', *The Financial Times*, 24th October.

Marsh, P. (1990a), 'The rising cost of coping with waste', *The Financial Times*, 5th March.

Marsh, P. (1990b), 'Rubbish disposal costs could rise substantially', *The Financial Times*, 17th July.

Marten, F. (1989), 'Gefährdet: das Müllwunder von Harburg', *Tageszeitung Hamburg*, 21st September.

Marten, F. (1990a), 'Warum die Müllgebühren wieder steigen', *Tageszeitung Hamburg*, 5th May.

Marten, F. (1990b), 'Es geht als doch: Aus Müll wird Gold gemacht', *Tageszeitung Hamburg*, 7th July.

Martin, R. (1986), 'Thatcherism and Britain's Industrial Landscape', in Martin, R. and Rowthorn, B. (ed.) (1986), *The Geography of De-industrialisation*, Macmillan, London, pp. 238-291.

Martin, R. (1987), *The new economics and politics of regional restructuring: the British experience*, paper presented to the University of Leuven, Belgium, April 1987.

Martinez-Alier, J. (1987), *Ecological Economics: Energy, Environment and Society*, Basil Blackwell, Oxford and Cambridge, MA

Marx, J. (1984), 'Gewerbliche Abfallbeseitigung in Hamburg', *Hamburg in Zahlen*, 8, pp. 214-218, Statistiches Landesamt der Freien und Hansestadt Hamburg.

Masser, I. and Williams, R. (1986), *Learning from Other Countries: the Cross-National Dimension in Urban Policy-Making,* Geo Books.

Massey, D. and Meegan, R. (1985), *Politics and Method: Contrasting studies in industrial geography*, Methuen, London and New York.

Meacher, M. (1975), 'Riddle of the great waste paper chase', *The Guardian*, 3rd April.

Meadows, D.H.; Meadows, D.l.; Randers, J.; and Behrens, W. (eds.) (1972), *The Limits to Growth*, Universe Books, New York.

Meister, M. (1990), 'MS Zanoobia: Eine Giftmüll-Odysee', in Spill, E. and Wingert, E. (eds.), *Brennpunkt Müll*, Sternbuch, Hamburg.

Melosi, M.V. (1981), *Garbage in the Cities: Refuse, Reform, and the Environment, 1880-1980*, Texas A&M University Press.

Mesarovic, M. and Pestel, E. (1974), *Mankind at the Turning Point: The Second Report to the Club of Rome*, Hutchinson, London.

Metropolitan Borough of Shoreditch (1925), *Report to the Electricity Committee on the Disposal of Refuse.*

Metropolitan Commission of Sewers (1849), *A report to the survey committee on street cleansing*, Reynell and Weight, London.

Meyer, F.A. (1901), *Die stadtische Verbrennungsantalt fur Abfallstoffe am Ballerdeich in Hamburg*, Friedrich Wieweg & Sohn, Braunschwieg.

Meyer, U. (1989), 'Kommunale Konzepte zur Abfallvermeidung - Ein

Überblick', paper presented to the conference *Ökologische Abfallwirtschaft*, 30th November to 2nd December 1989, Technische Universität, Berlin.

Miles, I. and Irvine, J. (1979), 'Social Forecasting: Predicting the Future or Making History?', in Irvine et al., *Demystifying Social Statistics*, Pluto Press, London.

Miller, K. (1990), 'Waste not, want not', *The Guardian*, 10th October.

Milton Keynes Borough Council (1990), *Materials Recycling Handbook.*

Ministry of Health (1929), *Report of an investigation into the Public Cleansing service in the administrative county of London*, HMSO, London.

Ministry of Health (1930), *Report of the cleansing committee*, HMSO, London.

Ministry of Health (1934), *Report of the cleansing committee,* HMSO, London.

Ministry of Health (1937), *Report of the cleansing committe*, HMSO, London.

Ministry of Health (1939), *Public Cleansing: Refuse collection and disposal; street cleansing. Costing Returns for the year ended 31st March, 1938*, HMSO, London.

Ministry of Housing and Local Government (1954), *Public Cleansing: Refuse collection and disposal; street cleansing*, costing returns 1952-53, HMSO, London.

Ministry of Housing and Local Government (1961), *Pollution of Water by Tipped Refuse: Report of the Technical Committee on the Experimental Disposal of House Refuse in Wet and Dry Pits*, HMSO, London.

Mintzel, A. and Oberreuter, H. (eds.) (1990), *Parteien in der Bundesrepublik Deutschland*, Bundeszentrale für politische Bildung, Bonn.

Morrison, H. (1949), *How London is Governed*, James Barrie Publishers Ltd., London.

Moser, M. (1990), *Environmental relief through waste prevention*, unpublished paper, Institut für ökologishes Recycling, Berlin.

Moser, C.A. and Kalton, G. (1971), *Survey Methods in Social Investigation*, Gower, Aldershot.

Mukhopadhyay, A.K. (1972), *The Politics of London's Water Supply 1871-1971*, unpublished PhD thesis, London School of Economics.

Mukhopadhyay, A.K. (1975), 'The Politics of London Water', *The London Journal*, 1, pp. 207-226.

Müller-Rommel, F. and Poguntke, T. (1990), 'Die Grünen', in Mintzel, A. and Oberreuter, H. (eds.), *Parteien in der Bunderepublik Deutschland*, pp. 276-311.

Mumford, L. (1961), *The City in History*, Secker and Warburg, London.

Myers, N. (1980), *The Sinking Arc*, Pergamon Press, London.

Nagel, E. (1981), 'The value-orientated bias of social inquiry', in Potter, D. et al., *Society and the Social Sciences*, Routledge and Kegan Paul, London.

Nairne, S. (1987), *State of the Art: Ideas and Images in the 1980s*, Chatto and Windus, London.

Narracott, E.S. (1974), 'The impact of plastics materials resources', paper presented to the conference *The Conservation of Materials*, 26th-27th March, Harwell.

Nathan, S. (1990), 'Not worth the paper', *LA Week*, January 18th, pp. 12-13.

National Soft Drink Association (NSDA) (1983), *The Soft Drink Industry of the United States: Statistical Profile 1982*, NSDA, Washington, DC.

Neave, H.R. and Worthington, P.L. (1988), *Distribution-Free Tests*, Unwin Hyman, London.

Newell, J. (1990), 'Recycling Britain', *New Scientist*, 8th September, pp. 46-49.

Newham, M. and Knight, S. (1991), 'A double dose of German recycling', *The Financial Times*, 30th January.

NIES (National Institue for Environmental Studies) (1978), *Source Separation for Resource Recovery: State of the Art*, National Insitute for Environmental Studies, Tsukuba, Japan.

Nilsson, K. (1991), *World-wide trends in solid waste incineration*, Alliance for Beverage Cartons and the Environment, London.

Norton, R. (1986), *Community Scale Recycling*, unpublished M Phil Thesis, University of East Anglia.

Norton-Taylor, R. (1982), *Whose Land is it Anyway?*, Turnstone Press Ltd., Wellingborough.

Odell, P. (1985), 'Energy and Regional Development: A European Perspective', *Built Environment*, 11, pp. 31-53.

OECD (Organisation for Economic Cooperation and Development) (1979), *Separate collection of paper, glass and metals at Hoje Tastrup, Denmark*, OECD, Paris.

OECD (Organisation for Economic Cooperation and Development) (1983), *Separate Collection and Recycling*, OECD, Paris.

OECD (Organisation for Economic Cooperation and Development) (1989), *Revenue Statistics of OECD Member Countries 1965-1989*, OECD, Paris.

OECD (Organisation for Economic Cooperation and Development) (1990), *The Role of Cities in Sustainable Development*, OECD, Paris.

OECD (Organisation for Economic Cooperation and Development) (1990), *Urban Environmental Policies for the 1990s*, OECD, Paris.

O'Hanlon, L. (1992), 'Time to shrink wrap', *The Guardian*, 9th October.

Ohashi, K. (1984), 'A study on volume reduction systems for plastic wastes', in Thome-Kozmiensky, K.J. (ed.), *Recycling International*, EF Verlag für Umwelt and Technik, Berlin, pp. 548-553.

O'Leary, B. (1987), 'Why was the GLC abolished?', *The Journal of Urban and Regional Research.* 11, pp. 193-217.

Ollier, K. (1988), 'Success for waste heirs', *The Municipal Journal*, 19th February, pp. 328-329.

Olsen, D.J. (1964), *Town Planning in London*, Yale University Press, New Haven and London.

Opschoor, J.B. and Vos, H.B. (1989), *Economic Instruments for Environmental Protection*, Organisation for Economic Co-operation and Development, Paris.

O'Riordan, T. (1981), *Environmentalism*, 2nd Edition, Pion, London.

O'Riordan, T. (1989), 'The challenge for environmentalism', in Peet, R. and Thrift, N. (eds.), *New Models in Geography Part One*, Unwin Hyman, London.

Ossenbrügge, J. (1988), 'Regional Restructuring and the Ecological Welfare State - Spatial Impacts of Environmental Protection in West Germany', *Geographische Zeitschrift*, 76, pp. 78-96.

Ossenbrügge, J. (1989), *Impacts of Environmental policies on Regional Restructuring in Industrialized societies. The Case of Hamburg Metropolitan Area*, unpuplished paper, Department of Geography, University of Hamburg.

Owens, P. and Owens, S. (1989), 'Resource Management', *Progress in Human Geography*, pp. 107-117.

Owens, S.; Amderson, V.; and Brunskill, I. (1990), *Green Taxes,* Green Paper No.2., The Institute for Public Policy Research, London.

Packard, V. (1960), *The Wastemakers*, David McKay Company Inc., London.

Page, T. (1977), *Conservation and Economic Efficiency*, John Hopkins University Press, Baltimore.

Parkin, S. (1989), *Green Parties: An International Guide*, Heretic Books, London.

Paterson, T. (1989), *The Green Conservative: a manifesto for the environment*, Bow Publications Ltd., London

Peacock, A. (ed.) (1984), *The Regulation Game: How British and West German Companies Bargain with Government*, Basil Blackwell, Oxford.

Pearce, D.W. (1990), 'In the market for action', *The Guardian*, 7th December.

Pearce, D.W. (1991a), *Blueprint 2: Greening the World Economy*, Earthscan Publications, London.

Pearce, D.W. (1991b), 'Saving the Tropical Rainforest: An Economic Approach', paper presented to the *Geography and Planning Research Seminar*, 5th December, London School of Economics.

Pearce, D.W. (1993), *Economic Values and the Natural World*, Earthscan Publications, London.

Pearce, D.W. and Walter, I. (eds.) (1977), *Resource Conservation: The Social and Economic Dimensions of Recycling*, Longman, New York.

Pearce, D.W.; Markandya, A. and Barbier, E.B. (1989), *Blueprint for a Green Economy*, Earthscan Publications, London.

Pearce, D.W. and Turner, R.K. (eds.) (1990), *Economics of Natural Resources and the Environment*, Harvester Wheatsheaf, London and New York.

Peet, R. and Thrift, N. (eds) (1989), *New Models in Geography*, Unwin Hyman, London.

Pepper, D. (1984), *The Roots of Modern Environmentalism*, Croom Helm, London.

Pepper, D. (1986), 'Radical Environmentalism and the Labour Movement', in Weston, J. (ed.), *Red and Green*, Pluto Press, London.

Pepper, D. (1989), 'Green Consumerism - Thatcherite Environmentalism', *New Ground*, Winter, pp. 18-20.

Perring, F.H. (1974), 'Changes in our Native Vascular Plant Flora', in Hawksworth, D.L., *The Changing Flora and Fauna of Britain*, pp. 7-27.

Pieters, R.G.M. and Verhallen, T.M.M. (1986), 'Participation in Source Separation Projects: Design characteristics and percieved costs and benefits', *Resources and Conservation*. 12, pp. 95-111.

Pinch, S.P. (1989), 'The restructuring thesis and the study of public services', *Environment and Planning A*, 21, pp. 905-926.

Poll, A.J. (1990), *Analysis of refuse from the kerbside collection area of Sheffield*, unpublished report, Warren Spring Laboratory.

Pollock, C. (1987), *Mining Urban Wastes: The Potential for Recycling*, Worldwatch Paper 76, Worldwatch Institute, US.

Pollock, G. (1990), 'Full Speed Ahead on the Recycle Path', *Readers Digest*, pp. 139-143.

Porritt, J. (1984), *Seeing Green*, Basil Blackwell, Oxford.

Porritt, J. (1986), 'Beyond environmentalism', in Goldsmith, E. and Hildyard, N. (eds.), *Green Britain or Industrial Wasteland*, pp. 340-350.

Porritt, J. and Winner, D. (1988), *The Coming of the Greens*, Fontana, UK.

Porteus, A. (1977), *Recycling Resources Refuse*, Longman, New York.

Porteus, A. (1984), 'Recycling in the UK - An examination of its feasibility', paper presented to the *Institute of Wastes Management*, annual conference, 5th-8th June, Torbay.

Porteus, A. (1987), *Recycling - technologies and strategies*, October 12th, Inaugural Lecture to the Open University.

Porteus, A. (1990), 'Municipal Waste Incineration in the UK - What's Holding It Back', *Environmental Health*. pp.181-186.

Potter, D. (ed.) (1981), *Society and the Social Sciences*, Routledge and Kegan Paul, London.

Pratt, A.C. (1990), *Varieties of theory and truth: the challenge of post-structuralism*, paper presented to the London School of Economics, Department of Geography, Postgraduate Reading Weekend, East Bergholt, Suffolk, 16th November.

Prestt, I. (1970), 'The effect of DDT on bird populations', in Warren, A. and Goldsmith, F. (eds) (1983), *Conservation in Perspective*, John Wiley, London.

Purcell, A. (1980), *The Waste Watchers: A Citizen's Handbook for Conserving Energy*, Doubleday, New York.

Rappe, C.; Choudary, G.; and Keith, L.H. (eds.) (1986), *Chlorinated Dioxins and Dibenzofurans in Perspective*, Lewis Publishers Inc., Chelsea, Michigan.

Rassmussen, M. (1991), *Waste to energy technology*, Alliance for Beverage Cartons and the Environment, London.

Rawstorne, P. (1989), 'Packaging: Common rules prove elusive', *The Financial Times,* 28th November.

RCEP (Royal Commission on Environmental Pollution) (1985), *Managing Waste: The Duty of Care*, HMSO, London.

RCEP (Royal Commission on Environmental Pollution) (1993), *Incineration of Waste*, HMSO, London.

Redcliffe-Maud Commission (1969), *Report of the Royal Commission on Local Government in England 1966-69*, HMSO, London.

Redclift, M. (1987), *Sustainable Development: Exploring the Contradictions*, Routledge, London and New York.

Reitz, P. and Fiolka, J. (1984), 'Design, Operation and Experiences of the Resource Recovery Center Ruhr (RZR) at Herten', in Thome-Kozmiensky, K.J. (ed.), *Recycling International*, EF Verlag für Umwelt und Technik, Berlin, pp. 275-284.

Rhodes, G. and Ruck, S.K. (1970), *The Government of Greater London*, George Allen & Unwin Ltd., London.

Richards, K.M. (1989), *'Landfill Gas - Working with Gaia*, Energy Technology Support Unit, Harwell.

Richmond Borough Council (1990), *Recycling sub-committee (Highways committee)*, 24th October.

RIPA (The Royal Institute of Public Finance) (1983), *Contracting Out in the Public Sector*, RIPA, London.

Risch, R.W.K. (1978), 'The Raw Material Supply of the European Community: The Importance of Secondary Raw Materials', *Resource Policy*. 4, pp. 181-188.

Roberts (1965), presidential address to the *Institute of Public Cleansing Annual Conference*, 1-4th June, Scarborough.

Roberts, F. (1974), 'Management policies for non-renewable materials resources', paper presented to *The Conservation of Materials Conference*, 26th-27th March, Harwell.

Robinson, A.J. (1974), 'Recycle and recovery', paper presented to *The Conservation of Materials*, 26th-27th March, Harwell.

Robson, W.A. (1939), *The Government and Misgovernment of London*, George Allen & Unwin Ltd., London.

Rockefeller Institute (1986), *Recycling in New York State: Status and Opportunities*, The Nelson A. Rockelfeller Institute of Government, Albany, NY.

Rose, F. and Wallace, E.C. (1974), 'Changes in the Bryophyte Flora of Britain', in Hawksworth, D.L. (ed.), *The Changing Flora and Fauna of Britain*, pp. 27-47.

Rose, R. (ed.) (1974), *The Management of Urban Change in Britain and Germany*, Sage, London.

Rosenhead, J. and Thunhurst, C. (1979) 'Operational Research and Cost Benefit Analysis: Whose Science?', in Irvine et al., *Demystifying Social*

Statistics, Pluto Press, London.

Rozcak, T. (1979), *Person/Planet*, Gollanz, London.

Rüdig, W. (1986), *Energy, Public Protest and Green Parties - A Comparative Analysis*, Unpublished PhD thesis, University of Manchester.

Rüdig, W. and Lowe, P.D. (1986), 'The Withered 'Greening' of British Politics: a Study of the Ecology Party', *Political Studies*, 34, pp. 262-84.

Ryan, A. (1981), 'Is the study of society a science?', in Potter, D. (ed.), *Society and the Social Sciences*, Routledge and Kegan Paul, London.

Ryle, M. (1988), *Socialism and Ecology*, Radius, London.

Sahm, L. (1984), 'The collection of separate components of domestic refuse and recycling', in Thome-Kozmiensky, K.J. (ed.), *Recycling International*, EF Verlag für Umwelt und Technik, Berlin, pp. 264-269.

Sandbach, F. (1980), *Environment, Ideology and Policy*, Basil Blackwell, Oxford.

Särlvik, B. and Crewe, I. (1983), *Decade of Dealignment*, Cambridge University Press, Cambridge.

Savas, E.S. (1979), 'Public versus Private Refuse Collection: A Critical Review of the Evidence', *Urban Analysis*, 6, pp. 1-13.

Sayer, A. (1992), *Method in social science: a realist approach*, Routledge, London.

Scheffold, K. (1984), 'Source separation of packaging - materials and recovery possibilities', in Thome-Kozmiensky, K.J. (ed.), *Recycling International*, EF Verlag für Umwelt und Technik, Berlin, pp. 796-801.

Schertz, W. (1984), 'Possibilities for separating and recycling disposable lined cardboard containers', in Thome-Kozmiensky, K.J. (ed.), *Recycling International*, EF Verlag für Umwelt und Technik, Berlin, pp. 784-789.

Schmidt-Alck, S. and Strenge, U. (1988), 'Glas - ein Pladoyer für Mehrweg', in IföR, *Abfall Vermeiden*, Fischer Taschenbuch Verlag, Frankfurt am Main, pp. 45-53.

Schomburgk, I.C. (1975), 'The development of conversion of refuse to energy innovation in Britain', paper presented to the *National Conference on Conversion of Refuse to Energy*, 3rd-5th November, Montreux.

Schulze, C.H. (1989), 'Der Umweltökonomische Ansatz', *Geographische Rundschau*, 41, pp. 318-323.

Schumacher, E.F. (1974), *Small is Beautiful*, Abacus, London.

Scientific American (1990), *Managing Planet Earth: Readings from Scientific American*, W.H. Freeman, New York.

SCLSERP (Standing Committee on London and South East Regional Planning) (1978), *Waste Disposal in South East England*, SCLSERP, London.

Scott, A. and Storper, M. (eds) (1992), *Pathways to Industrialisation and Regional   Development in the 1990s*, Routledge, London.

Seager, J. (ed.) (1990), *The State of the Earth: An atlas of environmental concern*,   Unwin Hyman, London.

Self, P.J.O. (1975), *Econocrats and the Policy Process*, Macmillan, London.

SERPLAN (The London and South East Regional Planning Conference) (1987), *Guidelines for Waste Disposal Planning in the South East*, SERPLAN, London.

SERPLAN (The London and South East Regional Planning Conference) (1988a), *Planning for Waste Disposal in South East England*, report of a seminar held 21st January, SERPLAN, London.

SERPLAN (The London and South East Regional Planning Conference) (1988b), *Waste Disposal in the South East Region: The Results of the 1987 Waste Monitoring Survey*, SERPLAN, London.

SERPLAN (The London and South East Regional Planning Conference)

(1988c), *Waste Recycling: A Regional Perspective,* SERPLAN, London.

Seymour, J. and Giradet, H. (1987), *Blueprint for a Green Planet,* Dorling Kindersley, London.

Sheridan, G. (1990), *Recycling in Hackney: Programme for the Inner-City,* London Borough of Hackney.

Shaw, G. and Wheeler, D. (1985), *Statistical Techniques in Geographical Analysis,* John Wiley and Sons, Chichester and New York.

Sheppard, G. (1990), 'Who will foot the bill for green rubbish?', *Transport Week,* 17th March, p. 26.

Shiga, M. (1975), 'Separate collection of household waste in Tokyo', paper presented to the *National Conference on Conversion of Refuse to Energy,* 3rd to 5th November, Montreux.

Shuval, H.I. (1962), 'Economics of Composting Municipal Refuse', *Journal of the Sanitary Engineering Division,* 7, pp. 47-56.

Simmonds, J. (1990), 'RECOUP (Recycling of used Plastic Conainers)', paper presented to the *London Recycling Forum,* 26th September.

Simon, J.L. (1981), *The Ultimate Resource,* Princetown University Press, Princetown, NY.

Simon, J.L. and Kahn, H. (ed.) (1984), *The Resourceful Earth - A Response to Global 2000,* Basil Blackwell, Oxford.

SIRR (Swedish Institute for Resource Recovery) (1975), *Households Contributing to Resource Recovery,* SIRR, Malmo.

Skitt, J. (1972), *Disposal of refuse,* Charles Knight & Company Ltd., London.

Smart, B. (1993), *Postmodernity,* Routledge, London.

Soja, E.W. (1989), *Postmodern Geographies,* Verso, London and New York.

Soper, G.A. (1909), *Modern methods of street cleaning*, Archibald Constable and Company Ltd., London.

SPD (Sozialdemokratische Partei Deutschlands) (1986), *Arbeit und Umwelt für Hamburg: Beschäftigungsorientierte Alternativen zur Standortpolitik*, Arbeitskreis Wirtschaftspolitik der SPD Hamburg-Eimsbüttel, Hamburg.

SPD (Sozialdemokratische Partei Deutschlands) (1989), *Berliner Koalitionsvereinbarung zwischen SPD und AL vom 13.März 1989*, SPD Berlin.

Spanos, A. (1986), *Statistical foundations of econometric modelling*, Cambridge University Press, Cambridge.

Spill, E. (1990), 'Das Supergift droht überall', in Spill, E. and Wingert, E. (eds.), *Brennpunkt Mull*, Sternbuch, Hamburg.

Spill, E. and Wingert, E. (eds.) (1990), *Brennpunkt Müll*, Sternbuch, Hamburg.

Stahel, W.R. and Reday-Mulvay, G. (1981), *Jobs for Tomorrow: The Potential for Substituting Manpower for Energy*, Vantage Press, New York.

Steiniger, E. (1984), 'Results of the Braunschweig model experiment on the combined recycling container for paper, glass and tins', in Thome-Kozmiensky, (ed.), *Recycling International*, EF Verlag für Umwelt und Technik, pp. 802-807.

Stewart, J. (1989), 'The Changing Organisation and Management of Local Authorities', in Stewart, J. and Stoker, G. (ed.) (1989), *The Future of Local Government*, pp. 171- 185.

Stewart, J. and Stoker, G. (eds.) (1989), *The Future of Local Government*, Macmillan, London.

Stoker, G. (1989), 'Creating a Local Government for a Post-Fordist Society: The Thatcherite project?', in Stewart, J. and Stoker, G (eds.), *The Future of Local Government*, pp. 141-171.

Studt, O. (1990), *Modellprojekt zur Eigenkomostierung im Stadtteil Altona*

1986-1989 des vereins nutzmüll e.V., Nutzmüll e.V., Hamburg.

Sudol, F. J. and Zach, A.L. (1988), 'Urban Recycling Problems and Solutions', *Public Works,* July, pp. 63-66.

Sweetman, J. (1979), 'Making Paper by Hand', in *Appropriate Technology,* Intermediate Technology Publications Ltd., UK.

Sychrava, J. (1991), 'Fair wind for renewable energy', *The Financial Times,* 5th September.

Tabasaran, O. (1984), 'Emissions from the Incineration of Solid Waste', in Thome-Kozmiensky, K.J. (ed.), *Recycling International,* EF Verlag für Umwelt und Technik, pp. 83-88.

Taira, K. (1969), 'Urban Poverty, Ragpickers, and the "Ants' Villa" in Tokyo', *Economic Development and Cultural Change,* 17, pp. 153-177.

Tattersley, P. (1990), 'Recycling in Denmark', *Environmental Health,* June 1990, pp. 158-160.

Taylor-Brown, T. (1990), 'BXL and plastics reclamation from household sources', paper presented to the *London Recycling Forum,* 26th September.

Tee, H.W. (1937), *London Cleansing: some observations on the reports of the London Cleansing Advisory Committee,* Institution of Municipal and County Engineers, London.

Teichert, V. (1989), 'Die Produktlinienanalyse: Möglichkeiten für ihre politische Implementation', paper presented to the conference *Ökologische Abfallwirtschaft,* 30th November to 2nd December, Technische Universität, Berlin.

Temple, F.C. (1943), 'Wealth from waste', *The Journal of the Institution of Municipal and County Engineers,* 69, pp. 405-13.

Thiel, W. (1988), *Kosten/leistungsaspekte und geeignete Einsatzgebiete der getrennten Naßmüllsammlung und Kompstierung am Beispiel Hamburgs,* unpublished thesis, University of Hamburg.

316

Thomas, C. (1977), *The Paper Chain: A Report on the Production, Use, Reclamation, and Recycling of Paper in the UK*, Earth Resources Research Ltd., London.

Thomas, C. (1979), *Material Gains: Reclamation, Recycling and Reuse*, Earth Resources Ltd., London.

Thomas, C. (1984), 'Conservation: Tackling unnecessary waste', In Wilson, D. (ed.), *The Environmental Crisis*, Heinemann Educational Books, London.

Thomas, D. (1990a), 'Tougher measures for illegal disposal', *The Financial Times*, 26th September.

Thomas, D. (1990b), 'Tenfold rise sought for renewable energy', *The Financial Times*, 1st October.

Thome-Kozmiensky, K.J. (ed.) (1984), *Recycling International*, EF-Verlag für Umwelt und Technik, Berlin.

Thome-Kozmiensky, K.J.(ed.) (1989), *Müllverbrennung und Umwelt 3*, EF-Verlag für Energie und Umwelttechnik, Berlin.

Thornhill, J. (1991), 'German packaging law condemned', *The Financial Times*, 28th June.

Townend, W.K. (1982), 'Waste Disposal in Greater London - Operational Developments since 1965', in *Wastes Management*, 72, pp. 229-235.

Townsend, E. (1974), 'Recycling glass: a not so simple task', *The Times*, 4th September.

Townsend, E. (1975), 'Ironies of the waste paper mountain' *The Times*, 16th July, 1975.

Townsend, P.; Corrigan, P.; and Kowarzik, U. (1987), *Poverty and Labour in London*, Low Pay Unit, London.

Trainer, F.E. (1986), *Abandon Affluence!*, Zed Books, London.

Travis, A. (1988), 'Westminster privatises £12 million refuse collection service', *The Guardian*, 5th October.

Trigg, R. (1985), *Understanding Social Science*, Basil Blackwell, Oxford.

Troge, A. (1984), 'Effects of a charge on drinks packaging on the environment and on business', in Thome-Kozmiensky, (ed.), *Recycling International*, E F Verlag für Umwelt und Technik, Berlin.

TUC (Trades Union Congress) (1989), *Towards a Charter for the Environment*, General Council Statement to the 1989 Trades Union Congress.

Tucker, D.G. (1977), 'Refuse destructors and their use for generating electricity: A Century of Development', *Industrial Archaeology Review*, 1, pp. 74-96.

Tunaley, C. (1990), 'A Local Authority View', *WARMER Bulletin*, 26, pp. 13.

Turk, T. (1989), 'Umsetzungsprobleme einer dezentralen Kompostierung', paper presented to the conference *Ökologische Abfallwirtschaft*, 30th November to 2nd December, Technische Universität, Berlin.

Turner, R.K. (1990), *Towards an integrated Waste Management Strategy*, Key Environmental Issues: Number Eleven in a Series, British Gas, London.

Turner, R.K. (1991a), 'Environment, Economics and Ethics', in Pearce, D. (ed.), *Blueprint 2: Greening the World Economy*, Earthscan Publications Limited, London.

Turner, R.K. (1991b), 'Economic instruments and solid waste management', *WARMER Bulletin*, 31, pp. 8-9.

Turner, R.K. (1992), *An Economic Incentive Approach to Regulating the Throwaway Society*, CSERGE Working Paper PA 92-05, UEA and UCL.

Turner, R.K. and Thomas, C. (1982), 'Source separation recycling schemes', *Resources Policy*, March, pp. 13-24.

Turvey, R. (1990), 'Waste Management and Control - The Envisaged Role of the Waste Regulation Authority', *Wastes Management*, October, pp. 775-786.

UK House of Commons (1984), *The Wealth of Waste*, Fourth Report from the Trade and Industry Committee Session 1983-1984.

UN Environment Programme (1978), *The State of the Environment*, UN, New York.

UN World Commission on Environment and Development (Brundtland Commission) (1987), *Our Common Future*, Oxford University Press.

UNESCO (1988), *Towards the Sustainable City?*, UNESCO, New York.

US Department of State: Council on Environmenmtal Quality (1982), *The Global 2000 report to the President*, Penguin, Middlesex.

Underwood, J.D.; Hershkowitz, A.; and de Kadt, M. (1988), *Garbage: Practices, Problems and Remedies*, Inform Inc., US.

Urry, M. (1989), 'Green issues pose dilemmas for pulp and paper industry', *The Financial Times*, 13th December.

Valette, J. (1989), *The International Trade in Wastes: A Greenpeace Inventory*, Greenpeace, Washington, DC.

Vaughan, D.A.; Anastas, M.Y.; and Krause, H.H. (1974), *An analysis of the current impact of plastic refuse disposal upon the environment*, Environmental Protection Agency, US.

Vaughan, D.A.; Ifeadi, C.; Markle, R.A.; and Krause, H.H. (1975), *Environmental assessment of future disposal methods for plastics in municipal solid waste*, Environmental Protection Agency, US.

Velzey, C.O. (1985), 'Measurement of dioxin emissions of energy-from-waste plants', *Waste Age*, 4, pp. 186-90.

Vick, E.H. and Flintoff, F.L.D. (1966), 'Refuse Disposal in Greater London', paper presented to *The Institute of Public Cleansing Annual Conference*, 7-10th June, Bournemouth.

Vidal, J. (1992), 'The new waste colonialists', *The Guardian*, 14th February.

Vining, J. and Ebreo, A. (1990), 'What Makes A Recycler? A Comparison of Recyclers and Nonrecyclers', *Environment and Behaviour*, 22, pp.

55-73.

Vogel, D. (1986), *National Styles of Regulation: Environmental Policy in Great Britain and the United States*, Cornell University Press, Ithaca, NY.

Vogler, J. (1980), 'Glassmaking as in the Time of Yore', *Materials Reclamation Weekly*, October18th, pp. 24-26.

Vogler, J. (1981), *Work from Waste: Recycling wastes to create employment*, Oxfam and Intermediate Technology Publications Ltd., London.

Von Schönberg, A. (1990), 'A Clear Issue: A survey of Glass Recycling in West Germany', *WARMER Bulletin*, 26, p. 7.

Ward, B. and Dubos, R. (1972), *Only One Earth*, Penguin, Harmondsworth.

Wakeford, T. (1990), 'Britain's Green Bill', *WARMER Bulletin*, 26, p.13.

Walker, P. (1992) 'What Can the government do to make recycling the first choice option for waste management?', paper presented to the conference *Waste Reclamation Credits - Landfill vs. Recycling*, 24th September, London.

Walker, R. and Storper, M. (1978), 'Erosion of the Clean Air Act of 1970: a study of the failure of government regulation planning', *Environmental Affairs*, 7, pp. 189-257.

Walsh, K. (1989), 'Competition and Service in Local Government', in Stewart, J. and Stoker, G. (eds), *The Future of Local Government*, pp. 30-55.

Waste Management Advisory Council (WMAC) (1976), *Report on Waste Paper Collection by Local Authorities*, HMSO, London.

Watt Committee on Energy (1990), *Renewable Energy Sources*, Report No.22, Elsevier Science Publishers, London.

Watts, M. (1983), *Silent Violence: food, famine and peasantry in northern Nigeria*, University of California Press, Berkeley, CA.

WEN (The Women's Environmental Network) (1989), *Dioxin: A Briefing*, WEN, London.

WEN (The Women's Environmental Network) (1990), *UK Paper Mills: Environmental Impact*, WEN, London.

WEN (The Women's Environmental Network) (1990), *A Tissue of Lies? Disposable Paper & the Environment*, WEN, London.

Wessel, K. (1988), 'Vermeidung von Abfall durch abfallarme Produktionsverfahren', in IföR, *Abfall Vermeiden*, Fischer Taschenbuch Verlag, Frankfurt amd Main, pp. 84-89.

Weston, J. (ed.) (1986), *Red and Green*, Pluto Press, London.

Weston, J. (1986), 'The Greens, 'Nature' and the Social Environment', in Weston, J. (ed.) (1986), *Red and Green*, pp. 11-29, Pluto Press, London.

Westra, G. (1984), 'Mechanical separation of municipal solid waste with the example of the plant in Zoetermeer', in Thome-Kozmiensky, (ed.), *Recycling International*, E F Verlag für Umwelt und Technik, pp. 252-257.

Whitebloom, S. (1991), 'No new GLC to run London', *The Observer*, 8th December.

Wiebe, A. (1989), 'Kommunale Steurungsintrumente für eine ökologische Abfallwirtschaft', paper presented to the conference *Ökologische Abfallwirtschaft*, 30th November to 2nd December, Technische Universität, Berlin.

Williams, L. (1990), 'CFCs: Recycling for reduction', paper presented to the *London Recycling Forum*, 14th March.

Williams, R. (1986), *Socialism and Ecology*, Socialist Environment and Resources Association, London.

Williamson, J.B.P. (1974), 'An industrialist's view of the recovery and recycling of materials', paper presented to *The Conservation of Materials Conference*, 26th-27th March, Harwell.

Winter, J. (1989), 'The 'Agitator of the Metropolis': Charles Cochrane and Early-Victorian Street Reform', *The London Journal*, 14, pp. 29-42.

Wirth, B. (1988), 'Kunstoffe: Problemaufriss bei der Herstellung, der Verwendung und Besietigung', in IföR, *Abfall Vermeiden*, Fischer Taschenbuch Verlag, Frankfurt am Main, pp. 38-44.

Wittern, I. (1990), 'Der Modellversuch Komposttonne (Grüne Nassmülltonne) in Hamburg - Harburg', paper presented to the conference, *Energie und Abfall*, 7-8th June, Neumunster.

Wix, P. (ed.) (1961), *Town Waste Put to Use*, Cleaver-Hume Press Ltd., London.

Wohl, A.S. (1983), *Endangered Lives - Public Health in Victorian Britain*, J.M. Dent & Sons Ltd., London

World Wildlife Fund et al. (1983), *The Conservation and Development Programme for the UK: A response to the World Conservation Strategy*, Kogan Page, London.

Wright, G. (1990), 'The compostable component in a curbside collection scheme', paper presented to the *London Recycling Forum*, 5th December.

WRWA (Western Riverside Waste Authority) (1989), *Waste Management Plan*.

Young, J.E. (1991), *Discarding the Throwaway Society*, Worldwtach Institute, Washington.

Young, K. and Garside, P.L. (1982), *Metropolitan London: Politics and Urban Change 1837-1981*, Edward Arnold, London.

Zagor, K. (1991), 'Rubbish industry smells new profit', *The Financial Times*, 29th May.